LIGHTING
THE
STAGE

LIGHTING THE STAGE

ART AND PRACTICE

SECOND EDITION

WILLARD F. BELLMAN
California State University—Northridge

Thomas Y. Crowell
HARPER & ROW, PUBLISHERS
New York   Hagerstown   Philadelphia   San Francisco   London

LIGHTING THE STAGE: Art and Practice, Second Edition

Library of Congress Cataloging in Publication Data

Bellman, Willard F
  Lighting the Stage.

  Bibliography: p.
  1. Stage lighting. I. Title.
PN2091.E4B39 1974   792'.025   73-18363
ISBN 0-8102-0040-6

TEXT AND COVER DESIGN BY JULES PERLMUTTER (STUDIO 17)
COVER COLOR SEPARATION BY RAMÓN SANCHEZ

CONTENTS

PREFACE TO THE SECOND EDITION XIII

PREFACE TO THE FIRST EDITION XV

PART I TECHNICAL ASPECTS OF STAGE LIGHTING

1 INTRODUCTION TO THE ART OF STAGE LIGHTING 3

Functions of Lighting 4

Psychological and Physiological Bases of Lighting 6

An Overview: Art, Meaning, and Mechanics 7

2 THE NATURE OF LIGHT 9

Light as Radiant Energy 9

Measuring Light 11

Producing Light by Incandescence 13

Other Methods of Producing Light 36

3 CONTROLLING LIGHT: REFLECTION 48

The Law of Squares 48

Specular Reflection: The Law of Reflection 49

Reflectors on Stage: Reflection in General Lighting Equipment 52

Specular Reflectors in Specific Lighting Equipment 57

4 CONTROLLING LIGHT: REFRACTION 66

Refraction in Plano-Convex Lenses 69

How Lenses Function in Spotlights 73

The Lens as a Converging Device 76

The Fresnel Lens 79

Lenses in Ellipsoidal Spotlights 85

5 COLORED LIGHT 89

What Is Color? 89

Light as a Physical Phenomenon 89

Sources of Colored Light on the Stage 93

Color Mixing 96

Selective Transmission and Reflection 101

Sensitivity of the Eye to Color 105

White Light 105

6 APPLYING COLOR THEORY TO THE STAGE 107

Plasticity: Colored Light and the Actor 107

Lighting the Acting Space as a Whole: Flood and Key 110

Lighting the Acting Space by Segments: Acting Areas 113

VII CONTENTS

7 ELECTRICITY IN THE THEATRE 122

History 122

The Nature of Electrical Current 123

Generation and Distribution of Electricity 131

Transformers 133

ac Power Distribution and Theatre Lighting 138

The Permanently Installed Stage-Lighting Control Equipment 148

Summary 156

8 ELECTRICAL SAFETY 157

Electricity and the Law: The National Electrical Code 157

The "UL" Label 158

Special Legal Obligations of the Theatre-Lighting Artist 159

Using Electricity Safely 160

9 MANUAL CONTROL OF STAGE LIGHTING 170

History 170

The Resistance Dimmer 174

The Autotransformer Dimmer 177

10 REMOTE CONTROL OF STAGE LIGHTING 186

Introduction 186

Remote Control 187

Remote Dimming 189

History of the Remote Control of Stage Lighting 190

Solid-State Control 195

Consoles 207

Glossary of Remote-Control Apparatus—Preset Consoles 218

Preset Control:
Concept and
Elaborations 223

Memory Systems 239

11 DISTRIBUTION
OF THE
CURRENT
FROM THE
DIMMERS
TO THE
LAMPS 273

The Dimmer Room
or Enclosure 273

Dimmer Utilization:
Flexibility and
Control Configuration 274

Types of
Interconnecting Panels 277

From the
Interconnection Panel
to the Lamp 286

PART II
DESIGNING
THE
LIGHTING

12 AESTHETIC
BACKGROUNDS 295

History of Modern
Design Concepts 295

The General Nature
of the Discussion
of Design 297

Procedure 297

13 DESIGNING
IN
SPACE
AND
TIME 303

The Designer 303

Dramatic Space 304

The Symbolic
Mode of Time 312

Paradox: The Prelude
to Insight 318

14 NONSYMBOLIC
ASPECTS
OF
LIGHTING
DESIGN 320

Attention 320

Depth Perception 322

15 LIGHT
AND
THE
ACTOR 326

The Development of
Directional Light
in the Theatre 326

Directional Light
and Acting 330

The Designer's Variables 336

16 LIGHT AND THE SETTING 355

Setting, Lighting, and Dramatic Space 356

Colored Light and the Set 360

17 LIGHT AND RHYTHMIC STRUCTURE 365

Dramatic Structure and Dramatic Rhythm 365

Climax, Tension, and Conflict 366

18 DESIGN PROCEDURES 371

Developing the Concept of the Play 371

Working with the Director 372

Development of the Lighting Plot 375

Mounting the Lights for the Show 394

19 CUES 397

What Can Be Expected of a Cue System? 398

Various Systems 399

Front-of-House Control as It Affects Cues 401

Cues with Preset Consoles 401

Cuing with Memory Controls 407

How the Designer Prepares for Cuing the Show 408

Training New Lighting Operators 409

"Technical Rehearsals" 410

Setting the Lighting Cues 411

20 EVALUATING
   A LIGHTING
   DESIGN   415

Categories of Criticism   415
Return to the Script   416

APPENDIXES

I PROJECTED
  SCENERY   418

Scenic Projection
Defined   418

Aesthetics of
Projected Scenery   419

Economics of
Scenic Projection   423

Earlier and
Simpler Applications
of Projection   430

Technical Problems
of Theatrical
Scenic Projection   431

Types of
Scenic Projectors   432

Lighting While
Using Scenic
Projection   454

Blending of
the Projection
and the Setting   457

Preparing Image Material
for Scenic Projection   459

II ORDERING
   LAMPS
   FOR STAGE
   USE   465

Economics   465

Current
Lamp-Ordering
Data   465

Data Needed for
Purchase of Lamps   466

III ALLOWABLE
AMPERAGE
IN COMMON
STAGE-LIGHTING
CONDUCTORS 467

IV LIGHTING THE
ARENA AND
THRUST-APRON
STAGE 468

BIBLIOGRAPHY 474   General Stage Lighting 474

The Aesthetics
of Stage Lighting 475

Light, Color,
and Human Vision 475

Scenography 476

Projected Scenery 476

Manufacturers of
Equipment Related
to Stage Lighting 476

INDEX 477

PREFACE TO THE SECOND EDITION

Essentially the attitude toward the art of stage lighting displayed in this revision of *Lighting the Stage* is unchanged from the first edition. The premise is that the arts of the theatre, including lighting, are *human activities*, that human insight and human sensitivity are at the core of theatrical work whatever technological assistance may be used to aid its creation. This position has been reinforced by the experience of teaching from the first edition and especially by developments in the American theatre. "Professionalism" is no longer synonymous with Broadway. It is true of theatres in many parts of the nation, as is shown in this edition by the variety of American lighting practices considered.

The technology of lighting however, has progressed at a constantly accelerating pace since the first edition appeared. A hint there that computer technology might enter the field of lighting control has now become a major section. And, as this edition goes to press, the computer seems likely to take over not only lighting control but all electromechanical devices on the stage. The console operator may evolve from a *repetiteur* into an interpretive artist of considerable stature. Indeed the computer may presage development of the master theatrical artist-interpreter many theorists have dreamed about.

The treatment of the technology of stage lighting proceeds from theory to application. For example, the reader will find that the study of refraction leads to a discussion of lenses and thence to their function in lighting instruments. A similar path leads from the theory of reflection to the various reflectors found in spotlights.

While no text can remain technologically current, one can hope that the basics of the presentation will enable the reader to put the latest technical developments to good artistic use. Finally, whatever the degree of technological assistance, the theatre is a *human* art, perhaps the most human of all arts. Insight and artistic genius can only become more important as the tools of the theatre become more sophisticated.

XIII

The following firms have been most generous in supplying illustrative material and technical data for either the first or the second edition or both:

Background Engineering
Berkey Colortran
Strand Century Inc.
Electro Controls
Electronics Diversified
The General Electric Co.
Harvey Hubbell Inc.
Kliegl Brothers Lighting

Panni of Austria
The Rank Strand Co.
Siemens AG
Skirpan Lighting
The Superior Electric Co.
Sylvania
Thorn of England
The Universal Screen Co.

The following individuals deserve special thanks for their assistance:

Herr Wolfgang Bergfeld
Mr. Patrick Byrne
Mr. Don Childs
Mr. C. N. Clark
Mr. Wayne Davidson
Dr. Ralph Duckwall
Mr. Eldon Elder
Mr. Lou Erhart
Dr. Gary Gaiser
Dr. Leonard Hall
Mr. Marvin Herbst
Mr. Thomas Hird

Mr. William Huling
Mr. Al Lynds
Mrs. Lucille Monson
Ms. Jonell Polansky
Dr. Joel Rubin
Mr. William Shearer
Mr. Robert Slutski
Prof. Josef Svoboda
Mr. Ron Swartz
Mr. Joe Tawill
Mr. Gene Williams

A special debt of gratitude must be acknowledged to my students and colleagues at California State University, Northridge for their support and encouragement in this project. Most of all, gratitude is due my wife and family without whose help and encouragement this edition would not exist.

PREFACE TO THE FIRST EDITION

This text is intended for the serious student of theatre lighting who wishes to gain a complete understanding of the tools, technology, and artistic considerations of that art. While it does not seek to force the lighting artist into any fixed pattern or scheme, it does make an effort to identify and deal with the aesthetic problems of lighting design. The discussion of design recognizes that the ultimate artistic effort is a product of the individual artist.

In the discussion of technology, every effort has been made to bring into focus the most recent developments as of the time of final preparation of copy. However, I am acutely aware that technological developments proceed far more rapidly than the preparation of a book. The reader must ultimately be referred to the latest technical publications of such companies as the General Electric Company and to papers published in technical periodicals.

The "tools" of stage lighting are varied indeed. Understanding their operation involves considerable basic theory in several areas of physics. The clearest understanding of each item of equipment will come from proceeding from theory to application. The section of the text on tools has been arranged according to logical development of theory instead of according to types of equipment. For example, the development of theory of lenses begins with a discussion of principles of refraction and proceeds into the application of that theory to lenses in the various spotlights and projectors. Theory of reflection, in turn, leads into the discussion of spherical and ellipsoidal reflectors. Thus the reader is led efficiently toward an understanding of these items in many applications with a minimum of repetition.

XV

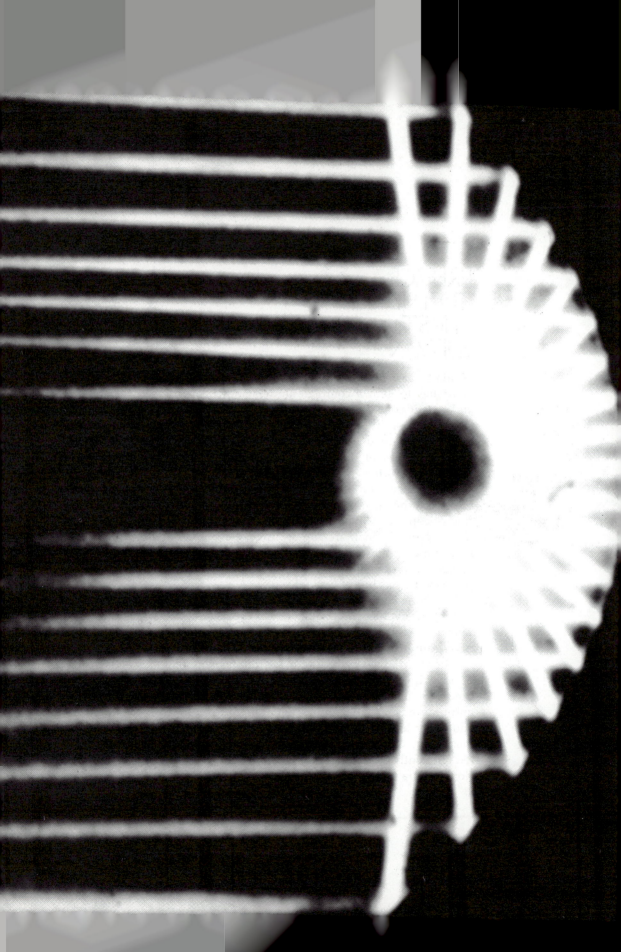

TECHNICAL
ASPECTS
OF
STAGE
1 LIGHTING

INTRODUCTION TO THE ART OF STAGE LIGHTING

1

All art exists, at least in part, because of man's need to express himself. It is probably true also that every art work exists in the form it does because the artist believed that no other way of expressing himself would be more effective. Why would a poet write a poem if his prose could communicate better? Any honest art work exists in its final form because that was the best and perhaps only form in which its creator could communicate what he wanted to say. The art of the theatre is no exception. The theatre exists as an art form because it can express certain ideas better than any other form, ideas best communicated by the living, moving, speaking actor.

The words "expression" and "communication" do not mean the same thing to everyone under all circumstances. Ask the telephone man what communication is and he will tell you it is the electrical-mechanical process that makes it possible for you to call up your Aunt Matilda and invite her over to dinner. As far as he is concerned, communication exists and is successful as long as the telephone works. If you pay your bill and the lines are working, you get through to your party. If you and Aunt Matilda can hear each other satisfactorily, communication is a success. This process is communication, but on an elementary level.

How about the artist? How does he communicate what he is compelled to express? Can the phone company supply him with an instrument that will electrically convert his thoughts and feelings to impulses that will mean the same to everyone on the line? Obviously not.

When Vincent Van Gogh examined a sunflower, he found in it some significant experience; he was best able to express this experience through color and form. There is no telephone for these thoughts. Van Gogh created the best device he could to communicate his experience of the flower: He painted "Sunflowers." But is this painting, like the telephone, a sure thing? Can Van Gogh be sure that his device will work, that everyone who sees it will think and feel as he did?

3

Artistic expression or communication is not sure and accurate as is the telephone. A work of art is a fusion of idea and emotion that is the product of the personality of the artist. You cannot understand it simply by picking up the receiver. You have to give something yourself; you are part of the communicative process. The circuit can be said to be complete only when your own personality has been fused with the art work, so what the artist has produced becomes a part of your life and your experiences. Then you will have received some part of what Van Gogh put into his painting. What the artist says and what you receive will never be the same and will never be completely different. What you get is Van Gogh's sunflower *seen through your personality*.

You understand a play or a painting or a piece of music only when you have made it a part of yourself, when you have given it a place in your life. You cannot expect it to pour itself out for you like a message from a telephone.

For two reasons, you must understand how an art work communicates. First, you must have an inkling of how lighting fits into the dramatic process of communication. This understanding will enable you to determine the limits of the art of lighting. Second, a knowledge of the intricacies of artistic communication will provide you with some of the tools you need to study the script and develop your lighting design.

Shakespeare said that the theatre consists of "two boards and a passion." Two boards — a place to play; a passion — human ideas and emotions. The passion is the combined property of the playwright and the actor. They create the passion, and with it the theatre. All else is secondary. Without the passion, no amount of scenery, lights, costumes, or anything else can make the theatre.

Theoretically, neither lighting, scenery, nor any of the other elements of the spectacle are essential to the theatre in the abstract. Any or all of them, however, may be essential for a particular play. Most plays were written with physical environment and illumination of some sort in mind. The playwright depended on them openly or tacitly. Modern audiences have come to expect the visual arts in the theatre. Unlike early audiences, who often saw plays without setting and lighting, modern audiences would be lost without them. Finally, although the visual production[1] may not be aesthetically *necessary* for a given play, it may be aesthetically desirable to make the play more effective.

Functions of Lighting

Now, given the actor and the playwright, what can lighting do for the theatre as an art? First of all, light enables all concerned to *see*. Seeing is elementary but necessary to a stage production. Only the spoken

---

[1] "Visual production" is often referred to by the French term *mise en scène* or the German *Inszenierung,* although both of these terms are broader in connotation.

words of the actor are independent of light and no actor on the stage likes to depend on his words alone. Seeing, however, is but a condition to the existence of drama on the stage, like the place in which the play is acted. The ability to see must be present, but in itself it can guarantee little to either the actor or the audience.

The moment seeing is thought of as more than mere visibility, art begins to enter lighting. It is not merely the seeing, but *what* is seen, *how* it is seen, and *how much* of it is seen that are important. In many cases what is not seen is even more important than what is seen. Max Reinhardt says, "I am told that the art of lighting consists of putting the light where you want it and taking it away where you don't want it."[2]

Controlling Focus of Attention

One of the powerful things that lighting can do is to control the focus of attention. Indeed lighting is the strongest device that the theatre has for this task. It is much more powerful than the blocking, or movement of the actors, that is usually worked out by the director. Movement of the actors which cannot be seen is of no avail. The lighting artist with his spotlights can move the audience's focus of attention about the stage just as surely as the motion-picture or television cameraman can aim his camera about a set and thus determine what part of it will be seen at any moment. We will discuss the psychological reasons for this control a little later.

Emphasizing Rhythm and Structure

A good play has rhythmic structure. It builds up to a climax and relaxes only to build up again to a higher climax. A play does this more or less regularly throughout its development until the final climax is reached; after the final climax it "unwinds" rapidly or slowly. This arrangement of climaxes is the rhythmic structure of the play. The lighting can heighten and emphasize that structure. It can make the climaxes higher in emotional intensity and can increase the contrast between them and the relatively relaxed moments between them. Lighting can also differentiate the moods of the various climaxes and sharpen their relationships. Thus the lighting artist must study the rhythmic structure of the play carefully.

Establishing Mood

Nothing except lighting, unless perhaps music, can more easily or more rapidly establish the overall mood of a play, its cheerfulness or

[2] R. E. Jones, *The Dramatic Imagination*. New York: Duell, Sloan & Pearce, 1941, p. 111.

its gloom. Frequently, color is the chief device in establishing mood, although light and darkness often suffice. Remember that few plays have exactly the same mood in the same proportion throughout their length. Mood, like rhythm, gains much of its artistic effectiveness through change.

Establishing Realistic Elements

Lighting can establish the time of day, the weather, the locale, the seasons, and many other environmental matters that pertain to the play. All such naturalistic phenomena are of unusual importance in realistic drama; they often provide symbolic accents to the action or motivate the characters. A good example of this sort of realism is found in Henrik Ibsen's frequent use of the foggy, cloudy Norwegian atmosphere as a device to elaborate character.

The presumption that these naturalistic phenomena are the only contribution that lighting makes to realistic drama is far from the truth. The problems of controlling attention, emphasizing structure, and the like, are not removed. These problems are complicated by the additional necessity that they be solved without allowing them to enter into the conscious awareness of the audience. In realistic plays, subtlety is of the essence.

This discussion of the functions of lighting is by no means exhaustive. It is not intended to do more than suggest generally what may be expected of stage lighting.

Psychological and Physiological Bases of Lighting

The power of lighting is rooted deep in the recesses of our psychological makeup and is apparently universal in application. Reactions to lighting environment are evident at an early age. Even the young child is attracted to light and feels disturbed by darkness. Unless the child is in familiar surroundings and assured of his security, darkness will often arouse fright. Bright lights and bright reflective surfaces are a source of amusement for him; his eyes follow them about perhaps even before he can focus clearly on anything. Somehow, darkness is associated with the unknown, with the disturbing feeling that all is not well. Darkness repels, or at least disturbs, while light attracts, or at least reassures. Shadow and gloom easily become symbols for what is unknown and, therefore, unpleasant. Thus it is no accident, but rather fundamental psychology, that tragedy is traditionally dimly lighted and darkly colored.

The reaction to color is similarly fundamental. This reaction does not develop quite so early in life (or perhaps it is not so easily detected), but warm and cool colors have a definite and roughly opposite effect on one's emotional states. The response is so pronounced that it affects one's perception of the temperature of his surroundings. Air-conditioning engineers, for example, have found that a room decorated in cool colors will feel several degrees cooler than a room decorated in warm colors, even though the temperature of both rooms may be the same. Workers with the mentally ill have found that a warm or cool color environment provides a stimulating or sedating effect which can help depressed or disturbed persons. Similar effects may be achieved on the stage by the proper use of color. Definition of "warm" and "cool" varies somewhat depending on the colors compared with each other. Refer to the color wheel, Plate VII. Note that the yellow-greens and purples are ambivalent; they will appear either warm or cool, depending on the contrasting color. This is of particular importance in the case of purple because tints of purple are often used to light acting areas. Sometimes the purple tint is contrasted to a salmon or rose color, in which case it becomes the cool color. At other times it may be used with a tint of blue or blue-green. Under these conditions, it becomes warm.

Reactions to light and shade and to color form the basis for most of the responses that an audience will make to stage lighting. Of course, principles of light and color may be used well or badly, but they continue to operate no matter how they are used.

An Overview: Art, Meaning, and Mechanics

The art of lighting, we have said, is dependent on the work of the playwright and the actor for its fulfillment. In production, the development of the lighting must parallel the decisions of the actor and director as they create the words and movements of the play from the script. The director controls the others; he will decide the exact relationship between the climaxes and between the characters. The actor will develop character, emotion, and all of the rest of the facets of his art, and the lighting artist will heighten these elements still more by the use of his powerful psychological media. The lighting artist can heighten climax and quicken emotions although he cannot create them.

The lighting artist's first move, like that of all other production artists, is to get a command of the play. He must make it a part of his emotional and intellectual experience. He cannot expect it to come to him in a flash or to be written out like the directions for making fudge. When he has mastered the script, he must see that his ideas parallel those of the other members of the production team. Remember that the script, like any other art work, is no sure communicative device. What each reader gets out of it will depend not only on what the writer put into it but on the emotional and intellectual makeup of the reader. This characteristic of art is one of the main reasons for the supremacy of the director. Someone must be the final authority for the interpretation of the script or chaos will reign.

How does the lighting artist, or anyone else for that matter, master the script? He does not do it by hard study alone. Neither does he do it by some mystical inspiration. He does it with a combination of careful study of the meaning of the script and a sincere attempt to feel and understand the emotions contained therein. He attempts to find common ground with the script by relating it to his own experiences, but he avoids the oversimplification that might lead him to a "moral" or maxim which he could assert as its "message." The play will have much to say, if it is good, but it will not say it in a blatantly oversimplified manner. The lighting man will develop his sensitivity to the images presented by the script and try to relate them to what may be shown on the stage. In the end, he will feel overwhelmed by the complexity of the script, yet awed by its structure and unity. If the play is one of the classics, he will constantly be amazed by the depth and complexity of what is apparently a simple drama. The truth is that he will never be in complete command of such a script, and the more he works with it the more it will challenge him.

This lack of complete command does not mean that there is no point at which he is ready to design the lighting for a production of the script. He must go on with his task aware that he has not felt and will probably never know and feel all that the script has to offer. Of course, a lesser play will offer a lesser challenge, but without giving its problems some study, no one should jump to the conclusion that a script is so simple that it is worthless.

In order to accomplish the artistic ends of successful stage lighting, it is necessary to become familiar with the tools with which the artist must work. He must know about light, the primary commodity of his art. He must understand quite a lot about electricity, by which he produces the light. He must discover the difference between the various pieces of equipment he will find on a stage and know why and how they work.

Let us use the word "mechanics" to mean all that pertains to the tools with which the lighting artist works: light, optics, electricity, equipment, and the like. No amount of mechanical ingenuity or dexterity can substitute for artistry in lighting. Neither can any modern miracle of electronic control make as much as one fragment of artistic lighting. The human being designs the lighting and it is he who is measured by the results. Except in rare cases, he cannot hide behind the lack of proper equipment; neither can he buy his way out of artistic slovenliness by purchasing fancy control boards and expensive dimmers. Such tools are desirable—they make the artist's job much easier—but they do not make the artist.

THE
NATURE
OF
2 LIGHT

Light as Radiant Energy

Light is the very essence of our art, yet we do not know precisely what it is or how it travels through space. We do not know precisely how the human eye perceives light, or how the eye separates the thousands of gradations of color and light and shade that we can see, yet our job is to control carefully these very perceptions. We must learn to mix colors with the subtlety of a chemist preparing a complex compound, and we don't know how the eye sees the results of our efforts! Yet we do know a great deal and much of it is helpful to our efforts.

Light, we know, is a form of energy, the capacity to do work. Light can make the needle of a photometer move and the grass grow; it can do work, so it is a form of energy. Moreover, it is a form of radiant energy; that is, it travels through space by a process called radiation. Related kinds of energy also travel through space in the same manner and have many of the same effects. This large array of energy is known as the *radiant spectrum*. We do not know precisely how this energy gets through space, but its movements have some of the characteristics of the movements of waves through air or water. There are periods or areas of greater concentration of energy followed by periods or areas of lesser concentration of energy, resembling ripples in water. In a pond, as a ripple passes a given point, there is an increase in the height of the water for a moment, a return to normal, a decrease below normal, and another return. This complete pattern of rise and depression is known as one wave. The length of a wave, a *wavelength*, is the distance between corresponding points of two successive waves — the crests or the troughs, for example.

9
Unfortunately, in terms of an orderly understanding of light, wave-

motion concepts fail to explain a number of important phenomena. For example, an attempt to explain the way in which a photoelectric cell responds to varying amounts or colors of light in terms of wavelength cannot be made to coincide with the observable data. This and many other physical observations have led physicists to evolve a complicated concept known as "quantum mechanics" which seeks to reconcile those observations compatible with wave theory and those apparently contradictory to it. Fortunately for the stage-lighting artist, his use of the physics of light will be almost entirely limited to those concepts which fall within the wave theory. The following discussion has been simplified by treating the wave theory as though it were a complete and adequate explanation of light.

The radiant spectrum is made up of a large variety of energy types which display many like characteristics in their travel through space. They vary in wavelength, however, from several miles to extremely minute portions of an inch for each wave. This spectrum is roughly illustrated in Plate I in the color section. On the graph, the various waves (if they are waves) are organized according to the length which they appear to have. Radio waves occupy one end of the line, X rays and gamma rays the other. As radio waves get shorter, they tend to act more like light, making microwave transmission of television programs and telephone conversations possible. These minute radio waves may be focused by reflectors just as light waves are. In fact, the same shapes of reflectors perform the same focusing in both cases.

Visible Light

The human eye is sensitive to an exceedingly small portion of this spectrum. The human body, however, can indirectly detect quite a bit more of the spectrum. For example, we cannot see the infrared rays whose wavelength is longer than 0.0000276 inch (7/10,000 millimeter), but we can feel many of them as heat. In fact, infrared lamps are used to produce rays that penetrate some distance into most objects, including human flesh, before they are converted to heat. Thus heat is produced where it can be most effective. Perhaps you have "baked out" a sore muscle with an infrared lamp. The heat worked on the muscle by penetrating deeply into your arm or leg and stimulating circulation more rapidly than a surface application of heat would have. For the same reason, infrared lamps are used to bake the enamel finish on automobiles dry in a few minutes. The heat produced inside the enamel dries it very quickly. At the other end of the visual spectrum in the violet region, the eye again ceases to be sensitive. The human skin, however, remains sensitive for quite a distance into the ultraviolet region. Some of these wavelengths produce sunburn, others make the skin develop dark pigments and produce a "tan." Of course man has developed indirect ways of detecting the rest of the radiant spectrum, or he would not know that it exists.

Kinds of Spectra

As you may have gathered, a *spectrum* is simply a display of a series of radiations lined up according to wavelength. If the display includes all wavelengths between the two limits or if the wavelengths shade subtly from one to another it is known as a continuous spectrum. If the display consists of sharply defined lines representing narrow bands of specific wavelengths, separated by darkness, it is known as a line spectrum. Since every element, when it is vaporized and made to radiate light, produces a set of lines as characteristic as a human fingerprint, physicists use line spectra for identification just as a detective uses fingerprints. This process of identification is known as the science of *spectroscopy*.

If we expand the portion of the spectrum that the eye can see so that we can examine it in detail, we find that it includes all wavelengths from 4/10,000 millimeter in length to 7/10,000 millimeter in length. Since fractions are hard to handle, scientists have devised two terms that are easier. The larger unit is the micron, a unit 1/1000 of a millimeter in length. In microns, the above lengths are 0.4 to 0.7 micron. A still smaller unit is used when the physicist wishes to be very specific about the wavelength of a light. When he gets specific he goes four more places to the right of the decimal point. To avoid all the extra zeros, he has coined the term "angstrom unit" (abbreviated "Å") which is 1/10,000 of a micron long. The above wavelengths would read 4000 and 7000 Å on this scale. A specific wavelength of light, for example that produced by a sodium-vapor lamp, will illustrate. This yellow light, produced by the "fog lights" often seen on super highways and bridges where fog is common, is made up of only two wavelengths, very closely related. They are:

Microns	Angstrom Units
0.58959	5895.9
0.58900	5890.0

The eye sees these as yellow. If we wish to be very accurate about the light produced by a source, we must describe the light in terms of the wavelength or wavelengths of the light produced.

Measuring Light

Light is a form of energy that must be converted into another form when it is to be measured. The light meter is a device for such conversions; it converts light into electrical energy and measures the electricity by means of electromagnetic effects which move the pointer of the meter. It is also possible to measure light by using its energy to produce chemical reactions on photosensitive materials and measuring the results chemically.

The Standard Candle

As in all systems of measurement, there must be some predetermined standard as a point of reference. In the case of light, this standard is the *standard candle*, once the quantity of light produced by a candle of special wax made to very close dimensions, with a carefully prepared wick.

The modern standard is a specially designed electric lamp operated at carefully controlled current under special conditions. In either case, the standard is arbitrary, that is, there is no unit in nature to which it can be compared, whereas the wavelength of light (vastly different from its quantity) has physical length. It is also important to note that the standard candle is really a unit of brightness and that the amount of energy present on the surface will vary with the wavelength. Thus a footcandle of blue light would contain more energy than one of yellow-green light because the eye is more sensitive to the latter. A *footcandle* is the brightness produced on a white surface one foot away from a standard candle, an arbitrarily chosen standard. One footcandle is quite a small amount of light; for example, a good reading illumination would be perhaps 30 footcandles at the surface of the book you are reading.

Light meters are usually calibrated to read either in footcandles or in some multiple which can be converted easily into footcandles. These meters are usually operated in such a way that they sample a small portion of the lighted area, considerably less than a square foot. Photographers call the operation "reading incident light." The operator must take a wide range of readings over an unevenly lighted surface if he wishes to get an accurate idea of the variations in brightness. Since absolute footcandle readings are seldom of value in stage lighting, the stage-lighting artist will usually be satisfied to use his meter to help him take better theatre pictures or to make relative readings to get some idea of the contrast range of his lighting. The motion-picture lighting artist will, of course, convert his readings photographically. The television lighting artist will sometimes need his meter for checking "minimum footcandle" readings. He may determine these on the basis of technical data concerning the sensitivity of the picture-taking tube-and-lens combination in use. Often he will operate from a rule of thumb set by long observation and practice to the effect that "the meter cannot read below 40 with the lens set at $f/5$." Practically, there will be so many variables that arbitrary conversion of meter readings to footcandles will only begin to solve his problems. Nevertheless, he will probably be much more concerned with absolute measurement of light in footcandles than his compatriots in the theatre.

The Lumen

Another term common to stage lighting is the "lumen," the quantity of light it takes to illuminate one square foot of surface to the brightness of one footcandle. In terms of electrical energy one lumen represents ±0.001496 watt, a small amount of energy. The most common use of brightness readings is in lamp catalogs where the term is often "initial lumens" or "lumens per watt," usually initial, or more rarely "cost per million lumen-hours." "Initial lumen output" is simply a measurement of the total number of lumens of light emitted from the lamp in all directions. It is up to the user to direct this light as efficiently as he can to where he wants it. The figure tells us the total amount of light produced by the lamp when it is new. As the lamp grows older, this output will drop off, giving rise to a more useful but rare figure, "mean lumens," which gives the user a better idea of the light output to be expected during the entire useful life of the lamp. "Lumens per watt" is a variation on the "initial lumens" figure which does the mathematics for us, converting the data into a form which focuses our attention on the efficiency of the lamp in converting electricity into light. "Cost per million lumen-hours" is a still more detailed efficiency figure which takes into account the cost of the lamp and the electricity it uses during the time it takes it to produce 1 million lumen-hours of light. If a lamp were large enough, it could do this by producing 1 million lumens of light for one hour, or by producing 500,000 lumens for two hours, or the like. The term "million lumen-hours" takes on more meaning when we realize that this is about the total light output of a 100-watt general service lamp during its entire life.

"Beam lumens" is another matter, one for much conjecture and argument because it is anybody's guess as to where the edge of the beam is. Only the most precise optical apparatus produces a knife-edge beam of uniform brilliance right to the very cutoff point. All stage spotlights produce a beam of varying density which tapers off into blackness with more or less rapidity depending on the type of instrument, its condition, and many other things. Thus a "beam lumens" figure means little unless other conditions are stipulated, for example, "beam lumens (average) to 10 percent candlepower." The engineer taking these measurements has averaged all of the variations in brilliance he found within the beam whose edge is defined as that place where the intensity of the beam drops below 10 percent of the brightness of the main portion.

Producing Light by Incandescence

We can convert light into electrical energy as we do in a light meter, or we can convert electrical energy into light. The problem in making light is to perform these conversions without too much loss of energy. The "lost" energy is not destroyed; it is merely changed to a form not wanted, and becomes heat in spite of everything the engineers can do. This heat is lost energy as far as light-making is concerned.

Man's oldest source of light other than the sun is fire. The light that comes from a pitch torch, from an oil lamp, or from a candle is incandescent. In a flame, light is made from heat that is produced when the fuel burns. Within the flame, burning particles are heated so hot that they radiate energy as visible light. Red-hot coals operate in the same manner; so does a red-hot poker.

The Coleman Lantern

A more modern incandescent source is the Coleman lantern. It is probably the simplest example of incandescence because the elements are clearly differentiated. A Coleman lantern consists of a heat source and an incandescent object placed within that heat source. The heat source is a gasoline blowtorch similar to the ones you may have seen a plumber use. This torch flame by itself will not produce enough visible light to be of any use. In the lantern the orifice of the tube from which the flame issues is surrounded by a "mantle." The mantle consists of a fragile mesh of chemical ashes which has the property of converting a large percentage of heat to visible light. When the Coleman lantern is working, the mantle emits a brilliant white light. Incidentally, when you buy a mantle for a Coleman lantern you get a little bag of cloth which you tie around the orifice of the torch and which burns the first time the lantern is used. The burning leaves the mesh of ash which becomes incandescent; the cloth was merely to hold the chemicals in place while you installed the mantle. In the Coleman lantern the heat source and the incandescent object are clearly separated. Also, the incandescent material is not consumed, as is most of the soot in a flame.

Electric Arc Lights

Another incandescent source, more like the flame than the Coleman lantern, is the electrical carbon arc. Heat for this source is produced by electrical energy which is forced to jump through air and carbon vapor from one piece of carbon to another. The carbon rods are called "electrodes." As the electricity passes through the space between the electrodes, it produces a great deal of heat which raises the temperature of carbon particles and of the ends of the electrodes themselves to the point of incandescence. The heat is so great that the carbon from the electrodes is gradually burned away, necessitating constant adjustment of the lamp. A modern carbon-arc lamp uses special electrodes which have "cores" of chemicals especially chosen for their ability to convert heat into visible light at high temperatures. The result is that a greater share of the electricity used is converted to light; that is, the result is increased efficiency. Modern arc lights are among the brightest stage-lighting sources available and are still in demand wherever a long throw (distance from light to actor) and a bright light are needed. An operator is necessary to keep the electrodes in adjustment but this is usually no problem because the operator's main job is to direct the beam of light wherever it is wanted. He is known as a follow-spot operator. Since arc lights are huge units, requiring special ventilation and always requiring special electrical apparatus, they are usually semipermanently mounted in a booth at the back of the theatre known as the spotting booth.

Arc lights were originally operated on direct current (dc) and many of the larger modern ones still are. Direct current heats one carbon electrode more than the other, producing a smaller, more controllable point source of light. Direct-current arcs are also less noisy and the dc source serves as a current limiter. Limitation of the current is necessary because an arc light, unlike an incandescent lamp, is almost a short circuit as far as its ability to draw current is concerned.

A modern development of importance to the lighting artist is the alternating-current (ac) arc-light follow spot. This device is relatively portable, highly efficient, and usually the most powerful source available to the lighting artist in a medium-size theatre. The instrument is not much noisier than its dc predecessors. The current-limiting apparatus is built into the base of the instrument, serving to lower the center of gravity of the relatively heavy lamp housing. The housing usually is equipped with a somewhat complex lens, iris shutter, and reflector system that will enable the operator to adjust the size of the beam over a wide range. Color changers are often built in also.

Arc lamps are rated in amperes, not watts (these terms are defined in the section "Electrical Mathematics" in Chapter 7.) The amount of current they draw is adjustable over a considerable range by changing the setting of the arc and the adjustment of the controller. Large dc arc spotlights may draw up to 250 amperes at about 30 to 50 volts.

The arc lamp was invented by Humphry Davy early in the nineteenth century but did not find use in the theatre until much later. It was the first electrical light source in the theatre.

CARBON MONOXIDE HAZARD

The reason that carbon-arc light sources, whether in spotlights or in motion-picture projectors, need special ventilation is that the carbon is only partially burned in the arc. The result is that the source emits carbon monoxide, a deadly but odorless gas. This is the same gas that is found in automobile exhausts. It can cause serious illness or death if breathed for any length of time. Safety laws require that spotting booths and motion-picture booths using carbon-arc sources be equipped with air exhaust systems. Such systems must be vented to outdoors and must be capable of removing all dangerous gases from the room. Since follow spotlights are often rented and used in temporary locations, especially the alternating-current type mentioned above, operators should be absolutely certain that proper ventilation is provided. Carbon monoxide poisoning is insidious; it can overcome a victim without giving any warning.

Properties of Incandescent Light

Before we begin our discussion of the incandescent lamp it will be helpful to understand some of the physical properties of the light which is produced by incandescence and the methods used to describe that light.

INCANDESCENT SPECTRA

We have already indicated that there are two kinds of spectra: line and continuous. Although the difference may not be apparent to the eye, a spectroscope can quickly distinguish between these two types. Line spectra are produced by gaseous discharges and similar phenomena, which we will discuss later; continuous spectra are produced by incandescence. Thus a spectrogram of an incandescent source will be like those portrayed in Plate IV. Wavelengths shade imperceptibly from one to another with no intervening sharply defined regions of darkness. If certain bands of wavelengths are missing, as in the case of white light passed through highly saturated filters, the borders will shade off gradually into darkness.

COLOR TEMPERATURE

Spectral analysis is the most accurate method of describing the color content of any light source. However, such analysis is often more detailed than necessary and tends to place the emphasis on the presence of individual wavelengths instead of the overall effect of the light on the human eye. Scientists have devised another method of describing the color content of white and near-white light which serves many purposes better than spectroanalysis. It is the Kelvin color temperature scale illustrated in Plate VIII and by the "black-body locus" near the center of Plate III. The system is based on comparison of the light in question with a standard. The standard, which is known as the "black body," is heated to produce light. The light then is compared with that of the source to be described.

Actually the emission of energy from a heated object is deeply involved in quantum theory and far beyond the scope of this text. It is sufficient for us to understand that when a material is heated it emits energy at increasingly shorter wavelengths, eventually reaching temperatures at which visible light is emitted. As this temperature is exceeded, the color content of the light varies in a predictable fashion that can be used as a standard for describing visible light. Since temperature is the variable which controls the light emission in this process, we describe the light emitted in terms of temperature. A special scale, known as the *Kelvin* scale (after a famous British scientist) is used. This scale begins at absolute zero (−273.1° C), the point at which there is no more heat energy in an object. The scale uses centigrade (Celsius) size degrees making the freezing point of water (0° C) 273.1° K and the boiling point of water 373.1° K.

The operative portion of the Kelvin scale for stage lighting may be best visualized by recalling the appearance of a piece of iron as it is heated, say over a gas flame. As its temperature rises, it begins to glow and first appears to be a dull red. This will be at about 800° K. As the temperature increases still more, the iron will turn to a yellow-white, at about 1000° K. It will emit warm white light at about 2600° K, if we are able to get it that hot. Of course, by the time the iron is emitting white light, it has melted. However, increasing its temperature still further would cause its light to become first whiter and then bluer.

Ultimately our piece of iron will cease to be a good example of the upper range of the Kelvin scale because we cannot get it any hotter by available means. Nevertheless, physicists have been able to continue the Kelvin scale up to extremely high temperatures by mathematical means. Furthermore they have been able to confirm these findings through such things as the observation of very hot stars.

Another means is available for producing high Kelvin temperature light: One may filter light of a lower temperature producing a remainder with a much higher color temperature. Light energy is lost in the process, but the result is high color temperature light without the need for a comparably high temperature source. This is precisely what is done in the theatre to produce blue light.

One of the ironies of color terminology is that the terms used to describe light according to its psychological effect are in direct semantic opposition to the terms used to refer to the Kelvin rating. Thus "warm light," which is yellowish in hue, refers to light with a rather *low* Kelvin rating (about 2200° K) and "cool light" is the term used to refer to light with a *high* Kelvin rating (about 3500–6000° K). The reader should also note that the Kelvin scale refers only to the color content of the light, not to the quantity produced. One may have a tiny amount of high Kelvin temperature light or a huge amount; the Kelvin number remains the same. This fact is somewhat confused by the property of the incandescent source which, because of its nature, tends to vary light output and color temperature at the same time. As the power is increased to a given incandescent lamp, it tends to produce both more light and light of a higher Kelvin temperature. This characteristic is not shared by many other sources.

The application of the color temperature scale to stage lighting will be evident as we examine the various types of lamps used and particularly the more recent development of the tungsten-halogen lamp.

Briefly, the color temperature of a lamp is an indication of the relative amounts of visible wavelengths available in the light it produces. See Figure 2-1 and Plate VIII. Note that incandescent lamps are deficient in blue wavelengths as compared to red. Even the 3200° K lamp (the color temperature of medium-life tungsten-halogen lamps) emits only about one-fifth as much blue as red. Thus it is more difficult to

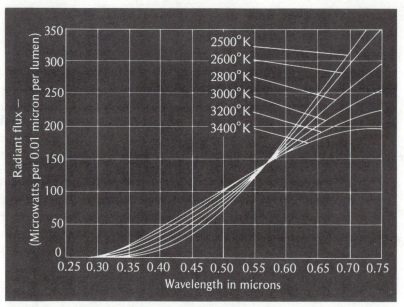

FIGURE *2-1*

Light Output. This graph shows the amount of energy, expressed as micro-watts, present at each wavelength of light being emitted from an incandescent lamp. While figures might vary slightly from lamp to lamp, these curves are typical. Note that visible red begins at 0.70 on the graph and that the deepest visible blue will be at 0.40. This graph illustrates the great advantage gained in blue light output by increasing the color temperature to 3200° K. Conversely it also shows the rapid diminuation of blue as a lamp is dimmed. Graph Courtesy General Electric Company.

produce high brightness levels of blue light on stage than it is to produce high levels of red light. Moreover, the color temperature of incandescent lamps drops as they are dimmed. This removes the already deficient blue end of the spectrum well ahead of the red end. Lamps tend to first yellow and then redden as they go out.

The Filament Incandescent Lamp

In 1879, Thomas Edison invented the first practical incandescent lamp. It consisted of a carbon filament made by charring a strand of bamboo fiber which was enclosed in an evacuated glass bulb. It produced about 1.4 lumens of light per watt of electricity, an efficiency of about 4 percent. Edison chose carbon for his filament because it has a high melting point, necessary because of the high temperature needed to produce useful portions of visible light.

The theory of Edison's lamp and all incandescent lamps since is quite simple. Electricity, when made to pass through a small wire of relatively high electrical resistance, will generate a great deal of heat. If the wire size and material and the amount of electricity are right, enough heat will be generated to cause the wire to glow white-hot, that is, to incandesce.

From the day of Edison's first lamp to the present day, there has been a constant struggle to get the hot filament to produce more visible light per unit of electricity fed into it and to prevent deterioration of the filament by sublimation.[1]

The search was soon on for materials that would not sublimate as easily as carbon in a vacuum. Osmium and tantalum were tried and found good, but they were prohibitively expensive. Tungsten lamp filaments were introduced in 1907. This metallic element represented a good compromise. Tungsten was relatively abundant and cheap. It had a high melting point, 6120° F. It sublimated rather slowly and it had the favorable property of emitting much of its incandescence within the limits of visible light.

In 1913 another solution to the problem of filament life was introduced. Gas pressure on the filament could be increased without burning up the filament by removing all air from the bulb and replacing it with an inert gas. Nitrogen was first used for this purpose, but today a mixture of nitrogen and argon is used because of more favorable heat convection characteristics. Introducing the gas did result in faster cooling of the filament because the gas carried the heat away from it, but this was more than offset by the increased temperature which was now possible in the filament and the higher efficiency which resulted. The gas-filled tungsten-filament lamp of 1913 had about 10 times the efficiency of Edison's first lamp, or 14 lumens per watt.

Since 1913, the efficiency of lamps has been further increased to more than 20 lumens per watt, largely by changes in filament design and increases in gas pressure in the bulb.

CONCENTRATED-FILAMENT LAMPS

Modern incandescent lamps represent more engineering effort than simply an increase in size and efficiency, however spectacular this increase has been. As far as stage lighting is concerned, the greatest single advance in modern lamp development came between 1910 and 1920. This advance was the development of, first, a method of making strong, ductile tungsten wire and, subsequently, a concentrated-filament projection service lamp using this wire. Until then, the incandescent lamp was strictly a general-lighting device on stage. No simple lens system can produce an evenly distributed, easily controllable pool of light on

---

[1] Sublimation is that process by which solids change directly to gases without first becoming liquids. For example, ice will slowly disappear by sublimation during the winter even though the temperature does not rise above freezing.

stage from a large, unsymmetrical filament. Instead of a pool of light, an out-of-focus bloblike image of the filament will be produced, which is of no value in lighting the stage. Theoretically the ideal light source for a lens system is a *point source* of light, that is, a powerful light emanating from one location with no dimensions. This mathematical point is physically impossible. However, the nearer the light source approaches this, the better the optical effect. The carbon arc was adopted for follow-spot use well before any other electrical spotlighting source entered the theatre. The light source from a simple carbon arc is relatively small; it may easily be less than a quarter of an inch in diameter. Since the source is essentially circular in shape and homogenous, the lens "sees" it much like a point and produces a circular pool of very usable light.

The development of the 100-watt concentrated-filament lamp in about 1920 ushered in the spotlight era. This same lamp also made possible such things as incandescent slide projectors, movie machines, various searchlight devices, and eventually the "sealed-beam" or "PAR" lamps. All of these devices depend on a near-point-source filament for their operation.

THE FIRST INCANDESCENT SPOTLIGHTS

While the power of the first concentrated-filament lamp was a mere 100 watts, in a few years these high-efficiency special-projection lamps were available in sizes up to 2000 watts. Availability led to the rapid development of lighting instruments to take advantage of these new light sources. First there was a series of plano-convex lens instruments.[2] The 100- and 250-watt types known as "baby spots" came earliest and were soon followed by the "spotlights." This term was for a time applied only to 1000- and 2000-watt "plano-convex" instruments.

All of these plano-convex spots used the globular, or "G-type," base-down lamp in its various sizes. During the late 1920s and early 1930s, these instruments were the main source of specific illumination on stage, now lit with electrically operated borderlights and footlights for the main flood of general illumination. The G-type lamps were designed to operate base down to keep the heated gases, which were by then standard in the envelope, from melting the base cement and ruining the base connections. Since the lamps were planned for base-down to horizontal operation, the filament supports were arranged with this position in mind and any radical departure from it often led to early failure because of sagging filament parts which touched together, shorted, and then failed.

MORE EFFICIENT INSTRUMENTS

During the 1930s pressure for more efficient lighting instruments led to the development of two types which led to changes in bulb shape and filament position inside the lamps. Both the ellipsoidal-reflector spot-

---

[2] So called because they use a plano-convex lens, flat on one side and convex on the other.

light and the Fresnel spotlight (see Chapter 4) were high-efficiency instruments. The Fresnel, in particular, demanded close lamp-to-lens distances and brought about the development of tubular bulbs. The ellipsoidal-reflector spotlight, with its very high efficiency, led to the development of the base-up lamp. This lamp presented two special problems: (1) the base had to stand extremely high temperatures without failing, and (2) the filament had to be supported from the top to prevent sagging and early failure. In addition, the operating temperature of both of these lamps had increased to the point where special hard glass was necessary for the bulb.

The development of the early Fresnel lens spotlight and the ellipsoidal-reflector spotlight heralded the proliferation of many specialized instruments and the lamps to operate them. Many of these instruments are still in use today and some of the specialized lamps for them are still being manufactured. However, a more recent development, the tungsten-halogen lamp, is rapidly superseding these early lamps. It will be discussed below. First we must examine some of the wide variety of conventional[3] lamps made for lighting instruments in the past 10 to 15 years and still in use.

Variations included a choice of several average-life figures (50 hours, 200 hours, and occasionally 1000–2000 hours), choice of color temperature (2600° K, 2950° K, and 3200° K), in two socket types, and in a great variety of wattages and filament configurations (see Figure 2-4). Many of these lamps are still carried in stock for sale. However, there is a gradual changeover taking place to the tungsten-halogen (T-H) lamp. New stage lighting fixtures are being manufactured around the T-H lamp exclusively and T-H lamps known as "retrofits" are being provided for older fixtures (see Figure 2-3a). Equipping an old ellipsoidal-reflector spot with a new T-H retrofit lamp does not make it into a modern instrument, but it does increase its efficiency somewhat and makes it possible to utilize it to the end of its normal life. As retrofit lamps are being manufactured and stocked, their conventional predecessors are being dropped from manufacturer's inventories. Thus the theatre lighting artist is forced to adopt T-H lamps whether he wishes to or not. For example, the 500-watt T20/70 lamp for Fresnel spotlights has become nearly unavailable as this edition goes to press. It has been superseded by a retrofit T-H lamp. However, many other conventional lamps remain available and we must understand their characteristics.

CONVENTIONAL LAMPS FOR STAGE-LIGHTING SERVICE

Stage lamps for specific lighting apparatus (spots, beam projectors, and the like) come in a wide variety of types, wattages, voltages, and color temperatures. Figure 2-2 gives the terminology for the various parts. As

---

[3] Since both the modern tungsten-halogen lamps and their predecessors are *incandescent* lamps, we will distinguish between them by calling the simple gas-filled incandescent lamps "conventional" lamps and the new tungsten-halogen lamps "T-H" lamps.

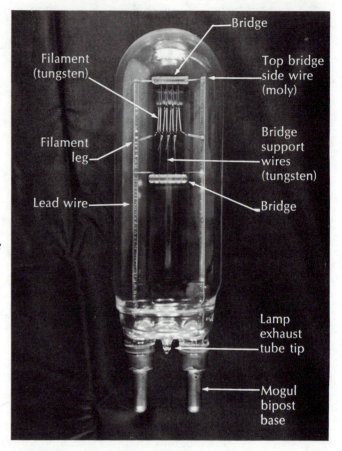

FIGURE 2-2
Parts of Conventional Stage Incandescent Lamp. Some details of concentrated-filament lamps, both conventional and tungsten-halogen, will vary with the manufacturer. See Figures 2-4b, 2-5a, and 2-5b for further variations in the structure of lamps. Photo by William Huling, California State University, Northridge Audio Visual Department.

the optics of spotlights became more and more exact, and as wattages increased, the original screw bases became obsolete because they could not assure exact placement of the filament with relation to the lens nor could they carry the heavy current needed to operate the larger lamps. The first departure from the screw base in stage lamps was the "prefocus base," pictured in Figure 2-3b. It has the great advantage of assuring that the filament will always face the lens exactly, as long as the lamp is properly inserted. Its current-carrying capacity is slightly greater than the screw base of comparable size and it can be reinforced to resist the effects of high base temperatures. At this point in the development of lamps for stage lighting, the current-carrying problem could be solved in the larger size lamps simply by increasing the physical size of the socket and lamp base from medium to large. Later increases in size and decreases in the amount of space available for sockets, plus what are apparently insurmountable difficulties in solving overheating problems in bases of prefocus and screw types, led to the development of the "bipost" base illustrated in Figure 2-3b (N and O).

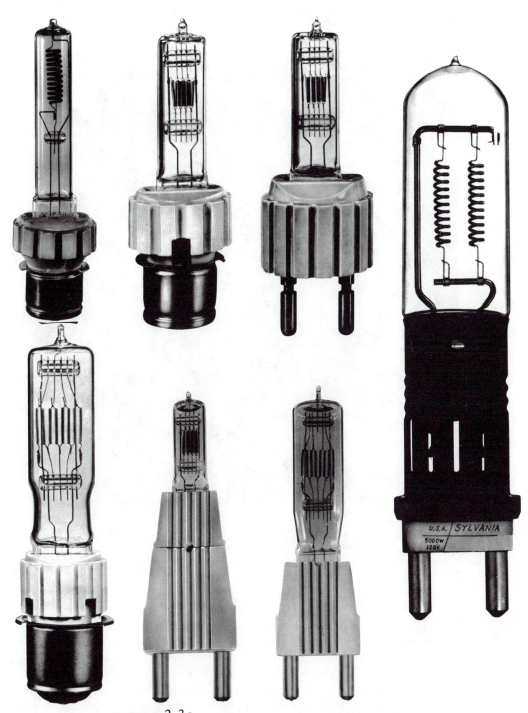

FIGURE 2-3a
Retrofit Lamps. These lamps were originally designed to allow owners of instruments designed for conventional lamps to convert to T-H lamps. However new instruments have also been designed around these lamps making the distinction between retrofit lamps and modern special-based T-H lamps academic. Sylvania Electric Products Inc.

23

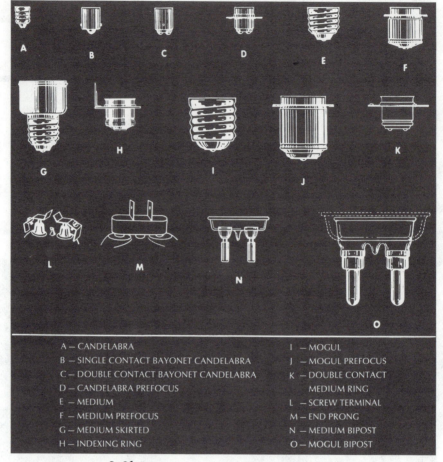

A — CANDELABRA
B — SINGLE CONTACT BAYONET CANDELABRA
C — DOUBLE CONTACT BAYONET CANDELABRA
D — CANDELABRA PREFOCUS
E — MEDIUM
F — MEDIUM PREFOCUS
G — MEDIUM SKIRTED
H — INDEXING RING

I — MOGUL
J — MOGUL PREFOCUS
K — DOUBLE CONTACT
      MEDIUM RING
L — SCREW TERMINAL
M — END PRONG
N — MEDIUM BIPOST
O — MOGUL BIPOST

FIGURE 2-3b

Common Lamp Bases. The above bases are commonly found on conventional lamps for the stage and on retrofit lamps. Prefocus and bipost bases will be most common. General Electric Company.

The bipost base was already in use in heavy-duty motion-picture and industrial types, and soon entered the stage-lighting field.

It is the experience of a good many professionals that the best base available for conventional lamps in either the medium or mogul size is the bipost type. It is almost completely resistant to failure from high socket temperatures and can, if well designed, carry large currents with ease.

None of these bases is foolproof in the hands of an amateur or a sloppy professional. All require care to see that the lamp is completely and accurately seated and that this has been done without forcing, which might break some part of the lamp.

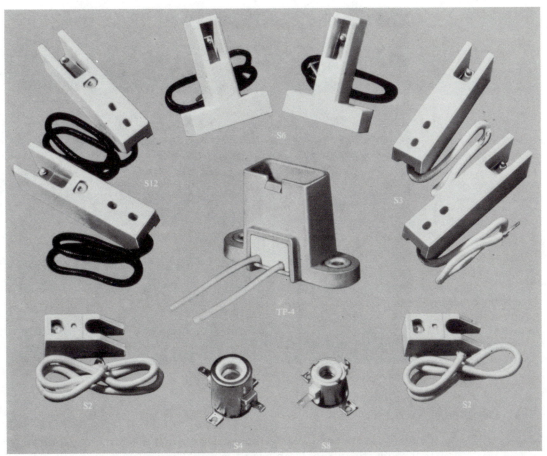

FIGURE 2-3c
Common Bases for Tungsten-Halogen Lamps. These bases have been especially engineered to control the operating temperature of the lamp seal and the base itself. Type TP-4, center, is the type most commonly found in modern spotlights using single-end T-H lamps. Sylvania Electric Products Inc.

MODERN TUNGSTEN-HALOGEN LAMPS

INTRODUCTION

As we begin our examination of the latest engineering improvements in the incandescent lamp, we must look at some of the difficulties with conventional lamps which led to this development. The problem centers around the interlocking relationship between lamp life and lamp efficiency. These terms are defined below.

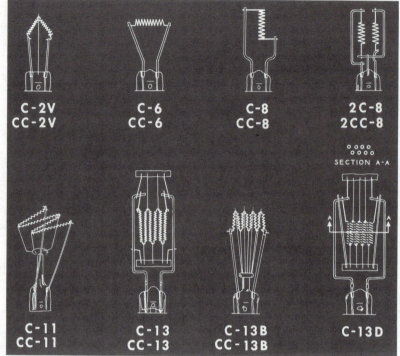

FIGURE 2-4
*Incandescent Lamp
Filament Configura-
tions. Particularly
note the concentra-
tion of light pro-
duced by the C-13
filaments.* General
Electric Company.

LAMP LIFE

Lamp life is stated in average hours. Thus a manufacturer may indicate
that a specific type of lamp has a life of 700 hours (a common figure for
household lamps). This means that if a large number of these lamps are
operated until they fail, the *average* life will be 700 hours. Individual
lamps will vary from this figure over a considerable range. Normally a
manufacturer of high-cost stage-lighting lamps will make good on
lamps which fail in the first few hours of use or on a batch of lamps
which can be clearly shown to average less than the stipulated figure.
The latter is very hard to establish under actual stage-lighting conditions.

EFFICIENCY

Lamp efficiency must be broken down into two types of data: *initial
lumens* and *lumen maintenance.* Initial lumens is a figure that can be
reported in either of two ways: *initial lumens* or *lumens per watt.* Since
the wattage of the lamp is always known, either figure can be easily
converted to the other. "Initial lumens" is a commonly used figure. It is
a number representing the entire lumen output of a lamp as it is emitted
in all directions. It is up to the user to gather the light for whatever purpose he has in mind. Normally this figure represents the average of a

considerable number of lamps whose light output has been carefully measured after a certain period of "aging" which causes the output to stabilize. The average total is reported in the following manner: "initial lumens—80,000." This figure would represent the output of a rather large lamp. The same data might be reported as "20 lumens per watt." This would represent the output of a hypothetical 4000 watt spotlight lamp (4000 × 20 = 80,000).

LUMEN MAINTENANCE

As we will see below, the lumen output of a lamp tends to drop as the lamp ages. In the case of conventional lamps, the drop is considerable. The term "lumen maintenance" is used to describe these data. This information is probably best conveyed in a graph plotting light output against lamp life. It is also frequently reported as the figure "average lumens." This, as the name suggests, is a figure reporting the average lumen output over the normal life of the lamp. It does not, however, indicate how the deterioration progresses during the lamp life.

LAMP LIFE AND EFFICIENCY

Incandescent lamps can be built for extremely long life but at the expense of very low efficiency. This difficulty arises from the fact that tungsten sublimates. "Sublimation" is the scientific name for the process by which a solid, when sufficiently heated, may be converted directly into a gas without passing through a liquid state. The process is speeded up by high temperatures and low pressure on the surface of the material—exactly the conditions that exist inside a vacuum lamp operating with a hot, highly efficient, tungsten filament. The result is what we have all seen inside "burnt out" lamps. The inside of the bulb is coated with a black, sooty material and the filament has thinned and broken, causing failure. Even before failure, the lamp was greatly reduced in efficiency by the sooty material and the thinned filament.

The black material is tungsten. It has sublimated from the filament circulating in the bulb as a gas until it condensed into a solid state on the relatively cool inner surface of the glass bulb. When enough of the tungsten has been removed from the filament to cause it to break, we say that the lamp has "burned out." This is actually a misnomer because no burning (combining with oxygen) has taken place. The tungsten is still chemically uncombined, although it has been removed to a useless place in the lamp. Burning does take place when a lamp has been accidentally cracked allowing air to enter the bulb. In this case the interior of the lamp will be clouded with a yellow smoke, tungsten oxide, when the filament is heated by turning on the lamp.

Early attacks on the sublimation problem resulted in the gas-filled lamp, which we have already discussed. Combining the concentrated filament with the gas-filled envelope resulted in the development of a large family of high-intensity lamps for theatre, motion-picture projection, and similar services.

COMPARISON OF STAGE AND GENERAL SERVICE LAMPS

In the case of general service lamps for household- and commercial-lighting purposes, the engineers have made a compromise in favor of long life and relatively low efficiency. Thus 100-watt lamps used in the home may be expected to last from 700 to 1000 hours on the average, when run at the voltage for which they were designed. When run at a lower voltage, their life will lengthen and their efficiency drop; at a higher voltage their life is shortened and their efficiency increased. This is the "teeter-totter" effect. In the case of concentrated-filament lamps for spotlights, the engineers have compromised in favor of relatively high efficiency and short life. More light per watt of power is produced from these lamps but the lamps must be replaced quite often.

In some of the more highly developed conventional lamps for stage and projection service, other steps have been taken to see that we get maximum light out of the bulb and onto the stage for the entire life of the lamp. For instance, in the "burn-base-up" ellipsoidal-spotlight lamps, a special metal screen often is installed above the filament to collect the sublimated tungsten, preventing it from depositing on the glass bulb and impeding transmission of light. Enclosed in other large lamps is a small quantity of sandlike material which may be swished around the inside of the bulb to clean the tungsten deposit off the glass and increase the effective light output during the remainder of the life of the lamp. However, the life of all of these lamps is still relatively short. Spotlight lamps range from 35 to 200 hours in average life.

CAUSES OF EARLY LAMP FAILURE

Most stage-lighting lamps give far more than the rated average life in actual practice because they are operated for a large percentage of their life through dimmers at reduced voltages.

Computations based on the following formula will show that the life of a lamp is rapidly increased as the voltage is reduced below its design value.

$$\frac{\text{life}_d}{\text{life}_r} = \frac{\text{volts}_d{}^{13.1}}{\text{volts}_r} = \frac{\text{lumens}_r{}^{3.86}}{\text{lumens}_d}$$

Subscripts d and r indicate the designed and the reduced values respectively.

As the formula shows, lumen output also drops off rapidly, but this output drop is the purpose of dimming. However, many stage lamps meet an untimely end because of poor handling by the operators. Probably the most common cause of early failure is the operation of lamps in a position too far from the one stipulated by the manufacturer. In the case of base-down lamps, operating them in any position that places the base higher than any portion of the filament may cause failure. Actually, if the lamp is operated in any position approaching this limit in a housing that hampers ventilation somewhat, early failure may come anyway. The second cause of early failure is the operation of too large wattage lamps in a given lamphouse. One should become suspicious of a high-wattage problem anytime lamps show signs of bulging after some hours of use. If the lamps are bulged, either the ventilation is not adequate or the reflector (in the case of Fresnel or plano spots) is out of alignment or both.

A third cause of early lamp failure is excessive vibration. Concentrated-filament lamps are precision devices, a fact which is reflected in their high cost. If these lamps are jarred unduly, especially when they are on, the parts may move enough to touch, causing a short circuit and destroying the filament. Operators should be especially cautioned about poking or bumping spotlights to make final adjustments in angle after the lights have become too hot to touch and the operator does not want to take the time to use gloves.

Still another cause of early failure appears only in those lamps equipped with prefocus and screw bases. These bases are found in most lamps under 750 watts in older theatres where equipment was bought before medium bipost bases were available for these sizes. These bases seem to be particularly susceptible to heat failure, which loosens the base from the bulb of the lamp. In most cases, such a faulty lamp continues to operate unless someone attempts to remove it, perhaps to replace it with a lamp of different wattage. When this happens the lead wires in the base of the lamp twist together, forming a short circuit and ruining the lamp for future use. Operators should be cautioned to be especially careful to avoid any extra strain on the base when changing lamps in prefocus sockets. This care will save most but not all of the lamps which have been overheated at the base.

THE HALOGEN CYCLE

The most modern stage-lighting lamps represent a new attack on the dilemma of lamp life versus efficiency. A means has been found to restore the sublimated tungsten to the filament. This is known as the "halogen cycle." Since it is the essential principle in the operation of all new stage-lighting lamps, we must understand it more fully.

The filament is a regular concentrated tungsten filament, although its configuration has been changed somewhat to improve the operation of the halogen cycle. Thus the lamp is still an *incandescent* lamp—it produces light by the conversion of heat energy into light energy. However, the conditions that control sublimation of this incandescing filament have been changed radically: (1) The atmosphere surrounding the filament contains a "halogen" in gaseous form. "Halogen" is the chemical family name for a group of elements consisting of fluorine, chlorine, bromine, astatine, and iodine. They are highly active chemically. Iodine and bromine have been successfully used in incandescent lamps. (2) The bulb of the lamp is much smaller than that of a conventional lamp. In earlier models of the T-H lamp this bulb was made of fused quartz and the halogen was iodine giving rise to the first name for these lamps: "quartz-iodine." This may now be a misnomer on two counts. The halogen may be bromine and the envelope may be hard glass, not fused quartz. Hence the modern generic term is "tungsten-halogen."

How the Halogen Cycle Works. When a T-H lamp is turned on to full power, the filament sublimates as it would in a conventional lamp. Tungsten vapor is formed in the atmosphere around the hot filament. This vapor migrates through the atmosphere of the lamp and deposits on the "cool" surface of the envelope (about 600° C). It is in this region that the halogen combines chemically with the tungsten forming gaseous tungsten halide. This removes the tungsten from the inside surface of the envelope as fast as it is deposited there. The gaseous tungsten halide diffuses into the atmosphere inside the bulb and eventually encounters the very high temperatures at the surface of the hot filament. This temperature decomposes the tungsten halide, depositing the tungsten on the filament and freeing the halogen as a gas to repeat the cycle. Thus the halogen serves as a "getter," removing the sublimated tungsten from the interior of the bulb and returning it to the filament from whence it came. Theoretically this cycle might proceed indefinitely with no loss of materials. The energy is supplied by the electrically generated heat provided to the lamp to make it incandesce. In the process, two of the main difficulties with the incandescent lamp have been removed: the filament no longer loses tungsten to the atmosphere surrounding it except for a small increment constantly in the halogen cycle, and the bulb is no longer blackened by tungsten deposits which reduce the light emitted from the lamp. Thus the lamp has high lumen maintenance.

The halogen cycle improves lamp life significantly. Nevertheless lamps eventually fail from one or more of the following causes:

1. Filament failure due to shorting. Filaments become shorted by the crystalline "whiskers" which are formed on the surface of the filament wire as the tungsten is redeposited from the gaseous state. If one of these crystals bridges the gap between two portions of the filament, a short circuit is formed.
2. Filament failure from erosion. The filament is eroded away at some point—usually a cooler portion—until it breaks and opens the circuit.
3. Seal failure. This problem arises from the high temperature which must be maintained at the envelope. The 600° C plus required to make the halogen cycle work causes the lead-in wire which is sealed into the quartz or hard glass of the envelope to oxidize. The powdery oxide breaks the seal and allows air to enter the inside of the bulb. When the lamp is turned on, the tungsten oxidizes, filling the bulb with yellowish smoke as the filament is destroyed.

The first two problems have not been completely solved at the present time. Many T-H lamps can be expected to fail from filament problems. The seal problem has been partially solved by means of special sockets designed to remove the heat from the seal and keep it as cool as possible. Such sockets are found in most T-H equipment (see Figure 2-3c). Their spring tensions are adjusted carefully to control the heat transfer from the pins of the lamp base to the metal parts of the socket. Any failure which causes socket burning or pitting and/or pin burning and pitting cannot be ignored. Putting a good lamp in a burned socket will only invite early failure. Damaged sockets must be replaced.

Difficulties can be expected if T-H instruments are operated in conditions of poor ventilation which increase socket temperatures. Costly lamp failures and socket damage are likely. Operating the lamps at overvoltage—sometimes occasionally done in scenic projectors—necessitates the careful adjustment of the forced ventilation to remove the added heat rapidly.

DIMMING TUNGSTEN-HALOGEN LAMPS

It is obvious that operating a T-H lamp at reduced voltage will lower temperatures throughout the lamp. If temperatures are lowered sufficiently, the halogen cycle will cease to operate. The envelope will blacken rapidly. If this condition were to continue for a considerable period of time, the lamp would first dim, the result of deposited tungsten on the envelope, and then fail. However, most stage lighting calls for the lamps to be brought up to full rather frequently. When a partially blackened lamp is brought up to full temperature, the halogen cycle soon clears the blackened envelope and restores the lumen output. The exact effect of such cycles of low-voltage operation and full-voltage clearing is hard to determine. It appears to have a rather small effect on the overall life of the lamps. One thing seems certain: If it is necessary to run T-H lamps for hours at reduced voltage because of the nature of the lighting design, it would probably be a good idea to run them at full up after each period of low voltage to restore the lumen output. Less than a half hour of full voltage operation should be enough.

Although seldom encountered in stage lighting, a condition which results in brief on-cycles followed by off-periods long enough to allow complete cooling will also cause T-H lamps to blacken. The cure is the same—run the lamps at full voltage for a period long enough to allow the halogen cycle to clear the bulb.

LIFE OF TUNGSTEN-HALOGEN LAMPS

In spite of the difficulties mentioned above, engineers have been able to design T-H lamps which have much improved life and lumen maintenance as compared to conventional lamps. Life improvements range from four times to as high as ten times that of comparable conventional lamps. The wide range is the result of the variety of options which lamp engineers have made available to users. They fall into three categories: long-life, medium-life, and short-life lamps. (See Figure 2-5 for typical modern T-H lamps.)

Long-Life Lamps. Lamps which have been designed to last up to 2000 hours are long-life lamps. They operate at relatively low color temperatures—about 3000° K as compared to 3200° K for short-life lamps. Their average lumen output is also significantly low compared to the shorter lived lamps discussed below, but the lumen maintenance feature of the halogen cycle makes them more efficient over their entire life than conventional lamps. Although these lamps may cost from two to three times as much as conventional lamps of the same output, their eventual cost of operation is much lower because they outlast the conventional lamp by as much as ten times.

These long-life lamps are often sold solely on the basis of economy. The cost accounting makes them appear to be the best buy by a wide margin, particularly when cost of relamping is figured into the account. If the fixtures are in an unaccessible location or one that involves costly shutdowns to allow relamping, the conclusion is inescapable. However, these are not the only factors to consider when evaluating these lamps for theatre applications. Following are some negative considerations:

1. Diminished output of these lamps combined with their relatively low color temperature may reduce levels of illumination below acceptable limits. This is particularly true of instruments being used as sources of cool light. If the theatre is limited in instruments and/or power available, long-life lamps may not be efficient enough to produce the light needed.
2. Long intervals between relamping are not entirely desirable if these relamping chores are the only times when the instrument is serviced. In many municipal auditoriums and school theatres, relamping is the only occasion for cleaning the instrument and changing the color medium. Gel, lenses, and instrument may be covered with dust and grime at the end of 2000 hours of operation. If long-life lamps are used, servicing must be made a part of a regular schedule. It cannot await lamp failure.

In short, lighting artists should not let cost accounting decide which lamp they should install with no consideration for other factors.

Medium-Life Lamps. T-H lamps designed with life comparable to or somewhat longer than that of the conventional lamps they replace are medium-life lamps. They have from about 150 to 500 hours rated life. By bringing the rated life down to these rather modest figures, the engineers are able to take advantage of the opposite side of the life versus efficiency dilemma. Medium-life T-H lamps are higher in efficiency and have considerably higher color temperature. They can be expected to produce about 10 percent more light and to have a color temperature of about 3200° K. The color temperature increase is more significant than it would first appear when this is applied to the production of cool light. Most of the lumen increase is at the cool end of the spectrum. Thus it is not uncommon that a 3200° K lamp will produce twice as much blue light under stage conditions as a 3000° or 2950° K lamp.

This increased efficiency makes medium life T-H lamps highly desirable on stages where total wattage is limited, perhaps by a restricted number of dimmer ways. Operating costs are higher than the cost of running the stage with long-life lamps, but light output is much improved.

Short-Life T-H Lamps. Lamps built with high efficiency as the primary consideration are short-life lamps. They usually have a life of about 50 hours and color temperature of about 3450° K. They are designed for photographic applications where high color temperature is the primary concern. "Indoor" color film has been standardized at 3450° K, and such lamps are vital to the photographer using this film. Their cost of operation is far too high, and their burn-out rate too risky for most theatre applications. Only occasionally can the theatre lighting artist justify installing such an expensive lamp in lighting equipment. However, he may find use for it in scenic projection equipment where high efficiency is absolutely necessary.

Theatre workers seeking emergency supplies of lamps from theatre supply houses or photographic concerns should be aware that they may find only 3450° K 50-hour lamps available. In addition to being outrageously expensive to operate and having early failure potentialities, these lamps will usually upset the color balance of the lighting if intermixed with long-life or medium-life T-H lamps, or with conventional lamps. In an emergency, the life of these lamps can be extended and color temperature lowered by operating them at reduced dimmer readings.

CHOICE OF LAMPS

The above information on lamp life can be best understood by examining Table 2-1 which summarizes the choices available to the lighting artist when he seeks lamps for a typical 500-watt ellipsoidal reflector

TABLE *2-1*
Available Lamps for a Typical 6-Inch Lens Ellipsoidal-Reflector Spotlight (Instrument: Century 1590 Series Lekolite; maximum watts: 750)

WATTS	BULB	GE ORDERING CODE	ANSI CODE	COLOR TEMP. (°K)	AVERAGE LIFE HOURS	APPROX. INITIAL LUMENS	OPERATING POSITION
250	T-12	250T12/8		2800	800	4,500	Base up to 30°
500	T-12	500T12/8		2850	800	9,000	''
500	T-12	500T12/9		2950	200	11,000	''
750	T-12	750T12/9		3000	200	17,000	''
500	T-4	Q500CL/P	EGE	3000	2000	10,450	any
500	T-4	Q500/5CL/P	EGD	3150	500	13,000	''
750	T-6	Q750CL/P	EGG	3000	2000	15,750	''
750	T-6	Q750/4CL/P	EGF	3200	500	20,400	''

SOURCE: Data from GE Catalog SS123, February 1973.

spotlight. This data is subject to change, but the number of choices is typical.

RETROFIT LAMPS

In addition to the three ranges of rated life offered to the buyer, two broad categories of lamps are presently being offered. The first is a completely new line of lamps which work in fixtures especially designed for T-H lamps. The second is a category known as "retrofit" lamps. These are T-H lamps to be used in older fixtures originally designed for conventional lamps. Such T-H lamps have sockets matching those on conventional lamps. These sockets often are fitted with extensions to raise the filament in the tiny bulb of the T-H lamp to the proper height above the bottom of the socket. (This distance is known as the Light Center Length—LCL.) In some cases the socket and extension of the retrofit lamp will be considerably larger than the bulb of the lamp itself. See Figure 2-3a.

OPERATING POSITION FOR TUNGSTEN-HALOGEN LAMPS

In most cases modern T-H lamps are made to be operated in any position, unlike their predecessors which were restricted to either "base down to horizontal" or "base up to horizontal" positions. Modern instruments made for T-H lamps usually are designed to operate the lamp axially. This makes it easier to obtain an even light field and greater efficiency with the T-H filament configurations. Retrofit lamps are a different story. Although the lamps themselves will usually allow any-position operation, the old instruments may have been designed with ventilating slots arranged for "base up only" operation or the opposite. Reversing this position may upset the ventilation enough to overheat the lamp and seals.

MIXING TUNGSTEN-HALOGEN LAMPS AND CONVENTIONAL LAMPS

In many theatres it is necessary to effect a gradual changeover from conventional lamps to T-H lamps. It is usually not feasible to discard existing inventories of conventional lamps, although some professional houses have done so by selling off the conventional lamps at a discount to schools, community theatres, and the like. This means that a designer may find that he has designed the color plot of a show around conventional 2950° K lamps and must relamp failed lamps with 3200° K T-H lamps. (In this regard the long-life 3000° K lamps offer an advantage.) Such a change may upset color balance if the relamped instrument is equipped with a gel that transmits a significant amount of blue light. The beam will be noticeably cooler than its conventional lamp counterparts. Regelling[4] with a slightly warmer color is the best solution be-

---

[4] "Gelling" is standard theatre terminology for replacing the color medium, whether the medium is gelatine or not.

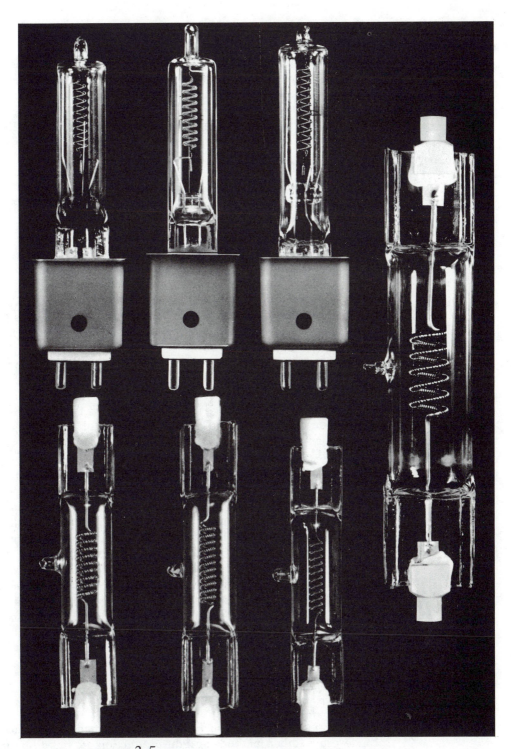

FIGURE 2-5

Tungsten-Halogen Lamps. Modern instruments of high efficiency have been designed around both the double-ended and the single-end lamps. These lamps are available in a variety of life and output ratings (see Table 2-1). Sylvania Electric Products Inc.

cause this will not upset the cues. An alternative is to operate the newly lamped instruments at lower dimmer readings to reduce color temperature. It is obvious that the shrewd designer faced with a mixture of conventional and T-H lamps in his spots will use the T-H lamps as cool sources wherever possible, thereby utilizing their increased efficiency in that region.

DETERMINING LIFE REMAINING IN T-H LAMPS

Along with their many advantages, T-H lamps have brought one disadvantage to the stage-lighting artist. It is no longer a simple matter to determine the approximate remaining life of a lamp. In the case of conventional lamps, one could note the amount of blackening on the envelope, and with a little experience, make a shrewd guess as to the probable remaining life. Significantly blackened lamps could be taken out of service or relegated to nonsensitive areas where their failure would not cause much trouble. Another method was to use old lamps for rehearsal periods and install new lamps only a few hours before opening—the few hours being enough to detect the rare early failures from faulty lamps.

No such alternatives are open to the user of T-H lamps. If any evidence of use is visible in a T-H lamp, it is nearly microscopic. Some authorities say that a close observer can see tiny crystalline deposits on the filament of a used lamp. These are formed as the tungsten is redeposited on the filament. The greater the amount of these deposits, the nearer the lamp is to the end of its life. Other authorities simply say that there is no visible indication of remaining lamp life. In any event, no casual glance at the lamp is going to produce an estimate of remaining life. A log of hours in service will not really solve the problem either because stage lamps are operated at widely varying voltages. This vastly complicates the computation of probable life. A computer would have to be programmed to take into account all of the variables in order to produce useful estimates of remaining life. As the matter now stands, lighting artists are going to have to live with a higher rate of unexpected failures until enough experience is accumulated by actual observation of the visible characteristics of failed lamps to enable some guesses to be made. In the meantime it would be wise to install lamps known to be near the beginning of their life in critical areas.

Other Methods of Producing Light

While perhaps 95 percent of all the light used on stage is produced from incandescence, other methods of light production are important to the lighting artist because of their potential for effect lighting and because of the possibility of future adaptation to stage lighting.

Producing Light by Gaseous Discharge

Everyone is familiar with the neon sign and its various brilliantly colored counterparts. We are also familiar with the sodium-vapor (yellow) and mercury-vapor (cold blue-green) street-lighting lamps that are common on superhighways and city streets today. Not many of these light sources presently appear on the stage, although it is hard to conceive of a modern commercial theatre without a neon-lighted marquee! Nevertheless, the stage-lighting artist will find use for these sources. They will become much more practical in the theatre of tomorrow.

Gaseous-discharge lamps all work on the same principle: When an electrical current is passed through a gas by increasing the voltage to the point where the gas becomes a conductor instead of an insulator (this point depends on the pressure of the gas, the temperature, and the kind of gas used), the gas glows with colors characteristic of that particular gas. For instance, the common neon lamp produces that red glow because the predominant visible wavelength produced by neon when it is made to conduct electricity is red. Within rather narrow limits, the total amount of light produced by a tube of gas depends on the amount of electricity forced through it. However, the principal factor determining the relative amounts of various wavelengths of light produced by a gaseous tube is the kind of gas and the pressure under which it is at the time of operation. For example, it is possible to vary, by adjusting the pressure of the gas, the light output of a mercury-vapor lamp so that most of the light falls into the ultraviolet wavelengths. One should notice, however, that the lamp will produce light consisting of typical line spectra for the element in use; the pressure will merely vary the amount of light in each of the various wavelengths. While these data seem a bit far removed from the needs of the stage-lighting artist, there are several quite practical applications. Mercury-vapor lamps are available which will produce a suntan, others will light streets, form the heart of the fluorescent lamp, or provide the blacklight (see the section "Blacklight: Ultraviolet Sources" in this chapter) frequently used on stage. All of these mercury sources use mercury vapor, but at various accurately determined pressures and with various types of glass envelopes and filters. In order to maintain the proper pressure within the mercury tube, rather limited variations in external temperature are stipulated for these lamps. Either too much or too little outside heat will impair their efficiency.

A complete explanation of the theory behind the production of light by gaseous-discharge lamps would be far too complex for this text. However, in very general terms, the light is produced by changes in the arrangement of electrons within the atomic structure of the gas. These changes are made by the passing electrical current. As these atoms and electrons return to normal again, "vibrations" occur which result in the production of light. The light produced will be composed of narrow bands of definite frequencies which make up the spectrogram of the particular material.

Since a gaseous-discharge lamp does not depend upon heat for the production of light, it is both more efficient in its use of electrical energy and more rapid in its response. As you know, large incandescent lamps have a very perceptible fade-out period after the electricity is turned off, and a short, but still perceptible, warm-up period when turned on. These lags (often more than a second) in the reaction of the light output of the filament to the electrical current tend to smooth out the flicker that might be caused by alternating current; in large lamps the lags obliterate the flicker completely. Compared to incandescent lamps, gaseous lamps operate instantly. Actually there is a lag, but it is measured in millionths of a second. The minuteness of these lags causes the gaseous-discharge lamps to produce what scientists call a strobo-scopic effect. Laymen call it a flicker, which is especially noticeable whenever a metallic object is moved in front of a dark surface.

The appearance is that of a series of overlapping images of the high-lights of the object. You may have noticed this effect in poorly designed fluorescent lighting. On stage it will be quite noticeable in the dim purple light visible from incompletely filtered blacklight sources. The flicker will probably bother the actors much more than the audience, but it can be an annoyance to both if quite a bit of metallic surface is lighted.

SHORT-ARC LAMPS

Gaseous-discharge lamps began as elongated tubes such as those in a neon sign. These have no application to lens systems. Now a new category has been developed. These are generically known as "short-arc lamps." Two of the earliest were the mercury-arc and the xenon-arc lamp. Presently there is an increasingly large family of such lamps, and they are finding more and more application in theatre lighting. Short-arc lamps operate by passing a relatively high electrical current through a tiny gap between two electrodes. The gap is bridged during the operation of the lamp by ionized gas which emits a brilliant light in the form of a line spectrum. Unlike the carbon arc lamp which actually operates in much the same way, nothing is consumed in the process, and there is no need to adjust the electrodes as they burn. Short-arc lamps (Figure 2-6) consist of heavy quartz envelopes containing heavy electrodes usually made of tungsten. This metal is chosen because of its high melting temperature. The arc is formed between the electrodes. The gas is contained in the envelope under high pressure. The result is a minute source of light of high efficiency (upward of 40 lumens per watt). Color of the light varies with the kind of gas used in the envelope and with

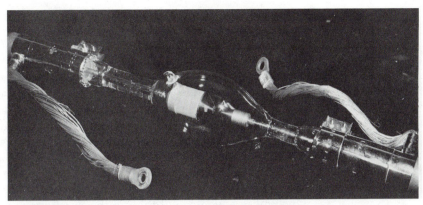

FIGURE 2-6
Modern Short-arc Xenon Lamp. This 4200 watt vertical-operation lamp is typical. It has a rated life of 800 hours, is ozone free and costs well over $500. Recently developed "HMI" lamps have the same general appearance. Lamp supplied by Background Engineers, Hollywood, California. Photo by author.

the pressure. In general, effective color temperature (the apparent color of the line spectrum to the eye) is high. In addition to the visible light, varying quantities of infrared and ultraviolet light are produced. Since the tungsten electrodes are heated in the process, a continuous spectrum also is emitted, although it is of relatively low intensity.

The mercury-arc lamp has not found much application in the theatre because of its cold, bluish light. The xenon-arc has been increasingly used in theatre lighting and in projection service. Although there is reason to believe that it will soon be superseded by safer, more efficient sources, it is described below because its characteristics will clarify the problems encountered in the use of short-arc lamps in the theatre. One should note in passing that there is also available and in use a long-arc xenon lamp. It produces a huge quantity of white light, and often is used for area lighting in such applications as parking lots. It is not commonly found in the theatre.

THE SHORT-ARC XENON LAMP

Short-arc xenon lamps found their first application in the theatre as high-intensity sources for scenic projection. They have been much used in such centers of advanced scenic projection as the Wagner Festspielhaus at Bayreuth, Germany, and the Salzburg Festspielhaus in Austria. This also led to the use of these lamps as single-source stage-lighting instruments — one lamp providing the entire lighting for a scene. More recently xenon lamps have been applied to follow spotlights, and have been extensively used as sources for motion-picture projection. At the present time most modern motion-picture theatres routinely use xenon sources because they provide a much more reliable light with a minimum of operator attention.

Advantages of Xenon. The greatest advantages of the xenon lamp are its high energy conversion efficiency, its small source size, and its high apparent color temperature. The high conversion efficiency makes it possible to utilize rather small wattages to produce large amounts of visible light. The tiny source size makes it relatively easy to design optical systems that catch most of the light produced and direct it where it is needed. The tiny source also makes possible a much more effective version of the square-law or lensless projector. This is a device which takes advantage of the fact that light spreads spherically from a source according to the law of squares—for each doubling of distance, the light covers four times the surface. If the source is small enough to resemble a point, objects placed in the light will cast sharp shadows which are magnified rapidly. Installing a xenon lamp in a square-law projector increases its efficiency and the sharpness of its image tremendously. The high effective color temperature of the xenon lamp is usually an advantage because follow spotting and projection frequently call for more blue light than the incandescent lamp can easily provide. At a color temperature equivalent of about 6000° K, the xenon lamp is an excellent source of blue light.

Disadvantages of Xenon. The first disadvantage of the xenon lamp is that it requires rather complicated electrical apparatus to operate it. It is a direct-current device. Stage-lighting current is almost universally alternating current. Moreover, the xenon lamp, unlike the incandescent lamp, is not self-regulating. When placed into an electrical circuit an incandescent lamp will only draw a limited amount of current as long as the maximum voltage is fixed. The gaseous-discharge lamp, such as xenon, will draw more and more current until something breaks down. This constitutes a short circuit unless controlled by some outside device. The control function is provided by the electrical device which converts the alternating current into direct current for the lamp. The equipment is known as a "power supply." It is heavy, bulky, and costly.

In order to start an xenon lamp, a special electrical device is required. It produces a jolt of very high voltage which ionizes the gas in the gap between the electrodes and allows the arc to start. Once this is done, the normal voltage of the power supply (perhaps 40 to 80 volts) will sustain the arc. This means that an xenon lamp, unlike an incandescent lamp, cannot be brought up gradually by means of a dimmer. Once on, however, the lamp can be dimmed or increased over a range from 10 percent of brightness to full. The color temperature does not change during this process of changing the amount of light.

An operating xenon lamp produces a wide variety of invisible light in addition to the visible light. Some of this is in the infrared region and represents wasted energy as far as stage lighting is concerned. Except for its heating effect on filters and the like, it is not harmful. The other end of the spectrum is a different matter. In the ultraviolet range, the xenon lamp produces lines of radiation down to the very short region where the ultraviolet light is highly dangerous to human beings. In this instance it approximates the radiation of sunlight in space. For this reason very high powered xenon lamps (up to 35 kilowatts or more!) have been developed for purposes of simulating radiation in space and testing space devices. These giants have not found their way into the theatre. However, even small xenon lamps produce these dangerous rays in limited quantities. The rays produce sunburn, eye damage, and also convert some of the oxygen of the air into ozone, a highly poisonous gas. A partial solution to this problem has been found in the manufacture of "ozone-free" xenon lamps. These lamps are equipped with an envelope which contains the dangerous radiation. They are much safer than other xenon lamps although a bit more expensive. Modern safety regulations require that any xenon lamp be operated in a well-ventilated enclosure which will remove all dangerous gases, and will not allow the unfiltered light to reach the operator or anyone else. Passing the light through ordinary glass lenses will filter out the remainder of the dangerous rays, making follow spotlights and scenic projectors safe to use.

The xenon lamp is a high-pressure device. While cold, pressures in the envelope can range up to 10 atmospheres (about 133 pounds per square inch). At operating temperatures the pressure may rise to 40 atmospheres. The result is that the hot lamp has the explosive energy of a small hand grenade. Even cold, the explosive power can drive fragments of the quartz envelope at tremendous speeds for short distances. As if this were not bad enough, it has been found that xenon lamps will occasionally explode while in storage without any apparent reason. Scientists call this effect "devitrification."

The result of all of these hazards is that complicated safety procedures are required by safety laws for the handling, installation, and operation of xenon lamps. They must be shipped in explosion-proof cases which may not be removed until the lamp is installed. To facilitate this, the electrode ends of the lamps protrude from the housing so they can be clamped to the electrical connections. Then the explosion-proof casing is cautiously removed. This process must be performed by a specially trained person dressed in protective clothing and wearing a protective face mask. No unprotected bystanders are allowed to be present. Once installed, the housing must be closed securely. It must be capable of withstanding the explosion of the largest size lamp that may be installed in the housing. No fragments may escape. The housing must also contain all radiation and be vented to remove the ozone. Finally, the housing must be so locked that it is impossible to open the door while the lamp is on. A blast of cold air from the outside might cause the lamp to explode. Clearly written warnings indicate that the door should be opened only by qualified personnel, and only when the lamp is cold. A special latch or lock must be provided to prevent unauthorized tampering.

In the face of these hazards and safety precautions it would seem that the xenon lamp would find little use in the theatre. The fact that it is still in use and that its successors are being rapidly put to use is evidence of the great value it has as a light source.

RECENT DEVELOPMENTS

There has been a constant struggle to produce arc sources which combine the characteristics of the xenon with safer operating characteristics and even more efficient light output. The most hopeful development to date has been the "HMI" lamps. Early engineering of short-arc lamps sought to place the purest possible gas in the envelope. For scientific applications this was highly desirable. However, the opposite procedure has been explored with good results for theatre and illumination purposes. Various metallic vapors are purposely introduced into the envelope. The combination of these vapors produces a complicated line spectrum which blends within the eye to produce an improved light. The process has reached the point where a source can almost be synthesized into a made-to-order spectral distribution. Such lamps, presently in the last stages of research and development, have over twice the efficiency of the xenon lamp and few of its drawbacks. They produce little heat, and little ultraviolet radiation. Moreover they are ac devices requiring only a ballast (to limit the current through the lamp) not a dc power supply. Color temperature approximates that of "equal energy white" (see Plate III) which means that there will be excellent color rendition. Such lamps provide a large amount of any visible wavelength needed with the use of filters. Unfortunately dimming changes the color output of these lamps in a complicated way, and they cannot be dimmed to very low intensities. They also require a high-voltage starter.

THE FUTURE OF SHORT-ARC LAMPS

It is obvious that the short-arc lamp will not replace the incandescent lamp as a general theatrical light source for a long time, if ever. However, it is equally obvious that these highly efficient lamps are going to be increasingly used in special theatrical applications where the incandescent lamp barely qualifies. Such cases are those where very efficient light output and small source are of primary concern. Projectors and follow spotlights are obvious cases. Other effects devices seem equally in need of this lamp. In such cases dimming will probably not be a function of the lamp itself. Mechanical dimming methods are presently available and in use, particularly in Europe. Liquid crystal and Polaroid devices offer even greater possibilities for intensity control susceptible to electronic remote control.

Producing Light by Fluorescence

Fluorescence is the property of a variety of materials to absorb energy from radiation of one wavelength and reemit this energy at another wavelength. Note that in the case of fluorescence the emission takes place only as long as the material is irradiated by the outside energy source. If emission continues after the radiation stops, the phenomenon is called *phosphorescence*. The property of fluorescence is the principle of both the fluorescent lamp and the various blacklight effects common in the theatre. In the case of the fluorescent lamp, the source of radiation is a mercury-arc lamp, a gaseous-discharge lamp using mercury vapor as the current-carrying gas. If the pressure of the mercury vapor is held very low, and electricity is passed through this tube, the mercury vapor will radiate light largely in the ultraviolet region (2537 Å). The conversion of electrical energy to ultraviolet light energy at this wavelength is much more efficient than any incandescent filament; often in the neighborhood of 60 percent of the electrical energy is converted into ultraviolet light. Some small portion of the energy is converted directly into visible light in the near-ultraviolet range.

The ultraviolet light produced inside the fluorescent tube then is used to irradiate *phosphors,* or powdered chemicals, usually phosphoric or boric salts of calcium, magnesium, cadmium, or zinc. These chemicals have the ability to fluoresce in the visible range. For example, calcium tungstate fluoresces largely in the blue region of the spectrum. As a general rule, conversion of lighting fixtures in a room to fluorescent will make it possible roughly to double the light intensity in the room without adding anything to the electrical load.

FLUORESCENT LAMPS ON STAGE

While the fluorescent lamp is rarely found in the United States theatre, it is quite common on European stages. Obviously, the fluorescent lamp is far too large to qualify as a point source, and therefore cannot be used as a source for a lens system. It is, however, a fine source of cool white or pale blue light, and much more efficient in the production of this light than the incandescent lamp. For this reason many European stages are equipped with a special bank of fluorescent lamps designed to produce a broad flood of cool "sky" light for cyclorama illumination. The instruments are designed solely for this one purpose, and they do a very good job. They are much more economical to operate than a set of three-color primary cyclorama lights, a saving further increased by the high cost of electricity in Europe.

Fluorescent lamps can be dimmed but not without certain alterations in circuitry. Transformer or magnetic-amplifier dimmers (see the section on "Autotransformer Dimmers" in Chapter 9 and the section "Magnetic Amplifiers" in Chapter 10) serve this purpose the best. The European cyclorama lighting systems mentioned above are equipped with specially adapted dimmer circuits which make it possible to regulate the intensity of the cyclorama light down to "out," and from "out" up to "full" with no perceptible flicker. Color temperature changes little during these dims.

Single-color cyclorama lighting using fluorescent tubes has never caught on in the United States. A very recent development is the adaptation of three-color primary fluorescent lighting to cyclorama lighting, particularly for television. There are great advantages in the use of fluorescent lamps for this purpose in television because of the high light levels necessary for good color picture quality. Conversion of the cyclorama lighting to fluorescent will reduce electrical loads significantly, including the air-conditioning load necessary to remove the heat generated by high wattage incandescent lighting. Unlike the incandescent lamp, the fluorescent lamp is somewhat inefficient at the red end of the spectrum. Therefore, two red tubes are used for each green and blue lamp, the opposite of the configuration for incandescent cyclorama lighting.

BLACKLIGHT: ULTRAVIOLET SOURCES

Another application of fluorescence on stage is that of *blacklight* effects. This use is not a future development, but a very common and spectacular effect today. The principle is much the same as that of the fluorescent lamp, except that the fluorescent materials are found on the setting, costumes, or even in the makeup of the actors. Ultraviolet light is made by one of several means and the fluorescent chemicals activated. The chemicals absorb the ultraviolet energy and reemit it in the form of visible wavelengths, usually in narrow bands of wavelengths selected for their brilliant color effects. The art of painting with fluorescent paints has progressed to the point that entire dioramalike scenes have been painted for display purposes and as "effects" in the "magic rides" of Disneyland. The effects range from bizarre and garish to subtle realism in such things as the portrayal of a city at night. In the theatre itself, spectacular variety shows such as the "Ice Follies" have used blacklight numbers for years with great effectiveness. In the production of serious drama, blacklight has found occasional application wherever supernatural effects are needed.

For blacklight effects, the best ultraviolet radiation is much nearer to visible light than that used to irradiate the phosphors inside a fluorescent tube. A wavelength of 3654 Å is considered best. With this in mind, sources are selected for the production of ultraviolet for blacklight.

THE ARC LAMP

Probably the oldest source for producing blacklight is a carbon-arc lamp. A high-intensity carbon arc produces a wide variety of ultraviolet radiations along with a large amount of visible light. This variety is evident to anyone who has been "sunburned" from excessive exposure to light from a carbon arc. Since ordinary glass is opaque to those wavelengths most likely to cause sunburn (but not to the near-ultraviolet region that causes fluorescence), stage arc lights present no serious hazard in this respect to performers. However, an operator exposed to spill light coming directly from the arc with no intervening glass might be burned. Now, if a stage arc follow spot is fitted with a filter that will block all visible light but pass the ultraviolet in the near visible range (including 3654 Å), the spot will produce an invisible pool of ultraviolet on stage that will activate any fluorescent materials present. Of course, the filter will have to absorb a tremendous amount of energy and reradiate it as heat, but the results in terms of stage effects will be good. Since this system utilizes existing stage-lighting equipment, and since the arc light can be focused easily and started instantly, this system is often used in spite of its inefficiency.

THE MERCURY-VAPOR LAMP

A more efficient source of ultraviolet radiation is a specially designed mercury-vapor lamp equipped with a filter to block visible light. This unit produces several times the ultraviolet of the carbon arc light, watt for watt. However, it has its drawbacks. First, it has a 10- to 20-minute warm-up period before it begins to emit ultraviolet light and, if it is inadvertently turned off, it must be allowed to cool before it can be started again. The warm-up period is not much of a handicap to a production with brilliantly lighted numbers preceding the blacklight because the ultraviolet sources are simply turned on well in advance of the time they are going to be needed. The effect of the ultraviolet light, which is relatively dim anyway, is washed out by the brilliant lighting. If it is desirable that there be a dimly lighted scene just before the blacklight scene, the only choice is to try to avoid any fluorescent materials in the dim scene. Any attempt to black out the fluorescent effect by turning out the ultraviolet sources will inactivate the sources until they have cooled to their starting temperature.

FLUORESCENT ULTRAVIOLET SOURCES

A third source of ultraviolet light is a special fluorescent tube which emits a large portion of its energy as near-ultraviolet light in the vicinity of 3654 Å. This tube is of great interest to us because it offers an example of the double use of the fluorescent phenomenon. The original light-energy source is the standard mercury-vapor arc found in all fluorescent lamps. The phosphors are chosen for their ability to convert this energy from 2537 Å to 3654 Å instead of converting it into visible light. Despite this, a considerable amount of visible light is produced which must be filtered away if blacklight effects are to be observed clearly. Such filters and the tube of the lamp itself must of course, transmit 3654 Å light. This "blacklight" then is used to produce fluorescent effects on stage.

Fluorescent blacklight tubes are commonly available in lamp supply houses. They cost somewhat more than regular fluorescent tubes because of the limited demand and the filter which is provided as a part of the lamp. These fluorescent tubes will operate in any fixture designed to take a standard tube of the same physical size and wattage. They are electrically identical to standard lamps. Thus any fluorescent fixture can be converted into a blacklight device simply by changing the lamps. Maximum efficiency will be gained by using highly polished chrome or stainless-steel reflectors in blacklight fixtures. These materials reflect the near-ultraviolet best.

These lamps can be dimmed by the same means used to dim visible-light fluorescent lamps. Operators should be cautioned against trying to dim fluorescent lamps, blacklight or normal, with unaltered solid-state dimmers. The ballasts which are integral parts of every fluorescent fixture, are transformerlike devices which will react unfavorably to the steep wave form produced by the solid-state dimmer. The results will be a noisy ballast and probably a flickering fluorescent lamp. Dimmer loading will also be difficult to compute. If special dimming apparatus is unavailable, the best solution is to turn the blacklight units on by a switch before the curtain opens, allowing them to start with their usual burst of light. The fluorescent effect will usually be masked by the normal stage lighting until the latter is dimmed down for the blacklight effect.

The advantages of this fluorescent source of ultraviolet light are economy, ease of operation, and easy availability of the parts. The disadvantages are that the fluorescent lamps produce a very broad spread of ultraviolet light that may reach into unwanted areas causing unexpected fluorescent effects and that these lamps will ordinarily be started, as are all other fluorescent lamps, by a sudden surge of power and of light. One solution to this problem is to turn them on before the curtain goes up and to mask their visible glow with bright light. Other methods will suggest themselves to the ingenious lighting artist as he experiments with the apparatus.

ULTRAVIOLET IN THE PRODUCTION

Use of any of the ultraviolet sources is no easy matter to be worked out during the last technical rehearsal. Even for the expert in the use of these materials, a great deal of experimentation and careful adjustment is usually necessary; the beginner should anticipate spending much time getting the effects working. One of the biggest problems is that many materials, not just those supplied by the manufacturers of fluorescent paint and fluorescent makeup, fluoresce naturally. Among these materials are human teeth, the vitreous humor of the eye, many organic dyes common in materials, inks, and paints, household detergents whose residues remain in laundered fabrics, and many other objects. While the fluorescent efficiency of these materials seldom equals that of the specially prepared paints, it is often disconcertingly high—just when it is not needed. Thus portions of the setting and costumes may glow vigorously with some bizarre and unexpected hue just when they are supposed to be blacked out! Every time an actor opens his mouth, a disembodied set of teeth will be visible to the audience if the rest of the stage is sufficiently dark. Even body makeup will sometimes glow slightly. Thus the introduction of ultraviolet light on stage may compel repainting of portions of the setting and props, alteration of costumes and even changes in business to conceal the whereabouts of actors in the darkness. Perhaps the most general problem is created by unwanted and uncontrollable fluorescence that takes place within the human eye. The effect of fluorescence of the vitreous humor is to create visible light within the eye itself. This light casts everything seen into a kind of luminous haze that disconcerts those who experience it because there is no way to focus the eyes upon it. If this haze effect is combined with the flicker of the stroboscopic effect by the presence of metallic moving surfaces, the stage is set for eyestrain and distraught actors.

The solution to all of these problems is long, careful preparation of both the materials on the stage and the actors who must work in the ultraviolet light. The results of this preparation will often be spectacular indeed.

Designing a dramatic production which includes the use of ultraviolet effects is something of a challenge in restraint. The tendency will be toward the garish or the obvious. The sheer contrast of brightly glowing colored objects against a dark background is enough to destroy subtlety. However, the background need not be totally black and the fluorescent pigments can be blended and shaded as subtly as any scene paint. It takes a great deal of time and experimentation, but it *can* be done.

Many of the magical effects demanded in children's theatre may be produced by the judicious use of ultraviolet light. Again, subtlety is the essential ingredient. Often careful blending of colors in natural and ultraviolet light plus careful fading can produce a transition from reality to "magic" that will remain within the theatrical framework of the play instead of raising the awestruck question, "How was that done?" Such scripts as *Beauty and the Beast, Rumpelstiltskin,* and *Greensleeves Magic* are cases in point.

3 CONTROLLING LIGHT: REFLECTION

The Law of Squares

Light, we have said, is a form of radiant energy. It travels through free space in straight lines until it is absorbed, or its direction is changed by some influence. Normally, it radiates from a source in all directions, forming what may be thought of as an ever-increasing sphere of illumination. As this hypothetical sphere increases in radius, the density of illumination on its surface decreases rapidly because the available light must cover greater and greater surface area. This decrease in light density as light moves away from the source is expressed mathematically by the *law of squares*. This law, which is derived from the mathematics of the increase in the surface area of a sphere as its size is increased, reads: *Light at the surface of a "sphere of surface radiation" decreases in inverse proportion to the square of the distance from the source.* For example, if a source will cause 16 footcandles of light to fall upon a surface 1 foot distant, the same source will provide but 4 footcandles of light at a surface 2 feet distant, and only 1 footcandle of light at a distance of 4 feet. The practical effect of this law is to rapidly decrease the available illumination as a light source is moved away, unless something is done to reduce the spreading of the light rays. Hence various engineering feats have been performed to make powerful spotlights possible for the stage. Without the optical engineering, moving a light source to the back of a large house would decrease the amount of light thrown upon the stage to a worthless glimmer.

Very recently, small sources have been devised which do not radiate light spherically, but instead over a very small solid arc of a sphere. The law of squares has not been rescinded; the application is only less "painful" in that all of the light produced already is concentrated into a very small "pencil of light" which does not appear to diverge rapidly.

However, if we consider this pencil of light as a very small conical segment from a very large sphere, which it really is, we find that the square law is still operative: Every time the cross section of the pencil of light doubles in width, the light decreases in intensity by a factor of four. We will also find that the distance from the source has been doubled. This law is important to us because it also applies in the case of narrow spotlight beams; all that the genius of the optical engineer has done is to increase the effective original distance from instrument to source so that a change of throw distance represents only a small percentage increase in total source-to-surface distance.

We have indicated that the basic reason for optical engineering of spotlight equipment is the law of squares. Without special optical equipment, the light from even the most powerful incandescent source will dissipate so rapidly as it moves away from the lamp that it will soon become useless. The following then becomes the basic engineering problem: How can the light from a spherically emanating source be gathered up and emitted from the instrument in a relatively narrow beam? If this problem could be perfectly solved, great efficiency and complete control of spill light would result. Unfortunately, a perfect solution is apparently far from possible.

The first step in controlling spherical emanation is to cut off and absorb the unwanted light. This process is wasteful, but simple. Only a light-tight housing with a hole for the useful light is needed. The primitive stovepipe spotlight occasionally found on poverty-stricken stages operates in this manner.

However, the waste of all but a small percentage of the lumens coming from a lamp filament is at least partly unnecessary. Reflectors and lenses can be used to gather up much of this "misdirected" light and send it to the stage. Since the operation of reflectors is simpler than that of lenses, we will discuss them first.

Reflection is a property of all solid surfaces and of many liquid and gaseous ones that enables them to turn a light beam to a new direction much as the cushion of a billiard table turns the course of a rolling billiard ball. Like the billiard cushion, the reflector always exacts a toll of energy; no reflector "bounces" all of the light that strikes it. Also, no surface, however black, succeeds in keeping all of the light energy that strikes it, although some black velours come very close to being perfect light absorbers.

Specular Reflection: The Law of Reflection

There are several types of reflectors. The one we usually think of first is the mirror. A mirror is a surface that changes the direction of the beam of light without otherwise altering the nature of the beam. It operates according to definite physical rules. In Figure 3-1, note that:

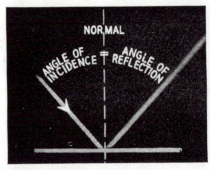

FIGURE 3-1

The Law of Specular Reflection. The drawing at the left illustrates the law in its simplest form. Note that the rays are also in the same plane. The drawing at the right illustrates the application of the normal to determine the angles when the reflecting surface is curved. Courtesy General Electric Company.

1. The *normal* is the line perpendicular to the surface at the point of reflection. If we are talking about a plane mirror, the normal is merely a line perpendicular to the surface of the mirror. If we are talking about a curved mirror, it is a line perpendicular to a tangent to the curve at the point of reflection. This difference is important to us because many types of curved mirrors are found in stage-lighting equipment and we must know how they work.
2. The *angle of incidence* is the angle between the normal and the beam of light as it impinges upon the reflector.
3. The *angle of reflection* is the angle between the reflected beam and the normal. The rule is this: *The angle of incidence equals the angle of reflection and they are in the same plane.* This rule is true of all mirror-type reflectors.

The technical name for mirror-type reflection is *specular reflection.* (Once upon a time a mirror was called a speculum.) Do not confuse this term with "spectral," which refers to color and the spectrum.

In addition to the mirror, there are three other types of reflecting surfaces. The types differ in the way light is scattered after striking them. Actually all three of these surfaces function according to the law of reflection, if we consider each tiny segment of the surface separately. The reflecting surfaces are made up of millions of these tiny reflectors, the total effect depending on how they are arranged with respect to each other. Thus a completely random arrangement of minute particles results in diffuse reflection. More orderly arrangements produce directional effects, described in detail below.

Diffuse, Spread, and Mixed Reflection

In diffuse reflection, the beam of light which strikes the surface is completely dispersed. Light emanates from the reflecting surface at the point of reflection as though the surface were a radiating body and proceeds in all directions according to the law of squares. White blotting paper and flat white paint such as whitewash are good practical examples of diffuse reflectors.

The beam of light is dispersed in spread reflection but a greater percentage of the light is reflected along the angle of reflection (figured as though the surface were a specular surface) than along any other line. The degree of spread and diffusion can be carefully controlled in the preparation of such surfaces. Thus these surfaces make ideal reflectors for stage use where a broad spread of light is needed but where distribution within that spread must be rigorously controlled. Borderlights and footlights are instruments used for such lighting and spread reflectors are usually found in use with them. "Anodized" or "Alzak" processed aluminum are the usual materials for spread reflectors. These patented processes are chemical means of producing accurately controlled spread-reflecting surfaces. Reflectors made by these processes are highly efficient and normally have a long life.

Mixed reflection is the bane of the stage-lighting artist's existence. It consists of a mixture of diffuse and specular reflection and usually is produced by varnished surfaces such as the stage floor or polished furniture. The specular component is the bogey. Mixed reflection usually results in reflection of a high percentage of the acting-area lighting upward onto the scenery or backdrops. As the actors move across the stage they interfere with this reflection and sometimes even cast inverted blurry shadows of themselves on the back of the setting. This situation is intolerable, particularly if projected backdrops are contemplated, because no projector is powerful enough to wash out acting-area light reflected onto the projection surface.

The solution is to remove or cover the mixed reflecting surface with a diffusing surface of low reflectance to eliminate the unwanted light.

The presence of mixed reflection in most varnished floors is one reason professional stages generally are unfinished. A highly polished floor is a detriment; a dark-colored, dull-finish wooden floor is much more desirable. Canvas gound cloths also are used to avoid reflections.

Efficiency of Reflectors

Not only do surfaces differ in the way in which they alter the direction of a beam of light, but they also differ in the efficiency with which they redirect the beam. Some absorb nearly all of the light that strikes them, reflecting only a minute fraction; others reflect nearly all of the light. The reflectance of a surface is the percentage figure which describes its efficiency as a reflector. If there were such a thing as a perfect reflector, it would have a reflectance of 100 percent. A perfectly black object would have a reflectance of 0 percent. Surfaces with a reflectance of over 90 percent are not uncommon and are considered high-efficiency reflectors. Black velour may have a reflectance of less than 1 percent and is considered one of the best light absorbers on stage.

Reflectors on Stage: Reflection in General Lighting Equipment

On stage, specular reflectors are found in spherical form behind the lamps in plano and Fresnel spotlights, as ellipsoids in ellipsoidal spotlights, and as paraboloids in beam projectors. Diffuse reflection is found in simple olivette-type floodlights but more important, it is the usual type of reflection from painted objects on stage, from costumes, and even from actors themselves. Spread reflection is found in general lighting equipment with Alzak or anodized reflectors. Mixed reflection is found in the case of varnished surfaces and similar materials and is avoided on stage wherever possible.

All general illumination equipment is a variation of the floodlight. This instrument is nothing more than a tin box with a light bulb in it. In earlier days of theatre lighting, tin-surfaced boxes were equipped with a number of small lamps and called *bunchlights*. A bunch of lights was the only way to get a lot of light; there were no high-wattage lamps. The interior of the box was painted flat white and the whole affair mounted on a stand for use on the stage floor. The successor to the bunchlight was the *olivette,* which was a similar box equipped with a single 1000- to 2000-watt lamp. The name probably came from the oval shape of the bulb of these lamps. Many of these units are still in use today and new ones can still be purchased. Olivettes usually are equipped for floor use, although they can be hung above the stage if desired.

Modern Floodlights

The modern version of the floodlight is the *parabolic* or *ellipsoidal flood* or, in television terminology, the "scoop." It consists of a reflector that looks roughly like one half of a large egg. A square frame is attached to the front of the reflector to hold metal frames containing color media or diffusing media. A socket assembly and mounting unit complete the floodlight. Modern floodlights come in 400-, 500-, and 1000- to 2000-watt sizes; they are very efficient and produce even distribution of light over a wide area, unlike the earlier floods. The purpose of any floodlight is to do just what the name implies, to flood the stage with light.

The more evenly distributed and brighter the light for a given wattage, the better.

Efficient light distribution in modern floodlights and in all of their adaptations to other general lighting apparatus depends on the exact control of spread reflection. Only the simplest and cheapest of modern floodlights are equipped with diffuse reflectors; all others have anodized surfaces, usually the result of the Alzak process. Alterations in the electrochemical operations of the Alzak process will result in variation of the surface from a specular surface to a diffuse reflector. Intermediate stages make possible the precise control of illumination needed for borderlights, footlights, and scoops.

Alzak surfaces offer little in the way of a maintenance problem to the lighting technician, whose main concern is to protect the relatively soft aluminum reflector from denting. Washing the surface occasionally with soapy water and drying it carefully will maintain the reflector's efficiency. No grit or polishing agent should be used.

All other general illumination equipment consists of adaptations of the floodlight or multiplications of the number of units. For example, in early days the stage was lighted from above and from the front by an adaptation of the bunchlight. Tin-surfaced troughs were equipped with rows of lamp sockets wired in three or more circuits. These troughs were then hung above the stage, extending from side to side, and called *borderlights* because they hung behind heavy cloth "borders" or masking curtains. They were also set into the stage floor at the very front and brilliantly lighted the feet and legs of downstage actors. Here they were called *footlights*. Except for the variations in mounting, both units were much the same. The lamps used in them were relatively small and were usually colored by dipping them in a colored lacquer (about like nail polish) and drying them.

Later refinements in the borders and foots (the names were soon shortened) resulted in less similarity, but they still remain enough alike so that in an emergency, the same unit can serve either function.

Modern Borderlights

Modern borderlights consist of a number of individual spun-aluminum reflectors mounted as close together as possible in a metal housing. Each reflector encloses a single lamp and usually is covered with a circular piece of colored glass called a *roundel*. This glass serves the double purpose of keeping one lamp and reflector clean and coloring the light. The receptacles are wired in three or four circuits, making it possible to turn on only the blue lights, or the red, or any separate color. Roundels are available in a number of colors of which red, green, and blue are usually the most useful.

A special type of borderlight also is made for the purpose of lighting sky cycloramas. A *cyclorama* is a curved cloth or wall used as a background of a stage set to suggest unlimited space. Cyclorama borderlights are usually more powerful and are especially designed to provide even illumination over a high curtain although they may hang only a few feet from the top of it. Similar units often are mounted near the bottom of the cyclorama to throw light upward from there.

Modern dramatic productions make very little use of borderlighting except for the sky cyclorama borderlight. Thus a stage intended for dramatic use only should not be equipped with an extensive borderlight system at the expense of other lighting equipment. Borderlights will not be nearly as useful as spotlights bought with the same amount of money. Probably a partial borderlight system consisting of removable units at the front of the stage immediately upstage of the act curtain and a cyclorama borderlight will be plenty. The downstage units can then be moved about to fit the needs of various plays, or removed entirely if they are in the way.

Modern Footlights

Footlights have undergone the same transformation as borderlights and are now made in much the same way, except that the wattages tend to be smaller. Where borderlights may run up to 500 watts per lamp in the large sizes, foots tend to run not much higher than 100 watts per lamp. Actually, on the dramatic stage, 100 watts is still far too much light. Many lighting experts have suggested that foots are completely unnecessary if spotlighting can be arranged from in front of the curtain at less than 45° to the level of the actor's head. Others suggest using partial footlights of very low wattage carefully controlled and removable or disappearing when not needed. In any event, most new stages spend too large a share of their slim lighting budgets on footlights.

Selection and location of footlights is a matter of concern whenever a theatre is being designed or revised. Whether the foots are to be permanently installed, or made portable so that the instruments can serve other purposes, the following criteria must be met:

1. The footlight instruments must produce an even blend of light from the various color circuits at very close range, preferably within 2 feet.
2. The flood of blended light from the foots should fill the proscenium[1] opening from side to side, and reach well above the heads of actors standing near the foots. It should do this without producing any noticeable spill light on the sides of the proscenium wall, or on that portion of wall or ceiling over the apron of the stage. In the case of a thrust stage, these requirements may result in an impossible situation if the actors must play very close to the foots. In this case, it is

---

[1] The proscenium is the opening through which the audience views the play in a conventional theatre. It is usually in the form of an elaborate arch built into the wall of the theatre faced by the audience, hence, "proscenium wall." There are many plans for theatres that do not require a proscenium.

probably better to depend on lighting the actors from overhead positions without the benefit of fill light from the footlights.

3. The footlight instruments themselves should not block the audience's view of the stage floor to any appreciable degree. A certain amount of projection above stage-floor level is inevitable. However, it should be held to a minimum.

Permanent footlights often are installed on hinged floor sections that close to become part of the stage floor when foots are not needed. Such instruments should be provided with interlock switches so that they cannot be turned on when they are closed. This disappearing footlight arrangement is expensive but convenient on a stage where footlights must be available but where they may not be needed for some productions.

Another good solution is to install carefully designed troughs for portable footlight units. The floor of these troughs should be tilted so that the units to be placed in them will meet all of the above requirements. Removable covers that are heavy enough to withstand ordinary stage-floor loads must be provided for the troughs. When the footlight instruments are not needed as foots, they may be used at other locations on the stage as borderlights, striplights, or as cyclorama footlights. Instruments that will meet these requirements are available from several manufacturers. However, various makes are not always interchangeable, so the troughs must be designed with a particular brand in mind.

Footlighting a thrust stage or a stage that is equipped with a large pit elevator that may be brought to stage level to become a thrust stage may require a double set of instruments or instrument troughs.

The Striplight

Floodlights, footlights, and borderlights complete the usual list of general lighting equipment found on the modern stage. Two other items must be mentioned. One of these is the *striplight,* a miniature borderlight unit, usually consisting of six or eight lamps in a trough. The unit is equipped with flanges or hooks so that it may be mounted vertically or horizontally on the back of a piece of scenery, and usually is used to illuminate entry areas, small alcoves, or the like. Striplights produce a flood of soft, nearly shadowless light whose color may be controlled either by coloring the lamps (if they are 40 watts or smaller) or by the use of color media. The striplight often is replaced by a small parabolic flood or a spotlight in modern stage lighting.

Reflector-Lamp Floodlighting

The last item to be discussed under general illumination is not an instrument, but a lamp. The *reflector lamp,* usually referred to as Type

"R," combines the properties of reflector and light source into one unit. The "R40" is most common. This funnel-shaped unit often is found in department store windows where its high efficiency and simplicity of operation make it desirable. The lamp consists of a filament, usually 150 or 300 watts, surrounded by a specially shaped glass envelope that has been partially silvered to form a reflector. The clear front glass is slightly etched to diffuse the light. The result is a floodlight complete in the lamp itself. All it lacks is a swivel socket. As a floodlight it is very efficient. However, this lamp is not well adapted for stage-lighting purposes. There is often considerable back spill, making some sort of housing necessary. Since R40 lamps are made of glass, they are quite fragile and are often broken during the rough usage on stage. Again this calls for a metal housing. Finally, the glass bulb operates at a temperature high enough to cause fire, so that the lamps must be protected from anything inflammable. The result is that a stage unit equipped for Type R lamps must be as heavy and expensive as one equipped for ordinary lamps. Since the reflector is an integral part of the lamp, every time a lamp burns out, you must replace the whole unit, a relatively expensive process.

There are available a number of makes of lamp holders for Type R lamps that cut down the back spill and provide for the use of color media. The holders usually are combined with a swivel socket to facilitate directing the unit. While most of these lamp holders are quite useful for store-window lighting and various types of decorative lighting, they are not rugged enough to stand the wear and tear of stage use. The swivel sockets soon lose their ability to hold the lamps in position, and the rest of the apparatus becomes bent or dented beyond repair. Thus the holders are usually a poor investment; their cost, plus that of the lamp, is nearly equal to that of a small floodlight or spotlight which would be much more durable and useful. The Type R lamps also are made in a "spot" type that produces a relatively narrow beam of light plus a wide spill. It cannot be focused except by changing the distance from the lighted area. It also has all of the disadvantages of the flood type. Reflector lamps often are said to be the "poor man's spotlight."

In contrast to specific lighting application, there are several good borderlight units available that are designed for Type R lamps. They have the advantage of extremely high efficiency. Moreover, their reflector efficiency does not drop with age because the reflectors are renewed with each relamping. Most of them are designed to take either Type R or the more rugged variety, the Type "PAR" lamp. PAR lamps are constructed with a heavy Pyrex glass envelope that is capable of taking the stresses that may occur when the hot lamp is doused by rain or a carelessly directed garden hose. The original purpose of these lamps was outdoor architectural lighting. However, their ruggedness makes them more adaptable to stage purposes than the R types. Dangers from breakage are greatly reduced when these lamps are used.

There are still drawbacks: PAR lamps weigh more than R lamps, they still get very hot, and their cost is considerably more than R lamps. Light distribution characteristics of PAR lamps are also different, but this is not necessarily a disadvantage because it offers the lighting technician a wider range of choices.

Both the R and PAR types are available in a wide range of wattages from 75 to as high as 1500 watts in certain cases. Proliferation of types has blurred the distinction between R and PAR to the extent that R-type envelopes may now be obtained of Pyrex glass, making them "waterproof." Pyrex does not materially increase their mechanical strength. To take advantage of the high efficiency of large reflector lamps, cyclorama striplights are available that are designed to use R56 or R64 lamps, 300 and 500 watts respectively.

The stage-lighting artist will find that he must keep up on the latest developments in this series of lamps if he wishes to take advantage of their great efficiency. New types and additional improvements are constantly appearing.

Specular Reflectors in Specific Lighting Equipment

Specular reflectors are the rule in spotlights, beam projectors, and all other optically precise equipment. While the precision of the Alzak process in producing controlled spread reflection is remarkable, that achievable in controlling specular reflection is nearly miraculous. Stage-lighting equipment, even the best of it, is but the crudest application of the art of the optical reflector maker. In the case of reflectors in large telescopes, accuracy to a fraction of a wavelength of visible light is possible.

In stage-lighting apparatus three types of specular reflectors are commonly found: spherical, ellipsoidal, and parabolic. Each has its special application.

Spherical Reflectors

Spherical reflectors are found in all but the poorest of plano-convex and Fresnel spotlights. The purpose of the reflectors is to increase the efficiency of the instrument by gathering up light otherwise lost in the housing and returning it through the filament to the lens. The optics of spherical reflectors is quite simple (see Figure 3-2). If a light source, say a concentrated filament, is placed at the center of curvature, light rays striking the reflector will be returned to the center of curvature and will continue to the lens. Theoretically this reflector should double the light output of a Fresnel spotlight. Practically, a 50 to 60 percent increase can be considered good, because the filament obstructs many of the returning rays and because the reflector is far from 100 percent efficient.

Notice that several practical needs must be met before the reflector will perform well.

1. Reflector, lens, and filament must all be on the same "optical axis," positioned so that a line can be passed through the center of curvature of the reflector, the center of the filament, and the center of the lens as shown in Figure 3-2. This line will then extend to the center of the pool of light produced by the spotlight on a plane surface at right angles to the line. If all parts are not on the same optical axis, a secondary pool of light will be formed and the entire system will lose efficiency.

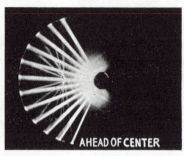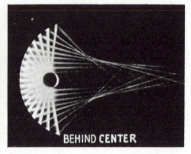

FIGURE 3-2a

The Spherical Reflector. With the light source at the center of curvature of the reflector the rays are reflected back through the source. This increases efficiency as shown in b *below. The amount of increase will vary from 40 to 60 percent with a monoplane filament and from 20 to 30 percent with a biplane filament. Note the rapid drop in efficiency or the change in light distribution or both when the source is moved away from the center of curvature.* Courtesy General Electric Company.

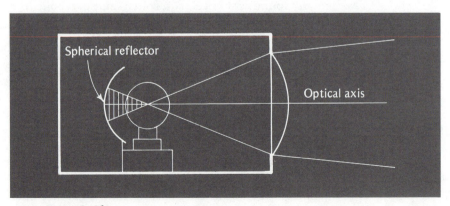

FIGURE 3-2b

The application of the spherical reflector to the spotlight is illustrated. Light saved by the reflector is shown by shaded angle. Efficiency is increased.

2. The distance from the reflector to the filament must be equal to the radius of the curvature of the reflector, or the reflector will produce a pool of light larger or smaller than that from the filament.

3. The reflector must have a useful diameter sufficient to encompass the largest cone of light to be used by the spotlight. In other words, the cone of light striking the lens when the spotlight is at flood position must be matched by the cone of light striking the reflector. If the reflector is too small for this requirement, efficiency will drop off as the spotlight is moved toward spread or flood position. This requirement can be met by manufacturing relatively large reflectors with fairly long radii, or by making smaller reflectors whose radii are shorter and thereby work closer to the lamp.

REFLECTOR MOUNTINGS

Most small spotlights are equipped with reflectors mounted at the back of the lamp carrier by means of a flexible metal bracket. This bracket is bent slightly to align the reflector whenever it needs attention. Larger and more expensive equipment may be fitted with setscrew adjustments to raise and lower the reflector and to move it forward or backward with reference to the socket. Such adjustments make possible aligning the reflector to fit a variety of filament positions.

ALIGNING SPHERICAL REFLECTORS

The easiest way to align a reflector in a Fresnel spotlight is to operate the instrument on a dimmer at a low reading. Dimming will reduce the possibility of being burned by the hot lamp and prevent the operator from being blinded by the bright filament. Rough adjustment can be made by looking through the lens and the filament along the optical axis while adjusting the reflector to an approximate position. Then the job can be finished by aiming the instrument at a blank wall to produce a circular pool. The position of the secondary pool should be noted and the reflector tilted until the two pools overlap perfectly. The results should be checked at flood position for the possibility that the reflector may not be the proper distance from the filament. Setscrews, if any are used, should be tightened.

Occasionally, the spherical reflector will get out of adjustment in such a way as to fall against the lamp. The results are often expensive. Usually the first effect is that the lamp cracks and fails. Sometimes cracking does not happen immediately and the reflector is heated to a red heat, destroying its surface. If the reflector is far out of adjustment, but not touching the glass envelope of the lamp, it will concentrate so much heat on a small area of the envelope that the glass will soften at that point causing a bulge. If the bulge touches the reflector, further losses occur. Thus it is a good idea to check the alignment of spherical reflectors frequently and to adjust promptly any instruments that display a secondary pool of light.

Ellipsoidal Reflectors

There are limits to the increase in efficiency which can be achieved with a spherical reflector. These derive mainly from the limiting factors surrounding plano-convex and Fresnel lenses, and will be detailed in Chapter 4. However, the reflective characteristics of the ellipsoidal reflector properly belong in our present discussion.

The ellipsoidal spotlight was developed because there was need for a still more efficient instrument than the Fresnel spotlight, particularly one essentially devoid of spill light. Since lens systems had been exploited as far as the economics of lighting instruments would allow, the reflector was developed. It was reasoned that even the most efficient spherical reflector missed a huge share of the light striking the housing of a spotlight. If more of this wasted light could be gathered up and passed on to the lens in a useful manner, greater efficiency could be the result. The catch is the phrase "in a useful manner," because it is not enough that beams of light be directed toward the lens opening in any random direction. The beams must arrive there in some orderly fashion, preferably closely resembling the direction of those beams of light coming from the filament.

THE ELLIPSOID

The reflective characteristics of an ellipsoid seemed ideal for this purpose. In order to understand them, we must turn our attention first to the geometry of the ellipse, then to its solid figure, the ellipsoid. An *ellipse,* the dictionary says, is "A closed curve, generated by a point moving in such a way that the sum of its distances from two fixed points [the foci] is constant."[2]

Thus, if one wishes to draw an ellipse, one may drive two nails some distance apart into a board. These nails become the foci. Then, by passing a loop of string around both nails, drawing it taut with a pencil at the outer limit, and using the string to limit the path, an ellipse can be traced. Note that the string meets the requirement of the definition that the sum of the distances from the foci remain constant. Now, if the ellipse is rotated about the axis passing through the foci, the result will be a solid, egg-shaped figure, the ellipsoid. Now imagine this figure cut by a plane between the foci. The resultant partial ellipsoid is the shape of the ellipsoidal reflector; with its interior coated to produce specular reflection, it is the "heart" of the ellipsoidal spotlight.

The reflective characteristics of the ellipsoid are unusual. Any wave motion originating at one focus and striking the inside surface will be

[2] *Webster's Collegiate Dictionary,* third edition.

reflected to the other focus. Both sound and light function this way in an ellipsoid.

THE ELLIPSOIDAL REFLECTOR AS A LIGHT GATHERER

If a concentrated filament is placed at one focus, all light striking the reflector will pass through the second focus. Not only will it pass through the second focus, but it will pass in an orderly manner, forming a cone of illumination as though it were emanating from a point source at the second focus (see Figure 3-3). Thus the ellipsoidal reflector offers the engineer two advantages at the same time: (1) It gathers up a far larger share of the light emanating from the filament than any combination of lens and spherical reflector and directs it toward the lens

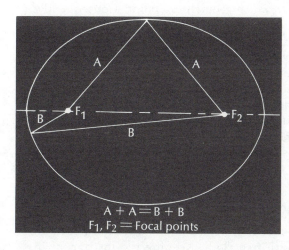

FIGURE *3-3a*
The Ellipse and the Ellipsoidal Reflector. There are two focal points in an ellipse (F_1 and F_2). The sum or the distances from these two points to any point on the curve is constant (A + A = B + B). Courtesy General Electric Company.

A + A = B + B
F_1, F_2 = Focal points

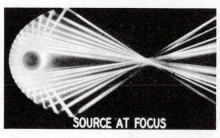

SOURCE AT FOCUS   AHEAD OF FOCUS   BEHIND FOCUS

FIGURE *3-3b*
The first drawing illustrates the proper place of the ellipsoidal reflector in an ellipsoidal spotlight: source at focus. Note the large percentage of the total light output of the lamp which is gathered and passed to the second focal point. The lens system is installed near this second focal point. The second and third drawings show the effect of moving and source away from the focal point. Note that efficiency will drop rapidly and that light distribution will be impaired. Courtesy General Electric Company.

in a useful manner; (2) it facilitates the use of lenses in an advantageous manner by providing a point source, the second focus, whose properties are much the same as those of a filament but with no glass envelope to get in the way. The result is that all light beams passing through the second focus of the ellipsoid can be caught by a lens and put to good use. The direct beam of light from filament to lens represents only a minute portion of the light in the beam of an ellipsoidal spotlight.

FLATTED ELLIPSOIDAL REFLECTORS

If filaments were really point sources, ellipsoidal reflectors could be manufactured with as much optical precision as their sale price would permit and the result would be great efficiency. However, the filament of larger incandescent spotlight lamps is in the neighborhood of one-half inch in diameter, far from a geometrical point! Consequently, manufacturers have sought methods of compensating for the light dispersion caused by the size of the filament. *Flatted* and *double flatted* reflectors have been the result. The ellipsoid is broken up into a series of small plane reflectors arranged to bounce light to the lens. The result is a more even distribution of light throughout the beam of the spotlight. Cost is, of course, increased. The smoothness of the beam is a great advantage when the instrument is to be used by itself and there will be no fill light to wash out any weak places. But it is doubtful that an audience can tell whether or not flatted reflectors are in use in cross-spotted acting areas, even without any blending light.

MAINTENANCE AND ALIGNMENT OF ELLIPSOIDAL REFLECTORS

Maintenance of the ellipsoidal reflector itself is simple. It needs an occasional wiping with a grit-free cloth. Keeping the instrument in alignment is more of a problem. Unless the lamp is accurately positioned so that the center of the filament is exactly at the first focal point of the reflector, the instrument will be inefficient, will often burn color medium as fast as it is installed, and will produce an unevenly distributed pool of light. At each relamping, especially if there is a change in wattage or in make of lamp or both, the operator should check the alignment of the reflector. The ideal way to check is to focus the instrument on an evenly colored surface which is at a right angle to the beam. Often the side wall of the theatre or the surface of the asbestos curtain will serve. With the instrument on and the lens sharply focused on the "screen," the operator carefully turns the adjustment screws in the socket housing seeking the most uniformly illuminated pool of light. Of course, the framing shutters must be entirely open during this operation. Whatever "hot spot" remains in the beam after adjustment should be located in the center. Once the beam is adjusted, the locking screw, if there is one, is set down and the instrument returned to service. Minor adjustments will often be necessary between relamping because of warping of filament parts from the heat.

Ellipsoidal spotlights should always be shuttered down in such a way that the center of the beam is utilized, even in the smallest pool. Shuttering down in this manner will produce the best possible efficiency and will equalize heat distribution on the framing shutters, thereby extending their life. Any ellipsoidal spotlight that must be operated for a long period of time with its shutters nearly closed should not be lamped at its maximum wattage. This down-rating will extend the life of both the framing shutters and the reflector, not to mention that of the lamp itself.

Parabolic Reflectors

Whereas the spherical and ellipsoidal reflectors are used in conjunction with lenses, the parabolic reflector is a complete optical unit in itself. The parabolic reflector came into use in stage lighting as an adaptation of searchlight equipment developed outside of the theatre. It is an efficient device for two reasons. First, it gathers up a high percentage of the light from a lamp and directs it usefully. Second, since there are no intervening lenses, there are no glass losses to "rob" the

 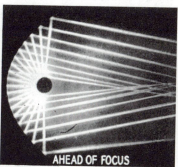 

SOURCE AT FOCUS   AHEAD OF FOCUS   BEHIND FOCUS

FIGURE 3-4

The Parabolic Reflector. The first drawing illustrates the correct operation of a parabolic reflector for stage purposes. The concentrated-filament source is placed at the focal point, making the beams essentially parallel. If the source were a true point, beams would be exactly parallel. Notice the high efficiency of the instrument, the result of the gathering by the reflector of a large share of the total light output of the lamp, and the fact that no light losses are introduced by the addition of lenses. The second and third drawings show the deleterious effect of allowing the source to move away from the focal point. Both efficiency and light distribution deteriorate rapidly.
Courtesy General Electric Company.

beam once formed. As in the case of the ellipsoid, we must return to geometry to understand the paraboloid.

THE PARABOLOID

A parabola may be described as the path of a point whose distance from a fixed point (the focus) and a line remains equal. If a parabola is rotated about its axis, a dishlike figure results. If a point source of light is placed at its focus, all light striking the reflector will be reflected as parallel rays and produce a cylindrical beam (see Figure 3-4). The addition of a spherical reflector facing the parabola will increase efficiency still more. Since parallel rays do not diverge, they should maintain their power through infinity. Actually, the cylindrical or "parallel" beams produced by stage parabolic reflectors do diverge slowly and also are diffused by dust and other matter in the air. Nevertheless, the beam from a parabolic reflector is the nearest approximation to actual sunlight or moonlight available on stage. Note that the rays from the sun and the moon are essentially parallel because of the great distance to these bodies.

THE BEAM PROJECTOR

Accurately formed parabolic reflectors form the "heart" of giant search-lights, often capable of throwing a beam of light for several miles. These instruments use a carbon-arc light as a source. The reflectors are made of glass, precisely ground to shape and silvered. On stage, the parabolic reflectors are usually simple Alzak-mirrored reflectors of aluminum and the spherical reflector often is replaced with a simple baffle to prevent unwanted spill light. Even with these limitations, the beam power of a parabolic *beam projector* as these units are often called, is higher in

FIGURE 3-5
Modern Beam Projector. This instrument produces near-parallel beams of light, utilizing a parabolic reflector with the filament of the lamp at the focal point of the parabola. Photo courtesy Rank Strand Electric, England. *Beam projectors are known as "beamlights" in England.*

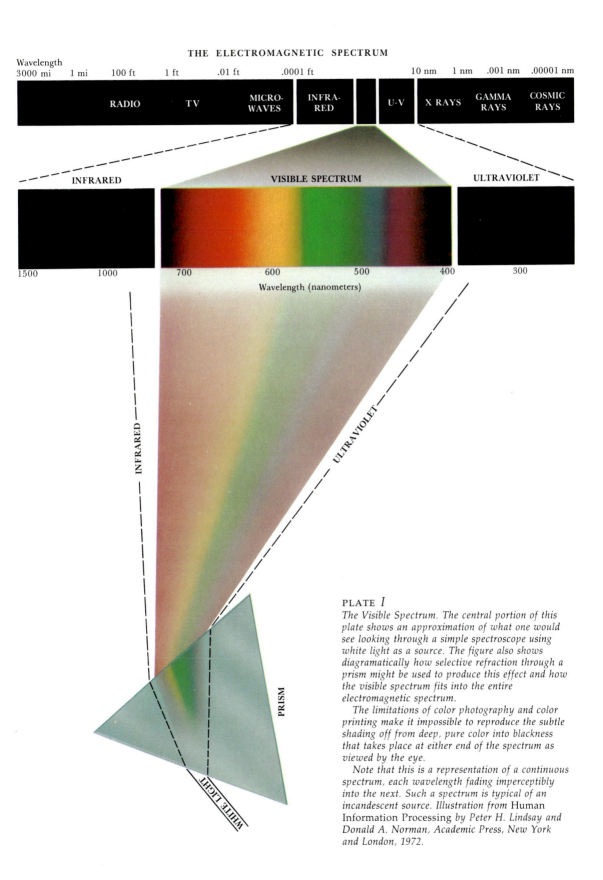

THE ELECTROMAGNETIC SPECTRUM

Wavelength
3000 mi   1 mi   100 ft   1 ft   .01 ft   .0001 ft   10 nm   1 nm   .001 nm   .00001 nm

| RADIO | TV | MICRO-WAVES | INFRA-RED | | U-V | X RAYS | GAMMA RAYS | COSMIC RAYS |

INFRARED   VISIBLE SPECTRUM   ULTRAVIOLET

1500   1000   700   600   500   400   300

Wavelength (nanometers)

INFRARED

ULTRAVIOLET

PRISM

WHITE LIGHT

PLATE *I*

The Visible Spectrum. The central portion of this plate shows an approximation of what one would see looking through a simple spectroscope using white light as a source. The figure also shows diagramatically how selective refraction through a prism might be used to produce this effect and how the visible spectrum fits into the entire electromagnetic spectrum.

The limitations of color photography and color printing make it impossible to reproduce the subtle shading off from deep, pure color into blackness that takes place at either end of the spectrum as viewed by the eye.

Note that this is a representation of a continuous spectrum, each wavelength fading imperceptibly into the next. Such a spectrum is typical of an incandescent source. Illustration from Human Information Processing *by Peter H. Lindsay and Donald A. Norman, Academic Press, New York and London, 1972.*

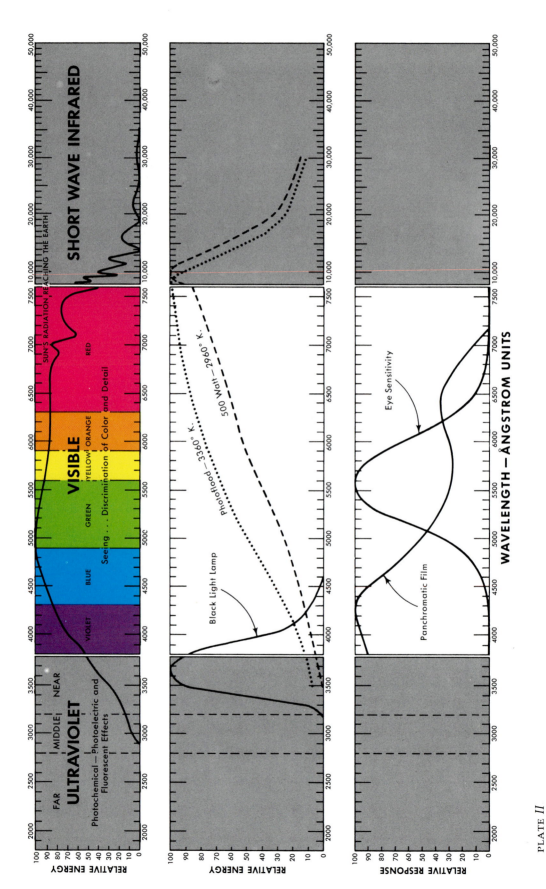

PLATE II

Lamps and the Spectrum. Simplified for this book from a comprehensive presentation published by General Electric Company.

PLATE III

The C.I.E. Chromaticity Diagram (Black-Body Locus). This diagram was produced by the C.I. E. (Commission Internationale de l'Eclairage). It is based on the three-color stimulus theory of color vision recently verified in the laboratory. Printing limitations make it impossible to achieve the clarity and brightness which the drawing represents. The reader will be able to increase his understanding of the diagram by imagining the spectrum in full brilliance and saturation wrapped around the curved perimeter as indicated by the wavelength figures.

Mixtures of two wavelengths can be plotted on a straight line joining their location on the diagram in the manner described for the color triangle (Figure 5-1). General Electric Company.

PLATE IV

Spectrogram. This plate shows graphically the significance of the spectrograms. The spectrogram for pale blue plastic has been superimposed over a representation of the spectrum. The varying area under the curve represents the relative amount of each wavelength. For instance, this diagram indicates that pale blue transmits only about 18 percent on wavelength 6000 Angstroms (shown as 600 on base line). This is a red-orange as the underlying spectrum shows.

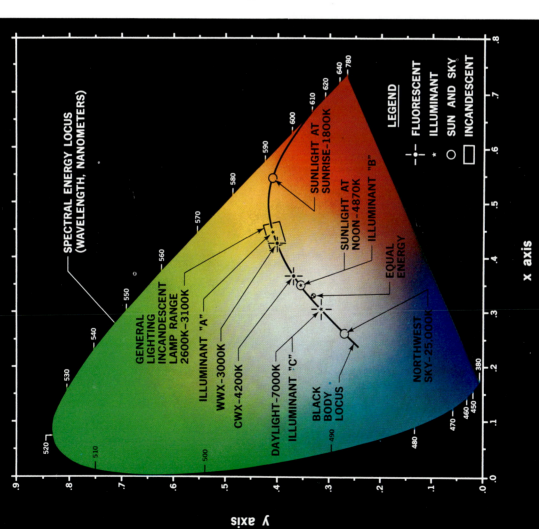

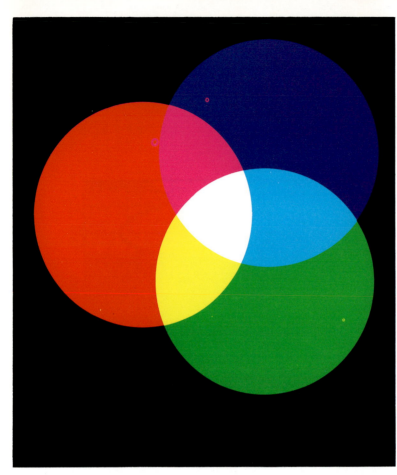

PLATE *V*

*Additive Color Mixing. Three
pools of light overlap on a white
screen; regular stage-quality
filters (Cinemoid) were used to
produce primary colors. The white
light is synthesized by mixing
stimuli produced in the eye by the
three primary colors. Adding
stimuli causes the brain to
respond as though the eye were
stimulated by all wavelengths in
equal (to the eye) portions. The
secondary colors are synthesized
by the combination of stimuli from
two of the three primary colors
mixed in equal (to the eye)
portions. This realistic
reproduction illustrates what may
be expected from mixtures of
stage-quality primaries rather
than light filtered through the
best-quality (and most expensive)
filters. These cyan and yellow
secondaries are not exact matches
for their spectral counterparts
because of the impurity of the
filters. (Lamp color temperature
was approximately 2950° K.)
Photography by William
Huling.*

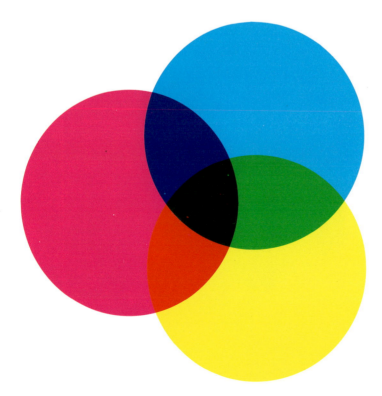

PLATE *VI*

*Subtractive Color Mixing. This
plate shows the manner in which
pigments operate by selective
transmission and absorption. It
reproduces an artist's rendering of
what will be seen when three
filters, each capable of transmitting two of the primary colors,
have been overlapped. These
filters, which match the
secondaries formed in Plate V,
are* magenta *(transmits red and
blue), often called "red" by
painters;* cyan *(transmits blue and
green), often called "blue"; and
yellow (transmits red and green).
These pigments, usually under
the names "red," "blue," and
yellow are the familiar primary
colors of painters. Note that the
mixture of all three pigment
primaries results in black, the
absence of light, the consequence
of blocking out or subtracting
of all wavelengths.*

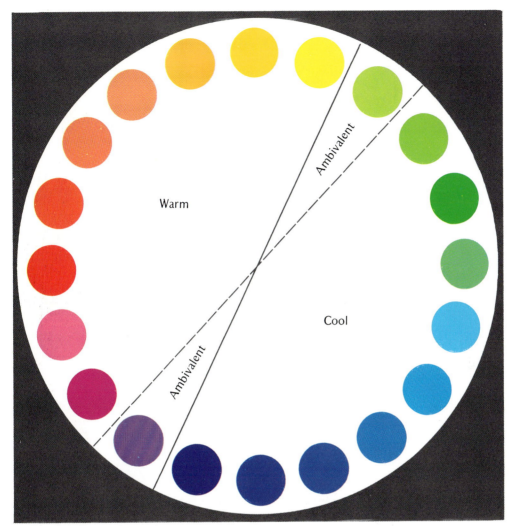

Warm

Ambivalent

Cool

Ambivalent

PLATE VII

Color Wheel. This is a photographic reproduction of a color wheel made from stage quality color media of moderate saturation. Acting area tints would be much paler in color than any of these colors. Note that tints of yellow-green and of purple can be interpreted as either "warm" or "cool" depending on the color with which they are contrasted.

PLATE VIII

The Kelvin Color Temperature Scale. This scale is the standard means of determining the color of near-white light. The color variations will most nearly approximate the actual situation if this plate is viewed under normal home incandescent light. Note that color temperature may be increased beyond that produced by the lamp by the use of filters. It is decreased by dimming in the case of incandescent lamps. Compare this illustration with the line labeled "black-body locus" on Plate III which is a more extensive representation of the Kelvin scale. General Electric Company (labels revised by author).

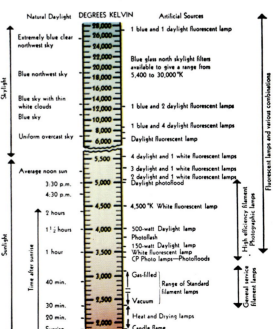

Natural Daylight — DEGREES KELVIN — Artificial Sources

Skylight

Extremely blue clear northwest sky

Blue northwest sky

Blue sky with thin white clouds

Blue sky

Uniform overcast sky

28,000
26,000
24,000
22,000
20,000
18,000
16,000
14,000
12,000
10,000
8,000
6,000

1 blue and 1 daylight fluorescent lamp

Blue glass north skylight filters available to give a range from 5,400 to 30,000 °K

1 blue and 2 daylight fluorescent lamps

1 blue and 4 daylight fluorescent lamps

Daylight fluorescent lamp

Sunlight

Average noon sun

3:30 p.m.
4:30 p.m.

2 hours

1½ hours

1 hour

Time after sunrise

40 min.

30 min.
20 min.

Sunrise

5,500
5,000
4,500
4,000
3,500
3,000
2,500
2,000

4 daylight and 1 white fluorescent lamps
3 daylight and 1 white fluorescent lamps
2 daylight and 1 white fluorescent lamps
Daylight photoflood

4,500 °K White fluorescent lamp

500-watt Daylight lamp
Photoflash
150-watt Daylight lamp
White fluorescent lamp
CP Photo lamps—Photofloods

Gas-filled
Vacuum

Range of Standard filament lamps

Heat and Drying lamps
Candle flame

Fluorescent lamps and various combinations

High efficiency filament
Photographic lamps

General service filament lamps

PLATE IX

A scene from a production of Simplicissimus *at Basel, Switzerland. Scenography by Analies Corrodi. Multiple projectors made possible the wide coverage and also the control over the montage of images. Photo courtesy Analies Corrodi by Hoffmann.*

PLATE X

Multiple Layer Projection. This plate illustrates a technique refined by Andrzej Majewski, a European scenographer. The scene is from a production of The Magic Flute *(Mozart) produced at the Wiesbaden Opera, Germany. The upper portions of the setting consisted of irregularly cut gauzes painted with various decorative designs. On and through these gauzes were projected abstract designs. As the projected images struck each gauze surface, they were partially reflected, showing an image to the audience, and partially transmitted, allowing an image to form on subsequent layers of fabric. This secondary image was altered by the shadow pattern of the gauze and the design on it. The result was a stage space in which the images seemed to exist in three dimensions. The same gauzes also allowed "fade-in" entrances when actors came between them. The production was directed by Heinz Wallberg, stage design by Andrzej Majewski, photo by author.*

PLATES *XI and XII*

Projection without projectors. These plates illustrate what can be accomplished in the way of scenic projection with nothing but standard lighting equipment. Plate XIII shows a production of The Rake's Progress (Stravinski) *done at California State University at Northridge. The "images" on the cyclorama are simply shadow patterns cast by the objects hanging near the top of the proscenium opening. The "projectors" were simply Fresnel spotlights with the lenses removed and equipped with incandescent lamps designed for motion picture projector service. These lamps were chosen because they have a very concentrated filament. Although the lamps were originally designed for use with forced ventilation there was no problem because they need never come up to full brilliance. The red filter did not require such color temperature. The bright area in the center of the cyclorama is the overlap area of the two beams. Scenography and photo by author.*

PLATE *XII shows another pseudo-projection. In this case the "image" if formed of beams from ellipsoidal reflector spotlights shuttered to narrow beam. These instruments were then angled to make the beams nearly parallel the cyclorama surface. The production was* The Poor Sailor (Darius Milhaud) *done at California State University, Northridge. Scenography and photo by author.*

PLATE *XIII*

Lighting for focus of attention. This plate shows a production of Turandot (Puccini) *done in Cincinnati. Direction by James de Blasis, scenery by Lloyd Burlingame, lighting by Jonell Polansky. Note how the focus of attention has been directed down right by a combination of setting and lighting. Photo: Babst.*

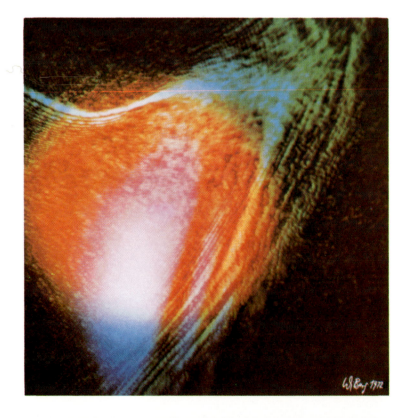

lumens per watt of electricity than that of any other stage instrument (see Figure 3-5).

The limitation of this instrument is that it can be focused only slightly. The focusing screw is mainly a centering device to adjust for various lamp dimensions. Any attempt to "flood" the beam produces first a ring of light, then a useless flare. Proper focus is that position where the beam is circular, even in distribution, and well defined.

Maintenance of parabolic reflectors is minor. Occasional cleaning with a grit-free cloth is all that is necessary. The one treatment these reflectors cannot take is overheating. If the instrument is so made that it is possible to run the focusing screw far enough to make the lamp touch the reflector, there is danger of this ruining both lamp and reflector.

PLATE *XIV*

Laser "projection." This photograph shows images generated by the phenomenon known as "interference." The images were produced by a laser device developed by Siemens (Germany). The light which forms the images is generated by lasers and is, of course, coherent light. This light is then sorted as to wavelength (to control color of the image), dispersed through a microscope objective, and then through movable plates of ripple glass. An almost infinite variety of images may be produced by moving the lens and/or the plate. Although there are certain somewhat predictable variables in the image-forming process, such as the focus of the microscope objective which determines the general dispersion of the image, experimentation is necessary to discover appropriate images for any given artistic purpose.

At this stage in its development, the laser device is too expensive, too bulky and its power and cooling water requirements too great to make it a practicable theatre device. However all of these problems should be quite rapidly alleviated.

The visible quality of the image does not lend itself well to photography. There is a vibrant granular quality in coherent light that cannot be caught in a still photograph; color purity is also much higher than modern reproduction techniques can handle. Finally, these images demonstrate none of the usual depth-of-focus problems associated with optical images formed by lenses. The image is "in focus" at any distance. Thus laser images are ideally suited to projection over three-dimensional objects and in space on smoke or aerosols. Since lasers of the power required to produce stage-worthy images are dangerous until the light is thoroughly dispersed, any actors or dancers playing in the image area must wear protective lenses. Possibly rear projection would solve this problem if design allows it.

Artistic potentialities of this device are only primitively developed. Since the images are powerful attention holders, it seems likely that the most promising applications will be in the field of dance staging and in opera. However little artistic experimentation has been done as yet.

The photo is courtesy Wolfgang Bergfeld of the Siemans Corporation, Erlangen, West Germany and Gerhard Winzer, Siemens, Munich.

CONTROLLING LIGHT: REFRACTION

Reflectors change the direction of a beam of light by bouncing it off a surface. There are two other ways of changing the direction of light: refraction and diffraction. Diffraction does not apply significantly to stage lighting and need not be discussed. Refraction explains the operation of lenses and must be studied.

Crudely stated, refraction is the bending of a light beam that takes place as it passes through a surface separating two different materials capable of transmitting light. For example, the surface may be that of a pool of water and the effect of refraction will cause a stick partially thrust into the water to appear to bend. Another example is the bending and distorting of the appearance of objects outside a window when the glass is of inferior quality, full of wavy imperfections. Most important to the lighting artist is this same bending of light through glass shaped purposely to alter the path of the light, that is, through a lens.

This crude descriptive definition of refraction is not adequate for purposes of understanding lenses. We must turn to the more exact language of the scientist and we must define some scientific terms related to light and optics.

A *medium* is a material that will, at least to some degree, transmit light. Note that our discussion of refraction depends on what happens to the light that passes through a medium, not that which is absorbed. Therefore, the same refractive principles may apply to a murky, nearly opaque piece of glass and to a clear piece of optical plate.

Optical density refers indirectly to the speed of light in a medium. The speed of light in a vacuum is about 186,280 miles per second. In air and other materials it is less than this.

The index of refraction is a number used to refer indirectly to the optical density of media. It is always larger than 1.000; the reason is that the index 1.000 is assigned to a vacuum, the condition under which light travels at maximum speed. Other materials have indices

larger than 1.000, indicating their higher optical density and the resultant lowering of the speed of light within them. Thus a material
which halves the speed of light would have an index of refraction of
2.000.

A *normal* is a line drawn at 90° to the tangent at the point where a
light beam strikes a surface. Note that if the surface is a plane, the normal is perpendicular to that plane. In the case of a curved surface, we
must refer to the tangent.

We are now equipped with those words necessary to make a more
exact definition of refraction: *Refraction is the bending of light rays
caused by their passage through a surface separating a medium of one
optical density from a medium of a different optical density, provided the
light rays are not traveling along the normal.*

Refraction will be *uniform;* that is, all rays will be bent the same
amount, if the light passing through the surface is all of the same
wavelength. Refraction will be *differential;* that is, bending will vary
with wavelength, if the beam of light is made up of various wavelengths. Differential refraction is the cause of chromatic aberration
(discussed later in this chapter) and is one of the ways in which spectra
are produced (see Chapter 5).

Practically speaking, the lighting artist is concerned exclusively with
those cases of refraction resulting from the passage of light from air to
glass and back to air. The index of refraction of air is so near to 1.000
that we may ignore the difference; that of glass will range from about
1.51 to 1.89.

Figure 4-1a shows a beam of light traveling at an angle to the first
surface of a piece of plate glass whose surfaces are exactly parallel. The
beam is shown at an angle because, according to the definition of refraction, if it were traveling parallel to the normal, no refraction would
take place. As the light beam passes through the surface, going from a

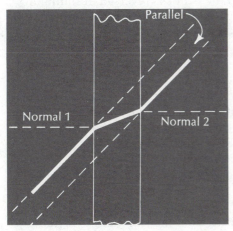

FIGURE *4-1a*
*Refraction. The path of a light "ray"
through air and a sheet of glass with parallel sides. The two paths in air are parallel.*

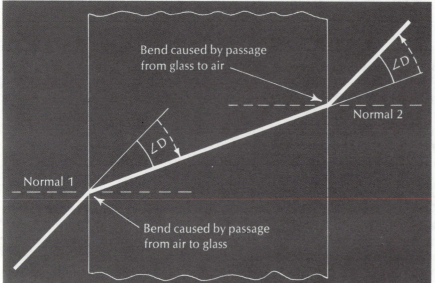

Bend caused by passage from glass to air

∠D

Normal 2

Normal 1

∠D

Bend caused by passage from air to glass

FIGURE *4-1b*
Magnification of Figure 4-1a with added detail. The ray that enters glass (denser medium) is bent from its original path toward the nor-mal, making Angle D. The ray that enters air (rarer me-dium) is bent from its original path away from the nor-mal, also making Angle D.

medium of low optical density to one of high optical density (air to glass), it is bent *toward* the normal. (Notice that the normal is on the side of the surface in the direction in which the light beam is traveling.) The amount of this initial deviation (a more exact word for bending) is indicated by Angle *D* (see Figure 4-1*b*). As the light continues toward the other glass-air surface, it moves in a straight line no matter how thick the glass is. At the second surface another change of direction takes place unless the new course happens to be along the normal to the second surface. If it is not along the normal, it will be bent *away* from the normal this time because it is now passing from a medium of high optical density (glass to air). The amount of bending will be the same in each instance because the ratio between the two densities remains the same. However, the direction of the bends is reversed, resulting in a new path in the air beyond the glass parallel to but offset from the original path. Thus Angle *D* is the same in each location in Figure 4-1*b*.

Although it is beyond the scope of this text, it will be of interest to many lighting artists to learn that each of the above described opera-tions can be mathematically computed with great precision if the char-acteristics of the glass and the wavelength of the light are known. The reader should also note that some of the light striking the glass surface is reflected instead of bent under all conditions. In certain cases the light may be completely reflected. Reflection results in a loss of about 10 percent of the light striking the lens under spotlight- or projection-operating conditions. Highly refined photographic and projection lenses can be treated to reduce this loss. Crude spotlight lenses are not worth the cost of the treatment.

It is important that the lighting artist note the fact that the bending takes place at the surface(s) of the lens. This principle is essential to an understanding of the Fresnel lens, a very important device in the theatre.

Refraction in Plano-Convex Lenses

Figure 4-1c transfers the information to a segment of a prism. Notice that the only difference is that the normal where the beam leaves the glass is now at an angle to the normal at the entry point. In the case of the parallel surface plate glass, the two normals were also parallel. When the normals are arranged as they are in Figure 4-1c the two angles of deviation no longer cancel; instead they are made to add. The result is that the beam of light is bent by an amount equal to twice Angle *D*. Although it will not usually refer to spotlight applications, the student should know that the above description has been simplified extensively and does not apply without many further qualifications when the beams of light strike the lens at relatively oblique angles. Figure 4-1d extends this process from prism to lens.

Three factors determine the amount of bending that can take place as the result of refraction: (1) the ratio between the indices of refraction—the greater this ratio, the greater the angle of deviation; (2) the angle between the norm at entry and the norm at exit from the inter-

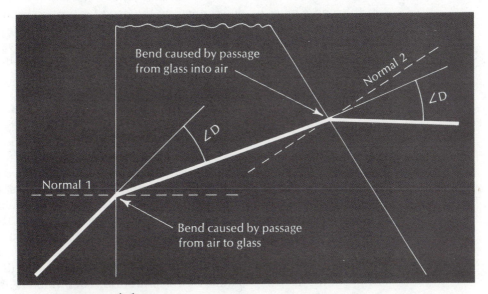

FIGURE *4-1c*
The path of a light ray through air and a glass prism with nonparallel sides. As in Figure 4-1b, the ray that enters the glass is bent from its original path toward the normal; the ray that enters air is bent away from the normal. But since the normals are not parallel, the paths in air are not parallel.

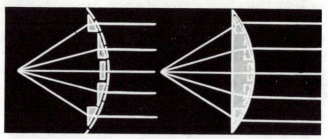

FIGURE 4-1d

The paths of light rays through air and a plano-convex lens. The lens may be regarded as a system of prisms each comparable to the prism in Figure 4-1c. The normals and the Angles D are not shown in these diagrams, but the ray paths are related to them as in Figure 4-1c. Courtesy General Electric Company.

vening medium—the greater this angle, the more the final path will vary from the original path; (3) the wavelength of the light—bending varies with wavelength, short rays (blue-violet) being bent more than long rays (red).

When the above factors are applied to stage lenses, we find that the only variable that can be applied effectively is that concerning the angular difference between the normals. The composition of the glass in the lenses must be determined by the need for heat resistance and stage usage requires that spotlight lenses handle all visible wavelengths equally well. In the case of plano-convex lenses, it comes down to this: The thicker the lens is made, the greater its light-bending power.

Describing the Refractive Power of Lenses

It is inconvenient to describe the bending power of a lens in terms of the angle of deviation or in terms of its curvature and refractive index. Thus a set of standard conditions has been adopted and lenses are described on the basis of their performance under these conditions. The standard conditions are: *Parallel* light rays are passed through the lens parallel to its optical axis (that is, at right angles to the plane surface of a plano-convex lens) and the distance from the optical center of the lens to the principal focus is measured. This distance is known as the focal length of the lens. Explanation of the terms of this definition is needed. The optical center is a point, usually within the glass of the lens, which geometrically determines the beginning of its bending effect. The *focal length* usually is defined as the distance from the optical center of a lens to its principal focus, measured in either inches or centimeters (see Figure 4-2). The *principal focus* is the crossing point for parallel rays. Since a lens is a two-way device, there are two principal foci for each lens. The *optical center* is a plane within the lens (in the case of positive lenses) which geometrically *appears* to be the plane on which all bending occurs. (Optically, bending occurs at the curved surface of the glass.)

Optical experts use a precise instrument known as an "optical bench" to make exact measurements to determine the focal length of a lens. Since stage spotlight lenses are crude optically and are made only in focal lengths separated by 1-inch increments, the lighting artist can utilize the conditions governing the determination of focal length on a much more primitive level. He needs only to seek out a source of relatively parallel beams of light (a lamp 100 feet or more distant or sunlight will be more than adequate) and pass the light through the lens or lens fragment to be measured. He simply measures the distance from the flat side of the glass to the sharply focused image of his distant object. This will roughly meet the conditions described above, coming close enough to enable him to estimate the focal length of the lens to the nearest inch, which is all that is necessary to enable him to order a new lens or to match up a couple of unknown lenses. Notice that it will make no difference which direction the light passes through the lens; the measurement to the flat side will come out the same either way.

Once the principal foci have been found and the focal length of the lens determined, we are able to describe its efficiency and bending power. As far as the simple lenses used in spotlights are concerned, the only other consideration is the diameter of the lens and this, of course, is determined by the make of the spotlight. Naturally, a larger diameter will allow more light to pass from the lamp to the stage and, given a strong bending power, the instrument will be able to concentrate this light on a small area. A typical lens specification for a spotlight would read *6 × 9 inch lens,* to define a lens 6 inches in diameter with a focal length of 9 inches. The manufacturer of the lens will have adjusted the curvature of the glass (with the index of refraction of the glass which he is using) to produce a 9-inch focal length and the stage-lighting technician need not concern himself with this. (Note that the designer

FIGURE *4-2*
Determining Focal Length. Standard conditions established as determinants of focal length of a lens. See also Figure 4-3c.

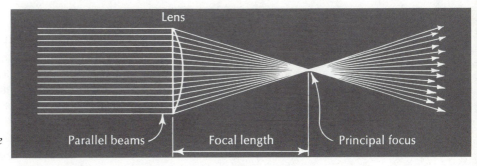

Lens

Parallel beams   Focal length   Principal focus

of high-powered projection apparatus *will* be concerned because the thicker the lens the less efficient and more liable to breakage.)

Photographers must use much more complicated lenses than lighting technicians. Thus they are in need of a more precise method of describing the efficiency of a lens at various adjustments. Several systems have been devised for this, the commonest of which is the f number system. In this system two numbers are necessary: the focal length of the lens and the f number. Once the lens has been fitted to the camera, the f number becomes the main consideration. The f number is simply the focal length of the lens divided by it *effective* diameter. Thus for a simple spotlight lens 6×12 inches, the f number is 12/6 or 2. Note, however, that this calculation assumes that light is passing through all of the lens. If the spotlight mounting takes one-fourth inch off the radius of the lens, the formula becomes 12/5.5 or 2.18. This does not seem very much, but it represents a loss of 8.3 percent of transmitted light. We will have reason to consider this rapid loss of light further when we study the efficiency of spotlights.

The photographer uses a device known as an "iris" to change the effective diameter of his lens. He does this to compensate for larger or smaller amounts of light which will be available to him and to adjust certain other focal characteristics of his lens. Since the focal length of his lens is fixed (unless he is using one of the new *zoom* lenses) he refers to this as changing the f of the lens and notes his exposure by f number and time duration. He may jot down "1/100 sec at f/6.3" for an exposure of a fast-moving object in fairly bright illumination. Another notation may read "1/10 sec at f/2.5." This setting would be appropriate for a rather dark scene with little or no movement.

While the stage-lighting technician may have little to do with photography on the stage, if he ever ventures into either motion pictures or television, he will find such "lens talk" vital to everything that is done and will soon learn that what the lens sees (and transmits to the audience) is sometimes vastly different from what the eye sees. Lighting technicians in these areas will do well to study photography long and diligently. Furthermore, if the lighting technician is to become proficient in the art of projected scenery, he will need to know a great deal more about the complicated lenses of cameras and projectors.

Chromatic Aberration

Earlier we noted that one of the three determining elements in refraction was the wavelength of the light. This, together with the difference in refractive index and the relationship between the two surfaces separating the media, determines the angle of deviation. No simple lens consisting of a single piece of glass is able to bring wavelengths of different lengths from the same source into focus on the same plane. If, for example, the lens is made to focus red waves sharply, the blue waves from the same source will be out of focus, appearing as a blue fringe around the sharp red image. If we focus the blue image, the red one blurs.

This same situation prevails inside the human eye. Its simple lens cannot bring the red and blue portions of an image into focus at the same time. However, we have become accustomed to viewing images with the red portion in sharp focus and the blue-violet portion slightly fuzzy. We do not notice this unless all of the colors in an image except the blue-violet are removed. Then the eye will try to focus on the blue-violet image and eyestrain will usually result. For this reason the stage-lighting artist usually avoids using pure primary blue light, with nothing to relieve it, except for short periods.

In the case of spotlight lenses, chromatic aberration becomes a problem only when the instruments are adjusted for the narrowest possible beam. Under these conditions, the pool of light will be ringed with color fringes and may even be streaked with color, making the instrument useless at this setting. The solution is to focus the instrument for a wider beam and install some type of beam-cutoff device well in front of the lens to get the narrow beam desired. Another possibility is to use an ellipsoidal spotlight for "pin spotting" since it will not display this fault.

How Lenses Function in Spotlights

We may now apply the theoretical material concerning refraction to the practical study of spotlight lenses. You will recall that the purpose of the optical parts of a spotlight is to gather up light radiating spherically from the lamp filament and to send this light to the stage. Let us consider a simple "stovepipe" spotlight for a moment, leaving out the spherical reflector for the sake of simplicity (see Figure 4-3a). Note that only that cone of light (A) which passes directly through the opening at the end of the pipe strikes the stage. The square law determines the amount of light reaching the stage and any attempt to narrow the beam

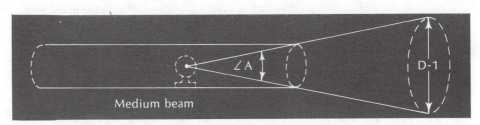

FIGURE 4-3a

Stovepipe Spotlight. Simplified drawing shows lamp in forward position producing large pool of light at short throw. Angle A represents efficiency of the instrument in this mode of operation.

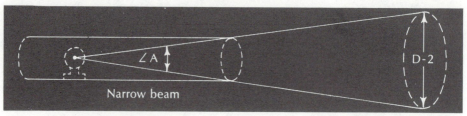

FIGURE 4-3*b*

Stovepipe spotlight with lamp moved to rear of housing to produce narrow pool of light for long throw. Angle A represents efficiency. Note reduction of efficiency produced by narrowing beam in this manner. Pool will be even dimmer than that illustrated in Figure 4-3a.

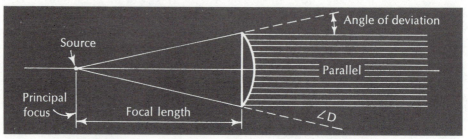

FIGURE 4-3*c*

Application of conditions established to determine focal length to plano-convex lens in spotlight service. Compare with Figure 4-2. Note that conditions are the same except that direction of light travel is reversed.

will result in still more light being wasted in the housing (see Figure 4-3*b*). The pool of light formed in Figure 4-3*b* is the same size as that in Figure 4-3*a,* but the throw is longer. The result is that a narrower angle of light is utilized, the pool is dimmer, and the efficiency lower.

Angle *A* in the diagrams graphically represents the efficiency of the light-controlling system; the wider this angle, the more efficient the system. An attempt to produce a smaller pool of light at the same throw will result in lowered efficiency because the lamp must be moved further back and Angle *A* narrowed. The pool will also be slightly dimmer because the lamp-to-stage distance has been increased by a few inches, and the square law decrees that the light must therefore become dimmer. To get a very small pool of light from this instrument at any workable throw means that we must reduce the efficiency to an intolerably low figure.

Now let us review the characteristics of the plano-convex lens with an eye to discovering what this lens can do to increase the efficiency of the stovepipe spotlight. You will recall the conditions under which the focal length of a plano-convex lens is determined (Figure 4-2).

Figure 4-3c reconstructs these conditions with the difference that the direction of travel of light has been reversed. A point source of light has been placed at the principal focus and the diverging beams which strike the lens are converged into a parallel beam by their passage through the lens. Thus Figure 4-3c emphasizes the *converging* power of the convex lens.

Figures 4-3d and 4-3e illustrate the two possible conditions that may prevail when a point source of light is *not* at the principal focus. In Figure 4-3d, the source has been placed farther from the lens than the principal focus with the result that an image is formed at some distance, q, from the lens. This distance will vary with the location of the point source, moving farther away from the lens as the source moves toward the principal focus and vice versa. As the source approaches the principal focus, we say that the image is at *infinity*, meaning that the

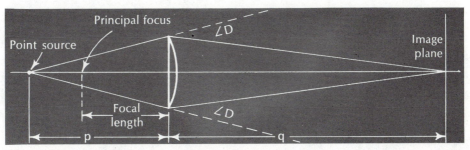

FIGURE 4-3d

The plano-convex lens as an objective lens. Drawing shows conditions under which lens will produce image and the mathematical quantities which will determine the location of that image.

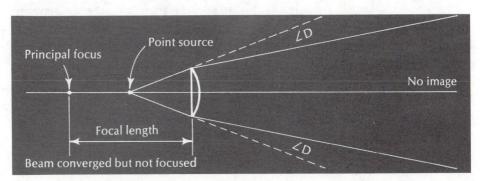

FIGURE 4-3e

The plano-convex lens as a condensing unit. Under these conditions no image can be formed. Within limits, the convergence will be determined by the focal length of the lens.

beam of light is essentially parallel. If an object such as a well-illu-minated photographic slide is substituted for the point source, its image will be formed by the lens. The plane on which this image ap-pears will be known as the *image plane*.

Under the conditions mentioned above the lens is described as an *objective* lens; that is, it is used as an *image-forming* lens. It is important to note that the term "objective" refers to the manner in which a lens is used, not to its optical nature, although satisfactory performance of a lens as an objective usually requires that it be highly refined and cor-rected. Most objective lenses are complicated and expensive pieces of equipment.

The relationship between objective lens, object, and image can be expressed mathematically with great precision. Since the stage-lighting artist may need to apply the formula when he is working with pro-jected scenery (see Appendix I), it is hereby provided:

$$\frac{1}{p} + \frac{1}{q} = \frac{1}{F}$$

In this formula, as indicated in Figure 4-3a, the terms are as follows: p equals the distance from the lens to the object; q equals the distance from the lens to the focal plane; and F equals the focal length of the lens.

The Lens as a Converging Device

Figure 4-3e illustrates the third possible position of the point source. Note that it is now closer to the lens than the principal focus. Under these conditions, the bending power of the lens is insufficient to make the diverging beams come to a focal point. However, the diverging beams are *converged* in an amount equal to the greatest angle of devia-tion produced by the lens. This angle is shown in Figure 4-3e. It is labeled Angle *D*. This angle represents the greatest bending power of the lens and is a constant factor in all situations. Note Angle *D* in Figures 4-3c, d, and e.

A lens operated in such a manner that it can only converge a beam of light, but not bring it to a focus, is called a *condensing* lens, or *con-denser*. The lens in a plano-convex spotlight and in the Fresnel spot-light is operated in this way. Most spotlight housings are made so short that it is impossible to move the lamp as far away from the lens as the principal focus. However, in the case of the arc follow spot, the housing is purposely made long enough so that the instrument can be *back focused*—the operator can move the arc back past the principal focus to a point where a defocused image of the arc becomes the pool of light on the stage. Back focusing is one of the two ways of dimming an arc light. The other is to spread the beam by moving the arc forward, but closing the iris, thereby losing most of the light inside the housing.

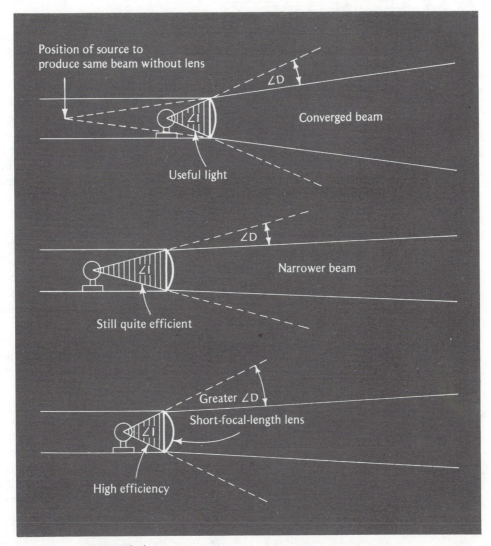

FIGURE 4-4

Application of Lenses To Increase the Efficiency of Spotlights. The top draw-ing shows the effect of the addition of a lens to a simple stovepipe spotlight. The result is a narrow, relatively efficient beam, the equivalent in size to a beam produced by moving the lamp well back in the housing. The other two drawings illustrate how still narrower beams can be produced either by moving the lamp back in the housing at a loss of efficiency or by changing the lens to one of shorter focal length.

Neither method will dim the instrument completely, but the beam can be reduced to the degree where it can be cut off without distracting.

Lenses and Efficiency

Now that we have detailed the optical nature of a converging lens, let us discuss its use with the simple spotlight and see what happens to the efficiency (see Figures 4-3a and 4-4). You will notice that the lamp has been moved quite near to the front of the housing and that (in Figure 4-4) the back portion of the stovepipe spotlight, which is no longer needed, has been removed. The dotted lines indicate what the spread of the beam would be if the lens were removed. This wide beam would be nearly useless on stage, and, if no lens were available, the lamp would have to be moved far back in the housing to narrow the beam. However, the lens will converge the beam according to its bending power, represented again by Angle D. The result is a beam of useful size and, even more important, a beam that is much brighter because the cone of illumination striking the lens, represented by Angle I, is as wide as it was before the lens was added. Nearly all of the light that formerly spread over the uselessly wide pool of light is now concentrated within the useful area. The only loss has been that absorbed by the glass of the lens and that reflected from its surfaces. This loss will amount to about 10 percent of the total light passing through the lens, far less than the amount gained by adding the lens.

Thus the converging lens makes possible a great improvement in the efficiency of a plano spotlight. Adding the spherical reflector, which we have left off in our example only for the sake of simplicity, makes the instrument a useful device indeed.

Refer to the middle part of Figure 4-4 for the results of moving the lamp back in the housing to produce a still narrower beam. Efficiency is still much greater than it would be in a stovepipe spotlight producing a similar beam. The lens will still gather a much larger cone of illumination right down to the point of a *pin spot* although there will be chromatic aberration with which to contend. However, if small pools of light are to be produced, a better solution is to seek greater converging power by using a lens of a shorter focal length as shown in the bottom part of Figure 4-4. The shorter focal length will enable the lamp to remain nearer the lens, retaining the large cone of light and the greater efficiency.

Since the beam of light from a spotlight will be divergent at all times, the longer the throw the wider the beam will become. For maximum efficiency, choice of lens must be based on the lens that will produce the beam size needed at the throw required and enable the lamp to operate as near to the lens as possible. The general rule for lenses used as converging devices is: long throw, short focal-length lens; short throw, long focal-length lens. Thus the converging power is matched to the beam spread needed and efficiency is maintained.

Further Improvements in Efficiency

It is obvious from the geometry of Figure 4-4 that the way to improve the efficiency of a plano spotlight is to increase the diameter of the lens and shorten its focal length. This arrangement will gather more light by capturing a larger cone of illumination and will converge this light into a narrow, useful beam. However, we soon run up against the limits of the plano-convex lens. Increasing the diameter rapidly increases the thickness at the center of the lens, even if our intent is only to maintain the focal length present, not to shorten it further. Large-diameter, short focal-length lenses are difficult to manufacture. The heat stresses set up in these large chunks of glass often crack them before the lens can be tempered. Furthermore, such lenses are heavy and the glass in them absorbs a lot of light. A vicious circle is set up: The absorbed light is converted to heat, creating stresses tending to destroy the lens. The result of this is that plano lenses with a diameter of more than 8 inches and a focal length much under 9 inches are not very practical for spotlight service even when the lenses are made of Pyrex glass to resist heat cracking. Since the reflector can only add a cone of light equal to that already subtended by the lens, there is a practical limit beyond which the efficiency of the plano spotlight cannot go.

The Fresnel Lens

The Fresnel lens represents a break through this impasse. Actually the principle is an old one, having been first applied to the design of light-house lenses to solve a similar efficiency problem. The basic principle derives from the physics of refraction. You will recall that the bending of the light takes place at the surfaces of the glass—not inside the glass. Around 1800, Augustin Fresnel, a French physicist, reasoned from this fact of refraction that most of the intervening glass could be removed from a lens without altering its refractive properties. He devised a segmented lighthouse lens whose curvature was that of a short focal-length plano-convex lens, but which used far less glass and lost much less light. More important still, it was not nearly as susceptible to heat breakage. Fresnel's technique was simple: He stepped back the curvature in ringlike steps to avoid extra thick glass (see Figure 4-5). The parts of Fresnel's lens were precisely ground to optical precision and carefully mounted in heavy brass holders to make up the lighthouse lens. The expense was enormous, but the life of a lighthouse lens is long and the benefits of its efficient operation are great. It was well worth the expense.

In the early 1930s the principle of the Fresnel lens was adapted to theatre lighting. However, little optical precision was involved. A theatrical Fresnel lens is not ground but cast in a mold. The lens is one

FIGURE 4-5

Development of a
Fresnel Lens. The
slope of the ring-lens
sections corresponds
to those of a thick
plano-convex lens.
Courtesy General
Electric Company.

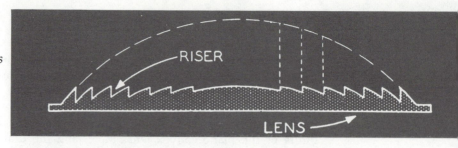

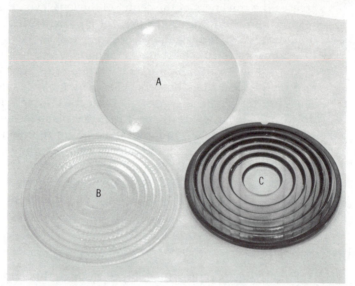

FIGURE 4-6a

Plano-Convex, Fresnel, and Oval Beam Lenses. A is a typical stage-
quality plano-convex lens. Such a lens is found in modern ellipsoidal
spotlights and in now outdated plano spotlights. B is a typical molded
Fresnel lens for stage use. Its surfaces are optically crude, therefore the
dappled pattern on the back has been added to smooth the beam and
soften the edges. C is a Fresnel lens with oval-beam cylindrical lens pat-
terns on its back surface. This lens has somewhat better optical properties
than the lens B. Thus its risers have been coated with black ceramic enamel
and its optical surfaces are sufficiently good to eliminate the need for
dappling. Photo by William Huling, California State University,
Northridge, Audio Visual Services.

piece of glass, not several, and it is cheap in price and poor in optical
characteristics. However, it is still a very efficient device. The Fresnel
lens (shown in cross section in Figure 4-5) is simply a piece of glass
molded following the Fresnel principle. Since the glass is crudely
molded and the vertical steps of the rings in the lens are not ordinarily
treated to prevent spurious refraction (in cheap lenses), a further optical
distortion is purposely introduced. This distortion takes the form of

dapplelike bumps cast on the "plano" side of the lens to smooth out the light output and soften the edges of the beam. More precisely made Fresnel lenses whose risers (vertical steps) have been opaqued with black ceramic enamel do not have these diffusing surfaces, and produce a sharper-edged beam [see Figure 4-6a (C)].

The great advantage of the Fresnel lens is that it is free of the limitations concerning diameter and focal length that hamper the plano lens. Diameter can be increased without the increase in thickness, and focal length can be shortened by simply changing the curvature of the front of each ring. Molded plastic Fresnel lenses are available from novelty houses which produce phenomenal magnifications with no apparent lens thickness. Examination of the grooved surface of one of these lenses with a magnifying glass will reveal that the "grooves" are really tiny Fresnel segments each bearing the curve of a tremendously thick plano-convex lens. Unfortunately such Fresnel lenses will not withstand the heat of spotlight service and are not used in stage lighting at this time.

Fresnel Spotlights

Installed in a spotlight housing, the Fresnel lens offers an immediate increase in efficiency. The focal length of the lens will be about half its diameter (because of manufacturing practice, this diameter-focal length

FIGURE 4-6b
*Modern Oval-Beam Fresnel Spotlight.
This modern Fresnel spotlight represents
late developments in efficiency and rugged
theatrical instrument construction.* Kliegl
Bros.

FIGURE *4-6c*
*Modern Fresnel Spotlight.
This instrument features a
metal ring in the place of
the usual focusing knob.
This facilitates operation of
the spotlight from below by
means of a pole with a
hook.* Photo courtesy Berkey Colortran.

relationship is the standard in the United States). The lamp will operate closer to the Fresnel lens than it probably ever operated with a
plano lens. Since the principal focus is very near the lens, housing can
be very short. Diameter can be increased enabling both lens and reflector to work at higher efficiency. Weight is actually reduced.

Since the Fresnel lens requires operation of the lamp very close to
the lens, it gave rise to the development of the tubular, Type "T" lamp.
The tubular lamp was needed because the older globe-shaped Type
"G" lamps could not get close enough to operate at maximum efficiency
without touching the lens.

The result of these changes is that the Fresnel spotlight, while it
operates on the same basic principle as the plano spot, is quite a different instrument. The Fresnel is shorter, tends to be larger in diameter
to accommodate the wide lens, has a tubular lamp, a larger reflector,
and, of course, a Fresnel lens. The light which it produces is brighter

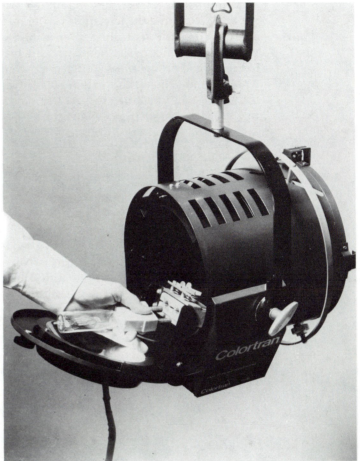

FIGURE *4-6d*
Modern Fresnel Spotlight Utilizing Retrofit T-H Lamp. This instrument also features a ring-focusing device — the metalic ring near the front — which allows focusing from any location near the spotlight. Note that the ring moves the lens instead of the lamp which remains fixed. Figure also shows proper method of handling T-H lamps; touch only the base. Photo courtesy Berkey Colortran.

by far, watt for watt, than a plano spotlight. However, there is considerable spill light and the edge of the beam is very soft, usually tapering off toward darkness over a distance of 4 to 6 feet. This light quality is an advantage when blending acting areas from on-stage positions, but makes the Fresnel all but useless for use in front-of-house (FOH) positions. Figures 4-6*b, c,* and *d* illustrate modern Fresnel instruments.

Oval-Beam Fresnel Spotlights

A recent addition to the Fresnel lens is the *oval beam* [see Figure 4-6*a* (C) and 4-6*b*]. The oval beam is produced by casting into the flat side of the lens a series of nonspherical ridges somewhat like those cast into the front of an automobile headlamp. These ridges serve the same purpose that the ridges serve in the auto lamp — they shape the beam into an oval pattern. Such lenses are often worth their price many times over in

small intimate theatres where the audience sits with "its knees in the acting area." Rotating the lens in its carrier makes it possible to cut acting-
area light much closer to the audience than the conventional Fresnel lens
would allow. Since oval-beam lenses are precisely made, they have flatted risers and produce less spill than the conventional types. Oval-beam
lenses are interchangeable with regular Fresnel lenses of the same diameter. A well-equipped theatre can carry a stock of both lens types, installing whichever suits the needs of the show at hand.

High-Quality Lenses Based on the Fresnel Principle

The high efficiency and low weight of the Fresnel lens have led to the
development of two more expensive types designed for use in ellipsoidal spotlights. The first of these is simply a precisely made Fresnel
lens with flatted risers. This lens has been ground to remove the worst
of the casting imperfections and is usually made of heat-treated glass
to insure a long life even in the hottest light beam. Since grinding the
broken curve of a Fresnel lens is difficult, another application of the
Fresnel principle has resulted in the *step lens*. In this lens, the excess
glass has been removed by stepping the flat, not the curved, side of
the glass. The result is a continuous curve identical to the plano lens,
but with a recessed flat side, making precision grinding easier. The
results are essentially the same — a highly efficient lens with some spill

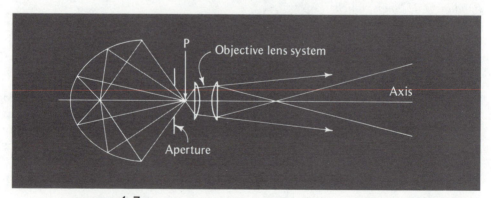

FIGURE 4-7a

*Application of Lenses to Ellipsoidal Spotlights. The drawing shows in
simplified form the manner in which plano-convex or step lenses are
applied to ellipsoidal spotlights. The objective lens (or lens system) is placed
so that its principal focal p point is slightly closer to the lens than the aperture. This makes it possible to focus an image of the aperture on the stage.
The image of the aperture is reversed and inverted as in any slide projector.
High efficiency results from the concentration of light in the aperture by the
reflector.*

FIGURE *4-7b* ·
*Modern ellipsoidal spotlight utilizing a
step lens for light weight and high efficiency because only two air-to-glass surfaces are involved.* Kliegl Bros.

from the setbacks, but lighter in weight and less susceptible to heat
breakage. Note the lens shown in the instrument in Figure 4-7*b*.

Lenses in Ellipsoidal Spotlights

Our examination of the optics of the ellipsoid led us to the conclusion
that this reflector could gather up a large portion of the light from a
filament and deliver it to a second focal point so that it would leave that
focal point in a wide but uniform cone of light. This cone of light must
then be converged upon the stage to form a usable pool of light. It is
also necessary to provide some way of adjusting beam size since the
cone of light will not allow much focusing by moving the converging
lens. The solution to this problem has led to the abandonment of the
converging principle entirely and to the use of crude objective lenses of
short focal length. The light moving toward the second focal point of
the ellipsoid is used to illuminate an *aperture*, a metal gate capable of
being formed to shape the beam. The lens system is arranged to focus
the image of this brightly lighted aperture on the stage. The second
focal point is placed so close to the lens system that all light from the
reflector is caught and passed on to the stage (see Figure 4-7*a*).

The result is a simple projection system. The reflector serves as the
light-gathering device, the aperture as the slide, and the lens system
as the objective lens. The stage becomes the projection screen. In fact,
simple images formed in sheet metal or painted with heatproof paint
on mica may be placed in the aperture and focused on the stage in the
same manner as a slide projector. However, the emphasis in the
ellipsoidal spotlight is on light-handling efficiency and beam shaping,
not on optical precision in handling images.

FIGURE *4-7c*
*Very recent ellipsoidal spotlight utilizing
die-cast aluminum parts, double-flatted
reflector, and double plano-convex lenses
for flat field and high efficiency.* Courtesy
Strand Century, Inc.

FIGURE *4-7d*
*A modern ellipsoidal spotlight designed to
utilize the high efficiency and optical
characteristics of the T-H lamp.* Kliegl
Bros.

The high efficiency of the ellipsoidal reflector brought about the development of the base-up spotlight lamp. This lamp has a very compact filament and is the most efficient lamp ordinarily used on stage. The base-up operation allows most of the sublimated tungsten to collect near the base where no useful light is emitted. Consequently, those parts of the glass that transmit light to the reflector remain relatively clean to the end of the life of the lamp. Modern ellipsoidal reflector instruments are shown in Figures 4-7*b* and *c*.

Still more recently, the tungsten-halogen lamp has been adapted to the ellipsoidal-reflector spotlight. Since this lamp clears itself of sublimated tungsten by means of the halogen cycle, there is no need for the added complication of base-up operation. Modern ellipsoidal-reflector spotlights designed around the properties of the T-H lamp may be operated in any position. One is shown in Figure 4-7*d*.

Lens Systems for Ellipsoidal Spotlights

Two types of lens systems are available in ellipsoidal spotlights. Both serve the same purpose: to focus the image of the aperture on the stage. The first type consists of a pair of plano-convex lenses mounted together, curved sides in, and serving as a single, short focal-length unit. These lenses should be heat treated or made of Pyrex glass since they must withstand considerable heat stress. The two lenses form a heavy but quite accurate objective system which results in a sharply edged beam with little spill light. The other type of lens consists of a single, highly developed Fresnel lens. Its risers are flatted for reduction of spill light. This lens weighs a great deal less than the two plano lenses and is much less susceptible to heat cracking. It produces slightly more spill and a slightly softer beam edge than the plano combination. Either lens system is quite satisfactory for front-of-house lighting. Under stage conditions it will be very difficult for the audience to tell which lens is in use. Cost is roughly the same for either system.

Alternate Lens Systems for Ellipsoidal-Reflector Spotlights

In addition to converting their lens systems to utilize the configurations of T-H filaments, engineers have also increased the versatility of modern ellipsoidal-reflector spotlights by providing alternate lens systems. Older instruments were manufactured with a single throw range in mind, although these instruments were often altered by ingenious technicians who installed different lenses to alter the throw distance. Modern spotlights often are equipped by their manufacturers with lens-tube holders that allow the installation of a variety of lens configurations. Each lens or set of lenses usually comes in its own lens tube. It is also possible to shift the lens assembly over a much wider range of settings in modern instruments making defocusing easier.

Although it is the practice of salesmen to demonstrate their ellipsoidal-reflector spotlights at sharp focus to best display evenness of field, lack of aberrations at beam edge, and sharpness of light cutoff, operators will more often want to use the instruments in a manner that will blend the light from each instrument imperceptibly from one area to another. For this purpose a good ellipsoidal-reflector spotlight should be capable of being defocused sufficiently to eliminate any trace of beam edge. In a well-designed modern instrument this can be done without compromising any of the sharp-focus features. The addition of interchangeable lenses increases the possibilities for soft focusing.

Selection of new instruments for purchase has been somewhat simplified by these developments. However the purchaser should carefully consider the efficiency matters discussed below and make sure that the instruments he is considering buying can be adjusted to operate at near top efficiency under all conditions for which he expects to use them. It is poor economy to operate an instrument shuttered nearly to zero efficiency instead of changing the lens configuration to improve its efficiency. This should be a telling argument for the purchase of auxiliary lens sets for spotlights.

Efficiency Considerations

Efficiency can be very high if the ellipsoidal spotlight is working under optimum conditions. Efficiency is at its best with the framing shutters completely withdrawn from the aperture to allow all of the light from the reflector to pass through the lens. Under these conditions the ellipsoidal spotlight will exceed the efficiency of the best Fresnel instrument. However, efficiency is not the only feature of the ellipsoidal spotlight. Flexibility in the form of variable beam shape is also a great advantage. No other instrument offers as easy adjustment to cut off flares of light or to fit a beam into a doorway. This spot can be adjusted to light almost any shape space needed by cutting off parts of the beam. Efficiency rapidly drops as the beam size is cut down. Nevertheless, it may be well worth the loss of efficiency to get the adjustment needed. The operator must be cautioned against running ellipsoidal spotlights with the shutters almost entirely closed for long periods of time. The energy cut from the beams must be dissipated within the housings, causing them to heat up rapidly. See "Maintenance and Alignment of Ellipsoidal Reflectors" in Chapter 3.

Selection of a set of ellipsoidal spotlights for area lighting from a beam or balcony position in the house should be made with care. Instruments should be fitted to the throw in such a way that they will operate in the "wide open" position most of the time. They will be more efficient and lamps will last longer if this is done. Instrument catalogs generally list ellipsoidal spotlights by maximum spot size at various throws. Select the nearest usable instrument. Because the ellipsoidal spotlight is usually the only instrument in the theatre whose lamp must be operated base up, extra cautions must be used when training a crew to mount them. The lamps are more than usually sensitive to damage from poor operating position.

5 COLORED LIGHT

What Is Color?

Strictly speaking, color is a human phenomenon. As far as physics is concerned, there is no difference except wavelength between radiation of 4000 Å and that of 7000 Å. However, the normal human eye sees the shorter (4000 Å) wave as blue-violet and the longer (7000 Å) as deep red. Thus, *color is the response of the eye to certain wavelengths of light.* Even this must be qualified by indicating a "normal" eye. Visual abnormalities may produce color blindness—the inability to distinguish between certain colors.

It is important to remember that color exists only when the human eye perceives *light* of certain wavelengths. Notice that nothing has been said about colored paint, pigment, dye, cloth, or anything except *light* itself. Clear understanding of this point is vital to our understanding of color mixing. Pigments are *not* color; they only have the property of sorting out light waves if these are present and thus producing the right combination of wavelengths to cause the eye to see color. However, without light of the proper wavelength, a pigment is helpless to produce color. Pigments do not create colored light; they only sort it out.

Thus color resides in the eye. How the eye sees color has been a matter of conjecture for years. Color perception is probably the most precise determination that our senses make. The wavelength difference between light of one hue and that of another is often a matter of only a few hundred-millionths of a centimeter, yet the trained eye of a color expert will never mistake one hue for the other. Anyone with normal vision can distinguish color differences only slightly greater.

Light as a Physical Phenomenon

89 Light, we have already observed, is but one small segment of a huge array of radiant energy phenomena all of which have certain char-

acteristics of wave phenomena and certain other less easily described characteristics.

While the physicists are prone to call the entire radiant array the spectrum (see Plate I in the color section) and to differentiate between variations in spectral displays as continuous spectra, line spectra, or interference spectra, meanwhile making little or no distinction between what the human eye can see and what it cannot, artists, photographers, and informed laymen usually use the term "spectrum" to refer to those wavelengths that the eye can see. For our use, then, the *spectrum* is simply an exact name for what we see in a rainbow or in the multicolored pool of light cast from a cut-glass dish in a beam of sunlight.

How Spectra Are Made

You will recall from the discussion of refraction that refraction is uniform only when a single wavelength of light is passing through a refractive surface. Differential refraction takes place whenever mixed wavelengths pass through a refractive surface, the result being the dispersal of the beam according to wavelength. While the details of this process are beyond the scope of this text, the reader should note that the blue wavelengths are bent much more than the red, bending being somewhat inversely proportional to wavelength.

We have already noted that differential refraction is the cause of chromatic aberration and that such aberration degrades the images produced by simple lenses, making it undesirable under these conditions. However, when it is our purpose to analyze the wavelength content of a beam of light, this dispersion can be used to advantage. The prism is a device for doing this. It consists of a piece of transparent glass, preferably with a high index of refraction, triangular in cross section and with its surfaces carefully flatted and polished. A narrow beam of light passed through a prism will be dispersed according to wavelength. If the beam of light contains all or most of those wavelengths visible to the eye, the dispersed beam will resemble an intense fragment of a rainbow. If the beam of light contains only a few groups of wavelengths, it will appear as a group of colored bands. In either case it is known as a spectrum.

See Plate I in the color section.

Spectral and Nonspectral Hues

A careful observation of the spectrum will lead to the discovery that there are colors which you have seen that do not appear anywhere on the spectrum. Thus it is inexact to say that the spectrum is "all of the colors the eye can see." The purples or magentas are completely missing. But if you were to overlap the blue end of one spectrum onto the red end of another, a complete array of purples would suddenly appear. Then all of the colors the eye can see will be present.

Careful thought will lead the observer to note that those colors the eye perceives in the spectrum are the result of single wavelengths striking the eye. Those seen in overlapping the ends of spectrum are the result of exposing the eye to *more than one wavelength at a time*. Those colors the eye sees as the result of exposure to a *single* wavelength (or a very narrow band of wavelengths) are known as *spectral hues* (colors); those that are produced in the eye as the result of the mixture of disparate wavelengths are known as *nonspectral hues*. This distinction would be simple if the eye were largely analytical in its reaction to colored light, as the ear is to sound (a trained musician can readily make out the notes in a chord), but this is not the case. The eye reacts synthetically to wavelengths, tending to see not colors but white as more and more wavelengths are added. Adding to the confusion is the fact that the eye can be "fooled" into "seeing" exact matches for certain spectral hues. For example, the right combination of red and green light will cause the eye to produce a sensation indistinguishable from that produced by spectral yellow. Thus the physicist and the physiologist may be speaking of different things when they mention "yellow" light.

The Color Wheel

The spectrum provides the physicist with an exact catalog of those wavelengths that the eye can see. In fact, until recent nuclear development, the wavelength of certain kinds of light was the most constant standard of distance available. Wavelength is still the most exact way of referring to those colors of light appearing on the spectrum. But the nonspectral hues cannot be referred to by wavelengths; they are mixtures. Thus artists are apt to leave the spectrum to the physics lab and refer to the *color wheel* (see Plate VII in the color section). The color wheel is, in effect, a spectrum curled upon itself with the nonspectral hues that are mixtures of red and blue inserted between those two colors. However, it usually is simplified into a series of color blocks termed primaries, secondaries, and sometimes tertiaries. These divisions are helpful to the artist in clarifying theories of pigment mixing. Since the lighting artist will be mixing light, not pigment, his most helpful system of denoting color will be the *color map* (see Plate III in the color section) or *color triangle,* either of which graphically charts the possibilities of mixing wavelengths. We will examine the color map in detail when we study the additive system of color mixing.

Color Identification

Because of the confusion generated by the myriad of popular color names and the fact that about 7,500,000 hues are distinguishable to the normal human eye, several systems of color denotation have been developed. These systems are rather widely used in industrial and some other applications, but they have never found much acceptance in the theatre. The two best known of these systems are the Ostwald and the Munsel systems. Both are based on a three-dimensional arrangement of colors by hue, saturation, and brilliance. Specific colors are referred to by a number indicating their geometrical location on a color *tree*. While such systems would be helpful in the theatre in describing color of pigments, the many degrees of brilliance possible in lighting far exceed the potentialities of any tree thus far derived.

Colorimetry is the science of analyzing and comparing colors for purposes of exact color denotation. Certain terms are important to the lighting artist.

Hue: That property of a color which distinguishes it from a grey of the same brilliance; for example, red, green, blue-green, and the like.
Saturation: Freedom from admixture with white.
Brightness: Difference from black (sometimes but less correctly called "brilliance"). Brightness of a pigment varies with the illumination it receives. Brightness of a surface is measured in footcandles.
Chroma: The combined qualities of hue and saturation. White, black, and grey have no chroma.

These terms will aid the lighting designer in being more exact in his description of color and in understanding the application of the Ostwald or Munsel systems.

Spectroanalysis

That portion of color science which has contributed most to the art of lighting is spectroanalysis. The instrument that performs this exact measurement of color content is called the *spectrophotometer,* an expensive and complex machine which measures the exact amount of each wavelength of light present in a sample. The instrument reports its findings in the form of a graph known as a *spectrogram.* Such spectrograms can be made from either opaque or from transparent colored objects. As far as stage lighting is concerned, spectrograms are the only exact means of describing the color characteristics of plastic color media now in common use. Spectrograms could, of course, be run for gelatine colors, but these vary too much from lot to lot to make it worth the cost.

Informed analysis of the spectrogram of a plastic color medium plus knowledge of the color temperature of the light passing through it will give the stage-lighting artist an almost exact idea of what wavelengths are striking any surface. This analysis will enable him to be far more exact about his predictions concerning the effect of the light on the pigment.

A spectrogram is simply a graph indicating the percentage of each wavelength present. Along the bottom of the spectrogram the wavelengths of the visible spectrum are lined up in order. Plate IV in the color section is an illustration of the spectrogram of a pale blue piece of color medium which has been placed over a picture of the spectrum for purposes of clarity. This spectrogram was made using the light from a spotlight lamp as the "standard white" for comparison. The percentage figures indicate the amount of each wavelength of light transmitted as a percentage of that in the standard.

One of the great advantages of the spectrogram is that it breaks coefficient of transmission figures down into artistically meaningful information. The coefficient of transmission (or reflection) figure given for most pigments simply tells us the overall percentage of white light that will be transmitted or reflected with no reference to color. Examination of a spectrogram will immediately distinguish colors, giving us wavelength-by-wavelength transmission factors. For example, if the spectrogram trace crosses the yellow line at 33 percent, we know that the material will transmit 33 percent of the yellow light that strikes it.

Sources of Colored Light on the Stage

Colored light on the stage is made in a spectacularly wasteful manner. White light is made by incandescence. All unwanted wavelengths are filtered out by passing the white light through various color media which convert the filtered wavelengths into heat. The remainder, minus an unavoidably lost portion of the desired rays, is used on the stage. In the case of some blue filters, the usable light produced by this process may drop below 1 percent of the white light put out by the lamp. Since lamps themselves are also rather inefficient, the percentage figure representing conversion from electricity to usable light on stage is infinitesimal. Nevertheless, this process is the only one presently available that offers enough flexibility and convenience to be useful to the lighting artist.

Stage Color Filters

GLASS

Three types of filters are used with modern incandescent lamps to produce colored light on stage—glass, gelatine, and plastic. Glass is by far the oldest color medium still in use in the theatre, and is still the most permanent and usually the best way to produce pure colors. The present use of glass is almost exclusively limited to roundels, slightly dished disks of colored glass made to fit into holders at the front of borderlight and footlight lamps. Roundels are available in pure red, green, and blue, and in a variety of secondary colors and tints. They frequently are embossed to form lenslike patterns or ridges that control the spread of the light they transmit.

Roundels are completely resistant to fading, unlike either gelatine or plastic. However, they are expensive, heavy, and susceptible to breakage. Therefore, they work best in permanently installed borders and foots. Since roundels are permanent, they must occasionally be cleaned of dust and grease. Temporary color media will usually be replaced before this becomes a problem.

GELATINE

Gelatine entered the theatre early and remains in use today. It is just what the name implies: Animal gelatine which has been purified, dyed, and dried in sheets. Modern "gels," as they usually are called, are generally treated with chemicals to make them less sensitive to changes in atmospheric moisture.

Gelatine must be considered a temporary color medium. The dyes fade and the material itself deteriorates rapidly under the heat of lamps. The cool colors are usually the worst offenders, probably because they absorb more energy from the infrared end of the spectrum. Gelatine is also apt to deteriorate in storage if the humidity gets too high or too low. If humidity is too high, the gelatine tends to stick together in a useless blob; if humidity is too low, the gelatine becomes so brittle it cannot be handled. Dry gelatine is salvageable. Simply increase the humidity carefully over a period of a few days and the gelatine will regain its pliability.

The greatest advantages of gelatine are its cheapness and high transmittance. It costs less than one dollar a sheet in most localities, and is available in a wide variety of colors. Light losses are generally lower when gelatine is used than for any other medium. Moreover, some very useful colors are available only in the form of gelatine. However, if exact color matches are needed, or color consistency is important, gelatine will not suffice. It varies from batch to batch and fades rapidly.

PLASTIC

There are two categories of plastic material used as color medium. The first, cellulose acetate, has been available for a number of years. The second, a Mylar-like material is relatively new. Both types have the advantage of considerable durability, resistance to moisture, and physical strength. Both cost substantially more than gelatine although this high initial cost may be outweighed by long life and the desirability of some of the colors.

CELLULOSE ACETATE

As compared with gelatine, cellulose acetate materials are highly durable. They are water and moisture resistant and have high mechanical strength. The moisture-resistant property makes plastic media almost a necessity for outdoor theatres where even a heavy dew would ruin gelatine. The high mechanical strength reduces the likelihood that a color medium will be poked out of a spotlight or broken if the color holder is dropped. The principal enemy of acetate plastic is heat. Under prolonged heat from a spotlight, the plastic slowly warps, the surface becomes distorted and diffuses the light. Finally the material becomes useless. However, this deterioration takes a long time.

The greatest disadvantage of acetate is its cost. It costs about twice the price of a similar amount of gelatine. Another disadvantage is that the light transmission factor of acetate media tends to be somewhat lower than that of comparable gelatine. This difference is not great, but may be significant when the lighting artist is struggling for every possible lumen on stage.

Although similar or identical color names are given to gelatine and plastic materials, the colors do not match. "Surprise pink," for example, refers to a different color in each of several brands of color medium. Once known, these differences are actually an advantage because they offer the designer a wider choice of colors. A well-equipped theatre should keep on hand a variety of colors in both plastic and gelatine. The acetate plastics offer a particularly good choice of colors in warm acting area tints—something rather lacking in gelatine colors, except for a few which fade rapidly.

MYLAR

Although Mylar materials are not exactly the same as the tough Mylar film used for such things as recording-tape backing, they resemble this material closely enough to justify using the name. This color medium is quite new. Only a small number of colors is presently available. The Mylar materials are thinner than the acetate media, their transmission factor is higher, and their durability is much greater. The greatest disadvantages are high cost and, at present, the limited number of colors available. Cost runs two to three times that of acetate plastic. Color purity is somewhat lower in the primary hues, but this is offset by a good choice of primary hues and the high transmission factor.

At their present prices, the best use for Mylar plastics is in those locations where color medium is changed only when it fails. For example, if a cyclorama is illuminated by scoops, these are usually fitted with red, green, and blue primary colors which remain in service from show to show until they fail. If gelatine or acetate plastic is used, the blue media will fail quite rapidly, the green somewhat more slowly, and the red only occasionally. Installation of Mylar material in such a setup will reduce replacements to a very low figure—perhaps every two or three years for a stage in heavy use. Under these conditions the high first cost of Mylar is more than offset by the long life. It will actually be the cheapest material to use.

Cost and Choice of Color Medium

The ultimate cost of using the various types of color medium is difficult to compute. Among the many factors to consider are cost, replacement policies which are governed by the amount of fading that the designer will tolerate, storage conditions, climate (i.e., the prevalent humidity), types of instruments in use, and the potential for salvaging the remaining life in colors removed from shows when they close. Obviously the lowest initial cost material—gelatine—will also produce the lowest ultimate cost in short duration usages where there is no potentiality for salvage. High-cost, long-life material such as Mylar will pay off best when used to the end of its life. The area between these extremes is so complicated with interlocking variables that the best policy is to let the color choice of the designer determine the medium.

Other Sources of Colored Light

It is obvious from the above discussion of color media that the stage needs a more efficient means of making colored light. The present system is wasteful of both electricity and materials. The fluorescent lamp offers hope of something better to come. The new "HMI" lamps (see the section "Short-Arc Lamps" in Chapter 2) offer the possibility of much higher efficiency in the production of colored light, particularly at the blue end of the spectrum. These sources produce light at nearly equal energy levels throughout the entire visible spectrum.

A source of colored light not commonly noticed on the stage unless color photographs are taken is reflection from colored objects. In nature almost all colored light is produced by reflection, but most of it goes unseen because the eye has adapted to it. A green lawn, for example, will produce a footlightlike flood of green light which illuminates shadows all around it. However, it may never be noticed until a color photograph is taken of someone standing on the lawn. Then the green shadows suddenly become apparent, much to the dismay of the photographer. Similar situations often prevail on stage, especially where brilliant saturated colors are present in the setting or costumes.

Color Mixing

Almost everyone has mixed paint, at least water colors, and inexactly claimed to be "mixing colors." However, they were not mixing colors, only color filters. One can mix color only by mixing the basic physiological responses of the eye. This mixing usually is done by presenting the eye with the stimulus of two or more wavelengths at the same time. However, it is possible to get the same effect by presenting the eye with successive stimuli, if these are close enough together in time to confuse the eye. Under very special circumstances, it is possible to present to the eye only black-and-white stimuli, rapidly and confusingly repeated, and get a "color" response. Thus color resides in the eye, in its reaction to light waves, not in pigments or dyes. Since the lighting artist, unlike the painter, uses light itself as his medium, he must understand more about the way the eye responds to color.

The Young-Helmholz theory of color vision originally was formulated by Thomas Young in the early 1800s; it has never been sup-planted and very recently has received confirmation thanks to modern developments of ultrasensitive electronic equipment. The theory—now largely established as fact—holds that human color vision takes place in the cones which form part of the light-sensitive retina of the eye. The rest of the retina is made up of rods, whose response is only to degrees of light and dark, not to color. The cones are less light-sensitive than the rods, but whenever light levels are bright enough for the cones to function, we see colors, if colors are present. There are three kinds of light-sensitive materials in the cones, with each single cone sensitive to either red light, green light, or blue light. Human color vision results from the response of these three kinds of receptors. This response is capable of sufficiently precise differentiation of responses to allow the eye to detect millions of color variations! Recent research at Harvard and Johns Hopkins has definitely established the existence of the three color-sensitive materials.[1] Research has also indicated that the color mixing actually takes place in the brain, not the eye, since different wavelengths can be presented to the left and right eye and the stimuli will be fused in the brain. However, these "mixtures" are not very stable, suggesting still more complex reactions. Lighting artists may wish to take advantage of this "two-eye" color mixing in studying the resultant colors produced by acting-area cross-spotting tints. Place a sample of one tint over each eye; look at a white surface to check the results. If they can be mixed (and this will depend on individual seeing apparatus) you can use this system to check out acting-area colors on setting, costumes, and the like.

The Primary Colors

The term "primary colors" refers to those colors which can be used to make any other color in a color system and which themselves cannot be made from other colors within the system. Although, in the last analy-sis, there is but one system of color mixing which embraces the entire phenomenon of human vision, it is common practice to refer to this system in two parts, treating each part as though it were a separate system. Thus the two parts are called the "additive system" and the "subtractive system." Each has its own set of primaries and sec-ondaries. Unfortunately, each is sometimes thought of as being op-posed to or incompatible with the other. This semantic difficulty we will have to dispel later.

The primary colors of the additive system—red, green, and blue—may be referred to by wavelength more exactly:[2]

[1] Paul K. Brown and George Wald, "Visual Pigments in Single Rods and Cones of the Human Retina." *Science* (April 3, 1964), p. 43ff; and "Three Colors, Three Receptors." *Scientific American* (May 1964), p. 60.

[2] Francis H. Adler, *Physiology of the Eye*, 3rd ed., St. Louis: The C. V. Mosby Co., 1959, pp. 702-772.

Primary Color	*Wavelength*
Red	About 6150 Å
Green	About 5200 Å
Blue	About 4470 Å

Fortunately, there is quite a span on either side of each of these wavelengths which will produce about the same results as far as the eye is concerned. Thus several sets of quite satisfactory primary color filters can be assembled. Remember that the *additive system* is concerned with the *mixture of stimuli in the eye*. This may be also thought of, but less accurately, as "mixing beams of light." As far as the stage-lighting artist is concerned, mixing beams of light is the only method at his disposal for controlling the stimuli given to the eye. He produces colored light by filtering, then mixes the colored beams to get the results he wants. Other additive color processes work by presenting different color stimuli in rapid succession, so rapid that the retentivity of the eye sends the stimuli to the brain as one mixed stimulus. Pointillism in painting some color-printing systems and color television depend upon the inability of the eye to distinguish tiny patches of color separately at a distance. Again, the brain is presented with a "single" stimulus.

The Color Map

While the exact details of color vision are still not entirely known, it is possible to "map" the responses with a good deal of accuracy. The color map, in its exact form, is shown in Plate III in the color section. Note that the colors have not been extended to the edges of the diagram because printing techniques do not permit accurate reproduction of these brilliant and pure hues. Colored light can produce such hues, and they are available to the stage-lighting artist. A less exact but easier to work with form of the color map, the color triangle shown in Figure 5-1, is simply an equilateral triangle with a primary indicated at each corner. Notice that both of these figures represent the colors as they appear on a continuous spectrum with the red and blue ends brought together to show what happens when these wavelengths are mixed. Plate V shows the effect of the color triangle as it usually is demonstrated for stage-lighting purposes. Three pools of primary light have been overlapped in such a way that they produce the secondaries and an area of white light in the middle.

The additive system always tends to work toward white; that is, the addition of more wavelengths tends to desaturate the colors, reducing them to tints. A perfect mixture of any three colors equidistant around the triangle will produce white. This fact is important to the stage-lighting artist, who must know how to produce colorful effects in multiple

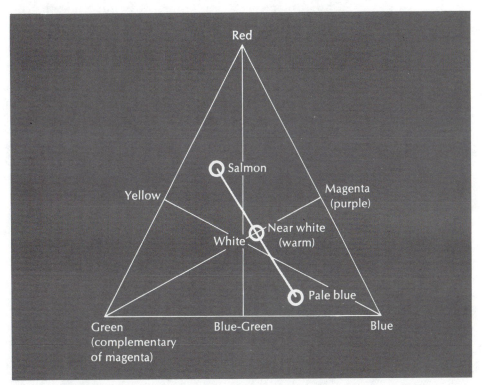

FIGURE 5-1

Color Triangle. Essentially a simplified form of the color map (Plate III). It is sufficiently accurate for most stage-lighting applications and much easier to use. The color names refer to light, not pigments. At each apex is a primary color and at each midpoint a secondary which has been produced by mixing equal (to the eye) portions of two primaries. Other tints and hues can be plotted following the example shown.

1. Locate the two colors of light to be mixed on the triangle either by reference to spectrograms or by estimating with the eye. Reference to the color map will aid this estimate.

2. Draw a line between the two colors. Note that it contains all mixtures of these two hues according to their proportions. For instance, a mixture of equal parts of each color will fall at the center of the line, a 2-to-1 mixture will result in a color two-thirds of the way toward the predominate color.

Subtractive color effects (light on pigment) may be approximated on the triangle by substituting black for white at the middle. Plotting will work as above except in the case of primaries in their pure form. Since any light primary can, by definition, contain only a narrow band of wavelengths of its own hue, any light primary will produce black when used to illuminate a pigment capable of reflecting only another light primary.

colors and how to produce near-white light for acting areas. If saturated multicolor effects are desired, it is important that the pools of color do not become mixed with each other. If they are allowed to mix, desaturation will result. Thus a polychromatic stage is one on which actors or dancers move from one color to another, not one on which they are bathed in all colors at the same time. Conversely, if we wish to produce a near white on stage, we purposely mix acting-area tints whose hues are complementary, that is, whose hues are found across from each other on the triangle.

Definitions: Primary, Secondary, and Complementary

The terms "primary," "secondary," and "complementary" are applied to colors of both the additive and subtractive system. General definition of these terms will aid in our discussion of the relationship between the two systems. We have already defined *primary* colors as those which can be blended to make all other colors in a system and which cannot be made by blending other colors within the system. *Secondary* colors are the result of mixing equal portions of any two primary colors. For example, an equal mixture of red light and green light upon a white surface will produce the secondary color, yellow. Similarly red and blue will make magenta, and blue and green will make blue-green. *Complementary* colors are, in the additive system, any pair of colors that add together to make white light. Magenta and green are examples of complementary colors, and are found across from each other on the color triangle (see Figure 5-1).

Additive and Subtractive Systems Interlock

Careful examination of the *colors*, not the color names, shown on the color map and in Plate V in the color section will reveal the relationship between the additive and subtractive system. *The primaries of the additive system are the secondaries of the subtractive system and vice versa.* The names of the colors create the apparent disparity between the two systems, not the colors themselves. The painter, for instance, will select a set of good primaries: red, yellow, and blue. However, if we match his primaries to the colors on the color map, we find that they come out to be about 5780 Å yellow, 4920 Å blue-green, and a nonspectral hue, a purple, roughly the complementary of 5080 Å green. Since painters' opaque pigments are notoriously impure, they may not work well, but if we will ask the painter to select a set of good primary watercolors from highly pure dyes, he will come up with a much closer approximation of the spectral references above, and they will mix predictably.

Selective Transmission and Reflection

In order to understand the effect of colored light on colored objects we must understand a bit about how colored objects become colored. Paint, dyes, and pigmented materials of all kinds exhibit either selective transmission or selective reflection: Colored objects have the property, probably as a result of their molecular structure, of allowing certain wavelengths to pass and of absorbing others, converting their energy into heat. Actually, it seems probable that selective transmission is the basic principle, whether the light passes through the object, or bounces back. We have already noticed the phenomenon called "mixed reflection." In this reflection, part of the light bounced off the surface of some material as off a mirror. This light has no color change wrought upon it. On the other hand, much of the light striking a mixed reflector passes some distance into the surface, being selectively transmitted through pigmented layers. Part of it is absorbed, according to the nature of the pigment, and the rest, now colored, is reflected out of the material in a diffuse manner. Examination of a piece of satin fabric of a deep color will illustrate this point clearly. Notice that the highlights, which are specularly reflected off the surface of the material, are unchanged as to color, while the rest of the light coming from the fabric is colored. All pigments and dyes apparently work in this fashion, whether they are mixed reflectors or not.

Thus the color of a filter or reflector depends on what wavelengths it transmits or reflects. The filter or reflector absorbs the rest. For this reason, the system of mixing dyes and pigments is called the *subtractive* system. No pigment adds color to a beam of light, although we inaccurately say "The pigment colors the beam," as though it were adding something. This leaves us with the semantic tangle that "adding color" to white paint really means increasing its light-*absorbing* power in certain wavelengths.

Subtractive Color Mixing

We are now ready to discover why stirring blue paint into yellow paint results in green paint, whereas mixing blue light with yellow light makes near-white light. When we are mixing paint we are mixing selective reflectors. We may also describe the paints as selective absorbers. The yellow paint looks yellow to the eye (under white light) because it absorbs the blue end of the spectrum leaving the red, green, and yellow waves to affect the eye. Since the eye will respond to this mixture as though it were all spectral yellow (about 5780 Å), we see yellow paint. Similarly, the blue paint, which is a painter's primary and thus matches something near 4840 Å on the color map, has the property of absorbing red. It reflects blue, green, and blue-green.

Mixing the two paints combines their absorptive characteristics, resulting in a mixture which absorbs all of the color map from yellow through magenta to blue-green. The remainder is what we see: green. Plate VI in the color section illustrates the subtractive effect of pigments. It is an artist's rendition showing what happens when three pieces of color medium with transmission characteristics of secondaries (cyan, magenta, yellow)[3] have been superimposed. Note that these relatively pure pigments will produce quite pure primary colors where two of them are overlapped. Inferior painter's pigments will not do this but produce muddy colors instead. For color-analysis purposes, white light is often assumed to be made synthetically of the three additive primaries. The effect of leaving out spectral yellow and spectral blue-green is negligible. However, there are times when the difference between spectral and nonspectral hues will be significant; fortunately not on the stage. Notice that any mixture of pigments that results in the absorption of red, green, and blue produces black. Lacking a spectrometer, the lighting artist can use this "total absorption" phenomenon to discover what colors are "leaking" through a set of three-color primary filters intended for cyclorama lighting. He simply superimposes the three filters, holds them in front of a powerful light source, and notes the results. Almost inevitably he will find that some red light is coming through even the best blue filter available.

This experiment in subtractive color mixing also points up another characteristic of the subtractive system; it tends to work toward black. This characteristic is, of course, reasonable when we realize that filters work by removing light and the absence of light is black.

Colored Light and Colored Objects

We are now in possession of enough data to predict with considerable accuracy what happens when any colored light strikes a colored object. All that remains is to systematize this information. The procedure for determining the results of a mixture of wavelengths on a colored object requires two steps. First, determine the wavelength composition of the light. For example, if we are dealing with yellow light made on the stage, we can be sure that it contains red, green, and spectral yellow, unless it has been made from red and green only by way of the three-color primary system. (The third possibility, pure spectral yellow, is very remote on stage.) The second step is to determine the absorption and reflection characteristics of the pigment under examination. For example, a magenta fabric would have the capacity to reflect red and blue; it absorbs the other hues. The rest is arithmetic. Subtract all colors absorbed from the list of those present in the light. What re-

---

[3] The term "cyan" is often substituted for the painter's term "blue" to avoid the semantic difficulty with this color.

TABLE 5-1
Color Names in Additive and Subtractive Systems

NAMES USED IN ADDITIVE SYSTEM	NAMES USED FOR SAME COLOR IN SUBTRACTIVE SYSTEM
Red	Red-orange or orange
Green	Green
Blue	Blue-purple
Magenta	Red
Yellow	Yellow
Blue-green (cyan)	Blue

mains will be the resultant color. In our example, the pigment can reflect only *red* of the wavelength available to it, thus the eye will see red. Be sure that you do not make the mistake of giving the pigment the property of *adding* a color to the light; it cannot do this. For example, our magenta pigment can reflect blue light, but there is no blue light available in pure yellow light. Remember, pigments can only absorb and reflect; they cannot add wavelengths not present!

Since most colored light and most pigments are far from pure, the usual result of analysis such as that above will be the conclusion that certain colors will be subdued or depressed and that others will be accented. Only occasionally will there be a complete shift from one color to another. Also, because most stage filters "leak" some red light, the common result of a combination that should theoretically result in black is a brownish-red glow. Colors can be neutralized to the point where the audience cannot identify their original hue, but they can seldom be "blacked out."

Color terminology problems make it difficult to discuss the effect of specific colors of light on specific pigments. Terminology overlaps in the additive and subtractive system in an unfortunate way. Since the lighting artist is likely to use colored light as the basis for most of his

TABLE 5-2
Colors Resulting from Colored Light on Colored Pigment

		INCIDENT LIGHT COLORS				
		RED	GREEN	BLUE	YELLOW	MAGENTA	BLUE-GREEN
PIGMENT COLORS	RED	Red	Black	Black	Red	Red	Black
	GREEN	Black	Green	Black	Green	Black	Green
	BLUE	Black	Black	Blue	Black	Blue	Blue
	YELLOW	Red	Green	Black	Yellow	Red	Green
	MAGENTA	Red	Black	Blue	Red	Magenta	Blue
	BLUE-GREEN	Black	Green	Blue	Green	Blue	Blue-green

work in color, he will probably want to consider the terms of the additive system as basic and equate those from the subtractive system to these. Table 5-1 equates the names given to the primaries and the secondaries of each system.

Using the names from the additive system, Table 5-2 is provided as a start in determining resultant colors from colored light on colored pigment, although most problems will fall outside the limited scope of the chart.

Colored Light and Color Contrast

Color contrast in stage design is a factor of many variables. Line, mass, texture, focus of attention through dramatic devices, and a myriad of other factors enter into the final effect of juxtaposing any two colors on the stage. However, lighting offers a variable to the designer that can alter contrast values in time, if necessary, or that can separate or bring together colors, particularly in costume and makeup, in a way that may save time and money. Several rules of thumb apply.

1. To heighten a color (increase its contrast with its background) give it lots of its own color to reflect plus enough white light to make the background look normal.
2. To depress a color, deprive it of its proportionate share of the wavelengths it reflects best (for example, to depress pinks, use cool, low in red, light).
3. To separate two nearly alike tints or shades, select the wavelength that is reflected most by one as compared to the other. This wavelength will heighten the one it favors and subdue the other. For example, if it is desired to separate two near-alike tints of pink, one slightly bluer than the other, blue-white light will heighten the bluish one at the expense of the other. Yellowish light will heighten the other, depressing the blue.
4. To "bring together" two nearly alike tints or shades, select a color of light they both reflect equally well. For example, reddish light would merge the two pinks mentioned above.

Notice that in all of these cases the principles of absorption and reflection have been applied to get practical results. In each case there will be some color distortion, but it need not be severe enough to be noticeable.

Another rule of thumb regarding color and contrast is that all of a color is none of a color. This rule is simply the extension of the optical principle of adaptation. If you flood the stage with red light, making everything either red or near black (remember that red light offers no choice—only red wavelengths are available), any red objects on the stage will be effectively subdued. Red objects will reflect the red light with great efficiency, but there will be no other color for the eye to contrast with the red and it will soon adapt as far in the direction of red as it can. Then red objects will be seen as grey or white, along with all other objects which are reflecting red. In effect, chromatic vision will be eliminated. The addition of one complementary highlight, say a single patch of blue or blue-green, will put things back into contrast again, although red objects will get no more attention than white objects and the focus will be on the blue-green patch.

Sensitivity of the Eye to Color

The eye is not uniformly sensitive to all wavelengths. Assuming that there is enough light to enable the cones in the retina to respond, the eye responds most sensitively to those wavelengths near the middle of the spectrum. Under daylight-vision conditions, the most sensitive area is at about the yellow-green wavelength 5600 Å. The sensitivity tapers off from this peak toward the 4000 Å and 7000 Å points in a manner much like the "normal curve" of statisticians' frequency distributions.

The relative insensitivity of the eye at the blue end of the spectrum adds to the difficulty of the lighting artist seeking a good blue sky. His troubles begin with the incandescent light, which is deficient in blue light because of its relatively low color temperature. This problem is compounded by the notorious inefficiency of pure blue filters and twice compounded by the insensitivity of the eye. See "Eye Sensitivity" in Plate II in the color section.

White Light

We have already mentioned the subject of color temperature in connection with our discussion of the incandescent lamp. However, the implications of color temperature for the making of colored light and for the perception of color values must be further discussed. Theoretical white light, that used for spectrophotometric comparison purposes and as a general standard, has a very high color temperature, about 6000° K. It is located at the point marked "equal energy" on the "Chromaticity Diagram," Plate III. It is so named because the light contains equal amounts of energy at all visible wavelengths. Its spectrogram would be a horizontal line at the 100 percent mark if the spectrometer were set to compare the sample with equal energy light. It would be steeply slanted toward the blue end if the spectrogram were a comparison with 2950° K light such as that in Plate IV. The rough stage equivalent of this is a mixture of equal parts of red, green, and blue primaries on a white surface.

Color temperatures far less than 6000° K will be accepted by the eye as white. However, these warm whites will exact their toll on pigments illuminated by them. Since the blue end of the spectrum is deficient, blue, blue-green, and, in extreme cases, even the green pigments will be depressed. Since the lighting artist consistently works with a white light of about 2950° K, he must expect that blues and blue-greens will be hard to make brilliant. More power will be needed to illuminate these colors and the results can be expected to suffer by comparison with the brilliance of warm colors in other scenes.

Adaptation of the eye to warm whites takes place quite rapidly, making the audience almost completely unaware that it is being exposed to rather warm light. However, this adaptation does not seem to compensate the cool colors as much as the optical descriptions of adaptation seem to imply it should.

APPLYING THE COLOR THEORY TO THE STAGE

6

After you have experimented with color media and lighting instruments long enough for the theories outlined to become realities, you are ready to study the detailed application of colored light to the stage. Probably the most useful place to start is with the use of colored light on the acting area.

The basic purpose of lighting the acting area is, of course, visibility. However, our earlier discussions have already shown that mere visibility—that is, the ability of the audience to see that there is an actor on stage—is not enough. The exact conditions of this visibility must be controlled and altered subtly as needed. Several factors are involved in this control:

1. The degree of plasticity (three-dimensional vision) that must be supplied by the lighting
2. The mood that must be established and maintained
3. The realistic effects that must be created and maintained within whatever limits the play seems to dictate
4. The amount of dimming or alterations to be performed on the acting-area lighting

Plasticity: Colored Light and the Actor

"Plasticity" is a term which was introduced into stage lighting many years ago to describe the ability of lighting to heighten the three-dimensional effect of objects, including actors, on the stage. Ultimately most of our theatrical depth perception comes from the perception of shadows. Of course, shadows can be artificially painted in on either scenery or faces, but this is a static device subject to being revealed for the sham it is by the superimposition of real shadows falling in a direction opposing the painted ones. Generally the modern theatre prefers that the audience see real shadows that have been carefully planned and occasionally augmented by the discreet application of a little paint.

Seeing real shadows in the theatre depends on the contrast between the shadow area, highlight area, and background. If the contrast is low, the shadow will have relatively little attention value and the effect will be one of flatness. If the contrast is high, the opposite effect, that is, high plasticity, will prevail. Similarly, if the edges of the shadow area are dulled by fuzzy lines from multiple sources, flatness will result; if these edges are razor sharp from a single point source, the plasticity will be heightened.

Color and Three-Dimensionality

So far it seems that the discussion is concerned with light and shade. What of color? Color is almost as great a factor in establishing contrast as directionality and brightness. In fact, most of the contrast apparent in color photography and color television is the result of color. If a color television scene were to be reduced to a set of equivalent-brilliance greys, it would seem flat indeed. Color contrast also exists in nature and helps us to see depth. Painters have known for years that shadows are not dead black except under very unusual circumstances. Shadows are colored and often contain a great deal of detail. Color contrasts between shadows and highlights will accent the third dimension just as surely as brightness contrasts, and will provide the added advantage of always allowing the audience to see into the shadows. This situation is common in nature. Consider your face as you stand on the lawn in the bright afternoon sunlight. If you look carefully into a mirror you will find that the sunlit side of your face (the highlighted area) is warmly illuminated. The shadowed side will be illuminated also by the much cooler light from the sky. The still deeper shadows under your chin will be illuminated by light reflected up from below—green light from the grass!

You have noticed by now that a shadow is almost never an area without light; it is only an area which has less light in proportion to some other area adjacent to it. This definition is important to stage lighting, because if we create shadows that are so dark or dense that we cannot see into them, we may undo the very effect we are trying to create. While we will certainly be aware of the three-dimensional quality of an actor whose face is half in highlight and half in total darkness, we will not get a very clear picture of the expressions on his face—the reason for the three-dimensional lighting in the first place.

Terminology: Key and Fill

At one time, the notion of "filled" shadows led to the concept of general illumination and specific illumination in stage lighting: Specific illumination created highlights; general illumination filled shadows. The terms "general" and "specific" are still useful, but are not as common as they once were, probably because there has been a shift in the technique used to produce these results, and this change has disrupted the terminology. Stage lighting was originally general illumination, that is, a flood of light thrown onto the stage to "see by." Before spotlights were available, there was no choice but to light the stage with border-lights and footlights. Later, as spotlights were introduced, specific illumination from these instruments was superimposed over the general illumination, creating highlighting. Modern practice in lighting dramatic productions is to depend on spotlights for both the highlights and fills. If borders and foots are used, they serve to blend the lighting and sometimes to tone the colors of the setting and costumes. The term "general illumination" has tended to remain attached to the equipment (borders and foots) which originally produced it, and has fallen into disuse. Its companion term, "specific illumination," which referred to spotlights, has also lost much of its value. Much more useful modern terms are "key" and "fill." These terms, unlike their predecessors, are not attached to any type of equipment, but instead, describe the function of any beam or flood of light, however produced.

Key or *key light* is that light which establishes the major direction of the illumination for the audience. Key light is manifested as a pattern of highlights and their related shadows on three-dimensional objects, including actors (see Figure 15-1).

Fill or *fill light* is the light that prevents the shadows from being black voids. Fill light usually has direction and can produce visible but secondary shadows.

Adjusting Key and Fill

Adjustment of the intensity of key and fill and the color of these lights has been the concern of lighting artists from the beginning of the spot-light era. The modern lighting artist will find that concern with key and fill will occupy most of his time. He will often provide himself with a variety of keys and fills striking at significantly different angles and equipped with a variety of carefully chosen colors—all of this for each segment of the acting space. In practice, the various systems or methods for handling key and fill light will be blended together to provide the degree of variety and flexibility that the artist desires. In order to study these methods we must separate and categorize them. First, there are those techniques which treat the acting space either as a single unit or only subdivide it into large segments. Second, there are those techniques which subdivide the acting space into many small units, carefully organized with regard to the needs of the play at hand. These small acting areas then are treated as design units to be adjusted individually or in patterns.

Note that the distinction between "acting space" and "acting area" is fundamental to this discussion. The "acting space" is the entire cubage of the stage which will be occupied by actors at one time or another during the production of a given play. Acting space is determined when the setting is designed and the masking placed. The term "acting area" refers to a small subdivision of the acting space usually made only for purposes of lighting. Occasionally the director will find that reference to stage location by the acting areas will be a convenience to both the designer and the actors. However, the student is cautioned against the assumption that the conventional "down left," "down center," "down right," and the like, pattern of reference used by actors and directors is the equivalent of an acting-area scheme. On a small stage these references may be a rough equivalent to the scheme, but these references are not specific enough for most large or more complicated setups. The designer will determine and name or number the acting areas as he needs them.

Lighting the Acting Space as a Whole: Flood and Key

It is obvious that the oldest method of illuminating the acting space was to flood the entire space with light from borders and foots. As soon as circuitry developed, it became possible to subdivide this flood of light roughly into upstage and downstage units and eventually on large stages into left and right. However, the edgeless nature of borderlighting and footlighting could produce no useful separation between these broad segments, and the result was only a matter of more emphasis in one part of the stage than another. The addition of spotlights to the lighting technician's array of equipment made it possible to be more exact.

Since footlights were the only illumination for that portion of the stage in front of the act curtain, this portion was poorly lit and received the benefits of the new spotlights as soon as they were powerful enough. The installation of front-of-house lighting evolved into the now standard professional practice of mounting banks of powerful spots on the front of the balcony. The angle of these instruments is usually quite low because of the architecture of the theatre. Only rarely will a balcony-front position be high enough to provide the optimum 38° to 45° vertical angle. Furthermore, no matter how high the balcony front is, the balcony occupants will be "looking down the beam" of the balcony spotlighting and will see it as essentially flat, shadowless light. The result is that balcony-front lighting is usually treated as a flexible and powerful flood of light. It often is subdivided into large segments and special single instruments are occasionally used, but the effect of this lighting is not sufficiently directional to have the quality of key lighting usually associated with an acting area.

The student lighting artist should not jump to the conclusion that balcony-front lighting is necessarily inferior because of its angle. Skilled professionals have long since proved the opposite. They recognize its nature and supplement it accordingly with spectacular success.

Since it is essentially a powerful, precisely adjustable flood of flat light to most of the audience, balcony-front lighting demands the addition of strong highlights. The two tools of the professional most used for this are the follow spot and side or tormentor lighting.

The Modern Arc Follow Spot

The modern arc follow spot is the most powerful light source in the theatre today. Its beam can cut through any other light on stage reducing the other light to the status of fill light. Although a follow spot's angle may be much the same as that of the balcony-front lighting, its directionality is clearly established by the intense beam it produces and by its movement. Thus it has the quality of a highly theatrical, highly directional key light that will take attention from all other lighting. In fact, it is so theatrical and so powerful in commanding attention that it is seldom successfully used in serious dramatic productions. It cannot be blended into the rest of the lighting well enough to allow the lighting artist to focus attention on the drama instead of the lighting. However, when spectacle is the order of the day, the follow spot comes into its own.

The use of balcony-front lighting with a follow spot reduces the problem of color selection to that of choosing a background wash of color appropriate to the spectacle being spotted. Attention will be riveted to the pool formed by the follow spot. The considerations discussed in Chapter 16 regarding the use of color on the setting and for toning will prevail. Facial color from the balcony-front lighting becomes mainly a matter of avoiding distracting or unpleasant distortion while maintaining a background for the follow-spot pool.

The choice of color for the follow spot itself will follow the precepts discussed under "acting-area colors" in the following pages. However, the designer must realize that the color temperature of an arc source is much higher than that of an incandescent lamp and that the color output of most acting-area colors will be several shades bluer when they are used on the arc light. Fading rate will also increase.

European Follow Spotting

A much different approach to the use of follow spotlights is found in European opera houses. A number of relatively low-power instruments equipped with incandescent sources are used as follow spots. Each instrument is specially equipped with lenses, irises, special shutters, and operator handles. The intensity and color of the follow-spot pool are kept within the general pattern of the lighting. The intent is to produce an accenting glow of light around key figures as they move about the stage with little emphasis on the fact that the pool of light is moving with the singer. Ideally, soft-edge pools are used.

Although European designers and directors often condemn the use of follow spots, they are still widely used. The technique can be very subtle, especially if special masks are used to shape the pool of light to a blurred ellipse outlining the figure of the actor or singer. With proper use of dimmers, proper color filters, and an alert, highly skilled operator, the results are nearly imperceptible. The tip-off, of course, is that the angle of the light varies every time the actor moves, and occasionally changes drastically as the actor moves out of range of one operator and into that of another. (Follow spotters are stationed in beams, side boxes, and on the light bridge.) The system has the advantage of getting a great amount of use out of a limited number of instruments—something always desired by European lighting artists who normally work with fewer instruments than American designers. It also makes adaptation to the constant changes of a repertory season much simpler; instruments are reangled from moment to moment. The following are the biggest disadvantages: (1) Moving pools of light are a distraction during dark scenes. European designers try to overcome this problem by the use of floor projections which extend the lighting design to the often raked stage floor and hide follow-spot pools. The results are good, but the follow pools are still occasionally seen. (2) Designers are deprived of a vitally important design element by this technique—design of key and fill light on the actor's face. It is rarely possible to provide the ideal lighting angle for a scene when follow spots are used.

Side Lighting

Side lighting is the other mainstay of the professional lighting artist when working with balcony-front lighting.[1] He will sweep across the stage with broad "brush strokes" of light providing keylight in quantity. Positions for such instruments will range from the usual tormentor location to special louvres at the sides of the forestage and to openings built into the side walls of the house itself.

Since side lighting is one of the most important tools in stage-lighting design, whether balcony-front lighting is used or not, our major discussion of it will be found in Chapter 15 where its design implications are treated in detail. The choice of color for side lighting usually is dictated by the same considerations that prevail for any key-fill lighting situation. On large stages there will be added the stipulation that side-lighting color medium must be of high efficiency to aid the

[1] For a detailed study of professional theatre-lighting techniques, the student of lighting should refer to the following: Joel E. Rubin and Leland H. Watson, *Theatrical Lighting Practice*. New York: Theatre Arts, 1954. Also Jean Rosenthal, *The Magic of Lighting*. Boston: Little, Brown, 1972.

powerful instruments in their task of reaching completely across the stage. The paler tints will usually serve as satisfactory side-lighting colors for lighting actors.

The use of side lighting as a design element as opposed to its use as actor lighting opens new and broader color possibilities. Choice will now depend on setting and costume color with little regard for facial colors.

Lighting the Acting Space by Segments: Acting Areas

Modern educational theatre lighting practice dates one of its fundamentals from the publication in 1932 of Stanley McCandless' book, *A Method of Lighting the Stage* (revised edition, 1947). In this book, McCandless introduced and developed the system of dividing the stage into "acting areas" for purposes of lighting. He devised a system of lighting these areas individually and then blending them into a carefully unified whole.

What Is an Acting Area?

An acting area is a workable subdivision of the total acting space of a given production. The size of the area is ideally determined by the degree of subdivision deemed necessary by the designer and, practically, by the capabilities of the equipment with which he must work. Thus a production that demands tightly controlled, carefully isolated bits of lighting closely allied with the blocking and acting—for example, a Greek tragedy—will require many small acting areas. A play that uses several large, but well-defined portions of the acting space at a time— for example, *Volpone*—will require much larger acting areas and will often treat these as groups. Acting-area size will usually range downward from a maximum of about 12 feet wide by 9 feet deep.

While any subdivision of acting space that is separately lighted could conceivably be called an acting area, common practice is to reserve this term for those units of lighting which form the building blocks of the entire lighting concept and which find repeated use in the production. The term "special" is used for those single pools of light which are used only briefly.

Since acting areas are the building blocks of stage lighting, a concept of the "normal acting area" has evolved almost directly from McCandless' first statement of the system. The normal point of reference is the lighting situation found in nature near noon on a sunny day. On such a day a person facing 45° to the sun will have one side of his face warmly lighted from sunlight and the other side coolly illuminated from the sky. The theatrical approximation of this lighting is diagramed in Figure 6-1. Note that as the actor stands in the center of the acting area facing full front, his head may be considered to be at the lower

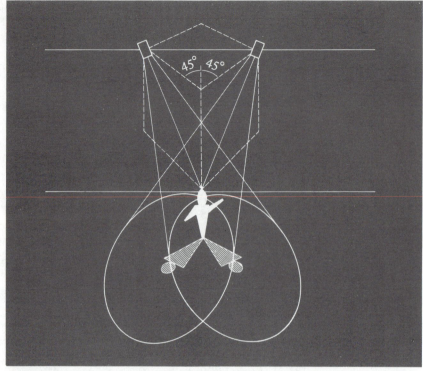

FIGURE *6-1*
Ideal Acting Area. This sketch shows the arrangement of instruments for the "ideal" acting area as seen from a viewpoint behind and above the actor standing in the center of the area. If one imagines a cube with its lower surface on the plane of the actor's line of sight straight into the audience and its upper corners at the ante-pro, the instruments will be located at those two upper corners. Thus they are 45° upward and 45° to the left or right of the actor's head. Actual locations are always approximate, depending on the architecture of the building and the wishes of the designer.

corner of a cube which extends upward and outward in front of him. The diagonal of this cube is on the center line of the acting area. Approximately 45° horizontally and vertically to his right and left are the two instruments lighting the acting area. When equipped with the proper color medium, one of these will form the warm key lighting, approximating the warmth of sunlight, and the other will provide the cool fill, representing skylight.

In lighting practice, as in nature, the angles and colors of the illumination vary a great deal. Actually the "standard 45° area" depicted in Figure 6-1 is more observed in departures from it than in any other way. Most designers will cite the figure 35° to 45° as encompassing the vertical angles regarded as standard in stage lighting. Angles higher or lower than these are often used but are not considered "normal." The horizontal separation of acting-area instruments by 90°, representing 45° each side of the centerline, is commonly desired by designers. However, the architecture of most theatres precludes this separation for all but stage center areas. The side walls of the house usually obstruct placement of lighting for the other areas.

Note that the acting area exists at *head level* of the actors in the stage space, not as a pool of light on the floor. The floor pools will cover considerably more area than the useful light at head level and will fall somewhat upstage of the useful light.

Architectural Limitations on Key and Fill Lighting

Certain architectural conditions will effect the use of key and fill. Horizontal sight lines are usually the most significant of these. The wider the seating area, the greater the difference in the audience's view of the actor's face from one side of the house to the other. In this regard, theatre-in-the-round presents the worst possible conditions for subtle lighting. It is impossible to more than vaguely suggest the same lighting on the face of the actor over 180°. Of course the back of his head will confront the other half of the audience at any given moment. Probably the best that can be done with subtle lighting in this situation is to limit strong key lighting to very high angles whose effect will appear somewhat the same from many directions. Side lighting is of little avail; it is effective only at relatively narrow viewing angles.

The influence of vertical sight lines upon facial lighting will depend on the configuration of the theatre. In a house with only one low balcony or no balcony at all, the difference in vertical sight lines from top of balcony to front of orchestra will not be insurmountable. But in an opera-house type of theatre with high balconies reaching nearly to the ceiling of the auditorium, part of the audience may actually be viewing the stage from a higher angle than that of the key lighting. This seating will result in reversed shadows for those persons above the lights, flat lighting for those looking down the beam of the lights (which may be mounted in the front of an upper balcony), and progressively better angles of view for those near the orchestra floor level. Such wide vertical angles, like wide horizontal angles, reduce lighting to illumination for a good share of the audience.

If these wide angles are coupled with great viewing distances, as they frequently are in large auditoriums, the lighting situation can be little more than a compromise in favor of some segment of the audience, usually those near the center of the orchestra level. Actor exaggeration and makeup can compensate to some extent for the loss of detail at great distances, particularly if aided by higher intensities of light and fairly strong contrasts. However, the bald fact is that huge houses do not offer the kind of subtlety that makes good facial lighting dramatically effective. The designer must resort to broader, more sweeping techniques, and trust that the actors will operate on the same scale.

Color of Key and Fill Light

The devising of color schemes for acting-area lighting or for the broad sweeps of key and fill lighting produced by side lighting and balcony-front lighting (or any combination of these) can be resolved into three systems for purposes of study. In practice, the designer will often use two or even all three systems together or blend from one to another as his needs require. These systems are (1) the complementary-tint cross-spotting system, (2) the related-tint cross-spotting system, and (3) the single-color system.

A discussion of the theory, advantages, and disadvantages of each system follows. All three systems are useful and workable; therefore, the designer will choose each to fit his needs and prepare to adjust to whatever difficulties are thus created in order to get the effect he wants.

THE COMPLEMENTARY-TINT SYSTEM

The complementary-tint system is the direct descendant of McCandless' original concept of the acting area. It requires the use of two instruments placed approximately as shown in Figure 6-1, equipped with tints carefully chosen to mix additively to a color very close to white. The actor's face, when he is facing front, is lighted with a warm light on one side and a cool light on the other, with highlights of essentially white light wherever both colors strike. The result is modeling which is a combination of both color and brightness contrast. Plasticity (three-dimensionality) is high. The effect can be quite naturalistic if the proper colors are chosen and visible motivating sources are provided so that the audience can relate the colors to them.

The choice of tints for this system is critical. Each color must be considered individually because it will exist by itself in shadow areas. Then the additive result of the mixture must be evaluated. It is this near-white mixture that will tone the setting and establish the warmth or coolness of the acting space. Moreover, the tints used must be relatively high in transmittance and ideally should fade at the same rate.

The final choice must be the result of careful testing of the additive effect on the setting, costumes, and makeup. A quick method of making such checks is to place a sample of one tint over one eye and of the second tint over the other. For most people, the result will be an additive blend of the two colors that can be used to test the combination. Be sure that the lighting used in the test is of the same color temperature (about 2950° K for conventional lamps, 3200° K for T-H lamps) as that of the stage lights.

In order that the student of lighting may be aware of the advantages and disadvantages of the complementary-tint system, the following list is provided. In practice, all of these advantages and disadvantages become relative to the production; therefore, the order of listing has no significance.

Advantages of the complementary-tint system include these:

1. The complementary-tint system can probably produce a higher degree of naturalism than most others under the usual working conditions found on stage.
2. The system offers a wide degree of flexibility in acting-area color variation if dimmers are available in sufficient number to allow colors to be dimmed separately.
3. Careful choice of tints can aid in alleviating minor makeup or costume color problems.
4. Mood in various scenes can be sustained by using judicious dimming to vary the color of the white light produced.
5. Plasticity will be high and consistently good over the entire acting area Since both color contrast and brightness variations contribute to plasticity, it will be effective from quite close to a considerable distance from the stage.

Disadvantages of the complementary-tint system include these:

1. There will be a strong tendency for the spill light from the acting-area lighting and the bounce light from the stage floor to tone one side of the setting warm and the other cool. Occasionally this toning will contribute to realism but more frequently it is a nuisance. Holding the setting well away from the acting areas, breaking it up with properties and other elements that do not show color changes, and even adjusting the scene painting are possible cures.
2. While all stage lighting requires precision in hanging and adjusting instruments, the complementary system is most sensitive to minor errors in these operations. Blending of color pools must be exact or color changes will take place whenever an actor moves from one place to another.
3. This system makes it difficult for the designer with limited equipment to conserve his spotlights by lighting little-used areas with only one spotlight.
4. The designer must be aware that dimming the complementary-tint system will result in deterioriation of the color contrast; the cool tint will shift toward warm as the color temperature drops, eliminating the blue output of the lamp. While deterioration of contrast is by no means a fatal flaw, it is one of the conditions with which the designer must cope. Occasionally he can convert the flaw into an advantage when a dim represents a shift to artificial lighting. How-

ever, the drop in plasticity will usually have to be compensated by the addition of other lighting.

5. If gels are used, fading will be a problem. Plastic media will alleviate fading to some extent. The difficulty is that with either medium the cool colors tend to fade faster, destroying the color contrast.

THE RELATED-TINT SYSTEM

Whenever the complementary-tint system is ruled out, there is still a need for augmenting the contrast or controlling mood or both by color, related-tint area lighting may be used. This type of lighting consists of using two instruments at substantially the same locations with relationship to the actor as the complementary-tint system, but equipping them with media that are quite closely related in terms of color. For instance, light pink and light salmon might be used. There are literally hundreds of such combinations ranging from those that are almost complementary to those that are nearly monochromatic. Mood, costume color, and makeup are the main considerations in a choice of a pair of colors. The only sure guide is experience and a careful study of the results as the colors are tried during rehearsal. In general, as the colors are farther apart on the color wheel, that is, as they approach being complementary, both the difficulties and the advantages of complementary-tint cross-spotting begin to appear. As the colors tend to be more and more closely related, the difficulties of complementary-tint lighting vanish and the special problems and advantages of monochromatic lighting gradually appear.

The advantages of the related-tint system are:

1. Lighting areas are easily blended; color differences are usually slight enough to make overlapping problems a matter of intensity adjustment only.
2. Warm related tints are relatively immune to the effects of reducing color temperature by dimming, although dimming will flatten the contrast.
3. Makeup and costume colors are easier to control because only one segment of the spectrum must be dealt with. More effective adjustments to control color contrast will be possible than with the complementary-tint system. Setting spill light problems are reduced to one color.
4. Mood effects are likely to be stronger, although any acting-area mood effect must be considered fugitive.

Disadvantages are:

1. Plasticity will suffer if the designer depends on color contrast for his three-dimensional effects.
2. Change of mood by dimming one side of each area is no longer possible.

3. Near-monochromatic effect places responsibility for contrast more definitely on other elements such as light and shade, makeup, costume color, set painting, and the like.

The final determination to use related-tint systems will have to be based on the designer's estimate of the potentialities for contrast control by other means. He cannot afford to produce a flat, two-dimensional stage picture. Given the ability to provide contrast, the designer may find that the great potentiality of the related color system for bringing together slightly disparate colors of costume and setting will weigh heavily in its favor.

A very useful pair is light blue-lavender used with salmon. These colors are a near-complementary pair, but the resultant color is much warmer than what is usually interpreted as white light. This warm tint is very useful for its mood and its favorable effect on skin tones. This combination is also more than usually susceptible to dimming without violent color shifts. Since both tints are warm (the salmon is much warmer, of course), the effects of fading are not as noticeable. All told, this pair is an excellent example of colors selected for a strong mood effect, good contrast effects, good dimming qualities, and a minimum of color distortion on the setting. These colors are far enough apart to demand careful angling and focusing, but they blend somewhat better than exact complementaries.

At the other end of the related-color scale is another example of a useful combination. This consists of using the natural output of 2950° or 3200° K lamps, perhaps slightly dimmed, as the cool half of the area and either salmon or gold tint as the warm half. These colors blend with ease and will distort the setting only slightly. The whole combination tends to favor the warm colors in setting and costume, but not drastically. Perhaps the greatest virtue of this combination is its efficiency. Since one instrument in each pair has no medium at all, it has an advantage of 10 to 30 percent in efficiency as measured in light reaching the acting area. This advantage is a tremendous help in building up bright sparkling lighting for comedy, particularly in a small theatre with limited equipment or power supply or both. Furthermore, the dispersing effect of color media is cut in half by removing one medium from each set. The result is somewhat like the lighting used in a modern jewelry-store window. Modern jewelers use clear glass lamps in silvered reflectors to provide concentrated bright sources which are reflected from the cut stones and polished metals of jewelry. The result is highlights of great brilliance.

Since efficiency is high, the effects of dimming this combination are not as drastic as in the case of complementary combinations. Of course, this effect is not without its drawbacks. Blue, green, and even subtle lavender costumes tend to appear somewhat "washed out" and mood will be limited to the brilliance of the lighting, not the color. However, for brittle comedy of manners, this situation is an advantage. Seeing conditions are also excellent for the subtle facial expressions which make high comedy successful.

THE SINGLE-COLOR SYSTEM

The single-color system is by far the simplest of all color systems, consisting of equipping *all* acting-space instruments with the same tint. This tint is usually a warm tone—perhaps pink, lavender, or salmon—although occasionally cool colors are chosen for stylized productions.
    The advantages of this system are:

1. Sheer simplicity makes it adaptable to many occasions. This color scheme often is chosen for the multipurpose stage during those periods between major dramatic efforts. Colors favorable to skin tones without makeup, usually pinks or lavenders, are chosen for this purpose.
2. The use of a single color makes possible major adjustments in color contrast of setting or costumes. Two related hues may be separated or blended as needed. The principle is simple: To blend two close hues choose a tint they both reflect equally well; to separate them, choose a tint one can reflect significantly better than the other. For example, to blend two close orange hues, choose a salmon or pale gold that will be reflected equally well by both. To separate these same pigments choose a tint favoring the one you wish to emphasize; for instance, a pale rose will accent the pigment nearest the red end of the spectrum.
3. Dimming will produce the same effect on all instruments in the single-tint system. Cool tints will shift to warm on low readings but balance will remain consistent.
4. Fading of color medium will be consistent through the system.
5. In the hands of beginners, or in a theatre poorly equipped with instrument mounting positions, this system will prove less susceptible to angling and focusing errors. This characteristic is no excuse for poor workmanship but it may be the only solace for those cursed with poorly designed plants.
6. Mood effects can be quite strong for the opening of scenes, although they will fade as the scene progresses.
7. The spill and bounce from a single-color system will tone the setting equally on all sides, presenting the least problem of the three systems.

    Disadvantages include:

1. Little variety in color can be produced unless other equipment is used.
2. Plasticity is purely a matter of brightness contrast except for what little color changes take place when one side of an area is dimmed.
3. Color of costumes, makeup, and setting must be adjusted to the

inevitable fact that one portion of the spectrum will be depressed by a single-tint system. Thus if warm colors are favored, cool colors will be greyed and vice versa.

Application of the Color Systems

What may seem to be disabling defects as we list the disadvantages of each system often turn out to be negligible in practice, particularly in the well-equipped theatre. For instance the apparent deficiency in plasticity in the single-color system may never be apparent if side lighting in some related color is added to the acting-area scheme.

Moreover, the lighting artist will soon find that he may blend and superimpose one system over another to produce vast ranges of possibilities that will challenge his artistic resources to the limits.

7 ELECTRICITY IN THE THEATRE

History

The history of stage lighting is considerably older than that of electricity in the theatre. The earliest plays, the Greek dramas, were played outdoors. However, this does not mean that lighting was of no consequence, if some authorities are to be trusted. It appears likely that some of the plays whose action begins at dawn (for example, *Agamemnon*) *did* begin their playing time at dawn, whereas the end of the trilogy, hours later in the dramatic festival, may have played to the setting sun. Even if these speculations are wrong, the playwrights were obviously aware of the great power of natural lighting changes over an audience, and used these as image devices with effectiveness.

Later, when the theatre moved indoors during the Italian Renaissance, artificial lighting became necessary, for visibility if not for effect. However, it was not long before early experimenters were devising special lamps, reflectors, and even color media by way of bottles of colored fluid. Still later, the Elizabethan theatre depended on natural light again, through the opening in the roof.

During the eighteenth century, with the advent of the great scenic perspectives of such artists as the Bibbiena family, lighting was intended primarily to illuminate the painted scenery. Shadows were the province of the painter, lighting was flat. It was also of low intensity and warm in color; examine the light from a candle to get the effect. Great scenes were played out during this era under the soft, flickering illumination of large numbers of candles. One source refers to the "candle hoop," a circular device which hung "in dripping radiance" over the heads of the actors. A little thought about the quality of this type of lighting will reveal one of the reasons for the rave notices about the scenic effects achieved by painting in perspective. Much was concealed in the murky shadows and low light levels.

More recently, the limelight was developed — radiation from a piece of lime heated to incandescence in the gas flame from a blowpipe. Since gas-air mixtures can be violently explosive (and the later gas-oxygen mixtures even more so), leaky piping in the presence of these hot flames leveled more than one nineteenth century theatre. Furthermore, rows of open gas flames hanging over the stage packed with inflammable wing and drop scenery would give a modern fire marshal nightmares. Theatre fires were common. The discomfort which came to those in the upper balconies from the hot fumes of poorly adjusted gas lights brought many theatregoers to the conclusion that it was not worth the risk.

In the nineteenth century, electricity appeared in the theatre. As a replacement for the rows of open gas flames, it met with early approval. However, things did not go so well for the early electrical substitute for the limelight. The first electric arc lamp was heartily disliked by many audiences and actors because of its cold, flickering light and its noise. The light was probably about like that produced by modern arc welding machines, and the noise was as bad or worse. The lamp's only apparent advantage was its relative safety. However, better arcs were developed and safety regulations made the limelight harder to justify. Eventually the electric arc spotlight became standard equipment for follow spot work.

The introduction of the incandescent lamp did not immediately bring in the spotlight era; early incandescent lamps had filaments that were unsuitable for use with lens systems. The incandescent spotlight had to await the development of the concentrated-filament lamp in 1920.

The Nature of Electrical Current

The history of the scientific and near-scientific study of electricity is too long and has too little relevance to the study of stage lighting to justify much attention here. However, some electrical terminology which we will find it necessary to use developed early in the history of electrical investigations. Since the easiest way to understand this terminology is to examine its history, we will do so. Early experimenters with electrical phenomena discovered what they termed two kinds of electricity. One could be produced by rubbing glass with silk, the other by rubbing amber with cat fur. The types were termed "vitreous" and "resinous" electricity. Much later, Benjamin Franklin suggested that vitreous electricity be called "positive," and resinous electricity, "negative." These terms still persist.

Modern experimenters have established that there are indeed two subatomic particles associated with electric phenomena. However, only one of these, the electron, moves about in the flow of electricity. The other, the proton, remains more or less fixed, providing the attraction that makes the electrons flow. Electricity is generated by detaching

TABLE 7-1
Conductors and Insulators

GOOD CONDUCTORS	POOR CONDUCTORS	INSULATORS
Silver	Tungsten	Glass
Copper	Carbon	Fiberglass
Mercury	Nickel-chromium alloys	Plastics
Brass	Silicon	Porcelain
Lead	Most nonmetals	Dry cloth
Water (impure)	Pure water	Paper
Aluminum		Rubber
Zinc		*Dry* wood
Iron and steel		Air
Most metals		Silicone rubber
Moist concrete		Teflon*
Moist earth		

NOTE: This list refers to the properties of these materials at stage-lighting voltages, that is, 120 volts. It includes materials commonly found in uses related to these properties in stage electrical apparatus.
* Trademark.

electrons from the atoms of materials by the application of energy, leaving the atoms in a state of unbalance; that is, there are more protons than electrons, and the result is a positive charge. Meanwhile, the extra energy which has detached the electrons causes them to accumulate at what is called the "negative" terminal. A semantic difficulty comes with the realization that the electrons flow from a place of negative charge to a place of positive charge. In this sense the term "negative" denotes a surplus of electrons and the term "positive," a shortage.

The energy in an electrical current is not atomic energy. The electrons are not destroyed in the process of using electrical energy any more than the water which drives a mill wheel is destroyed. It is the energy of flow that is used up; the electrons ultimately are reattached to atoms. If more electrical energy is needed, more energy must be applied to detach the electrons again, giving them new energy of flow.

Conductors and Insulators

Not all materials part easily with electrons from their atoms to produce a flow of electrons. Those materials that do allow electron flow we term "conductors." Their electrons are detached easily and little energy is "lost" (converted to some other form—usually heat). Other materials part with electrons only with difficulty and with considerable loss of energy in the form of heat. These materials are known as poor conductors. Still other materials will release only a few electrons under any conditions. Such materials, called insulators, are used to isolate conductors from each other to keep electricity where we want it. Table 7-1 lists common conductors, poor conductors, and insulators for stage-lighting voltages. Note that many of the poor conductors and insulators can be forced to carry electricity if enough voltage is used. Even a vacuum will conduct electrons if the voltage is high.

Since the process of generating electricity is somewhat complex and we can only gloss over the scientific aspects of it, it will be easier for us to defer examining it until we know more about the way electrons flow through conductors.

Electron Flow

Electrons are said to flow whenever they move about in such a way that unbalanced atoms (those with more protons than electrons) are restored to balance. While any free electron can contribute to this restoration (assuming only one was needed), the effect of this movement toward a state of balance ultimately is reflected back to the initially unbalanced electron. Thus it is possible to refer to various electrical charges as conditions in which there are related surpluses and deficiencies of electrons. The total number of electrons in the entire system is constant, but the number disassociated from atoms represents the unbalance or surplus; the number of electron-short atoms, the deficiency. To understand the basic facts of electron flow, the student must remember that the effect of electron movement is always to restore balance, not merely to move about. Unless the potential path of electron movement is so arranged that electrons can restore balance between a surplus and a related deficiency, nothing will happen. For instance, connecting the positive terminal of one dry cell to the negative terminal of another will not result in the restoration of any unbalance; restoration can be effected only if the two unbalanced situations represented by these two cells are completely interrelated by also connecting the remaining terminals (another positive and negative). For like reasons, an electrical circuit cannot be made to work simply by providing a path through which the electrons can flow to a lamp or motor or whatever. *A return path is necessary.* Otherwise the unbalance cannot be rectified.

This basic pattern—surplus electrons, flow path, return to electron source—is known as a circuit. Each circuit acts independently; the surplus from one cannot satisfy the deficiency of another. Of course, electrical circuits (a circuit is a complete pattern of flow from surplus to deficiency) can be combined and intermixed with fantastic complexity, but ultimately each deficiency must be related to its own surplus. In its primitive form, a simple circuit consists of some generator of electricity, a conductor to allow the electrons to flow, insulation to keep it in that path, something to use the electrical energy, and a return conductor to allow the electrons to return to the generator. Let us consider each of these briefly.

THE GENERATOR

A *generator* is a device for converting some other sort of energy to electrical energy. The process may be as simple as the friction which serves to generate electricity when we scuff across a carpet on a dry day, or it may be a chemical reaction taking place inside a dry cell or an automobile battery. The device may be the dissimilar metals in a thermocouple or the inside of a photoelectric cell or silicon cell (solar cell). But it is most likely to be a magnetic device for converting energy of motion into electrical energy. No matter what the energy source, the common characteristic of all generating devices is that they produce related surpluses and deficiencies of electrons. Electron surplus and deficiency produces the pressure (volts) which drives the electrons through the conductor to the device using the power. This device may be a motor, a lamp, a radio, or any of the thousands of other devices that convert electrical energy into other useful forms of energy.

A circuit is essentially a circle; the electrons are "pumped" back to the negative terminal by the energy fed into the generator and the path is completed. Probably the most common practical application of a simple circuit is the dry-cell flashlight. The generator is one or two dry cells. Dry cells are chemical-electrical devices in which energy is stored in the form of chemical compounds that give off electrical energy as they combine with each other inside the cell. Once this combination has exhausted the available chemicals, the flow of electricity ceases and we say that the dry cell has "run down." Then we usually throw the dry cell away because it is not worth the trouble to regenerate it, although this is possible.

The zinc can of the dry cell carries a negative charge (surplus of electrons) and the brass button in the center (which is connected to a carbon rod) a positive charge. The negative charge flows through the metal case of the flashlight (or through a plastic-covered metal strip in some cases) to the switch. When the switch is closed, the electrons flow to the lamp, through the filament, and back through the brass button at the top of the battery to the inside of the dry cell.

The only additional part the flashlight contains compared to a primitive simple circuit is the switch, which makes it possible to break the circuit, saving the energy for those times when it is needed.

In stage lighting, we must deal with circuits carrying much more electricity than the one or two dry cells in a flashlight can produce. The puny current of these dry cells can do no harm so no safety measures need be taken. But if the source of power is large enough potentially to do harm, the simple circuit must have adequate insulation to protect those using it from danger, and must contain some "safety valve" to shut it off in case of uncontrolled flow. Otherwise heat could be generated so rapidly that the whole apparatus might be destroyed. This safety valve can be a fuse or a circuit breaker, either of which will shut off the flow in case of dangerous currents. These devices will be discussed in detail in the section "Overcurrent Protection" in this chapter.

Note that the sequence of the parts in a simple circuit may be changed considerably with no effect on the circuit. For example, it makes no difference whether the switch comes before or after the lamp. Since all electrons must make the complete circuit, either location will do. Likewise, note that whatever quantity of electrons flows through one part of the circuit, this same quantity must flow through all parts. The current-using device (in this case the lamp) is usually the limiting device and determines the flow through all parts.

SERIES AND PARALLEL: VARIATIONS OF THE SIMPLE CIRCUIT

Relatively minor variations of the simple circuit usually fall into two types: *series circuits* and *parallel circuits* (see Figure 7-1). In a series circuit there may be a number of current-using devices, but they are so arranged that the entire current must flow through all of them. A string of Christmas tree lights of the "indoor" type is often wired this way. If one lamp burns out, the entire circuit ceases to work. The advantage of series circuits is that they enable the power used to be equally divided among several lamps (or other devices), and only one wire need be strung between lamps.

The other variation, by far the more common in stage lighting, is the

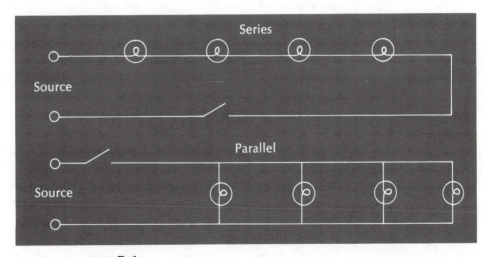

FIGURE 7-1
Series and Parallel Circuits. These schematic drawings show the principle involved in each of these two basic circuits. The series diagram shows the manner in which a series circuit provides only one path for the electron flow. Any break cuts off the entire flow. The parallel diagram shows typical alternate paths provided by parallel circuits. Interruption of any one path (for instance a burned-out lamp) cuts off flow in that path but does not disturb rest of circuit.

parallel circuit. In this circuit a number of paths which may be of different power ratings, are available to the electrons after they leave the switch. As long as any one path is operating, some current will flow. When more than one path is in use, the current will equal the sum of all operating paths. Of course, the great advantage of this circuit is that a single lamp failure does not cut off the entire system. Two conductors must reach each lamp, however, which often uses up more wire.

Electrical Mathematics

The ease with which electrons flow through conductors varies according to the material the conductor is made of, the size of the conductor, and the pressure applied to the electrons. These variations can all be expressed mathematically. First, the various units must be defined.

Ampere: Unit of quantity (amp). An ampere is that quantity of electricity which will deposit 0.001118 gram per second of silver when flowing through a neutral silver-nitrate solution. Note that this is an absolutely measurable quantity.

The ampere may be thought of as the *unit of flow* of electrical current. In this sense it is analogous to "gallons per minute" in describing the flow of water through a pipe. The above technical explanation is far more exact.

Volt: Unit of pressure. A volt is that amount of electrical pressure necessary to form a current of one ampere through one ohm of resistance.

Ohm: Unit of opposition to flow of current, *resistance.* Resistance is a property of conductors. One ohm of resistance to flow of electricity is that amount which will allow only one ampere of current to flow at a pressure of one volt.

The mathematical relationship between these three electrical units is known as *Ohm's law,* after its developer:

$$E = I \times R$$

in which

E = electrical pressure
I = quantity
R = resistance

The letters E, I, and R are nearly standard among scientists and electrical engineers. They are worth memorizing, as is Ohm's law. Ohm's law is fundamental to all electrical phenomena, being analogous to the physicist's standby, $F = m \times a$ (force equals mass times acceleration). Ohm's law and its variations describe the basic relationships that exist among voltage, current, and resistance in any electrical circuit. It is a truism among electrical engineers that any electrical device, no matter how complex, can be reduced to a number of simple circuits, each explained by Ohm's law.

The stage-lighting artist will seldom use Ohm's law *directly,* because the unit he works with most (watts) has already been derived from the basic law. However, each computation he makes to determine proper wattage, for example, will be an indirect application of Ohm's law.

As in any mathematical equation expressing three interrelated quantities, if any two of the three are known, the third can be computed. Thus, if a voltage of 100 is applied to a resistance of 100 ohms, a current of 1 ampere will flow. If the resistance is reduced to 10 ohms, the current will increase to 10 amps.

$$100 \text{ (volts)} = 10 \text{ (ohms)} \times 10 \text{ (amperes)}$$

Simple algebraic variation of the formula will enable the student to compute any of the variables from the other two:

$$I = \frac{E}{R}$$

or

$$R = \frac{E}{I}$$

Since the lighting artist will occasionally have to determine the resistance of a number of electrical lamps in a series or a parallel circuit, he should know how to apply Ohm's law in these cases. Figure 7-1 illustrates the flow of electrons in these circuits. The algebraic formulas for computing them are below. In both cases, R represents the resistance of the entire circuit and r that of each of the various components. Since the common condition of stage lamps is that they operate in parallel, the effect of the formula

$$\frac{1}{R} = \frac{1}{r} + \frac{1}{r} + \frac{1}{r} \cdots$$

is that the wattages of the lamps are simply added to find the load. However, in the case of a series circuit, such as a string of Christmas tree lamps of the older type, the resistance of the string must be computed and then Ohm's law used to find the current for whatever voltage is being supplied. Once the current has been determined, the wattage can be found by applying the power formula.

The formula for determining the effect of resistance connected in series is:

$$R = r + r + r + r \cdots$$

THE POWER FORMULA

While Ohm's law describes the most fundamental situation in the flow of electricity in a simple circuit, another formula will be of more frequent use to the stage-lighting artist: the *power formula*. This formula is used to describe the rate of energy usage in an electrical circuit. A variation of it is used by the power company in computing your light bill.

The energy available in any electrical circuit (watts) is the product of the amount of electrons flowing (amperes) times the pressure of their flow (volts). The term used to describe a unit of this electrical energy is the "watt." The formula is:

$$W = E \times I$$

in which

W = energy available
E = electrical pressure
I = quantity

The same relationship may be stated using the initial letters of the units of energy available, electrical pressure, and quantity:

$$W = V \times A$$

in which

W = watts (energy available)
V = volts (pressure)
A = amperes (quantity)

THE KILOWATT AND THE KILOWATT HOUR

Since the watt is a rather small unit, it is commonly referred to in a unit of 1000 watts known as the *kilowatt*. Because kilowatts represent a measure of flow at any given instant, a time factor must be added to enable the power company to total up the entire amount of power used over a given period. The time factor unit is the *kilowatt hour*, any amount of electrical energy that totals up to the energy equivalent of 1000 watts of power flowing for one hour. For example, one might operate a 100-watt lamp for 10 hours, using up 1 kilowatt hour (KWH) of electricity, or one might operate 6000 watts of lamps for 10 minutes, using up the same amount of energy. The cost of operating any electrical device may be computed once the wattage is known and the price per KWH of power is determined. Such prices range from less than one-half cent per KWH in localities with hydroelectric resources to 12 to 15 cents per KWH in localities using coal to generate steam to operate electrical generating plants.

For example five 500-watt spotlights, two 1000-watt floodlights, and 2500 watts of borderlights are to be operated on a small platform stage. What will operating costs per hour be if electricity costs 4 cents per KWH?

For the five spots	5×500 =	2500 watts for 1 hour
For the two floods	2×1000 =	2000 watts for 1 hour
For the borders		2500 watts for 1 hour
For the total		7000 watts for 1 hour

7000 watts = 7 KW
7 KW × 1 hour = 7 KWH
7 × 4 cents = 28 cents

To use the listed combination of lamps at the 4-cent price will cost 28 cents for each hour of use.

Note that lamp costs might easily exceed this figure if high-intensity concentrated-filament lamps were operated in the spotlights. A cost of 20 to 30 cents per hour per lamp is not unusual.

THE HEAT FORMULA

The most basic formula having to do with electrical safety is the *heat formula*. This formula describes mathematically how electrical energy is converted into heat as it passes through a conductor:

$$\text{Heat (in calories/second)} = 0.24 \ I^2R$$

Note that voltage does not appear directly in the formula, although of course it has had a part in figuring the amperage. The factor 0.24 is a constant number that has been determined by careful experimentation which converts the arithmetical product I^2R into calories. *Particularly note the I^2 portion of this formula.*

Generation and Distribution of Electricity

Generation and transmission of power are interlocking matters. If it were possible to generate the electricity needed in the theatre on the premises or very nearby, many problems would never arise. However, the need for vast amounts of hydroelectric power, the necessity of steam-generating plants for large amounts of cooling water, and the sheer size of generating plants today makes it nearly impossible to locate them in the immediate vicinity of users of power. The result is that the conditions of use of electrical power are established to a considerable degree by the necessity of transmitting it over vast distances efficiently and safely. This science has been until very recently almost exclusively centered in the science of *alternating current.* For much of the development in this area, we are indebted to the inventor and scientist, Charles Steinmetz.

The *alternating-current generator* is the starting point in our discussion of power generation. Generators must be driven by some "prime mover"—a water turbine, a steam turbine, a diesel motor, or any other source of mechanical energy large enough and constant enough to meet the demands to be placed upon it. Theoretically, it makes no difference what turns the generator, but practically the machine must be capable of maintaining precisely the same number of revolutions per minute no matter how heavy the load is that may be impressed upon it or how rapidly that load may change in size. One of the marvels of modern engineering may be witnessed by those who visit a large power plant at starting or stopping time for large plants in the area. In the minutest fraction of a second, the load upon the generators may increase many times over (or drop). Yet these giant machines are so sensitive that they adjust themselves almost instantly, maintaining such precision that electric clocks may be operated from them, deriving their precision from the generator, and remaining exactly on time.

These generators all operate on the same basic principle: *When a conductor is placed within a moving or changing magnetic field, an electrical potential will be produced in that conductor.* If there is a path available, current will flow and energy may be derived from the conductor. The electrical energy comes from the energy of movement supplied to the generator; thus the prime mover supplies the force—the magnetic field merely provides the conditions for conversion of energy of motion to electrical energy.

The current and voltage of the electrical energy thus generated will depend upon a number of variables; among them are the speed of movement of the coil and the strength of the magnetic field.

Parts of Generators

Since rotary motion is by far the easiest and most efficient to maintain, generators are rotary devices. Most small ones consist of fixed magnets (permanent or electrical) mounted so that they surround a rotating shaft that carries coils of insulated wire. The current is generated in the coils and must be removed from the rotating assembly (called an *armature*) by means of a sliding connection. This device consists of a series of insulated copper or brass rings surrounding one end of the shaft. Two are provided for the two ends of each coil of wire. Bearing against these rings as they rotate are graphite "brushes"—blocks of graphite with electrical connections attached. Graphite has the two necessary qualities of being slippery and a conductor of electricity. Thus, with a minimum of wear, the electrical current is removed from the moving part of the generator and sent upon its way.

The electricity coming from these graphite brushes in almost all large power plants in the United States is known as *alternating current.* It is so named because the rotary motion of the generator has produced rapid pulses of flowing electrons which move first in one direction and then the opposite as they race over the wires from one generator pole to the other. These alternations are arranged to take place 60 times each second, hence the name *60-cycle alternating current.* Although modern generators are huge, immensely complicated devices, they function as though they contained only three coils of wire rotating in a single magnetic field. This produces three pulsating currents, each lagging slightly behind its predecessor in time. Electricians call this *three-phase current.*

Alternating Current Compared with Direct Current

How is alternating current different from that coming from a battery? There are no waves or alternations of direction in the battery current.

Its electron flow is a continuous, orderly movement from negative to positive. Indeed, there are many differences, and some of them are of great importance to the stage-lighting artist. But as far as flowing through wires and transmitting energy are concerned, both the direct current from a battery and the alternating current from our generator are highly efficient. Electron flow through conductors is so fast that reversal of direction every 1/120 of a second is almost insignificant. It is true that the peak voltage reached for a fraction of a second at the 90° and 120° points in each cycle does not represent the true average of the voltage and will not act the same as the peak voltage of a dc circuit (which *is* the *only* voltage). To compare these two voltages, we must divide the peak voltage, say 155 volts, by 1.41 to get the voltage equivalent to that of a dc circuit.

$$\frac{155}{1.41} = 110 \text{ volts}$$

But once this operation has been performed—and most ac voltmeters do it for you—the application of Ohm's law, the power and heat formula, and others, will be exactly the same for alternating current as for direct current, as long as no other factors enter into consideration.

Note that alternating current has the unique quality of reversing direction every 1/120 second, passing through a moment of "off" or "no voltage" as it changes direction. This reversal makes many of the theatrical lighting-control devices work.

Transformers

Probably the most important invention of all those based on the properties of alternating current is the transformer. This device has made possible the relatively simple, efficient transmission of huge quantities of electrical power over vast distances. Until very recently, transformerlike devices were the mainstay of lighting control in the theatre. They still remain vitally important today.

How does a transformer work? What does it do? For our answers we must return to the basic theory of operation of the electrical generator: A conductor which is moving in any magnetic field, or which is placed in a changing magnetic field (*movement* equals *change* under these circumstances) will have an electrical potential developed within it. There is also an important corollary to this: Whenever an electrical current flows through a conductor, a magnetic field will be set up around that conductor. The field will vary with the strength of the current.

These two basic facts make it possible for the transformer to be, in effect, a generator without moving parts. A transformer operates by converting the incoming alternating current back into a fluctuating magnetic field. This field is then used to produce new electrical current or currents whose characteristics need by no means be related to those of the incoming power, except that no more power can be taken out of the transformer than is fed into it. New voltage/current relationships representing the same amount of energy can be developed. The power can be subdivided into several separate circuits, each with its own characteristics, grounding can be removed or established, and many other variations can be wrought on electrical energy by transformer action.

Transformer Parts

The mechanical arrangement of a transformer is as follows: A magnetically variable "core" is provided, made up of very soft iron plates whose magnetic properties will change with the strength of any magnetic field in which they are placed. Note that if steel were used, it would become permanently magnetic and resist further change. The reason for arranging this iron core in plates instead of in a solid piece will be apparent shortly. Two or more coils of insulated copper wire are wound around the iron core. If the transformer is to be efficient, the coils must be as compact and closely spaced as possible. Note that there is *no* electrical connection between the coils. The ends of the several coils of wire are brought out to a terminal block on the surface of the unit. Often the entire inner assembly is then enclosed in a steel casing which is filled with insulating material. In the case of large power-distribution transformers, this material takes the form of dry oil that prevents moisture from reaching the insulation on the wire. The oil is circulated through tubes protruding from the surface of the unit to cool it. The result is the familiar "tank with radiator tubes" seen in power switchyards or in a smaller version without radiator tubes hanging from a power pole in an alley. The inside of the case of small transformers is often filled with asphalt, which prevents moisture from entering but offers little heat dissipation.

How Electrical Energy Passes through a Transformer

Let us follow the course of electrical energy through a transformer. Power is fed into it through one of the coils, called the "primary." The incoming power is converted into magnetic energy producing several important effects.

REACTANCE: BACK EMF

The magnetic field generated and concentrated in the primary affects the flow of current in the primary itself. Without this effect, the primary would be little more than a short circuit, because it is merely several hundred feet of low-resistance copper wire. If this same wire were strung out straight and alternating current applied to it with no intervening resistance to control the flow, it would draw several hundred amperes and melt quickly. However, when the wire is wrapped around the core, only a fraction of an ampere will flow, due to the effect of the constantly changing magnetic field that the current generates in the core. This field "reacts" on the primary, producing an opposite and almost equal voltage to that coming in. This voltage is known as "back electromotive force" (back EMF). It "bucks" the incoming flow of power much as though the resistance of the coil had been increased greatly. Unlike resistance, this "reactance" merely prevents the flow of power; no heat is produced in the process. The only heat generated in the primary will be that coming from the slight resistance of the wire and its amount can be computed by the usual heat formula. Naturally, engineers keep the resistance of transformer coils low, depending on non-heat-forming reactance to hold down the flow of current.

CORE LOSSES

The magnetic field produced and sustained by the small current flowing in the primary also affects the iron core itself. This core of soft iron is a conductor of electricity as well as magnetism. Since it is large in cross section, it will have very low resistance. Therefore, while the electrical current the changing magnetic field "induces" (the scientific term for conversion of changing magnetic energy to electrical energy) in it is of low voltage, current can be high according to Ohm's law. This high current will be squared in the heat formula and will result in a great deal of wasteful and dangerous heat in the core. Thus, a means must be found to prevent the core from being a low-resistance conductor of electricity without raising its resistance to magnetic energy. Fortunately, most electrical insulation is easily penetrated by magnetic energy. The solution is to "laminate" the core, building up hundreds of thin plates of soft iron, each insulated electrically from its neighbors by a thin layer of varnish. Because only very low voltages are encountered, this varnish is insulation enough. Magnetic energy easily penetrates the varnish and the core retains its magnetic properties.

Heat losses in the core are thus reduced to a minimum. The only problem raised by this process is the possibility that the laminations of the core will vibrate against one another because of the magnetic forces in them. This vibration can cause an annoying hum and possibly loosen the parts of the transformer dangerously. The solution is twofold: (1) Use the insulating varnish to "glue" the laminations together; (2) tightly bolt the laminations together, keeping them in a state of compression. Since neither of these measures will stop vibration entirely, transformer devices will make noise and some of them have to be checked periodically for loose connections and even loose lamination clamps—a job the theatre electrician should not overlook.

TRANSFERRED ENERGY

The other coil or coils wound around the core of a transformer are called "secondaries." Secondaries are intended to do what the core should not do: reconvert the magnetic energy into electrical energy. Their resistance is also kept low because this electrical energy is intended to be withdrawn from the transformer for use elsewhere—it should not heat up the secondary.

Mathematics of Transformers

The important function of a transformer is to alter voltage/current ratios without altering the product of these significantly. The factors in the power formula

$$W = V \times A$$

are mathematically varied while keeping W constant.

The changes in voltage that take place in a transformer are directly proportional to the ratio of number of turns of wire in the primary and the secondary. Thus

$$V_1 : V_2 :: N_1 : N_2$$

in which

V_1 = the voltage in the primary
V_2 = the voltage in the secondary
N_1 = the number of turns in the primary
N_2 = the number of turns in the secondary

If there is more than one secondary, each is treated as though it were the only one for purposes of computing voltage changes.

Assuming that the wire in the secondaries is of sufficient size and the transformer is efficient, the amperage available in the secondary is *inversely* proportional to the turns ratio. Thus

$$A_1 : A_2 :: N_2 : N_1$$

in which

A_1 = the amperage in the primary
A_2 = the amperage in the secondary

Note that if there is more than one secondary, the amperage reflected to the primary will be the *sum* of those in the secondaries as converted individually by the turns ratio.

STEP-UP AND STEP-DOWN TRANSFORMERS

A *step-up* transformer is one that is designed to increase voltages and decrease amperages. For example, one might pass 1000 watts through such a transformer, putting in 10 amperes at 100 volts, and taking out 1 ampere at 1000 volts. The turns ratio would be 1:10 in such a transformer. Remember that the turns ratio does not reflect the exact number of turns, but only the mathematical ratio between primary turns and secondary turns. Such a transformer, if it were efficiently designed, might have 500 turns in the primary and 5000 in the secondary. Fewer turns, but in the same ratio, would result in poor conversion of electrical energy to magnetic energy and, thereby, poor efficiency.

A *step-down* transformer is designed to reduce voltage as the power is passed through it. There must be fewer but heavier turns of wire in the secondary than in the primary if efficient design is to be maintained. A special exception to the efficient design consideration is found in such devices as the doorbell transformer. Only a small amount of low-voltage alternating current is needed to operate a doorbell. By purposely designing a step-down transformer of low efficiency, it is made to serve as a current-limiting device in addition to its step-down function. Thus the doorbell transformer usually drops 120 volts ac to 12 volts ac, but limits the current available in the secondary to a fraction of an ampere.

Theoretically, one might operate a step-up transformer in reverse and make it into a step-down transformer. This reversal is sometimes possible in certain audio applications. However, the fine wire in the secondary of a step-up transformer might be poorly adapted to the amount of current it might be asked to carry if it were connected as a primary. In the case of a step-down transformer converted to step-up service, the insulation in the erstwhile primary might break down under the voltages impressed upon it as a secondary. Finally, transformers usually are designed with the location of the various coils in relationship to the core determined by the function they are intended to perform. Changing that function generally will upset the efficiency of the transformer.

POWER TRANSFORMERS

The huge transformers designed for transmission-line use are among the most efficient devices made by modern engineering. They are often well over 95 percent efficient—a figure seldom approached by other energy-converting machines. The great advantage of transformers to the transmission of alternating current is their ability to alter voltage/current relationships with little loss of power. Reflection upon the heat formula ($c = 0.24 \, I^2 \, R$) will show the advantage of being able to do this. Let us suppose that it is necessary to transmit 1,000,000 watts of power some 500 miles from Boulder Dam to Los Angeles, where it will be used as 120-volt lighting service (assume line resistance of 1 ohm per mile—500 ohms). For the purposes of our example, let us round off the 120 volts to 100 volts so we can check the mathematics in our heads. Converting and substituting the heat formula:

$$1,000,000 \text{ watts at } 100 \text{ volts} = 10,000 \text{ amperes}$$
$$c = 0.24 \times 10,000^2 \times 500 = 100,000,000 \times 0.24 \times 500$$
$$100,000,000 \times 0.24 \times 500 = 12,000,000,000 \text{ calories of heat per second}$$

This heat would be generated in the Mohave desert, which scarcely needs it! The cost of transmission would be prohibitive since only a trickle of energy would ever reach Los Angeles. Thus early city dc systems never expanded very far from the generating plant. Now, let us see what would happen if we would change our 1,000,000 watts to high voltage, say 1,000,000 volts. Again substituting in the formula after working out the amperage:

$$1,000,000 \text{ watts at } 1,000,000 \text{ volts} = 1 \text{ ampere}$$
$$c = 0.24 \times 1^2 \times 500 = 0.24 \times 500 = 120 \text{ calories per second}$$

This almost incredible mathematics of high-voltage transmission of power explains the great importance of the transformer—the device which makes this possible. Power transmission is worked out in this way: Power is generated at no more than about 18,000 volts at the generator because of the problems of insulating moving parts. Then, immediately outside the generating plant, the power is stepped up by passing it into the primary of a huge transformer. The secondary of this transformer has many more turns of wire than the primary. The result is that the new current is of higher voltage and lower amperage. The loss at this transformer, which generates only a bit of heat and a slight hum, is minimal.

The rest of the energy is transformed into high-voltage power and fed to the 500 miles of transmission lines. These lines are heavily insulated and protected against lightning. While the lines are expensive, they are highly efficient, delivering almost all of the power to the transformers at the other end. Here, in the outskirts of the city, the energy is stepped down by passing it into transformers with fewer turns of wire in the secondary than in the primary. These secondaries must be of heavier wire, however, for they will have to carry more amperage, if we are to retain most of our 1,000,000 watts. In most cases, the stepping down is a two-step process. The very high voltage of the long-distance transmission line is dropped to perhaps 6000 to 8000 volts for distribution around the city. Then, in every block or in every large building, another step-down transformer reduces the voltage to the 120-volt lighting current needed.

Only very recently has it been possible to raise dc power to very high voltages for transmission across the country. This new process is at this time, reserved for unusually long hauls of immense amounts of power. The transmission-line transformer is still the mainstay of power distribution.

ac Power Distribution and Theatre Lighting

The above information on transmission lines is important to the lighting artist because: (1) it will aid his understanding of transformer applications in the theatre, and (2) he must work with the conditions that the protection of long-distance above-ground transmission lines from lightning impose. What about lightning? Transmission lines cost millions of dollars and take years to build. Yet they can be destroyed in a flash, and the generator with them, by a bolt of lightning. This hazard is terrible to contemplate, so safety measures are taken. Lightning is essentially a huge electrical spark of incredible energy but short duration. The type that threatens transmission lines is that in which the spark passes between a cloud and the earth. Since lightning, like all other electricity, takes the path of least resistance, the electrical engineers take pains to see that the path of least resistance leads well away from their expensive equipment. They use several methods. One is *grounding,* which will be discussed in some detail. Another is to block the flow of lightning in the conductors of the transmission line. The conductors are provided with special coils at their ends which represent only a minute obstruction to 60-cycle current, but present high resistance to the lightning. Also, "spark gaps" are often provided which are too wide for the transmission-line voltage to jump, but which the lightning can leap with ease. Note that voltages in a lightning bolt are huge, even when compared with high-voltage transmission lines.

GROUNDING

Grounding is always provided in addition to the other protections. "Ground" in one sense is the earth; a grounded conductor, also often called a *ground,* is a wire that is firmly attached to the earth at frequent intervals over its entire length. This wire is the path of least resistance for any lightning that gets into the line, and the engineers make sure that it offers mighty low resistance to lightning!

The final step in this protective program is to make the grounded conductor a vital part of the electrical circuitry of the entire power system so that the easy path to ground is always nearby. To understand this step, we must look a little further into the nature of the circuits coming from the power plant.

THE GROUNDED COMMON NEUTRAL

A simple generator has only one coil of wire and one magnet; those in a power plant have to be more efficient. Thus, power-plant generators have a number of coils and a number of magnets, always multiples of three coils and three magnets, wired to act as though they were three. If we imagine three coils on a laboratory generator, evenly spaced around the shaft, we will find that these coils are 120° apart on the shaft and that the current produced in them when the machine operates will be 120° apart. Engineers call the current from each of these coils a *phase,* and call a generator that produces three such currents a *three-phase generator.* They describe each phase as being 120° behind or ahead of its partners. It would be possible to treat each of these three currents coming from a three-phase generator as though it were coming from a separate generator and to keep the wiring separate all the way to the lamps and back. However, this arrangement would result in a needless waste of wire. Examination of the current relationships in these three circuits indicates that the three never add together at their full strength. Whenever one of them is flowing heavily, another is very light, and a third is of opposite polarity and tends to cancel, making it possible to combine one conductor from each circuit and make one wire do the work of three. The saving in copper far outweighs any complications which might arise. The common connection is grounded, aiding the safety program against lightning and, in the bargain, gaining the additional current-carrying capacity of the earth itself. (This capacity is ignored in computing wire sizes, but it is still there.)

Electricians commonly term the wire which is the common grounded connection the *neutral*. Any wire whose voltage is above that of the earth is known as *live* or *hot*, particularly if the voltage is high enough to be dangerous.

Since this *three-phase 60-cycle alternating-current* supply is standard throughout the United States, and the grounding of the common wire is standard nearly the world over, the electrical worker must be aware of its implications: *Whenever your body is attached electrically to the earth, it is already connected to the common terminal of every grounded generating system in the world.* Only one more connection is necessary for electrocution!

As this three-phase power is distributed around the country, any one, two, or three phases may appear, depending on what is available at the point of delivery and on the needs of the user. Theatres are usually large users of electricity and tend to get the kind of power supply that a factory gets. All three phases and the common neutral appear at the main switch of the building. Smaller installations may find themselves supplied with two hot wires and the common or, perhaps, only one hot wire and the neutral. As long as 120 volts is needed for lighting service, the neutral will appear in the system. If only higher voltage motors are to be used, the neutral may not show up. Let us examine each of these power-supply systems in detail because the lighting artist may have to connect his equipment to any of these supplies when he travels with a show from place to place.

THE TWO-WIRE SYSTEM

The two-wire system is nearly obsolete today, but many are still found in older residences and small commercial buildings. One "live" wire and the common (or neutral) are brought into the building from the wiring in the street. These services are too small for any but the most primitive of stage lighting; consequently, the lighting artist who must work within the limitations of such a service will need to know every trick of the trade to eke out enough light to do anything at all. His first move will be to install high-efficiency, short-lived lamps of the lowest possible wattage in his equipment. Then he will determine the maximum load which the service can safely bear and plan to stay within it. Almost inevitably, the stage-lighting man will find it impossible to work with a two-wire service for long. Most of these services provide only 15 to 30 amperes of power and are frequently overloaded before the theatre system is even connected.

THE THREE-WIRE SYSTEM

As far as the power company is concerned, the three-wire system is still only a single-phase system because its power is usually supplied from one of their hot transmission lines and the common. However, a different type of transformer hookup is used. (Almost inevitably today, this system is used to feed whatever two-wire services are remaining.) The primary of the step-down transformer is a single coil of wire properly sized for the power company's distribution voltage. However, the secondary consists of a heavy coil of wire with enough turns to step the primary voltage down to about 220 volts. Then the *center* of this coil is grounded. Note that this change in grounding is possible because the current in the secondary is electrically unrelated to the current in the primary. The result of grounding the center of this secondary is that we have two live wires whose voltage fluctuates above and below that of the grounded midpoint in exactly opposing fashion. This grounding makes it possible for the return current from *both* hot wires to be carried in the neutral conductor with no increase in its size over that of the hot wires. Again, the engineers have saved wire. This system is known as the *110–220- (or 120–240-) volt, single-phase, three-wire feed.* It is common in medium-sized installations, including many theatres. The cancellation properties of the two waves as they return in the neutral make it desirable for lighting wiring in buildings and wherever the load on the two live wires can be balanced so that little current actually flows through the neutral.

THREE-PHASE, FOUR-WIRE SYSTEM

The three-phase, four-wire system embraces all three circuits coming from the generator. Whatever transformer arrangements have been interposed between the power plant and the service entrance point, the three live wires and the neutral return are present. The neutral serves all three live wires and may, under certain theatre-lighting conditions, have to be larger than any one of the live wires.

Three-phase systems are common in large industrial plants where they often are used to operate motors with no neutral wire included. The theatre electrician must beware of such systems in large buildings because the service equipment may resemble that used for the 120-240-volt, three-wire system. However, voltages between hot wires on the three-phase system are different. Measurements taken between any two live wires will show 208 volts. Voltage to the neutral is always about 120. Therefore, when three-phase systems are used for theatre lighting, all three hot wires are referred to the neutral (ground) for 120 volts.

Three-phase services are desirable in new installations because they offer the greatest amount of available capacity for the least amount of installation cost. Moreover, they make possible highly efficient motor installations for air conditioning, power tools, and the like.

Service Entrance Equipment

The term "service entrance equipment" is used to designate the electrical equipment which brings the electricity into a building from the tie-point of the power-line drop on the roof or side wall, and provides for its metering, shutoff, and safe distribution to the interior of the building. The beginning of this equipment marks the point of distinction between wiring supplied by the power company and wiring supplied by the builder of the building. Generally, the power company brings the live wires to the building and attaches them to fittings provided by the builder. From this point on, the builder provides everything except the meter itself. The meter is provided and mounted by the power company after whatever legal requirements for safety inspection have been met. A "service" is a set of wires representing one of the several types of electrical feed. It is not uncommon for a building to have more than one service because of different rates of charge for various applications of electricity.

Generally, the service entrance equipment in the building is located as near to the point where the wiring enters the building as is practicable. There is no overcurrent protection of any consequence for whatever wiring comes ahead of the service entrance equipment. A short in these incoming lines is rare, but if one happens it can be disastrous.

Frequent locations for service entrance equipment are in basements, backstage areas, storage rooms, on outside walls, or the like. The wires from the roof or outside wiring point are brought to the entrance equipment by means of a large steel pipe. This pipe is used to carry electrical wires and is known as "conduit." It looks like water pipe, but is considerably softer and much smoother on the inside to facilitate pulling wires through it. For interior use, several other lightweight types of conduit often are used—light steel or aluminum tubes or, in some cases, flexible coverings. The tubing is known as "electrical metallic tubing" (EMT), and the flexible material by various trade names such as "B-X," "Greenfield," and others.

THE METER AND THE MAIN SWITCH

At the service-entrance-equipment location, the first thing that happens to the power is that it is passed through the meter, unless there are multiple meters, in which case a main disconnect switch sometimes is installed. However, power companies usually like to meter the power as soon after it enters the building as possible, taking their chances with any rare short circuits that might ruin the meter. Meters are available for two-, three-, and four-wire services up to fairly large sizes. When the load gets too large to be practicable for passing through the meter, a transformer is used that passes some fixed portion of the current to the meter, thus measuring it indirectly. Such transformers are common in theatrical installations. After the meter, the power passes through the *main switch*. This switch disconnects the entire building as far as that particular service is concerned. Note that other services in the building may still be live. The main switch usually is equipped with the main overcurrent devices, one for each hot line in the service. If these devices are fuses, they will work separately, hot wire by hot wire; if they are circuit breakers, it is likely that they will be interconnected so that a failure in any one hot wire will turn all of them off.

The main switch and overcurrent devices represent the last-resort electrical protection for the building. The switch and fuses or breakers must be large enough to carry all of the current that will be drawn from the service at the time of maximum use. Usually they are sized much larger than this to allow for future load increases. In older buildings where this room for expansion has been used up, adding to the theatre-lighting load can be an expensive proposition. Service entrance equipment is exceedingly expensive, and increasing its size is a major wiring change.

From the main switch onward, there are almost as many configurations of equipment as there are installations. However, certain general categories of equipment, listed below, are nearly inevitable in a theatre building.

GENERAL BUILDING SUPPLY

The general building supply is usually a major subdivision of the power coming from the main switch, supplying power to room lighting, utility outlets, and other general equipment throughout the building. Usually this system has nothing to do with the stage lighting, although utility outlets and some work lights backstage usually are fed from this supply so that janitors can work and perhaps rehearsals be held without activating the theatrical lighting equipment.

POWER AND/OR MOTOR SUPPLIES

Power and/or motor supplies are special supply lines taken directly from the main for operating large motors such as air-conditioning units, blowers, and the like. These lines are usually either 240- or 208-volt lines without the neutral appearing at the motor, and are often quite heavy.

HOUSE-LIGHTING SUPPLY

The house-lighting supply is a separate supply that feeds the theatre house lights. Usually it is carried through dimming equipment and thence to the house lighting. Note that the law usually requires that the house lighting be supplied independently of the stage lighting so that a failure in stage lighting will not plunge the house into darkness and cause a panic.

STAGE-LIGHTING SUPPLY

The main for the stage lighting serves as the last overcurrent protection for stage lighting. It is also the point where the entire stage-lighting system can be turned off for major repairs. This switch should not be used as a stage-lighting master switch for blackouts, even if it is located backstage. Subsupply switches of the types used to subdivide service entrance wiring are not intended to be operated frequently under load, and will fail if used in this manner.

EMERGENCY LIGHTING

Some theatres will have a subdivision of the main allocated for emergency lighting. Others, depending on the law in their locality, will be provided with a separate service from the power company for this purpose. Emergency lighting will be detailed later.

The Neutral Bus and the Hot Bus Bars

All of the above switch gear, and often much more like it, will be found enclosed in steel cabinets near the main switch. Each supply will consist of a switch and fuses or a heavy, multiple-pole circuit breaker. At the bottom of the cabinet, or in a separate enclosure, will be found the neutral bus. (In older locations, the neutral bus often is enclosed with the rest of the wiring.) The bus is a large copper bar to which are attached all of the neutral wires for the various loads and from which a heavy wire runs to the neutral connection below the meter.

Often the subfeed switches above are arranged around a series of bus bars—heavy copper bars, uninsulated except where they are supported—which serve to carry the heavy current from the main switch to the subfeeders. Bus bars usually are arranged so that minor mechanical changes in the various switches or breakers make it possible to "tap off" either 120 volts, 240 volts, or 208 volts as needed.

Main switches and supply bus bars are of considerable importance to the touring stage-lighting artist. He must frequently attach his equipment to these in order to draw off enough power to operate his lighting. Also, in a permanent theatre situation, the main service equipment will usually be a mystery to all but the theatre lighting man and perhaps the plant engineer. Since theatrical lighting failures tend to happen at night, and plant engineers usually quit at 5 P.M., the lighting man is usually his own emergency man.

Testing Services for Hot and Neutral Connections

Since the stage electrician must often hook up portable equipment, and since the arrangement of service equipment varies greatly, the only safe way to proceed is to test each hookup point carefully before making any connections. This procedure is recommended even in the few stages where a bull switch is provided. This switch, often called the "company switch," is intended as a tiepoint for portable switchboards. The bull switch *should* have no other equipment attached to it and should be clearly marked as to voltage, phase, and capacity. More often than not, these precautions have not been taken, and the company switch is as much of a mystery as the service entrance equipment. Thus, the following series of five instructions should be followed:

1. *Test for hot and grounded wires.* These tests can be made with a voltmeter, but a pair of 120-volt 30-watt or smaller lamps in a couple of "pigtail" sockets, wired as shown in Figure 7-2, will often be better. In all of the following operations, the operator should be very sure that he handles only the insulated portions of the test lights or voltmeter.

    a. Locate a known ground—a cold water pipe; the frame of the switchboard, if it is relatively modern; part of the steel framework of the building, if it is of steel construction; or the like. If in doubt about the ground, place one end of the test lamp on a known hot wire or bus and the other lead on the ground in question. If both lamps light to half brilliance, the ground is adequate. If a voltmeter is used, the voltage between the hot line and the ground should read between 110 and 120 volts.

    b. Once the ground is known, attach one end of the test lamp to it for the next part of the text. Then touch the other lead to the various wires or bus bars under test. Half-brilliance in any such test indicates a hot wire. Anything more than half-brilliance should be viewed with extra caution. In any of the standard feed patterns, such a condition often indicates serious trouble, which may be confirmed by a voltage check. Any unknown wires which show no voltage should be temporarily categorized as probable grounds. Note the number and location of the hot leads or buses; this will aid in identifying the type of service with which you are dealing. In modern systems, the odds are that the electrical ground will be an easily identifiable ground bus, attached to a wide assortment of white wires. The largest of these will lead

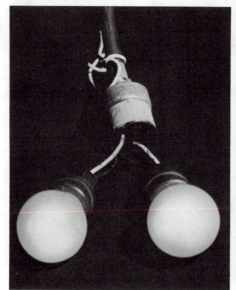

FIGURE 7-2

Pigtail Tester. The two photos above show the construction and operation of a typical pigtail tester. Tester is being used to check voltages at a connector. Left photograph shows approximate brilliance of tester when it is reading the voltage of a 120-volt circuit. Right photograph shows same tester reading a 240-volt circuit. Refer to Table 7-1 for a summary of conditions possible in using the tester, and comparative voltages indicated. Photo by Herbst.

toward the meter and eventually back to the feed transformer outside. Such ground buses should be double checked before assuming that they are what they appear to be, however.

c. Check for grounds. All lines which do not show a voltage when tested with the known ground will fall into two categories: They are either open lines or grounds. If they are grounds, the test lamp will glow when it is connected between them and a hot line. If open lines, they will not work in any test and should be viewed with suspicion because they may be fed by some path not on at the moment, but liable to come on unexpectedly. Time clock controlled feeds for exterior lighting are an example of this sort of equipment. Usually such lines and buses will not appear in the same panel with continuously operating equipment, but they will appear just often enough to trip up the unwary.

2. *Determine the type of service.* The number of live buses in a system will be a hint as to the type of service encountered. Refer to the summary of services. However, conversion of older equipment and

TABLE 7-2
Voltage Tests Using Two 120-Volt Lamps in Series as Pigtail Tester

CONDITION TESTED	LAMP APPEARANCE	VOLTAGE READ
1. Both buses from same phase	Out	0
2. Two buses from one phase, 120-240 feed, fed from two outside leads of transformer secondary	On full bright	240 volt
3. Both buses from one side of above feed	Out	0
4. Both buses from hot leads of three-phase system	About ¾ full	208 volt
5. Hot bus and grounded bus	Half brilliance	120 volt

NOTE: The above voltage readings may vary several volts without any cause for alarm. However, if voltages are significantly higher than normal, lamp life may be shortened.

changes in hookup to stretch a limited feeder capacity sometimes lead to some strange combinations. For instance, two hot lines and one neutral would probably be assumed to be single phase, 120–240-volt service. This may or may not be the case; the two hot lines may be two of a three-phase system, or they may both come from one-half of a larger 120–240-volt system. Voltage checks will tell the difference. The double test lamp will aid in this, but the difference between 208 and 240 volts is sometimes hard to determine with lamps alone. If it is necessary to use the test lamps without a voltmeter and thus determine the difference between 208 and 240 volts, it is a good idea to provide a third 30-watt lamp (or whatever size is being used in the tester) operating at 120 volts for comparison. See Table 7-2 for the test and voltages to be determined. Remember that you are testing from one hot wire to what may very well be another hot wire. This combination may present a lethal voltage, so be careful.

3. *Determine if any direct current is present in the panel.* Direct current cannot be identified by a lamp test, but its presence can be determined by the use of an ac-dc voltmeter which will, of course, read the correct voltage only when properly set to ac or dc. Examination of labels on motors and equipment in the building will also reveal the presence of dc lines.

4. *Determine the amount of power that may be drawn from the lines to operate a stage switchboard.* If the hookup point is a bull switch, it is possible that the rating plate will give this information. However, it is more likely that the electrician will have to inquire from local authorities, and it is not unlikely that he will have to add up the load already being drawn from the service, subtract this from the capacity of the system as determined by the main fuses or breakers, and plan to work with the difference.

5. *Hook up the control board through the portable lines. Always connect*

the ground or neutral first. This procedure makes sure that no voltages over 120 will appear at any lamp connections in the stage equipment. Also connect the equipment ground for the system to a secure ground such as the frame of the service entrance equipment or a cold-water pipe. *Do not ground to gas lines or hot-water lines!* These lines may not be properly grounded themselves. An equipment ground should not be hooked to the neutral bus. It is intended to back up the electrical ground by functioning no matter what may happen to the latter. Do not defeat this purpose.

The Permanently Installed Stage-Lighting Control Equipment

The usual purpose of the service entrance equipment, as far as the stage is concerned, is to feed to the stage-lighting control system enough power to meet its needs. Power is fed through the subfeed leading to the stage. Usually this subfeed will be led directly to the stage-lighting control system with no intervening breaks or branch-offs. At that location, another switch or breaker is installed to control and protect everything from there on. Since this breaker is usually more accessible to the stage electrician, it is considered a good idea to size it somewhat smaller than the one at the subfeed portion of the service entrance. Then, in case of a breakdown, the odds are that this accessible breaker or fuse will open instead of the relatively inaccessible one at the service entrance position. A huge short circuit[1] will often open *both* fuses or breakers, however, so the stage-lighting man must be able to get to both switches in an emergency.

At the stage-lighting control cubicle, which may be backstage or under the stage if remote-control equipment is used, the house lighting will branch off if it has not been given a separate feeder of its own. The next rank of branch-offs will be for stage lighting proper, of which there will be at least two categories, occasionally three.

1. Nondim circuits are circuits controlled only by a switch or a remotely operated switch. Their output will go from this switch directly to the lamps, usually by way of an interconnecting system.
2. Dimmer "ways" are circuits that pass through dimmers and thence to the lamps, again by way of an interconnecting panel in most cases.
3. Control circuits (occasionally found) are taps from the stage-lighting feed that supply power for relays, remote-control consoles, and the like. While they are small in capacity, they are vital to remote-control

---

[1] *Short circuit:* An uncontrolled flow of electricity that will result in damage if the source of power is large enough. With the power of huge generating plants available, shorts (common abbreviation) in stage lighting often cause explosion and fire (see "Short Circuits," Chapter 8).

systems. An open fuse or breaker in a control circuit may disable all or most of the system.

In some systems, the stage-dimmer circuits and even the nondims may have heavy master switches controlling them. Older boards may have so-called *color masters* — huge switches originally designed to control all of the red, white, and blue lamps in the foots and borders together. Sometimes these switches were provided with fuses, sometimes not. The switches usually serve little purpose in modern stage-lighting operations.

Overcurrent Protection: Fuses and Circuit Breakers

All electrical circuits attached to the power lines must have some sort of overcurrent protection; there must be some automatic device that will turn off the power in case too much begins to flow. If not protected, equipment may heat up and catch fire or even explode in a flash. Overcurrent devices are of two types: fuses and circuit breakers. Fuses are the older and simpler of the two. A fuse consists of a purposeful "weak link" in the electrical circuit, intended to heat up and break harmlessly before any other damage is done. The working part of the fuse is a piece of solderlike wire, usually with a thin portion in the middle. The size and composition of this wire are carefully adjusted so that the wire will overheat and melt when more than a specified number of amperes flow through it. Obviously, if the fuse is to be accurate, the metal in it must have a sharp melting point so that it will change quickly to a liquid and fall apart. The rest of a fuse is simply an enclosure to prevent spattering hot metal and sparks when it "blows" and mechanical arrangements to hold it in place in the circuit. There are two common mechanical types: plug and cartridge. The plug fuse is a common device in home lighting. It screws into a socket much like a lamp, and has a glass or mica top so that the interior may be inspected. This characteristic provides an advantage over other types in that inspection of a blown fuse will often give a hint as to the cause of the failure (see Figure 7-3). If the metal has simply melted and dropped out of the center portion of the fuse, an overload heated it up rather slowly to the breaking point. Overloading is a common stage problem easily corrected by cutting a lamp or so off the circuit. If the interior of the blown fuse is blackened or opaqued with metallic smoke, the fuse went out from a short circuit. Under this condition, a huge amount of amperage tried to get through the fuse and literally exploded the wire inside.

Other types of fuses display the same two types of evidence, but they must be disassembled to examine them. However, the problem of containing the explosive force of a short circuit blowout in larger amperage fuses is too much for the tiny glass container of a plug fuse. Fuses over 30 amperes in capacity are not available in plug type. Instead, *cartridge*

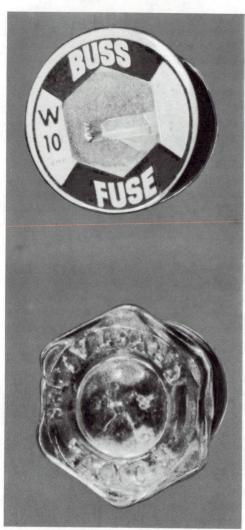

FIGURE 7-3

Blown Plug Fuses. This photograph will aid the reader in distinguishing between plug fuses opened by an overload and those opened by a short circuit. The upper fuse in this picture was purposely opened by subjecting it to a slight overload until it blew. Note that the central portion of the fuse wire melted out leaving a clearly visible break. The lower fuse in the photo was purposely subjected to a simulated short circuit. This sudden surge exploded the fuse wire, blackening the entire face of the fuse. The break cannot be seen. This condition is typical of fuses opened under short-circuit conditions. Photo by Herbst.

fuses are used. These fuses consist of the same inner element of fuse wire, but the container is a tube of heavy fiber. Electrical contact in smaller sizes is made by two brass ferrules at the ends of the fuse (see Figure 7-4, no. 5). In sizes over about 60 amperes, the ferrule is fitted with heavy copper or brass blades which serve to make the connection. Larger sizes are made with replaceable "links," the fuse metal portion. Links make it possible to avoid the necessity of replacing the entire assembly for every blowout, and also make it easier to stock fuses in many sizes because only the links need be altered to change size. Since cartridge fuses must be pressed into and pried out of the clip connectors that hold them into a circuit, they are more hazardous to the electrician who must service them. A "fuse puller," a plierlike device of insulating materials, is worth the investment for safe insertion and removal of cartridge fuses.

A variation of the cartridge fuse is the *miniature fuse*. This device resembles the cartridge fuse except that it is about one-fourth inch in diameter and about one inch long (see Figure 7-4, no. 3). The covering tube is glass so that it can be inspected. Such fuses are common in automotive work where they operate on low voltages and rather high amperages, and in electronic work, where they are used to fuse small currents accurately. In stage lighting, the 5- or 10-ampere size is occasionally used to protect small autotransformer dimmers. The electronic-equipment types may be found in control circuits for remote-control apparatus.

Fuses are categorized by amperage ratings, voltage, speed of response, and mechanical type. The following summary by mechanical

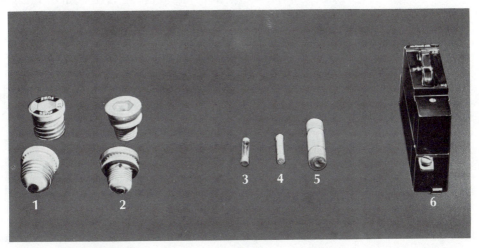

FIGURE 7-4

Typical Fuses and Circuit Breaker for a Stage. The above photograph depicts only a few of the many types of fuses and circuit breakers available. These few are usually encountered in stage lighting. (1) Typical plug fuse used to protect circuits of 30 amperes and under. (2) Fusestat used in the same way as plug fuse. But the Fusestat of each rating fits only its special socket, defeating any attempts to alter fuse size. (3) Miniature cartridge fuse occasionally found in small stage circuits and often in control circuits. (4) Ceramic miniature fuse occasionally used to protect small dimmer circuits. (5) Standard cartridge fuse for heavy-duty circuitry. Fuse shown is usually available up to 60 amperes. Larger sizes have larger housing and blades to fit socket at each end. (6) Typical top quality thermomagnetic circuit breaker; these are excellent for stage use and come in a wide variety of amperage ratings. Photo by Herbst.

types will give the reader some indication of types common to the stage. Examination of the fuse section of an electrical-supply catalog will convince the reader of the multiplicity of types and sizes of fuses available.

PLUG FUSES

Plug fuses are available in 5-ampere steps from 5 to 30 amperes. These fuses have medium speed of response, slow enough to "ignore" tungsten surges or motor-starting currents, and fast on major short circuits.

Plug fuses are available nearly everywhere. They are economical and reliable. Under heavy loads they may be worked loose by the ac vibration, causing overheating of the fuse contacts and fuse blowouts at less than rated capacity.

Their main disadvantage is the ease with which wrong-size fuses may be inserted in the circuit. Since the price is the same regardless of size, the layman often figures the 30-ampere size a better buy and uses that everywhere. More sophisticated users, with a poor appreciation for safety, purposely overfuse to avoid separating loads.

"Bridging the fuse" with a penny under it or a bit of brass jumping the base connections of the fuse itself is illegal and dangerous. *There is no excuse for such practices!*

FUSESTATS

Fusestats (a trademark name) are basically the same device as plug fuses, but with alterations to avoid the problem of replacement with the wrong size. When Fusestats are installed for the first time, the electrician inserts a special nonremovable adapter in the fuse socket that was designed to take plug fuses. This adapter must be chosen to match the proper fuse size for the circuit in which it is inserted. After the adapter is in place, a Fusestat of *only* the proper size can be installed in that particular socket. The adapter can be removed only by destroying it. Fusestats usually are slightly slower in action than plug fuses and have a spring-loaded device which breaks the fuse wire rapidly once it does soften.

Fusestats are not as readily available as plug fuses. They are not adaptable to circuits where occasional changes in fuse size are proper. The sizes of Fusestats parallel those of plug fuses, but their cost is slightly higher.

CARTRIDGE FUSES

Heavy power types for lighting service are available in a wide assortment of sizes from about 3 amperes upward. (Note that they overlap ratings of plug fuses.) The smallest size available goes to 30 amperes, the medium-size to about 60 amperes. Neither of these sizes has blade-type contacts. From 100 amperes upward, blades are used and fuses are frequently renewable. (Smaller sizes seldom are renewable.) From 60 amperes to about 200 amperes, size is adjusted to changing links. Over 200 amperes, larger and longer links are used and a larger fuse body is provided. Some nonrenewable types are filled with a powder to damp the arc in case of heavy shorts. Links for larger sizes are available in wide variety of capacities. The lag (speed of action) is usually medium in duration, long enough for tungsten surges. Both quick-blow and slow-lag types are available for special applications. The stage-lighting artist may find use for the quick-blow types to protect silicon-rectifier circuitry.

Instrument and automotive cartridge fuses are miniature glass-tube types available in a tremendous variety.

CIRCUIT BREAKERS

Fuses have been the mainstay of overcurrent protection since the early days of electrical distribution. However, more recently, the circuit breaker has become more common and, for the theatre, more desirable. Circuit breakers serve the same purpose as fuses without being destroyed in the process. They are heat or magnetically activated switches that automatically turn off whenever the current passing through them exceeds a specific amount. As they turn off, the operating handle is released in such a way that the breaker cannot be held in "on" position. After the overcurrent situation has been cleared, the breaker is restored to its closed position merely by pressing the handle all the way to the "off" position and then back to "on." Small-size circuit breakers have much the same appearance as switches (see Figure 7-4, no. 6). Indeed, they can be used occasionally as switches, but they are not ordinarily intended as off-on devices to control the circuit.

Circuit breakers are available in almost any size from a fraction of an ampere to thousands of amperes. The latter are incredibly fast-acting, complicated devices used to protect power lines and generating stations. Stage circuit breakers will seldom have a capacity of more than 1000 amperes per pole.

Unlike fuses, circuit breakers may be mechanically linked together so that a number of them will operate as a unit. Thus two-pole and three-pole breakers are common in service entrance and motor control equipment.

For stage-lighting purposes, circuit breakers are far superior to fuses mainly because of the speed and accuracy with which service may be restored after an overload. Probably the most frequent cause of outages in the theatre is the overload caused by inadvertently attaching too many lamps to the same circuit. Often the operator is aware of his error at nearly the same instant that the circuit goes out of service. He will usually lose little time rectifying this mistake. However, if a fuse must be replaced, there will be a considerable time lag before the circuit is back in duty. With a circuit breaker protecting the circuit, this lag is cut to a minimum. Furthermore, sizes can be accurately adjusted. Breakers can be calibrated to any load.

However, there are some disadvantages. First is cost: The initial cost of a circuit breaker as against a comparable fuse and socket is much higher. Over a period of time, the breaker tends to catch up because occasional outages cost nothing to restore. However, a series of serious short-circuit blowouts may cause a breaker to go out of calibration. With this change, the breaker almost always changes to a lower amperage capacity; therefore protection is not lost. But theatre circuits are often loaded to within a few watts of capacity, and a breaker that is slightly under its rating may go out unnecessarily.

Breakers may be had in a wide variety of response times. Common practices in stage lighting is to use a slow-lag breaker. This device will ignore momentary overloads and surges from cold lamp filaments. However, extra-long lags should be avoided. They may ignore minor overloads until well into the third act — and then open!

Economically priced circuit breakers are almost always designed to operate on a heat principle. A bimetallic strip is heated by the current passing through the breaker. When it reaches a certain temperature, it warps enough to trip the mechanism, opening the circuit. Economically priced breakers and all fuses have a common fault: They will open at currents well under their capacity if they are operated in an extra-warm area. This response is one reason that breakers or fuses were mounted well away from the dimmers in a resistance control board. As noted in our discussion of fuses, loose connections can cause the same false blowout situation.

Best quality circuit breakers have both thermal and magnetic mechanisms in them and are so arranged that they are much less heat-sensitive. They are worth the money.

MAGAZINES

Overcurrent protection is usually located adjacent to the switch controlling the circuitry up to that point. This location makes it easy for the electrician to shut off the power to the fuse mechanism while changing fuses. Where large numbers of fuses or breakers are needed, they are installed in a separate steel cabinet with its own locked doors. Such cabinets sometimes are called fuse or breaker "magazines" (see Figure 11-1a). In the case of stage-lighting installations, these magazines should be quickly accessible to the stage electrician — not hidden in a broom closet somewhere. If fuses are installed, a supply of the various sizes needed should be quickly at hand. In any case, each device should be clearly marked as to the circuit that it controls.

Determining the Size of Overcurrent Devices

The general principle in sizing fuses or breakers is that they are chosen to protect the weakest portion of the circuit needing protection. In the case of lighting, the lamp is the only part of the system which is capable of protecting itself. As long as the voltage does not rise above the proper limits, the resistance of an incandescent lamp will prevent any more than the rated amount of power from passing through. Even in the unlikely event of a large rise in voltage, the lamp will draw more current, but is unlikely to do anything more damaging than to burn out prematurely. Thus, fuses are not sized for lamps in circuits. However, the rest of the circuit depends on the resistance of the lamp to protect it from excess current. In an ordinary stage-lighting circuit, the resistance of all parts besides the lamp will be so minute as to be negligible. Therefore, a short circuit that bypasses the lamp will cause severe damage. To prevent all such damage, a fuse or breaker is installed. If the device is sized to protect the most vulnerable equipment in the circuit, it will automatically protect the rest of the circuit.

Various parts of electrical circuitry are rated in different ways: Lamps, most dimmers, many switches, and outlets are rated in watts. Wire, bus bars, and many other connections are rated in amperes. Since fuses and breakers are inevitably rated in amperes, it is up to the electrician to make whatever conversions are necessary in order to determine fuse sizes.

PROTECTING DIMMERS

In a stage-lighting circuit, the dimmer will probably be the weakest or most vulnerable device. Its rating in watts will have to be converted to amperes and a fuse or breaker installed to protect it. If there is no dimmer in the circuit, chances are that the wiring itself will be the vulnerable point. Consult the wire-size table in Appendix III for allowable currents in common types of wire. With respect to copper conductors, note that the strength of the insulation, not the size of the conductor, is the determining factor. Copper may be heated to a red glow without melting it. However, most insulation and probably the building would be on fire long before that.

SAFETY VERSUS EFFICIENCY

There is often a considerable discrepancy between the *safe* current for a circuit and the *efficient* one. Moreover, the law may enter into the situation, insisting on certain maximum fuse sizes no matter what the wire size may be. For example, a long run of wiring to the ceiling position of a theatre might present this situation: The lamp to be operated is a 1000-watt spot. On the basis of lamp size and dimmer size alone, a No. 16 wire and a 10-ampere fuse would do the job. The local electrical code will probably insist that no branch circuit in the theatre be smaller than No. 12 wire, which can safely carry 20 amperes. The extreme length of the run indicates that unless excessive voltage drops are to be suffered, No. 10 wire (30 amperes) should be used. The final result will be a circuit wired with No. 10 wire, fused to protect the 10-ampere, 1000-watt dimmer. Note that if the dimmer is removed from the circuit, or replaced by a 2000-watt unit, the fuse can be increased to 20 amperes. This amperage may be the legal maximum, even though the No. 10 wiring can take 30 amperes.

In permanently installed wiring on or off stage, a new set of fuses or breakers must be installed whenever wire size is lowered. Thus, branching off four 1000-watt circuits with smaller wiring from a large 50-ampere subfeed will require new fuses to protect the smaller wire size. Be sure to remember that the fuse protects only that wiring and equipment which is *beyond* it in the circuit. A short between a fuse and the generator will simply bypass the fuse.

Portable stage wiring must meet many of the same rules as permanent wiring, but there are some exceptions. Probably the most common exception is that stage properties may be wired with No. 18 or even smaller cord to a point out of sight of the audience so that they will look authentic. At that point, however, most local ordinances insist that the prop lamp be connected to a heavy-duty stage cable, at least No. 14 in size, and in many locations No. 12. On modern stages it is usual practice to allow no portable wiring smaller than No. 12, no matter how small the load, except for props on stage. In older theatres the previous standard of No. 14 cable prevails.

Summary

As the length and diversity of the previous discussion indicate, the application of electricity to stage lighting is a complicated business. The lighting artist will frequently find it necessary to call upon the skills of a licensed electrician, an electrical engineer, or a specialist in electronics. The ideal theatre plant would be able to avail itself of the services of each of these individuals at any time, leaving the lighting artist free to concern himself with design. Since most theatres are far from this ideal, the lighting artist must be able to make his own emergency repair, and to function independently when he is part of a touring company to the extent of making his own board hookups and protecting himself, the traveling equipment, and the local equipment from damage.

A final note of caution should be added: Anytime the lighting artist has doubts about the safety of any electrical operation he must perform, such as making a power hookup, he should call in an electrician. Then he should learn how to do the job properly because sooner or later, he will have to do it on his own.

8 ELECTRICAL SAFETY

Electricity and the Law: The National Electrical Code

The laws of physics are not the only laws of concern to the stage-lighting artist; state, county, and city laws will have considerable influence upon him. Some people are inclined to flaunt the laws of physics and to ignore good common sense. Man-made laws are contrived to protect us from this folly. In the area of electrical safety the protection takes the form of building and safety "codes." While these codes are of local nature, they usually have their origin in the recommendations of a nongovernmental group known as the National Fire Protection Association. This organization prepares and publishes a model electrical safety code titled the "National Electrical Code." The code, as it is commonly called, is revised on a 3-year schedule with opportunities given to all interested parties to make comments and suggestions on every revision. Each edition is a complicated legalistic document several hundred pages long, including a section on theatrical wiring practices and theatrical equipment. Copies of the code are usually available from a local library or can be purchased by writing to the National Fire Protection Association, 60 Batterymarch Street, Boston, Massachusetts 02110.

Several things must be made clear concerning the code. First of all, the code has no legal status in its own right; it is merely a group of recommendations by a nonlegal body. However, it almost invariably is written into law by local or state governments, giving it the status of a law wherever it is adopted. The lighting artist must be very sure that he understands the local laws because there is a tendency to write local standards that are still more restrictive than the code. Such standards then take precedence over the code in those areas where they specifically apply. The lighting artist, particularly when making recommendations for new construction or alterations in a lighting system, must familiarize himself with all laws governing theatre usage. Often he will find that such legal knowledge will work to his advantage. Theatre wiring is a rather specialized area which may not be included in the local laws except under the clause referring the reader to the National Electrical Code for "other applications."

The "UL" Label

Another organization connected with the National Fire Protection Association, is the Underwriters' Laboratories, Incorporated.[1] This organization tests electrical equipment for safety, granting the use of the "UL" label to those pieces of equipment that meets its minimum standards. Note that the Underwriters' Laboratories is concerned only with the safety of equipment, not its durability or efficiency. The cost of testing the equipment is borne by the manufacturers who submit it for testing. Testing expense is apt to run to thousands of dollars for a single piece of equipment. Moreover, each model change requires new tests. Thus manufacturers of lighting equipment usually limit the submission of items for testing by the Underwriters' Laboratories to standard-line, mass-produced devices which will remain in their catalogs long enough to compensate for the high cost of testing. About 80 percent of the catalog entries of the two major lighting-equipment manufacturers bear the "UL" label. Special items and new equipment frequently do not bear the label. Therefore, the absence of the "UL" label does not necessarily mean that the product is unsafe if it is a new or relatively uncommon item.

Manufacturers of components to be built into switchboards or remote-control consoles occasionally submit their products to the Underwriters' Laboratories. Such tests are even more expensive, often running to tens of thousands of dollars. More frequently, component manufacturers leave it up to the company that builds their products into control boards to determine whether or not they wish to have tests run.

The result of these conditions is that the "UL" label is not a clear-cut test of electrical safety in the field of stage lighting. Its presence should be sought for those items such as cable, connectors, and regular-line catalog items. It cannot be expected to appear on new or seldom-sold items. Thus the lighting artist will have to make the final determination of the safety of a piece of equipment by studying specifications, examining samples, interviewing those who have used the equipment, and possibly by running tests of his own.

Just as the National Electrical Code is often superseded by local law, the safety tests of the Underwriters' Laboratories may not be considered sufficient in certain areas. Municipalities, for instance, may require independent tests according to their standards before they will

---

[1] Underwriters' Laboratories, Incorporated, 207 E. Ohio Street, Chicago, Illinois 60611.

deem a piece of equipment safe and legal for installation within their boundaries. Again, such testing is expensive. The lighting artist specifying new equipment in such a legally restricted area must be prepared to comply with the local laws, either using equipment already approved, or seeking special approval for that equipment he desires.

Special Legal Obligations of the Theatre-Lighting Artist

The theatre operator owes his first responsibility to the audience; the audience members are his guests and he is legally obligated to protect them. The theatre operator's second obligation is to protect the life and limb of his own personnel and then to concern himself with the equipment and the show. Therefore, the lighting artist will find that extra-stringent regulations apply to any electrical equipment operated in the house or over the heads of the audience; for example, falling color holders are a menace anywhere, but they must be prevented, by use of wire mesh, from falling upon the audience. Frequently, lighting recesses in the ceiling of the house have to be protected with a fire wall as secure as any surrounding the auditorium. Backstage, however, instruments may hang in the open with only the roof of the theatre over them.

Emergency-Lighting Tests

Since panic is equally as dangerous as fire, the theatre-lighting artist must observe all precautions to prevent it. Emergency lighting must be kept in working order and tested frequently. Usually tests must be logged for the perusal of the inspector. All equipment must be up to standards and available for inspection at any reasonable time. Remember that fire inspectors have the legal power to close the show and to issue a summons if necessary.

Special Effects

Any stage effect involving the illusion of open flame is likely to become the job of the lighting man. Laws concerning candles, lanterns, and the like, are becoming stricter all the time. Generally, battery-operated devices will fulfill the open-flame function safely and effectively. Adaptations of the circuitry of a flashlight will do the trick.

Stage lightning is another safety problem. The old standby of the theatre, the carbon arc, is often no longer legal. Even if it is, the electrician should consider substituting something safer. A bank of low-wattage lamps with a rapid-switching device or a number of photo-flash lamps will often be just as effective and a lot safer. Adaptations of the photographer's strobe light offer a still better (but expensive) solution to this problem.

Using Electricity Safely

Electricity is dangerous. There is no possible way to conjure away this fact. Electricity can produce destructive heat, set buildings afire, or explode equipment with demonic fury. Electrical shock can take life and electrical burns can maim. These are facts the stage-lighting artist should never forget.

Electricity is so common in our homes that we tend to forget its danger. Yet the power available at any home light socket is more than enough to set a fire or to kill. On stage, many times more power than that from a home socket is available almost anywhere. Let us examine the chief dangers involved in the use of electricity and the safety precautions that these dangers necessitate.

Electrical Heat

We have already seen how electricity can be converted into heat by passing current through resistance. We have also seen the astronomical way that heat increases with amperage. Inevitably, whenever heat is generated by electricity, either by intent or by accident, the current or the resistance, or both, have increased. Fuses or circuit breakers can protect against increase in current within a circuit. However, they cannot protect against an increase in the resistance of a circuit. While the heat does not increase with the square of the resistance as it does with the square of the amperage, another insidious pattern makes increases in resistance almost as dangerous. Assume that a slightly loose connection develops in a stage connector. Heat will be generated at this point in the circuit because of increased resistance. This heat will cause oxidation of the copper or brass parts loosely in contact with each other. Oxides of metals have higher resistance than the pure metals and the resistance will rise still further. More heat will be generated and the vicious circle will spiral until a wire or part burns off, the insulation breaks down and a short occurs, or until fire breaks out.

This insidious heating of loose connections is often the cause of mysterious electrical fires that occur in the middle of the night in older dwellings. Probably a loose connection has been smoldering for months before it reaches the ignition point. Fortunately for the theatre, the stage-lighting equipment is seldom on except when there is an operator in attendance. Therefore, middle-of-the-night fires are not so common. However, failure of connectors and burned connections in equipment are a hazard. Even though the operator is there to stop the fire, the show often is interrupted. Also, this type of heating can ruin such expensive equipment as dimmers, high-priced connectors, and the like. It is not a very pleasant experience to have to throw away a $100 transformer dimmer with a perfectly good coil because the end has been burned beyond repair by a loose connection.

OVERLOADS

Next to loose connections, the greatest dangers to continuous operation of stage equipment are the overload and the short circuit. Overloads can be prevented by calculating loads carefully to see that they do not exceed capacities and by thinking before plugging in that "one more lamp." See Chapter 7 for details on circuit breakers and fuses.

SHORT CIRCUITS

Short circuits all have one thing in common: The resistance of the circuit is reduced to nearly zero and huge quantities of electricity try to flow through a circuit not designed to handle them. Unless the fuse or breaker opens immediately, fire and explosion will result. For instance, the power available at a 400-ampere bus is sufficient to vaporize the insulation of several hundred feet of No. 14 wire, blasting it out of the conduit in flames before the copper conductor will burn off. A building might easily be set afire along several hundred feet of conduit inside walls and under floors! Even a momentary short circuit inside a connector which results in burning off a few strands of copper and does not even open a fuse can leave the connector smoldering.

Short circuits are of two general types: shorts and "grounds." Both are equally dangerous, but the distinction between them will aid in their detection and prevention. A *short circuit* results when a path is formed from one live wire to another of a different phase, or to the neutral. This path can be formed by the twisting and tearing of the insulation of an old stage cable, for example. When the insulation is broken and the conductors touch, a short circuit has been formed. The short will occur the moment the power comes on to that circuit! A *ground* results when a live or hot wire comes into contact with some conducting material that is electrically attached to the earth (of course, this contact must happen in a grounded system). When contact takes place, the electricity takes the low-resistance return path to the generator instead of following the proper path. A ground will result in an uncontrolled flow of electrons only if it takes place in a conductor leading to a load. If the ground takes place in the return line, the load will continue to operate and the operator may not be aware that anything has happened until the connection heats up by resistance effects.

GROUND-FAULT DETECTORS

The fact that considerable amounts of electricity may flow through a ground fault without any interruption of the usual operation of a piece of equipment, and that this flow may constitute a shock hazard, has led to the development of *ground-fault detectors*. These devices, which are often combined with circuit breakers, offer a higher level of protection against shock in locations where operators are apt to be grounded during their normal activities. One of the first locations that has been cited for application of ground-fault detectors has been swimming pools and the area immediately around them. Obviously, a person swimming or standing barefoot on a wet concrete deck surrounding a pool is well grounded. If such a person handles a metal part, say the support for the diving board, and this part is carrying current to the earth from a ground fault, the person may offer an even lower resistance path to the errant current than the support metal, and he may receive a dangerous shock. Similar conditions may exist in areas paved with concrete, such as theatre shops, below-stage areas, and the like. Although water may not be present in quantities as copious as those around a pool, a damp concrete floor is a sufficiently good conductor to make the situation potentially dangerous. It seems likely that as the price of ground-fault detectors drops and the concern for safety rises, they will tend to supersede fuses and circuit breakers, whose function can be included in the ground-fault detectors.

Ground-fault detectors work by carefully comparing the amount of current flowing into a load circuit through the "hot" wire with the amount flowing back through the neutral serving that circuit. If the two currents do not match by a very tiny margin, the device shuts off the current.

The difference between a ground-fault detector and a circuit breaker, as far as the lighting artist is concerned, is that the neutral serving the circuit passes through the device along with the live wire. This represents a departure from the past practice of terminating the neutral (white) wire from every load circuit directly to a large neutral bus bar. Cost of installation of ground-fault detectors is higher than circuit breakers because of the more complicated wiring. This cost increase is compensated for by a greater degree of safety for operators.

Prevention of Shorts, Grounds, and Loose Connections

Two principles of prevention are paramount: Use good equipment and practice preventive maintenance. These same principles will also assure good operation and long life of the equipment. Safety problems usually arise in the theatre when short-term plans are made and budgets are cut to the bone. "Temporary" installations have a way of becoming permanent, and inferior equipment that was planned to "last out the season" often remains to threaten several other seasons.

Safe equipment begins with proper design. While design is not the province of the stage-lighting artist, he often must evaluate various pieces of equipment offered for purchase. Careful study of detailed specifications will aid in this process provided the suppliers have a reputation for meeting their specifications consistently. Additional valuable information can be gained by arranging an interview with those who use such equipment regularly. Users will often be aware of weaknesses that neither specifications nor examination could reveal. Still another indication of reliable equipment is the availability of stock repair items within easy shipping distance and at reasonable prices. Unfortunately, stage lighting is sometimes plagued with manufacturers who constantly change their designs, abandoning the owners of superseded equipment to the mercies of the custom builder of repair parts, whose prices are high and service often slow.

CUT-RATE LIGHTING EQUIPMENT

The lighting artists with a limited budget is particularly warned against cut-rate spotlights and substitutes for spotlights using the PAR- or R-type reflector lamps. Such equipment is usually not worth the freight one must pay to get it. PAR lamps have many good uses including some that the stage-lighting artist may wish to try, but they cannot be focused nor their spill light cut down without more auxiliary equipment than is economically worthwhile. Cut-rate louvre devices alleged to make spotlights out of PAR units may partially do the job, but they will be far too flimsy for stage use if the price is worth considering. A far better buy for the limited budget is secondhand equipment that was made by a reliable manufacturer. Often such items can be had at an extremely low price. Replacement parts will be available and often the equipment can be restored to nearly new efficiency at the cost of a few new parts and some time in the repair shop.

One more caution regarding the reflector lamps: These instruments operate at very high glass-bulb temperatures and offer a far greater fire hazard backstage than a conventional spotlight. Most fire regulations take this into account and place additional restrictions on their use. Also, the danger from lamp breakage is greater because there is no housing to protect those underneath from hot broken glass. These units are really display-lighting instruments meant to be used away from active people and moving scenery. Reflector lamps unprotected by specially designed stage-type fixtures do not belong on stage. There are, however, a number of borderlight or striplight fixtures designed to take advantage of the long life and high efficiency of PAR lamps. There are also specially designed fixtures that allow the installation of PAR lamps in the ante-pro position for use as rehearsal lights. Both of these types of fixtures take the high temperature and the fragility of PAR lamps into account, and are designed for safe operation.

VENTILATION OF HOT EQUIPMENT

Given basically well-designed equipment, further safety precautions must be taken during operation of the equipment. *Ventilation* is a major consideration. The wattage rating on spotlight housings is based on reasonable movement of air around the housing. Instruments that are to be operated in enclosures with poor ventilation should be down-rated. Not only will the buildup of heat create a safety hazard, but the life of the lamps will be shortened and often the bulbs will heat to the softening point, bulge, contact the reflector, and ruin it as they crack. Damaged equipment can be expensive and failures will plague the show. *Observe the wattage restrictions printed on lamp housings!* They are usually close to the limits as it is.

WIRE SIZES AND LOADING

Legal restrictions regarding the loading of various sizes of wiring and cables sometimes vary from place to place. The determination of what constitutes a reasonable safety margin is a matter of opinion, subject to the judgment of local governing bodies. Nevertheless, the highest legal load indicated for a cable or set of wires should not be exceeded. Doing so will often void insurance in case of trouble and is certainly flaunting the law. The law assumes that equipment is in reasonably good repair—in fact, this clause is usually part of local codes. Therefore, it is only sensible to downrate old cables which are near the end of their safe life.

WET LOCATIONS

Stage-lighting equipment is generally extra-heavy-duty gear, but it is not intended for use in wet locations. Outdoor theatres should be particularly alert to this. Fiber stage connectors, for example, that might have a life of 30 years on a dry indoor stage, may disintegrate overnight if left lying on wet ground. Rubber, Neoprene or plastic covered cable and water-resistant connectors are the solution, but they are not intended to operate under water. Only special (and expensive) fittings will do this. Most spotlights are designed to afford maximum ventilation but not to shed rainwater. Special roofing must be provided against rainstorms. Even with these precautions, reflector life will be reduced by dampness.

On the indoor stage, water effects should be treated with extra caution. Equipment must be water resistant, carefully and frequently checked, and usually replaced often.

ALTERNATING CURRENT VIBRATION

Alternating current is a constant source of maintenance problems. Every conductor is subject to constant 120-cycle vibration. This vibration loosens connections, warps heat-softened parts, and does other damage. Annual or biennial checking of all interior connections on control boards will often save transformer dimmers from untimely destruction. Fuses in magazines should be tightened occasionally. Plugging panels must be constantly watched for loose connections. Stage connectors should have their prongs cleaned periodically and the split portions spread slightly to assure good connections. Twist-lock connectors may be checked during operation by feeling for unusual warmth. Any connector that is heating should be tightened at once.

Electrical Shock Hazards

Most of the above safety precautions are concerned with preventing untimely failure of equipment or dangerous buildup of heat, or both. Electrical shock is a more direct and immediate hazard. Probably about half of the electrical shocks that occur in the theatre come from ignorance of or contempt for the dangers of electricity. We tend to forget the fatal power that is available at every outlet, or to feel that we are somehow immune to its effects. Thus it is not entirely uncommon to find an electrician with calloused hands who has the habit of testing for 110-volt current with his thumb! True, he only feels a slight tingle — usually. But one mistaken poke at a high voltage bus bar or one contact with a 110-volt line which has become crossed with a high-voltage primary and he will be finished. High-voltage breakdowns do occur and high-voltage bus bars are sometimes in cabinets with lower voltage equipment. The savings on a couple of pigtail sockets and two 30-watt lamps is not worth the risk.

HOW MUCH CURRENT IS FATAL?

Electrical shock kills and injures by overwhelming the minute electrical impulses of the nervous system. Heat also plays its part. The amount of damage done depends on the part of the body involved and the amperage which flows through it. Voltage, as such, is relatively harmless without appreciable current. Therefore, the body can stand the passage of several thousand volts of static electricity generated from sliding over a rug with no more than minor annoyance.

In the past, authorities have often stated that currents of 1 or 2 amperes at 120 volts or more are usually fatal. More recent research has found that a much smaller amount of current can, under certain conditions, kill. Fortunately these conditions are not common on stage, but the danger from shock is hard to overemphasize when it has been proven that currents as small as one hundred thousandth of an ampere and voltages as low as 40 volts have killed! It is all a matter of what part of the body is included in the circuit — something one would not want to investigate by the trial-and-error method.

Most electrical shocks are really grounds by way of someone's body. Practically all generating systems are grounded, thereby making a connection with everything and everybody in contact with the earth. Any contact with electrically live parts will result in a shock. A general precaution is to assume that you are grounded unless you are certain that you are not. Structural steel, plumbing, concrete floors, frames of electrical gear, steel battens and rigging equipment, covers to floor pockets and outlets, equipment associated with sound amplifiers, and the like, are all nearly certain to be grounded. Indeed, most laws require that they be securely grounded. Then if an insulation breakdown occurs within them, a short will be caused and a fuse opened warning of the danger.

To avoid the dangerous situation of passing the electrical current through vital parts of the body, electricians who must work on live parts make a practice of using only one hand and keeping the other in their pocket, well away from grounded parts. On stage it should seldom be necessary to work with live equipment, but when it is necessary, one must be sure that no part of the body is grounded.

Common Backstage Hazards

Two common occurrences backstage often result in shocks. One is the attempt to check out, without disconnecting it, a spotlight whose lamp has burned out or which has a socket lead burned off. *Always* unplug the spotlight at the end of the asbestos cord. Thus, it is disconnected where you can see what is happening while working on it. Turning off the circuit at the control board is not adequate protection. Someone may turn it on! Remember that many high-intensity lamps have live parts around the base when they are inserted in the socket. Lamp the instrument while it is disconnected, then plug it in.

Worn insulation is the cause of the second common shock hazard. The problem usually occurs where the lead-in wires enter a lighting instrument. Considerable wear takes place at this point particularly in the case of Fresnel spotlights whose lamp is moved back and forth on the socket carriage as the instrument is focused. If the hot wire wears through first, the entire housing of the instrument may become live at full line voltage. If a neutral wears through, a ground fault will occur. Either situation can be dangerous. For years this problem has been aggravated by the necessity for using asbestos insulation on lead-in wires. No other material could withstand the heat in the instrument. Asbestos resists abrasion poorly and lead-in failures were a common occurrence. Recently new materials have been introduced which promise to reduce the probability of such failures. Silicone rubber insulation, which resists heat to about 600° F, and fiberglass fabrics have been combined to make a much more durable insulation for lead-in wires. However, theatres will have instruments equipped with asbestos insulated lead-ins in use for years to come, and even the new materials will eventually fail. When such a failure occurs on an instrument mounted on a grounded batten, there is no hazard; if the hot wire is shorted, the fuse will open immediately, or if the neutral is shorted, a ground fault will occur. However, if the instrument is mounted on an ungrounded floor stand, or if the ground-faulted instrument is removed from its batten, the situation becomes more dangerous. An operator may provide the path to ground with fatal results.

To permanently prevent this situation and similar hazards, many municipalities have adopted rules requiring an *equipment ground* for all portable equipment. Such rules parallel the rule requiring that the frame of all permanently installed equipment be grounded. The equipment ground is maintained any time the instrument is connected by carrying a third wire in all cables. This third wire leads from a secure ground at the outlet end to a ground connection at the frame of the instrument. Anytime the instrument is plugged in, it is also grounded. This additional expense is worth the cost. In a three-wire cable, the color code is as follows: black means *hot*; white means *neutral*; green means *equipment ground*.

All connectors must have three poles for this service and all outlets must accept them. There is in progress a gradual changeover to this system in household wiring. Most portable electrical apparatus is now sold with three-wire cords and a "U" ground plug. An adapter is supplied to enable the user to attach the machine to a standard duplex outlet. The extra wire from the adapter should be attached to the coverplate screw in the center of the outlet. This extra wire will ground the equipment if modern wiring practices have been followed. Such a practice is highly desirable in case of outdoor electrical equipment. Newer wiring is now being installed with "U" ground outlets whose ground connection is properly grounded to the earth. Such outlets will be found on new stages in many areas, where they are provided for utility and cleaning service.

Solid Neutral

In earlier days of electrical wiring it was common practice to put a fuse in the neutral line—a safe practice in two-wire services where loads might conceivably "pile up" on the neutral and overheat it. However, with the advent of three- and four-wire systems, the fused neutral became a hazard and present practice calls for the "solid neutral." The neutral conductor is never broken by switchgear, breakers, or fuses unless all live phases are cut off at the same time. Even then it usually is left connected. The reason for this system is that inadvertently opening the neutral will place a higher voltage across the entire lamp load. The voltage will distribute itself according to resistance. The result will be very high voltage on whichever part of the system has the lowest load. Lamps will be destroyed and motors burned out. A similar situation will develop if the neutral is opened in a three-phase system. The solution is to make it impossible for the neutral to be opened unless the power is off. Fuses and breakers are removed from the neutral and it is securely connected to the ground at the service entrance point. The stage electrician on tour will occasionally find a vestige of earlier days in the form of a main switch with fuse holders for all three or four blades. The one carrying the neutral will have the fuse replaced with a length of copper tubing, or it may be bypassed completely with a heavy piece of wire. Obviously, the stage electrician will not alter such changes—they do not represent an attempt to bridge a fuse to destroy its protective power. However, they do provide him with a good clue as to the identification of the neutral bus.

Dead-Front Systems

Earlier control boards in and out of the theatre were often potential electric chairs. Electrified copper was everywhere. Modern law requires just the opposite. The entire operating surface of the control board must be "dead," that is, no live parts can be within touch. One should be able to approach the equipment in darkness and feel for a switch with no danger of shock. The same thing is true of modern service entrance equipment. Since most dead fronts are metal, they are securely grounded. Theatre-lighting gear may have ventilated sides and backs provided that screening is used to prevent anyone from touching live parts.

Trouble Shooting

Electrical emergencies will arise backstage—usually at crucial times. The skilled stage-lighting expert will plan for these in advance and have a course of action in mind. The first priority in any emergency is safety of the audience and the theatre staff. Next comes the show. No amount of misguided enthusiasm for "the show must go on" should be allowed to reverse this order.

However, stopping the show will seldom be necessary if proper safety precautions have been taken in advance and good lighting practices have been followed. For example, most vital lighting areas on the stage should be illuminated by more than one instrument. Thus a lamp failure will not completely destroy the show. Furthermore, old lamps near the end of their life should be relegated to nonvital areas where their failure will not be so critical. Crucial lighting areas should be re-lamped regularly. An unexpected short circuit in otherwise properly sized and installed wiring will cause only a momentary flash and cut off only one circuit. However, if the entire theatre has been loaded to the verge of overload, the short may black out the whole place.

Even in the most reliable of lighting systems, a dimmer will occasionally fail. Thus the prudent lighting artist will hold at least one dimmer way in reserve and instruct key staff members how to put it into service in a hurry.

Panic Lighting and Battery Systems

As far as major power outages are concerned, two "backup" systems are usually required by law. The first is a "panic" system for the houselights. This system controls a switch which automatically cuts the houselight feed to a separate circuit from the stage feeder and bypasses the houselight dimmers in the process. Thus the house can be lighted even if the entire stage-lighting system fails. The second backup system is still more automatic. Its heart is a set of heavy-duty batteries installed in the basement. These batteries are kept charged to a voltage about 110 volts dc. They feed special lamps installed in key locations to provide enough light for occupants to leave the building. Such lamps must be installed in the house of every theatre without natural illumination. In case of a major power failure, a special relay trips, turning on these emergency lights. The batteries have enough reserve to allow several hours of operation without recharging. As soon as the regular power comes on again, the emergency system cuts off and begins to recharge the batteries. In some cases the battery system will be replaced by a special generator system arranged to come on the moment the regular power source fails. Such generators must be occasionally started up to keep them in good working order. A rigid maintenance schedule must also be followed.

A self-contained emergency system is available at a reasonable price for small theatres. It consists of a battery, a charging apparatus, and two or more automotive lamps that produce a sufficient light to illuminate a considerable area. The entire package is mounted on a shelf where the emergency lights can be directed effectively and the ac cable plugged into an ordinary convenience outlet. As long as ac power is available at the convenience outlet, the charger keeps the batteries up and the lights remain off. The moment the outlet goes dead, the lights come on. These systems are adequate for small or temporary theatres. They may frequently be seen installed in department stores where there are no windows to light the way out of an emergency.

9 MANUAL CONTROL OF STAGE LIGHTING

History

Even the beginnings of modern stage lighting involved some sort of control apparatus; gaslights had to be turned on and off for convenience and safety, if not for artistic reasons. Since gas valves, by their nature, are devices that may be gradually turned off, graduated control came naturally to gaslighting; "dimming" of the lights by turning down the gas was commonplace from the beginning. However, completely extinguishing the flames meant relighting by hand or by means of pilot lights with the flash usually associated with such an operation—certainly not a very artistic process! Nevertheless, gaslighting "control boards" did achieve a kind of subtle control from their maze of valves and pipes.

The introduction of electricity into the theatre in some ways represented a setback in control. Whereas gaslighting had been controlled by a valve that served as an off-on device and as an intensity control all in the same piece of equipment, early electrical boards brought a separation of these functions. The result was a divided control board with all switches, fuses, and master and submaster switching on one board and the dimmers as a separate apparatus some distance removed. These old switchboards were both impressive and deadly. Frequently the face of the switchboard was a fine polished piece of marble with the open knife switches carefully mounted in polished copper splendor in neat rows on its surface. The bright metal blades of the larger master and submaster switches seemed to have been designed by a fiendish mind so that the distance from one live piece of copper to another matched the span of the operator's hand perfectly. An uncautious grab for a switch resulted in a mighty jolt across the knuckles if the operator was lucky and perhaps electrocution if he happened to be grounded elsewhere. To increase the hazards, these shining death traps were

170

usually installed in a murky corner backstage and lighted by a single dim lamp, if at all. Adding insult to potentially grievous injury, the position was usually such that the operator could see little or nothing of the results of his efforts to light the stage.

Meanwhile, still further in the darkness and even less likely to afford visibility of the acting area was a metal rack heavy with dimmers. These resistance units produced vast quantities of heat in the process of dimming the lights and were sensitive to load. If not loaded to about 80 percent of capacity, they would not dim out the lights. Consequently, still more heat was generated backstage and still more electricity wasted in "phantom loads"—spare lamps, heaters, and the like—operating backstage to "fill out" a dimmer to its capacity so it would dim out a lamp on stage.

It would be nice to assume that all of the above is history and that we could smile indulgently at the past and enjoy our superior equipment of the present. However, the one great virtue of this old equipment was its rugged construction. The result is that there is still much of the older equipment in use today. Many traveling professional companies are still using resistance dimmer boards whose only improvement over the 1920s is that they no longer present live parts to the operator, and that the switches and dimmers are in the same enclosure. Only very recently have there been any serious attempts to adapt the SCR dimmer to "road board" use. Such adaptations can take advantage of the fact that a modern SCR dimmer may weigh one-tenth what a resistance dimmer of the same capacity would weigh. Controls can be grouped into a console in whatever configuration is desired.

Although "live front" boards are rapidly becoming a rarity, there are probably still a few in existence. The law cannot always force their removal unless repairs or renovations are needed. Lighting technicians must still occasionally cope with this heritage of danger.

Subdivisions of Early Control Boards

The earliest of the electrical control boards were geared to the stage-lighting apparatus of the day—general illumination apparatus consisting of row upon row of borderlights and, of course, a set of footlights. The only effective spotlighting unit was the follow spot, an arc unit that could not be dimmed anyway. Thus the dimmers were solidly wired to the various circuits of lamps in the borders and foots and ganged by way of master and submaster switches into color patterns. This arrangement is known as a nonflexible control board. The standard pattern was red, white, and blue foots and borders. Obviously this arrangement had more to offer as a patriotic symbol than as a means of mixing colors additively, but warm white, blue, and purple were the three colors most used for review numbers. The equipment served its purpose. The present-day user will find that adjusting the wattage of the red and blue circuits and substituting green for white will result in a workable (but not very efficient) three-color primary system.

However, the system provided almost no control for spot lighting. Usually there were a few "floor pockets"—iron boxes equipped with huge 50-ampere "stage plugs" divided into "arc" and "incandescent" categories by means of a pin which kept the two types from being interchangeable. The arc pockets were wired directly to heavy switches to supply power to backstage arc lights—usually floodlighting units. The incandescent pockets were grouped by means of a color code into units, one large resistance dimmer per color group. These units were intended to operate big incandescent loads made up of *bunchlights* (tin-surfaced boxes with ten or more 100-watt lamps) or *olivettes* (simple tin-surfaced box floodlights, usually of 1000-watt capacity). Bunchlights and olivettes were arranged as sidelights in color patterns to match the borders.

Flexible and Nonflexible Control Boards

The floor pockets represented the only flexible circuitry on the old stage. In this application, the term "flexible" means that the dimmer may be loaded with an instrument plugged into its outlet as opposed to permanent or nonflexible circuits where the wiring leads directly from the dimmer to the lamp sockets. Since these old-fashioned pockets were controlled by resistance dimmers, usually of high capacity, their flexibility was still extremely limited by the need for heavy loads if the dimmer was to function. Also the habit of color grouping a number of positions on both sides of the stage reduced the number of control circuits to three or six depending on the elaborateness of the setup.

The next major change in control-board design was to bring the separate elements back together where they had started in the mechanical simplicity of the gas valve. The result was the "integrated control board" with dimmers and their associated switches in some rational order in the same unit. However, the only change was the integration of dimmer and switch; the same pattern of circuitry and the same inflexible wiring directly to the lamp sockets prevailed.

Making Older Boards Flexible

Many older installations have been or can be made much more useful. The entire dimmer bank can be made flexible by disconnecting the load wiring leading to the borderlights, pockets, and the like, and interposing some type of interconnecting panel, allowing any load to be attached to any dimmer. This change, relatively minor in most older boards, will increase their usefulness greatly. However, it is usually necessary to add fuse protection to each load circuit to make it safe.

FIGURE 9-1
Front and Rear Views of Now Obsolete Inflexible Resistance Dimmer Board. Notice spacing of dimmers necessitated by heat produced and large handles provided to enable the operator to move all the dimmers together by mechanical interlock. (This control board has now been replaced.) University of Wyoming.

Also local ordinances often look upon such a change as renovation and insist that the board be brought up to modern safety standards (at least dead front) at the time of the change. Thus, the alteration to make a permanent board flexible is likely to burgeon into a major electrical job if the original board was not safe to operate. However, there are a great many control boards that were installed about 40 years ago which are quite safe but totally inflexible (see Figure 9-1). The bitterest irony is that such systems are still occasionally being installed by those unfamiliar with modern theatre lighting. Such systems are 40 years obsolete before they are even turned on!

The Resistance Dimmer

Early dimmers were almost always resistance units. These dimmers dim lamps by reducing the flow of current through them to the point where the heat produced in the filament is no longer sufficient to produce visible light by incandescence. Current still flows, but not enough to light the lamps. Practically, it takes about four times the resistance of an incandescent lamp to reduce the flow sufficiently to dim it out. Some authorities cite five times the resistance of the lamp as the proper figure. The exact amount depends somewhat on what is considered to be a negligible glow of the filament at the "out" position.

How the Resistance Dimmer Works

The resistance dimmer operates by gradually inserting additional resistance into the lamp circuit until current flow is reduced sufficiently. Since the remaining current is still flowing through both the dimmer and the lamp, both still heat up. The dimmer heats the most because it has the largest share of the resistance. Heat will be generated according to the heat formula.

At intermediate points between full on and blackout, the resistance wire in the dimmer will be asked to carry larger amperages, although over less resistance. Since the heat will vary by the square of the amperage, these large amperages will produce still larger quantities of heat. Thus resistance dimmers get hotter at intermediate points than they do at blackout. Moreover, many good resistance dimmers have a *flipper switch* at the low reading point that cuts off the remaining current completely.

Load Sensitivity

All resistance dimmers are load sensitive because of the inescapable mathematics of resistance circuitry. The "four times the resistance of the lamp" ratio can be satisfied for any given lamp load with only one dimmer size. For example, a 1000-watt lamp draws 9.33 amperes at 120 volts:

$$\frac{W}{V} = A \quad \text{or} \quad \frac{1000}{120} = 9.33$$

Its resistance is

$$I = \frac{E}{R} \quad \text{or} \quad \frac{120}{9.33} = 12.86 \text{ ohms}$$

By rule of thumb it takes 4×12.86 or 51.44 ohms to dim to black.

Therefore, the 1000-watt dimmer will have to be made up of wire able to carry about 10 amperes and of sufficient resistance to equal roughly 50 ohms. (Note that there is some "give" in the "four-times" rule.) However, if we try to dim a 500-watt lamp with the 1000-watt dimmer, we run into difficulties. There is no problem involving danger to the equipment because the dimmer can handle twice the capacity and the lamp is self-limiting as long as the top voltage (120) is not exceeded. However, the four-times rule has been violated: A 500-watt lamp has twice the resistance of the 1000-watt lamp, or 25.72 ohms approximately.

Four times this resistance equals 102.88 ohms, twice that available in the 1000-watt dimmer. The result is that the dimmer will only partially dim the lamp. Since it is not feasible to change the resistance of the dimmer, the only way to make the 1000-watt dimmer work is to load it with additional wattage (phantom load) so that its resistance will equal four times that of the entire load and it will be able to black out the circuit.

The Resistance Dimmer as a Master Dimmer

Notice that each addition to the load on a resistance dimmer will change the ratio between the resistance of the dimmer and its load. This change in ratio causes a new set of dimming characteristics to be developed for each load change. For this reason the resistance dimmer is limited in its ability to function as an electrical master dimmer. An electrical master dimmer is simply a large dimmer so connected that its output feeds a number of smaller dimmers which, in turn, feed lamps. The large dimmer controls all lamps feeding through it and can dim them out no matter what the setting of the individual dimmers—provided that it is properly loaded if it is a resistance dimmer. The loading is the catch. Any change in the setting of one or more of the individual dimmers will alter the amount of current drawn from the master. This change will be reflected as a change in dimming characteristics. For example, if the master dimmer is set at 8 and one of the individual dimmers is moved from 4 to 10, the change will cause all other lamps feeding from the master to dim slightly. This will happen because the increased load will come closer to the ideal 4 : 1 loading ratio for the master. This "pulling," as it is often called, limits the use of a resistance master to fade-in and fade-out operations in which the dimmer is used to bring on or take out a preset arrangement but is not left in the circuit to produce pulling if individual changes are to be made. At "on" position, resistance dimmers are effectively out of the circuit.

Because of this limitation, resistance dimmers were never extensively used as master dimmers. Instead, manufacturers developed mechanical means enabling the operator to move a number of dimmers simultaneously. In the United States this device took the relatively simple form of a slotted shaft common to all dimmer handles in a single row. Each dimmer handle was fitted with a movable dog that could engage the slot in the shaft, or could be held clear depending on the rotation of the handle. A worm drive or a large handle, or both, were attached to the shaft to give the operator the leverage he needed to move many heavy dimmer parts at once. This system is still common in both resistance and autotransformer boards. Its limitation is that all dimmers must be at the same reading while they are engaged in the shaft. Proportional dimming[1] is impossible. The nearest approximation to it that can be obtained is to set a series of dimmers which are at different readings in such a way that the dog will engage the slot in the shaft when it lines up properly. Then the topmost dimmer is engaged and those at lower readings are picked up as the shaft rotates toward dim position. This setting levels out the readings as the dim is accomplished. The reverse of this procedure is still more difficult. Individual dimmers must be disengaged from the shaft as they reach their predetermined settings. This procedure often requires the assistance of two or more operators.

In Europe elaborate clutch arrangements were devised making possible proportional dimming and even cross-dimming (some lamps going on and others off) from the same shaft. This development made mechanical "faders" possible wherein one handle would dim out one bank of lamps and dim in another at the same movement. The faders added greatly to flexibility of control, but did not overcome the basic necessity of loading resistance dimmers to capacity. The only practical solution to this problem was to have available on the control board a large variety of sizes of resistance dimmers so that loads could be matched to proper-size dimmers. This arrangement was attempted, but seemed to lead always to compromises and forced grouping of circuits on the board by load value instead of function, making operation more difficult.

---

[1] Proportional dimming consists of reducing or increasing the intensity of a group of lights on several dimmers while maintaining the proportion or ratio of intensities that originally existed between those lights.

Mechanical Arrangement of Resistance Dimmers

The mechanical arrangement of the resistance dimmer has changed only a little over the past 30 to 40 years. Originally a resistance dimmer was nothing more than the simple "rheostat" of the physics laboratory: a coil of nichrome wire, chosen for its high resistance, wrapped around a cylinder of heat and electrical insulation material. The ends of the coil were provided with terminals and a simple slider was arranged to move along the coil including more or less of the resistance wire in the circuit as needed. In theatrical use, these rheostats soon turned out to be too flimsy. The slider would arc as it passed over the resistance wire, causing pitting and quick destruction. Furthermore, large loads and heavy currents developed too much heat in the coil for safe operation. Consequently, the rheostat was refined by cementing the resistance wire to a slate disk which was an electrical insulator but much more able to dissipate heat. The cement covered the wire and the slider moved over a series of brass buttons (known as steps) brazed to the resistance wire and allowed to protrude up through the cement at frequent intervals. If there were too few steps, the lights flickered as the slider traveled from one to another; 120 was considered an adequate number. Later the slate disk was replaced by a cast-iron disk and the cement by porcelain enamel which was baked onto the wire and backing at the same time. Still later, the cast iron was replaced by steel, lowering the weight somewhat. The arrangement of the resistance wire continued in about the same manner as in the first slate disk dimmers.

The Autotransformer Dimmer

The introduction of the autotransformer dimmer opened the way to the solution of most of the problems associated with the resistance dimmer. First, the dimmer generated little heat, making possible compact boards which were more easily located within sight of the acting area. Second, it was totally non-load-sensitive. Electrical mastering became completely practical. Finally, the autotransformer dimmer was stepless, resulting in smooth dimming. Good but expensive resistance dimmers were substantially smooth, but many inferior ones were jerky and jumpy.

The first autotransformer dimmers were merely laboratory units that had been brought into the theatre by enterprising amateurs in stage lighting.[2] The professional theatre was largely excluded from this development by the presence of direct current in most New York and Chicago theatres. Autotransformer dimmers work on *alternating cur-*

---

[2] Note that by this time the reactor dimmer (a remote-control unit of great weight and cost) had been installed in a few locations including Rockefeller Center in New York. In Europe the Bordoni system was in use. See p. 185.

rent only. The early autotransformers were ill-adapted to stage use because their mechanical operation necessitated turning a dial about 340°. Thus only two dimmers could be run at a time by an operator, and then a completely smooth dim was difficult because of the wrist movement involved. Furthermore, large ones were heavy and often moved with difficulty. However, their biggest handicap was lack of ruggedness. These dimmers were really laboratory instruments developed to set voltages at the test bench, not heavy-duty devices intended for thousands of changes of reading and the rigors imposed by heavy-handed stage electricians. The sliding contact or "brush" was the chief culprit; it wore out easily or was damaged by banging the dimmer to "full-up" or "full-out" position. While the brush itself was cheap and easily replaced, if it was not attended to immediately, the entire dimmer could be ruined.

Theatrical Adaptations of Autotransformer Dimmers

As soon as autotransformer manufacturers became aware of the demand for their products in the theatre, they began to design them with the theatre in mind. The first improvement was to add a rack and pinion gear to the units and to arrange their mounting so that they would fit into standard resistance-dimmer banks (see Figure 9-2). This

FIGURE 9-2

Autotransformer Dimmer for Installation in Theatre Control Board. Dimming capacity of this unit is 6000 watts. It has been designed to fit the standard mountings designed into commercially built boards since the days of resistance dimmers. The handle may be operated independently by the shaft arrangement pictured or it may become part of a mechanical interlocking arrangement allowing the operator to tie an entire row of such dimmers to a common shaft. To do this their settings must all be the same. Courtesy of The Superior Electric Company.

change resulted in lever-operated dead-front autotransformer boards that were mechanically identical to earlier resistance boards. The boards usually were wired in the same inflexible manner and equipped with mechanical master handles as though the autotransformer were nothing more than a heatless and stepless resistance dimmer. The heatless factor was ignored because the same mountings were used and the boards came out the same size although ventilation was no longer a major problem. There are a great many such boards in use today. This practice was unfortunate because the best features of the autotransformer are overlooked. Probably some of the best adaptations of autotransformers to stage lighting were those boards assembled by skilled theatre technicians out of commercially available parts but with careful attention to the potentialities for master dimming.

Although there are thousands of autotransformer theatre lighting control systems in use today, the autotransformer is rapidly becoming obsolete. Some are still being made to satisfy the needs of those who insist on their installation and for replacement of dimmers in existing installations, but it is now more economical to manufacture and install electronic devices. We will discuss these later.

The following discussion of autotransformer devices is included for the lighting artist because the many installations now in use will undoubtedly remain in service for a long time. Lighting artists will have to know how to use and service these control boards. Major new installations of autotransformers are, however, almost a thing of the past.

Commercial Autotransformer Control Boards

Manufacturers soon discovered the market which was being created in the little theatre movement by the introduction of the autotransformer dimmer. "Package units" soon came on the market and dominated the little theatre lighting-control area for a long time. Such a unit is illustrated in Figure 9-3. This type of unit is still commonly found in smaller theatre installations, and may even be found in large installations where it can serve as a supplementary control device when additional dimmers are needed. Note that transfer switches make it possible for any or all of the six 1000-watt dimmers to be fed from the master dimmer or from the power line. If no master dimmer is needed, it is possible to use the 6000-watt unit as another individual dimmer by throwing a transfer switch which passes its output directly to a set of outlets or even to use it to control another board.

Variations on such circuits are nearly infinite. Two master dimmers may be used to obtain cross-fading. Package units of individual and master dimmers can be made up and interconnected in any manner that preserves the safety of the equipment. All of this flexibility is possible because the autotransformer dimmer is a voltage-setting device and will maintain the same output voltage, regardless of load, up to

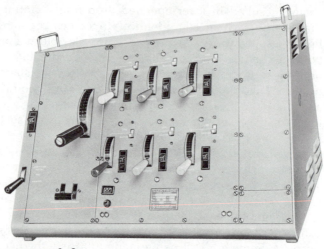

FIGURE 9-3a

Autotransformer Control Board. This control board represents a typical configuration of dimmer control using autotransformer dimmers. The handle at the very lower left edge of the board controls the function of the master dimmer making it available as a separate dimmer when not needed for master dimming. Such autotransformer boards are rapidly being superseded by solid-state package boards, some of which now include simple memory facilities. Courtesy of The Superior Electric Company.

capacity. Individual circuits can be switched or dimmed on and off a master with no change whatever in other circuits on the same master. Furthermore, the autotransformer dimmer is highly efficient. The only power that flows except that through the load is a small magnetizing current roughly equal to 1 percent of the capacity of the dimmer. The heat loss amounts to little more, whereas a resistance dimmer may dissipate as much as one-fourth of its capacity as heat.

How the Autotransformer Dimmer Works

Since the autotransformer has been until recently the standard unit for all direct-control (as opposed to remote-control) boards, it is necessary to know in detail how it operates. We must elaborate considerably on our discussion of back EMF in Chapter 7. You will recall that back EMF is the result of the effect of the changing magnetic field in an ac coil upon the coil itself. The result of this effect is that, if the coil is properly designed, the back voltage induced in the coil is almost equal to and of opposite polarity to that of the incoming current. The effect, of course, is that only a minute amount of electricity flows through the coil—just enough to sustain the magnetic field and to offset heat losses. The coil of an autotransformer dimmer is designed in this manner, but there is no secondary coil. If we measure the voltage available at various points along the autotransformer coil, we find that the effect of the bucking voltage is distributed along the coil in such a way that every voltage from 0 to 120 is also available somewhere on it. All that is necessary is to add a slider to tap off the varying voltage.

Elimination of the secondary saves weight, bulk, and expense with only one minor loss. Note that in the case of the two-coil transformer, the primary circuit is completely isolated electrically from the secondary. If one line of the primary is grounded, this is not reflected in the secondary, which may be considered as a new and independent electrical circuit drawing its energy from the magnetism in the core. However, in the single coil of the *auto*transformer, the grounding is associated with the output because the same wiring is common to both input and output. The primary and secondary circuitry are not clearly differentiated and it is not so easy to call the output a "new" circuit. This situation leads to some extra safety precautions, but these are no great handicap compared to the savings effected by eliminating a secondary.

Mechanical Arrangement of Autotransformer Dimmers

In practice, the autotransformer dimmer usually consists of a coil of insulated copper wire wrapped around a highly efficient laminated iron core. The outer surface of the coil has the surfaces of the wire bared and a graphite slider just wide enough to cover two wires at the most is arranged to move across it. The slider must be narrow so that it will

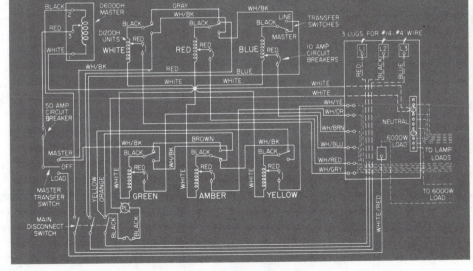

FIGURE *9-3b*
Circuit diagram for the control board shown in 9-3a.
Courtesy of The Superior Electric Company.

not contact more than two wires at the very most and it must have enough internal resistance to prevent excessive current from flowing through the closed loop formed when it does touch two turns at the same time. This loop is a potential heat source because it represents a closed circuit of low resistance to current induced in it by the changing magnetic field. The only thing that keeps it from destroying itself is the resistance of the graphite slider (brush). Thus the thickness of brushes is limited and their current-carrying capacity for large dimmers is achieved by making them long but thin. This construction makes them the most fragile part of the dimmer.

Generally the coil of the autotransformer is toroidal (doughnutlike) in shape since this is most efficient magnetically. The slider may be anywhere on the coil or even on contacts wired to it as long as the "loop" problem is taken care of.

Innovations in Control Board Location

The introduction of the autotransformer dimmer came at the same time that a number of related developments were challenging the traditional location of the control board backstage. Theatre architecture was changing; the proscenium was no longer the only format. Theatre-in-the-round and thrust stages were being designed. Concepts of lighting based on the ideas of Adolphe Appia were being put into use. These concepts demanded a close relationship between the lighting changes and movements of actors. It was increasingly difficult to accomplish such cues via a stage manager who could see little and a lighting crew who could see nothing. Therefore, it was argued that the place for the lighting control was at the back of the house where the operators could have about the same view of their work that the audience received. Cues could then be taken from directly observed business on the stage, and relayed by telephone from backstage when necessary. Although skeptics scoffed at this rational approach, it has become almost the standard for modern theatre construction in spite of the fact that some houses are still being built with the controls backstage.

The autotransformer dimmer fitted this new location well. It was heat free, almost noiseless, and well adapted to package units that could be used to fit old houses with back-of-house controls. In new installations it served well because it was adaptable to console-type control boards which could be placed in front of the operators like a desk.

Modern, highly reliable communications systems, now including closed-circuit television, have reduced to insignificance the early worries of those who feared a breakdown in communications between light booth and backstage. In fact, many of the functions of the stage manager located backstage have migrated to the "light booth" (it now includes sound equipment, video, effects controls, and perhaps even a computer). Advanced speculation looks toward the day when one back-of-house console will control all staging elements, lights, sound, effects, moving scenery, lifts, revolves, and whatever else the designer can conjure up.

Potentialities of Autotransformer Control

The autotransformer dimmer is a sensitive control device. Given enough of them, properly circuited to allow proportional mastering, a well-trained light crew can perform any operation the mind of the designer can create. The job may take several operators trained to the precision of a *corps de ballet,* but it can be done. It will be far easier if the control board is located where the crew can see the results of their work.

Characteristics of Autotransformer Dimmers: Voltage versus Light Output

The nature of autotransformer dimmers is that they alter the voltage they put out linearly with respect to the movement of the operating handle. Since the light output of the lamps is somewhat nearer to an exponential curve with regard to voltage, it is a common characteristic of autotransformer units that the bottom half of the scale—1 to 5 on the usual dimmer scale—offers roughly one-third of the total light available; the top half contains the rest. Theoretically this division sounds like more of a handicap to smooth dimming than it turns out to be in practice. Operators soon adjust to this state of affairs, and if they are not told about its existence, are often unaware of it. Some makes of larger autotransformer units have been wound with a *tapered* coil to overcome this difficulty. In such a coil the distribution of windings is altered so that fewer windings are encompassed in the movement of the slider from 1 to 5 than from 5 to 10. This distribution is a convenience, particularly in master dimmers where subtlety is critical.

OPERATIONAL PROBLEMS AND MAINTENANCE

Probably the chief mechanical danger to smooth dimming of a large autotransformer dimmer is the inertia of the relatively heavy parts that must be moved to change the reading. In 6000-watt dimmers there is a perceptible "flywheel effect" that tends to make the operator overshoot his mark occasionally, carrying him past the specified reading. Also, slight departures from the proper tension on the pivot mechanism can cause the dimmer to drift toward its off position or to offer sticky resistance to movement if it is too tight. These are relatively minor maintenance chores, but they may brand an innocent control board operator with ineptness when the dimmers really are at fault. Consult the maintenance instructions for the particular brands of dimmers for details in adjusting tensions.

General maintenance chores with autotransformer dimmers consist of frequently checking the brushes for wear and replacing brushes immediately on any dimmer that develops a flicker or sparks perceptibly during operation. Connections to and within the dimmers should also be checked often because the magnetic field causes constant vibration. Occasional dusting of the slider contact is permissible and desirable under dusty conditions, but no lubricant should be applied to the slider surface unless instructions specifically call for it. Generally any grease or oil on the slider surface merely holds dirt and speeds the time when the dimmer must be removed from the control board and carefully cleaned with solvents and perhaps the slider surfaces polished with crocus cloth. This operation should be performed only by a carefully trained and most responsible maintenance man.

Autotransformer dimmers have long life—not as long as that of resistance units, but often as long as the useful life of a theatre today. The main causes of failure are loose and worn brushes which have been allowed to arc and thus destroy part or all of the copper windings upon which they bear, loose connections in or under the connection plate of the dimmer which result in overheating and destroy parts, continuous overloading, and heavy handling. Of course, incorrect wiring or connection to a dc circuit can ruin a brand-new dimmer in a fraction of a second. Since smaller sizes are relatively inexpensive, it is common to discard them if they develop any major fault. Larger units can be rebuilt with good success if the windings have not been damaged.

A symptom of old age in the autotransformer dimmer is inability to carry the designed load without overheating and often without dropping the reading of the lamps further than the setting indicates. These symptoms indicate that the copper surface of the windings which contacts the sliding brush has worn away materially. No economical remedy is available for this but the life of the dimmer can be extended by downrating it to perhaps 50 percent of its original capacity and carefully maintaining good brushes in it. This procedure will often stave off incipient disaster until the end of a season or until the budget will stand the price of a new dimmer.

SWITCHING SURGES

A word of caution is in order for those who attempt to repair or renovate autotransformer control boards. The magnetic principle on which autotransformers operate makes them produce large surges of current when they are turned on or off by a switch controlling their input. This is exactly the condition of a switch installed to choose between "master" and "line." It must turn the power to the transformers off and on in rapid succession. Standard "T" rated switches used for house and industrial wiring will not withstand this surge for very long. They fail spectacularly in a flash of fire and smoke. The best solution is to install switches supplied as replacement parts by the manufacturer of the original equipment, or to install industrially available switches designed to control fluorescent-lighting circuits. Properly designed fluorescent-light ballasts have surge characteristics very similar to those found in autotransformers, and switches designed for this service will work well. "T" rated two-way household switches should be installed only as an emergency stopgap measure; early failure may be anticipated.

Multislider Dimmers

It is appropriate to digress for a moment from our discussion of lighting control in the United States to note what was happening in Europe, particularly Germany, during this period (1920–1940). Development of the autotransformer in Europe took a different turn than in the United States because of certain basic patent rights that were not made available to the United States until after World War II. These patents covered an ingenious combination of the step-down power transformer that supplied the stage and the transformer dimmer known as the "Bordoni System." Under this arrangement the 110- or 230-volt coil (European stages often supply higher voltages to lamps than those supplied in the United States) was wound on the outside of the step-down transformer and its surface bared much as the surface of the coil in an autotransformer dimmer is bared. Then multiple sliders were arranged to operate on this surface, each of them feeding a stage-lighting circuit. Of course, each slider was provided with overcurrent protection equal to its current-carrying capacity. Since this system involved proximity to the primary distribution voltage (perhaps 6000 to 8000 volts) the whole affair was enclosed in a room in the basement and the sliders operated remotely by complicated wire-and-pulley arrangements, susceptible to some degree of mechanical mastering. Such a system must be said to meet the minimum requirements of remote dimmer control although most of the advantages of electrical remote control do not accrue.

Since World War II, the patent on the multiple-slider system has been available in the United States. Since United States safety standards frown on the proximity of high voltages, the only application has been in the multiple-slider autotransformer unit. Purchasers of this unit should be aware that, while it has all of the usual advantages of autotransformers, it also offers certain complications in computing the load imposed upon it. Two factors must be considered: (1) the overall capacity of the unit and (2) the capacity of the individual slider. Usually the capacity of the entire unit is less than the sum of the capacities of the sliders. Thus the existence of six 1000-watt sliders does not mean that there are six 1000-watt dimmers available. More than likely, the overall capacity is nearer 4000 watts.

10 REMOTE CONTROL OF STAGE LIGHTING

Introduction

Major developments in the remote control of stage lighting began in the United States at the end of World War II. Technological spin-off from the war and the presence of a large supply of war-surplus parts at low prices spurred a period of intense development. This has now resulted in the replacement of manually operated dimmers by electronic devices. These electronic dimmers have become so cheap that they have superseded manual devices even in locations where there is no need for remote control, such as dimmer-switch installations for controlling a single light in the home.

Moreover, cost is rapidly decreasing to the point where control-board designers are questioning the notion of the interconnecting panel or patch bay. In the near future it will probably be cheaper to provide a dimmer for each load circuit than to install a patch bay. Control interpatching will allow for a rational arrangement of controllers. A bit farther in the future another possibility seems likely: The interpatch function may be taken over by a computer device which will scan a rack of dimmers assigning them to lighting changes as needed. A dimmer will serve a given circuit only for as long as it is needed, then be released by the computer to await further service elsewhere. Such search and assign operations can be performed faster than an operator can move a controller handle calling for a dimmer.

The present state of the art suggests that the era of remote control is soon going to blend into the era of computer-assisted theatre. The theatre artist will be able to design, cue, and operate not only the lighting but the entire visual production from a console elaborately provided with memory devices, simulators, and other forms of computer technology that will enable him to control functions now under the guidance of several people because it is presently nearly impossible for one artist to cope with this many cues at once. Such computer-assisted control may well bring the Appian concept of the theatrical master-artist into possibility.

Before we look toward these ideas of the future, we must look at the concept which has made it all possible: *remote control.*

Remote Control

The idea of remote control of electrical circuitry is not new, either in or out of the theatre. For many years it has been common practice to use simple remote control to avoid placing huge main switches backstage, and to make it possible to switch houselights on and off from a number of locations. Similarly, motors and heavy loads of all sorts have been controlled by small remote switches for a long time. A brief study of these simple situations will clarify the concept of remote control, help in the understanding of these circuits which are still standard in theatres, and serve as an introduction to more sophisticated remote applications.

In the simplest form, a remotely controlled switch is simply an on-off electromagnet that pulls or pushes the handle of a large switch. Whenever the power is fed to the coil of the magnet, the switch is closed, and whenever the magnet power is turned off, the switch opens by spring pressure. Of course the opposite situation would be just as easy to arrange. There are advantages even in this simplest system that make it worth the additional expense and complication of the electromagnet. These advantages are:

1. The large switch can be located wherever the demands of a short run of the heavy feed and load wires indicate, as long as it is accessible for occasional servicing. This saves a considerable sum of money that might be spent to buy long runs of heavy copper wire and the conduit in which they would have to be run. For a 200-ampere houselight main, for example, this might mean a saving of $5 to $10 per foot of wiring run.
2. Large switches are noisy. Hence the need to locate them well away from the stage and house can be met by using the remote switch.
3. Many large switches must be turned on and off with considerable force—if they are not, they tend to spark badly and wear out before the end of their normal lifetime. Timid operators may be apt to approach them indecisively and damage them. The electromagnet can be counted on to operate the switch with precision every time.
4. The large size of the main switch would make it unsightly. A small control switch will be no more obvious than any home light switch.

Already an impressive list of arguments favoring remote control has been assembled and we have cited as an example the most primitive of the lot. Economics alone will often determine the use of remote switches for houselight control, stage mains, and the like. In order to understand the full potentialities of remote switching, let us examine some of the refinements of the remotely controlled switch. These switches are commonly called *relays* or *contactors*. The latter term usually is applied to them when they are used to control motors. In that application they generally combine the functions of control switch and circuit breaker.

The simple relay described above has certain disadvantages for practical use, the chief one being that the coil must be energized either all the time the switch is on or all the time it is off. This necessity complicates coil construction because heating from both resistance and induction will occur. Induction can be avoided if the relay is operated on direct current, but unless a supply is already at hand, obtaining it will create a needless expense. Coils for 110-volt ac are easy and inexpensive to make, and work well for intermittent service. The solution to the problem is mechanical. A latching device is provided so that all the coil has to do is to turn the switch to on or off, and it is held there mechanically. This arrangement can be achieved with one coil and a latching device that alternately latches the switch on and off. The control switch at the remote location becomes merely a push button. Every other push turns the circuit on, and every other one off. This arrangement is satisfactory whenever the operator of the switch can see the results of his work, and when an occasional mistake in turning the circuit on or off will do no harm.

A more precise way of doing the job is to use two electromagnetic coils. One turns the switch on and is latched mechanically. The other releases the latch and spring tension opens the switch. In this case the remote position consists of two push buttons, one for on and one for off. Each is spring loaded and makes contact only while held down. Current flows in the coils only for a fraction of a second and heating is no problem. Also on-off operation is always certain. Now let us examine the added potentialities of the latching or two-coil relay, or both:

1. Since the remote stations are only small momentary-contact buttons, these may be duplicated as many times as necessary. There is no longer the danger that the coil will be left on for long periods of time to overheat. Thus the houselights, for example, can be controlled from positions right and left backstage, from the back of the house, from the projection booth, and perhaps from the box office. At each station only two small buttons are needed and the wires leading to them can be small. It is common practice to go to the additional expense of installing pilot lights in locations where the results of pushing the buttons cannot be seen. These lights are usually very small lamps operated from the same circuit as the houselights, but they may be fed from a separate circuit operated by another set of contacts on the relay.

2. Another advantage of the relay is that it can operate many circuits at the same time, in various combinations of on and off, from the same coil. Until recently, telephone exchange circuitry consisted of

an elaborate arrangement of relays that made the connections to complete a call by following the instructions of the dial signal.

3. Master switches and lockout switches become easy and cheap to install. For example, a small switch cutting off the power supply for the coils of a large number of relays (still a rather small amount of current because each coil uses no more than about one-half an ampere) will effectively lock off a system without the necessity of turning off the main switch and perhaps disturbing clocks and other such devices that should run continuously. Master switches can be arranged that will control groups of relays either depending on the setting of individual switches or overriding those settings. Thus a series of "nondim" circuits of stage lighting can be controlled in groups or singly. Tiny "two-way" (SPDT) switches provide the options of "on," "off," or "master" for each circuit. The relay equipment is merely a series of simple off-on locking relays which obey the command of whatever pulse of current comes their way. *Note that there is no large master switch or relay although its function may be served by setting all of the individual controls to "master" and operating another small switch marked "master."* Understanding of this principle is exceedingly important to further understanding of remote control. The function of master control is, in a remote system, taken over entirely by small equipment—no large master switch is needed for control. Of course in houselighting control and the stage main switch, there is a large master relay because it is necessary that one be able to cut the entire system off the power line for servicing. However in the case of such things as a group of nondim circuits, a series of small motor controls for a fan system, or any one of thousands of other applications, there is no master relay; the master button merely controls the power supply to each of the many individual relays. This feature alone often makes remote-control systems desirable economically.

Notice that remote control opens vast possibilities for multiple-control locations, otherwise impossible control locations, and for the ganging together of controls. Furthermore, additional control such as submastering becomes quite economical of both money and space since only small toggle switches or push buttons are needed. The ingenious reader will soon see further possibilities for flexibility by using multiple-contact relays to control still other multiple-contact relays, for sequencing events electrically by use of time-delay devices, and for other operations. This way leads to all of the potentialities of automation.

Remote Dimming

Note that until now our discussion has centered around switching. Relays are devices for turning a circuit on or off. One of their virtues is the speed and precision with which they do this. Thus relay applications on stage have been limited to houselights, stage master and sub-master circuits, and to nondim circuits. Even in the case of the house-lights, on-off control is not theatrically desirable, but often is used with or without the addition of dimming equipment because of the need for multiple-location control. The addition of a special set of contacts or a special relay to the system makes possible a "panic" system that will override any other setting of the houselights, and provide light for the audience in case of emergencies.

Motor-Driven Dimmers

Remote adjustment of the intensity of a lighting circuit involves more complications than off-on control. However, where speed of change need not be varied, a relatively simple system has often been used. A fractional-horsepower electrical motor can be geared down to a slow speed and attached to the shaft of an autotransformer dimmer or a group of such dimmers on a common shaft. The motor must be reversi-ble and limit switches must be provided at the full-on and full-off positions of the dimmer so that the motor will not try to turn the dim-mer further than it will go. Remote locations are simply two push buttons marked "raise" and "lower." The operator holds down the appropriate button until the lights are set to the reading he wishes. A pilot light or voltmeter may be provided to aid the operator if he can-not see the lighting circuit being controlled. Note that there is no con-trol over the speed of change except by "pulsing" the control button to operate the motor in a series of small starts and stops. This pulsing usually is seen as uneven changes in the lighting and in any event cannot speed up the change, only slow it down. Such controls were often installed for houselight dimming or for sequenced patterns of dimming of lights in such things as illuminated fountains. Here relays operate various dimmers in sequence, each taking its cue from the movement of the previous one in the sequence.

Since control over the rate of change is vital to stage lighting, this simple motor-driven mechanism has never found use in a stage-light-ing control. Several variations of this motor-driven mechanism were tried on stages, but all exhibited limited speed of control and usually considerable delay in responding to signals for change. Their expense and complexity militated against further refinements and they were never very common.

History of the Remote Control of Stage Lighting

In the years since the end of World War II the development of remote-controlled devices for stage lighting has proceeded at a rapid and some-what erratic pace. Since many of the various devices developed are still in use throughout the country, it is necessary to examine them in de-tail. Fortunately the principles involved in their operation are, for the most part, applicable to the latest dimmers. Therefore, the following brief history will serve to introduce the reader to equipment which he may encounter and to principles which will aid his understanding of new equipment.

The Saturable Reactor

It is almost axiomatic of developments in the area of stage lighting that the first development of whatever device is under discussion takes place far from the theatre and with little thought of theatrical application. This is the case regarding the first successful remote-control dimmer. Actually it predates the autotransformer dimmer somewhat. Relatively early in the study of ac phenomena, the *saturable reactor* was developed and refined as a means of subtly controlling large amounts of current. This device then was applied to the control of high-current welding circuits, motor controls, and similar devices that called for precise control of large amounts of current. Ultimately it was used in the theatre.

HOW SATURABLE REACTORS WORKED

The saturable reactor used a relatively small amount of direct current to control a huge amount of alternating current. The control was effected by magnetizing the laminated iron core of the transformerlike coils of the reactor with direct current. The continuous magnetism produced by the direct current destroyed the back EMF that would otherwise have been produced in the coils by the alternating current. Without the back EMF, the coils will conduct the alternating current offering only their resistance to the flow, a negligible item. The magnetizing direct current is fed to the reactor through a special control coil that contains a large number of turns of fine wire making it possible for a small direct current to saturate the core magnetically. As this direct current is increased, the back EMF is reduced and the lamps fed by the reactor come on.

Early saturable reactors were operated by controlling the direct current through small resistance dimmers. This primitive control system suffered from all of the loading problems of any other resistance system and made mastering difficult.

REFINEMENTS IN CONTROL OF DIRECT CURRENT

It was not long ago before researchers realized that they might gain great advantages by producing the direct current in controlled amounts using circuitry common to radio power supplies. Fractions of amperes of direct current were being produced and exactly controlled in radio and associated circuits using vacuum tubes. These amounts were nearly enough to control a saturable reactor. By substituting a small amount of certain gases for the vacuum in a tube rectifier, larger amounts of current could be controlled, although with certain complications beyond the scope of our present discussion. These tubes, named *thyratrons*, produce direct current in relatively large quantities and can control it closely under the proper conditions.

At first, thyratron tubes were available only in small sizes. These were used to produce and control the amount of direct current fed to the control coils of saturable reactors, one or two thyratrons providing a separately controllable dc source for each. Since the amount of direct current was somewhat larger than previously had been available for this use, the speed of the reactors was increased significantly by the brute-force technique of feeding them heavier direct current. But the greatest advantage was in the control circuitry. The heavy ac controller was twice removed from the remote device in the hand of the operator. That remote controller now was analogous to a volume control in a radio set—essentially a voltage-setting device which told the thyratron how much direct current to feed to the saturable reactor. The controllers no longer exhibited the loading problems they had when they were simply miniature resistance dimmers. The door was now wide open to every kind of grouping and multiplying of controls that the mind of ingenious switchboard designers could conjure up. A single reactor might, at times, answer the command of as many as a dozen controllers acting together. None of these controllers was called upon to handle significant amounts of current. All were miniature devices. As in switching by relays, the mastering functions were completely absorbed in the remote devices and the power-handling equipment remained simply a rack of individual reactors obeying master commands in unison and individual commands separately. Unlike a manual autotransformer board, there was no need for a huge master dimmer to handle the whole load. Only a master controller was needed.

DIFFICULTIES WITH SATURABLE REACTORS

As far as the potentialities for organizing control consoles to fit the artistic demands of stage lighting instead of the engineering demands of heavy current-carrying equipment was concerned, the millennium had arrived. However, the thyratron-controlled saturable reactor still was far from perfect. It lagged rather dismally. It was heavy and very expensive. Only a few were installed.

Thyratron Tube Dimmers

The next step was the development of thyratrons capable of producing and controlling large amounts of current themselves. It was soon apparent that these could be operated in pairs to control an ac circuit of the capacity of small- and medium-sized stage-lighting circuits. The control device became the dimmer. The reactor was relegated back to the spot-welding room except for the largest of lighting loads.

This pure thyratron dimmer was largely the result of research and development by George Izenour of Yale University. It brought instantaneous control to stage-lighting remote systems for the first time. However, cost and noise were still high and the life of the large thyratron tubes—the heart of this dimmer—was limited. Nevertheless, these boards were rather widely accepted in installations which could afford them, and some of these are still in operation.

HOW THE THYRATRON DIMMER WORKS: GATING

In spite of the rather short life of the thyratron dimmer as the ultimate in remote-control units, it will be wise to learn something of its operation because the application of this information will help us to understand its modern replacement. The thyratron is essentially a gating device; it "opens its gate" and allows current to flow under certain circumstances. It does not directly control the amount of flow, only when that flow commences. The only way that the flow can be stopped in a thyratron once it has "fired," that is, current has commenced to flow, is to turn off the power outside of the tube. Fortunately this automatically happens twice for every cycle of alternating current as the voltage goes to zero and reverses direction. Thus if a thyratron can be told to start carrying current halfway through a pulse of alternating current, it will carry the current for the rest of that pulse and return automatically to its nonconductive state as the voltage goes to zero (see Figure 10-1). Since it will conduct current only in one direction, it cannot fire during the next half wave pulse because the polarity is wrong. Therefore it rests for 1/120 second or more and fires again with the coming of the next pulse whose polarity matches its hookup. Operating singly, a thyratron could be made to produce controlled pulses of current, all in the same polarity, for every other half cycle of the incoming alternating current. Two of them together are commonly used to fire alternating half cycles and thus take advantage of every pulse in the alternating current. These intermittent pulses of electrons are evened out by the lamp filament which heats up in proportion to their average value. The smaller the increment from each half wave that is allowed to flow, the dimmer the lamp. Firing-control devices for thyratrons are essentially voltage-setting devices that ultimately determine when, during each half wave, a tube will fire and thus how much energy will reach the lamps. These devices were already in existence well before the development of large thyratrons capable of carrying lamp loads themselves.

TUBE BOARD PROBLEMS

The greatest virtue of the thyratron dimmer was its speed and its nearly complete lack of sensitivity to load. The greatest difficulty with the "tube board," as these came to be known, was its high cost coupled with the unknown life of the tubes, although experience has now shown this to be long. Replacement cost of the tubes was high. Failures were hard to anticipate; techniques were worked out that eased this situation somewhat. In the case of television work, the rapid change from nonconductive to conductive state in the tubes, produced electronic noise problems in the television gear and necessitated the addition of filters which added still more to the cost. Finally, the tubes had a warm-up time of several minutes which had to be rigidly observed — time-delay relays were installed to assure this. This delay meant that the entire tube bank must be "warmed up" in advance of the use of even one dimmer, which used up the life of the tubes and also consumed rather large amounts of power keeping the tubes warm. A power outage, however short, meant that the entire warm-up cycle had to be repeated.

Figure 10-1 illustrates not only the operation of a thyratron dimmer but that of all more recent remote-control units. All operate on the principle of "gating." This means that the dimming unit controls the power flowing to the lamp by an on-off action. The timing of this action determines what percentage of each ac cycle passes to the lamp and this in turn is averaged by the lamp in its light output. The steep wave front caused by the change in condition of the gate from off to on is the major cause of both electronic and acoustical noise from circuits operating from such dimmers. Note that it always takes two gates to take advantage of both halves of each cycle of alternating current.

Magnetic Amplifiers

While the tube boards were being developed (there were others under development at the time Izenour put his on the market), the transformer manufacturers were not inactive. They went quietly about the job of developing the primitive saturable reactor into a highly sophisticated control device. More was at stake here than the stage-lighting control market. Advances in electronics made the market for accurately adjustable power-control devices broader every day.

The first major breakthrough for the transformer developers came with post-World War II development of new magnetic alloys that were much more sensitive to magnetic fluctuations than anything previously available. These were produced in thin tapes which made the lamination of a highly sensitive core into a winding job instead of a sheet metal job. The thin tapes also reduced eddy-current losses to new minimums. The result was new saturable reactors of higher speed and greater efficiency.

These reactors were then piled electrically one atop the other to produce the *magnetic amplifier* wherein their final full-power stage was equipped with silicon rectifiers. These rectifiers also were a postwar development—a device that allowed current to flow in only one direction much like a thyratron but using the junction layer between two

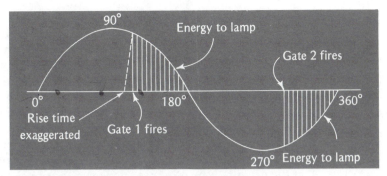

FIGURE *10-1*

Gating Devices. This drawing illustrates how thyratrons, SCRs, and triacs "chop" the normal sine wave to govern the amount of current reaching the lamp. The left portion of the illustration also shows in exaggeration the nature of "rise time." The actual rise time of an unaltered SCR or triac is so fast that it could not be illustrated in proper scale on a drawing of this size.

kinds of silicon alloy. They were inert, stable devices of very long life and were relatively inexpensive. It was obvious that these developers were aiming at the most vulnerable points in the thyratron's defenses—its limited life and its warm-up requirements.

The result of this development was a device with no moving parts, no vacuum or gaseous tubes with their warm-up and heating losses, a minute time lag measured in hundredths of a second, and with the fantastic ability to control thousands of watts of alternating current with about 0.004 ampere of current at 0 to 10 volts dc.

Like the saturable reactor, the magnetic amplifier was heavy and expensive. But it was soon developed into an efficient, relatively maintenance-free, long-life device whose cost was significantly lower than that of the tube dimmer. It required no warm-up time, and the current it drew to keep the magnetic field saturated was considerably lower than that which the tubes required for filament heating. For these reasons, the magnetic amplifier soon replaced the tube dimmer as market leader during the 1950s. It enjoyed almost exclusive control of the market during that period in both the United States and in Europe. Its low control-current requirements and nearly instantaneous response offered console designers the opportunity to concentrate their efforts on devising control devices with a minimum of concern for the engineering difficulties produced by control-current problems.

Solid-State Control

The magnetic amplifier was to have only a short period of prominence in the lighting-control market. Thyratron tubes were obsolete, but the transistor and its many descendants were rapidly coming into their own. The transistor, which was developed in 1947–1948 by William B. Shockley and others, is a device based on the current-conducting properties of semiconductors. These are materials which, under certain conditions, exhibit the property of conducting electricity in one direction only. It was discovered early in the 1930s that application of voltage at right angles to the conducting layer of some semiconductors had a controlling effect on the current they were carrying. These findings eventually resulted in the development of the transistor, a device which produces the same type of control over the flow of an electrical current that the vacuum tube provides. However, the transistor has no vacuum, requires no heater, and works at much lower voltages. It is also much smaller. Unfortunately for lighting control, it is a low-current device.

The Silicon-Controlled Rectifier (SCR)

One of the outgrowths of the development of the transistor was the development of the silicon-controlled rectifier. (The SCR is known as the "thyristor" in Europe.) It functions in a circuit almost in the same manner as a thyratron. It gates the current in the same way and has the same property of controlling only the time when the current begins to flow, not the cutoff point. SCRs soon were manufactured in sizes capable of handling stage loads. Dimmers were constructed using pairs of them in circuits much like those used for thyratrons. Early SCR dimmers had some unfortunate characteristics which have since been largely overcome. They were extremely sensitive to surges and reverse voltage pulses. Hot patching (plugging a lamp into a live circuit) would often destroy them.

ADVANTAGES OF MODERN SCRs IN DIMMERS

In a properly designed circuit, the modern SCR has the following advantages over the magnetic amplifier and earlier dimmers:

1. Low cost. No other device can presently match the cost of SCR dimmers per watt of lamp load controlled. As a result, magnetic amplifier dimmers are no longer manufactured in the United States, although they are still being made in Europe.
2. Small size and light weight. SCRs are tiny devices; one capable of handling 12,000 watts is only about the size of the end of one's thumb. It weighs a few ounces. Unfortunately the auxiliary equipment needed to operate the SCRs is much larger and heavier than the SCRs themselves. Nevertheless, an SCR dimmer will be much lighter and less bulky than a magnetic amplifier or an autotransformer dimmer of like capacity.
3. Efficiency. There is no need for heater current; SCRs dissipate rela-

tively little heat and cause relatively little drop in voltage. Ninety-seven percent overall efficiency is not uncommon in SCR dimmers.

4. Long life. SCRs are an inert device with a long life if operated in a properly engineered circuit.

DISADVANTAGES OF SCR DIMMERS

SCRs generate objectionable noise of three types. The almost instantaneous response which they have (far faster than required for stage lighting) generates hum at the dimmers themselves which may be particularly objectionable in package units.

They also generate radiation at radio frequencies which may enter the circuitry of sound systems and cause intolerable interference. The wave form produced by the gating action (Figure 10-1) is the culprit. The vertical portion of the graph at the point where the SCR fires represents an exceedingly fast change in current value. This generates the noise. The same wave form can cause lamp filaments to "sing." Lamp sing is more troublesome in T.V. studios where the lamps may be near a sensitive microphone, but it can cause trouble in theatres too. Filament sing is caused by the rapid change in current value as the SCR fires; however, it is aggravated by certain types of filament design. To alleviate this problem, lamp manufacturers make what are known as "low noise" lamps for use in places where lamp noise is a serious problem. Such lamps cost more than regular lamps.

SCRs are inherently sensitive to surges. Early SCR dimmers were somewhat notorious for this problem. An inadvertent hot patch or a line surge might destroy the SCRs. Modern engineering has reduced the problem but at the cost of adding expensive and bulky parts to dimmers. Much more conservative ratings of SCRs have proven to be one of the best solutions.

SCRs are sensitive to heat. SCRs have a top temperature limit which cannot be exceeded without near-instantaneous destruction of the SCR. This problem is related to their sensitivity to surges. Dimmer banks must be kept cool. In many cases manufacturers recommend air conditioning the dimmer room and may install an interlock which will cut off the system if the air conditioning fails.

In spite of these difficulties, the SCR has become the standard dimmer unit in the United States and England and is encroaching on the magnetic amplifier on the continent. To some extent, the SCR is being superseded by the triac in the manufacture of small-wattage dimmers.

The Triac

The triac is a device using the conducting properties of silicon much in the manner of the SCR. However, unlike the SCR, only one triac is required to make a dimmer. Separate portions of the triac conduct current in each half of the alternating-current wave; the control layer is common to these.

There is considerable engineering controversy about the triac as a theatre dimming device. Some manufacturers use them in their small-wattage dimmers (say, under 3000 watts); others will have no part of them. Skillful engineering and willingness to make adjustments for engineering quirks of triacs which are beyond the scope of this text, seem to be at the center of this controversy. The dimmer buyer would be well advised to consider the overall reliability of the manufacturer and his willingness to guarantee his product as more important than whether or not he uses triacs in some of his dimmers. As far as operation of the dimmer is concerned, there is no perceptible difference between a dimmer made with SCRs and one made with triacs.

TRIACS IN NONTHEATRICAL DIMMERS

Because of their adaptability to simple circuitry and their low cost, triacs have become almost the standard device in small wall dimmers designed for nontheatrical use. Such dimmers are now even being made small enough to screw into a lamp socket below the lamp and control its intensity. While wall dimmers are not intended for theatre use, many of them do appear in little theatres. Users should not expect theatre-dimmer performance from them. They generate more noise of all types and have little of the surge resistance of theatre dimmers. Of course, their wattage capacity is low and should probably be down-rated even further for theatre applications. In many cases the finned aluminum wall plate is the heat sink for the triac and can be expected to get quite warm.

Modern Solid-State Dimmers

A well-engineered, properly installed modern solid-state dimmer is a very reliable device whose tiny control current and sensitivity open the way for concentration on designing a console around lighting functions, not engineering problems. Many such dimmers are being manufactured. However the pressure of the marketplace and some very real differences of opinion about what constitutes a satisfactory dimmer have also led to the manufacture for sale of a number of less-than-satisfactory units. It should be clear that the following discussion refers to stage-lighting dimmers, not to wall dimmers adapted to stage use.

Buying dimmers for a theatre is not a simple task. Most buyers are advised to retain the services of a good theatre consultant if they intend to spend a sizable sum for dimmers. His fee will be more than compensated for by long-term savings. The following discussion is offered in the hope that it will help to substantiate the arguments of a would-be purchaser for retaining a consultant. It will also give the buyer some idea of the issues to be considered.

COST OF DIMMERS

In the day of manually operated dimmers, cost varied almost directly with capacity in watts. This situation started to change with the manufacture of magnetic amplifiers and has now altered almost completely. At this stage, the cost of a low-quality dimmer of, say 12,000 watts, may be equal to or even less than the cost of a high-quality dimmer of half that wattage. Moreover, cost of dimmers within a single quality range may vary only slightly as the wattage is doubled. Fortunately the general cost of dimmers has been lowered and is still dropping, so that dimmer cost is now a much smaller percentage of the cost of a lighting-control installation than it once was.

SURVEY OF SPECIFICATIONS FOR SOLID-STATE DIMMERS

The following paragraphs deal with a subject fraught with considerable controversy. Engineers and large users of dimmers differ markedly in their approach to the problem of specifying a good solid-state dimmer. Reasons for disagreement are many: unresolved matters of engineering study, personal differences concerning such subjective judgments as "tolerable" noise level, matters of economic policy in manufacturing techniques, and the like. To try to dispel some of these disagreements and to aid the buyer of dimmers in his difficult task, this writer devised a questionnaire which was sent to all major manufacturers and to a major purchaser of dimming systems. A number of answers, varying in detail, were received. The following represents an effort to compile this data, noting significant discrepancies and disagreements.

NOISE PROBLEMS

The first part of the questionnaire was directed toward the problem of noise, acoustic and electronic, generated by the steep wave front produced by SCRs. All replies agreed that the practical solution lay in the proper design of a choke. A choke is a transformerlike coil of insulated copper wire around a laminated iron core. The back EMF generated in this coil tends to increase the time it takes for the current to rise to its maximum when the SCR fires. Thus the "rise time," i.e., the time the current takes to rise from zero to full value after the SCR fires, becomes a measure of the noise which might be generated by the dimmer.

Measuring Rise Time. Rise time is stated in microseconds (millionths of a second). Figures between 250 and 1000 microseconds are common. However there is considerable variation in the manner in which the rise time is measured. A number of conditions are involved in establishing a standard method of measurement. These include such things as defining the start and finish of the rise, determining exactly when in the half-cycle of alternating current the measurement should be taken, establishing load conditions, evaluating the electrical characteristics of the supply line to the measurement apparatus, and other factors. In an effort to standardize these conditions a group of reputable engineering organizations have agreed upon a set of standards. This group includes the Illumination Engineering Society (IES), the National Electrical Manufacturers Association (NEMA), and the Institute of Electrical and Electronic Engineers (IEEE). The standard accepted by this group includes stipulations that the measurements should be made from 10 percent volts, at 90° firing angle (the worst noise condition), and other details. Unfortunately not all dimmer manufacturers have accepted this reasonable standard. In an effort to illustrate the extent to which different measurement techniques will effect the figures given for rise time, Ray Ruble, of Strand Century Inc., ran rise-time measurements on the same choke using the various techniques. The results, shown in Table 10-1 will give the reader some idea of the difficulty to be encountered in trying to compare the results of various measuring techniques.

TABLE 10-1
Rise Time in Microseconds

LOAD (WATTS)	A	B	C	D
150	400	260	175	175
500	650	420	325	320
1000	700	525	450	430
1500	700	550	480	450
2000	700	575	500	450
2500	650	550	500	450

A: Measured from 0 percent rise to 100 percent rise.
B: Measured from 0 percent rise to 95 percent rise.
C: Measured from 0 percent rise to 90 percent rise.
D: Measured from 10 percent rise to 90 percent rise—IES/NEMA/IEEE standard method.
NOTE: Rise time at 0 percent rise, 150 watt load, changes because of other variations in the methods of measurement.

Since there are many other factors which vary as these measurements are taken, the reader should not assume that this table can be used to "translate" rise-time figures from one method of measurement to another. It is reproduced merely to illustrate the degree to which figures may vary using the same choke.

It is obvious that a potential buyer should insist that rise times quoted by the various bidders be based on the same method of measurement, preferably that adopted by the engineering associations. It is equally important that the buyer be assured that the measurements were made by a competent and well-equipped measurement laboratory, preferably an independent organization. One dimmer manufacturer indicated in his reply to the questionnaire that he had little faith in many of the measurements cited, even in some cases by his own organization!

Load as It Affects Rise Time. Table 10-1 indicates that the rise time varies over a wide range as the load is changed on a dimmer. Rise time tends to increase with load, but not linearly. Thus a dimmer may display a satisfactory rise time and perform quietly while fully loaded, but may have a low rise time and be noisy at low load. Since dimmers in theatre use are commonly operated at less than full load, the IES/NEMA/IEEE standard requires that measurements be taken at 50 percent load. A still better display of dimmer characteristics can be made by preparing a graph which compares rise time with loads.

Firing Angle. Firing angle refers to the point in the cycle at which the SCR fires (see Figure 10-1). The worst condition as far as the generation of noise is concerned, is the 90° point. (It is standard practice to refer to points in the cycle in terms of degrees of rotation of a simple generator producing a sine wave.) Ninety degrees represents the peak instantaneous voltage and thus the greatest potential change during the firing of the SCR. This 90° point is best determined by an oscilloscope; merely stipulating a peak voltage is not accurate enough.

Variations within Rise Time. A simple statement that "The current rise time is 300 microseconds at 20 percent load and 800 microseconds at 90 percent load" is not sufficient. A careful display of the curve representing the rising current during these periods might bring out the fact that the rise is anything but linear. There may be periods of slow change followed by periods of rapid change. There may even be ringing or oscillations. Since rapid change in current value is the source of noise, it is important that such changes within the rise time be smoothed out by a well-designed choke and circuitry. Unfortunately, there is no industrially recognized way of indicating these variations. One authority, William Shearer of the Canadian Broadcasting Company, a large purchaser of dimmers for television applications, says that the specifications should indicate that there be no rapid pulses or ringing. Another, Steven Kleinlein of Electro Controls, Inc., says that there should be no point in the curve where the rise in current exceeds 250 microamperes per microsecond. Examination of the oscilloscope display itself while the dimmer is being varied over a wide range of load conditions and settings would be a good method of testing this item, provided the equipment were properly set up and the observer were trained in examining oscilloscope displays.

What Is a Satisfactory Rise Time? No simple answer can be given to the question "What is a satisfactory rise time?" because of the many variables discussed above. Given assurance that there are no rapid current changes, ringing, spikes, or other aberrations in the rise-time curve, and given the IES/NEMA/IEEE method of measurement, a rise time in the neighborhood of 300 microseconds at 20 percent load and of 600–800 microseconds at 90 percent load would probably bracket most quality dimmers. However, good quality quiet dimmers of some types can be expected to vary considerably from these figures. Key factors are the skill with which the measurements are made and the reputation of the manufacturer for consistency in his product.

Another approach to the problem of evaluating noise from SCR dimmers has been taken by the British Broadcasting Corporation (BBC). Its engineers have devised a means of measuring with considerable accuracy the noise produced by SCR dimmers under normal working conditions. This measurement serves as a measure of both electronic and acoustic noise. Instead of stating the noise level in terms of rise time, which is, as we have seen, not a complete description of the problem, the BBC system results in a statement of noise as microvolts. These are measured on a meter attached to their standardized measuring circuitry. The technique developed by the BBC is detailed in their pamphlet, "Interference caused by Thyristor Dimmers. Its measurement and maximum acceptable limit in a television studio."[1] This same report indicates that the BBC has solved most of its interference problems by using a specially designed microphone cable in conjunction with high-quality dimmers.

If at all possible, prospective buyers should test samples of dimmers being considered under conditions as nearly resembling those contemplated as possible. For example, in small open-stage theatres, it is quite important to determine exactly how annoying the hum from a dimmer pack will be. This is not merely a factor of loudness, but also of the frequencies involved in the hum and the acoustics of the room. Similarly, the amount of electronic noise that can be tolerated in a T.V. studio will depend, among other things, on the wiring layout of lamp circuits and microphone runs. The alternative to such testing on location is to be sufficiently conservative in writing specifications to eliminate any reasonable chance that interference will develop.

SURGE PROTECTION

There are a variety of conditions under which heavy currents or abnormally high voltages can be imposed upon a dimmer. Modern engineering has brought under control the problem of moderate voltage surges (caused, for example, by switching off a large motor) as they pass through SCRs. Current surges are a different sort of problem. Originally SCRs were exceedingly sensitive to such current surges as those caused by hot patching a lamp load. If the filament is cold when hot patched, it can produce a surge which may exceed ten times the normal hot current of the lamp. However, there is a problem which overshadows this one. Many modern theatres draw their current from exceedingly heavy power lines through large step-down transformers. If a short circuit appears in a large, heavily wired load, for example the output of a 12,000 watt dimmer, a huge current may flow through it. This current may actually exceed the capacity of the dimmer breaker to interrupt it, causing major damage to the entire system. Or the dimmer breaker may work, but the huge current flowing through the short before it can operate may cause serious damage. Moderately rated SCRs may be

---

[1] BBC Planning and Installation Department Report No. S.P.I.D./TV/1968/4.

literally blown to bits and the entire system badly damaged. Obviously, if this large surge problem is solved, the lesser problem of hot-patch surges will also be solved. The solution to the large-surge problem— sometimes known as a "crowbar short"—lies in a combination of providing enough inductance in the system to hold down such large rushes of current and the choice of SCRs with very large surge ratings. A 3000-ampere surge rating for any SCR up to and including 12,000-watt dimmers is a reasonable compromise between economics and safety. Coupled with such high-rated SCRs must be an inductor, an air-core choke, capable of holding the surge current within this figure. Given these conditions, the normal circuit breakers or fuses in the system should be able to react to massive shorts before other damage is done. Obviously any hot-patch problems will have been solved.[2]

Another device sometimes used to limit overcurrent in SCR dimmers is known as a "phase-back" circuit. This is a special circuit in the dimmer that senses overcurrents and "phases back," i.e., turns down the output of the dimmer, limiting the current to a safe amount. One such system is arranged to begin to take effect when the current increases to a few percent over the rated capacity. When it senses more current than the dimmer is rated to handle, it has the electronic effect of moving the dimmer-control handle toward zero, reducing the current. If limits were not placed on this system, it would render the overcurrent protection of the dimmer inoperative by holding output current to the nameplate rating of the dimmer no matter what happened to the load. This would be both dangerous and illegal because it would mean, for example, that a 12,000-watt dimmer could feed its full current output through a short circuit indefinitely. To prevent such a situation, the phase-back circuit is arranged to sense the amount of increase in current as an overload increases. It makes increasingly larger cuts in dimmer setting up to about 300 percent of normal current draw. Above this point, it shuts the dimmer down completely allowing no current to flow, if the regular fuse or circuit breaker has not already done this.

In spite of these precautions in the design of phase-back circuitry, many authorities will have no part of it. They still feel that it may increase the risk that a short circuit may continue to flow longer than the absolute minimum time that a circuit breaker requires to detect it and turn off.

REGULATION

"Regulation" is the technical term referring to the ability of a dimmer to maintain normal output under a wide variety of circumstances. It must be evaluated with reference to several variables:

1. Output voltage at various dimmer settings as it varies with the load imposed on the dimmer. This variation should be small, 3 percent or

[2] Data supplied by Mert Cramer, Berkey Colortran, Inc.

less from a minimum output to full load. Some authorities say that there should be no more than 1 volt variation under any load change from zero to full load. The best way to display this information is by way of a graph showing curves comparing output volts to various load percentages. Conditions of measurement should be clearly stated.

2. Output voltage at various line voltages. This type of regulation recognizes that the line voltage feeding the theatre may vary considerably, either up or down from the stipulated normal. While theatrical dimmers are not intended to be voltage regulators—i.e., special devices for correcting deviations in line voltage—they should have the effect of minimizing line voltage changes. A half-volt variation for each 5-volts change in line voltage seems a reasonable maximum figure except for conditions in which the line voltage is significantly lower than normal. Under these conditions, the dimmer should put out the line voltage at top settings (not boost the voltage) and return to its normal output for settings below those which equal or are less than the low line voltage. Again, the conditions of measurement should be clearly stated and comparisons should be made on the basis of like measurements.

3. Regulation at very small loads—minimum load. This refers to the ability of the solid-state dimmer to handle extremely small loads even at high dimmer capacity. Unlike the autotransformer dimmer, the electronic dimmer cannot be expected to handle all loads down to the tiniest lamp without losing some of its regulation. However it should be possible to handle a small spotlight, say 500 watts on a large (12,000-watt) dimmer without trouble. It should also be possible to control, without flickering or other distractions, loads much smaller than 500 watts. For example, it is often necessary to control the brightness of a property lamp with perhaps a 30-watt lamp. This may have to be done on a large dimmer because none other is available. While it may be unreasonable to expect the dimmer readings to be exactly the same at this tiny load as they would be at more normal loads, control should be possible. In some cases, especially with very small loads, it may be necessary to "ghost load" the dimmer with a few hundred watts to establish control.

4. Regulation under various thermal conditions. This refers to any drift in settings that may occur as a result of heating or cooling of the dimmers themselves within the limits set by the manufacturer. Such drift should not result in any change that would cause the dimmer to exceed the performance specifications listed under Number 5 below. Some authorities insist that thermal drift be unmeasurable.

5. Tracking with reference to control voltage. This refers to the ability of two dimmers receiving the same control voltage to produce the same output. A good standard is to insist that two dimmers operating from the same controller track each other within 1 volt from zero to full.

GROUND-FAULT PROTECTION

At the present time codes do not require that dimmers be provided with ground-fault detectors (see Chapter 8). Manufacturers are reluctant to include this feature because of the increased cost per dimmer. (One authority sets this at about $35–$50 per dimmer.) There is also the possibility that a very small ground fault may cause a sensitive detector to interrupt a circuit vital to a production. The Canadian Broadcasting Corporation suggests that the ground-fault detector be set to warn of a ground fault but not to clear the circuit. This decision is thereby left to a human being who can decide whether the continuity of the show is more important than the ground fault.

OTHER FEATURES OF SOLID-STATE DIMMERS

While the above specifications represent the most vital issues in the choice of solid-state dimmers, there are a number of other features built into many of them which should be investigated by the potential purchaser.

MODULAR CONSTRUCTION

Most solid-state dimmers are built as plug-in modules to facilitate replacement or servicing. Such plug-in arrangements should assure that the grounding pins connect before any current-carrying parts engage. Normally the plug-in feature also extends to the control-signal input part of the dimmer. This is the portion which contains the electronic circuitry that makes it possible for the minute signal current to control the SCRs. Modern manufacturing practice calls for this circuitry to be mounted on a printed circuit card which plugs into the dimmer chassis. Some manufacturers make this card removable from the front of the dimmer; others require that the dimmer be removed from the rack and disassembled to remove the card.

SERVICEABILITY

It is inevitable that dimmers will from time to time require service. Modular construction makes this much easier, but there are usually certain parts of the system that do not lend themselves to modular, plug-in construction. For example, it should be possible to remove and replace SCRs with a minimum of difficulty. Whether the potential buyer plans to do his own servicing or hire someone to do it, time and money will be saved by a dimmer constructed to enable a workman to get at parts easily.

ADJUSTMENTS

Some dimmers come from the factory adjusted and no provision is made for field adjustments. Others provide screw-locked adjustment points for such things as changes in dimmer curve, quiescent state voltage, and gain adjustments for variations in signal voltage. Test points for taking voltage readings should be available if adjustments are to be effected with ease.

OUTPUT CURVE

There has been a great deal of controversy over the "best" output voltage curve for theatre lighting control. The original standard, linear voltage, which came automatically with autotransformer dimmers, has to some extent been replaced by the "square-law curve." The latter approximates a light output which is linear with relationship to the setting of the controller. See Figure 10-2. Light output in this sense is that perceived by the eye, not a physical measurement. Most dimmers are either adjustable to these curves with variations, or can be supplied with whatever curve is desired by the user. A recent investigation tends to reveal that much of the controversy over dimmer curves is subjective; when presented with a variety of curves unidentified and randomized, most operators were unable to clearly identify the various curves. Either the linear or square-law curve offers the operator a reasonable control over the lighting. Most operators who have begun their lighting careers with autotransformer controls will find the linear curve more familiar. It offers somewhat more control at the low readings at the expense of rapid change in light near the top of the scale.

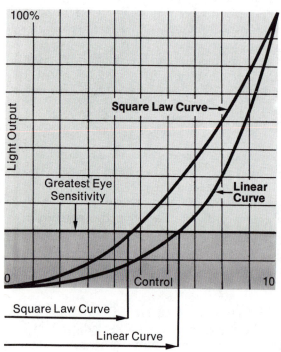

FIGURE 10-2

Dimmer Control Curves. This graph compares the two most common control curves provided by dimmer manufacturers. The curves show the light output of a lamp at various settings of the controller from 0 through 10. The "linear curve" is the oldest and most common since it is the standard curve for almost all autotransformer dimmers. The voltage varies linearly with the dimmer setting. The "square-law curve" represents a more recent attempt to make each increment of change (e.g., from 2 to 3 or from 8 to 9) on the controller produce an approximately equal light change as seen by the eye. Courtesy of Berkey Colortran.

Summary

It is obvious from the above discussion that the choice of a set of dimmer specifications is, even for an expert, a difficult thing indeed. The best evidence is careful testing of the equipment under circumstances closely resembling those in which it is to be used plus careful comparison of data developed from skilled tests done to the same standard on all equipment under consideration. In most cases the assistance of a qualified theatre consultant is recommended.

Consoles

Before the advent of remote control, the design of lighting-control boards was almost exclusively a matter of electrical engineering. Resistance or autotransformer dimmers were installed according to engineering requirements, such as heat dissipation, short electrical runs, electrical code specifications, and the like. The operator of the control board had to make the best of what engineering had provided him. The first improvement along the line of fitting the design of the control board to the needs of the operator came with the addition of interconnecting panels between the dimmers and the load circuits. This addition, within the limits of dimmer size and number, enabled the operator to group together design-related circuits, such as the circuits representing a series of closely related acting areas. More convenient operation was possible because the operator no longer faced the necessity of reaching for the dimmer operating Area I at one end of the switchboard and that operating Area III at the other. If several operators were needed—and they frequently were—they could be assigned sections of the board representing various lighting functions. For example, one man might control those dimmers representing cyclorama color. Another might handle downstage acting areas, a third, upstage areas, and so forth.

Of course there are many such installations still in operation at the present, and most stage-lighting artists can regale one with stories of complicated effects worked out by applying arms, legs, teeth, and elbows to an old board in order to move enough dimmers at one time to get the job done. The significant thing is, however, that the job was done! Any approach to sophisticated lighting-control consoles that overlooks the fact that the artistic sensibilities of the operator are more important than gadgetry, and that the potentialities of relatively primitive systems are fantastic in the hands of an artist, misses the most fundamental tenet: Human beings, not machines, create art.

Modern remote-control dimmers have largely removed the necessity for console designers to concern themselves with engineering; they are free to consider the console as an interpretive instrument designed to accommodate the needs of a human operator. However, in doing this the console designer will be well advised to keep in mind that the most elaborate and costly console does not, in itself, make more elaborate or more artistic lighting possible—the best it can do is to free the minds of the designer and the operator from concerns over mechanical and personal handicaps brought about by awkward arrangement of controls. Indeed, a basic precept for the modern console designer to follow is that the console should be to the operation of lighting what a fine violin is to a virtuoso—an almost invisible link between the concept and its interpretation.

Three Approaches to Console Design

There are at least as many ways of arranging a console as there are those who concern themselves with the problem. The art of lighting has not reached the happy state of that of violin playing—we are still in the early stages of designing the instrument. Thus there is controversy. Much of it revolves around the fact that there are a variety of conditions under which operators are expected to run consoles. The following discussion attempts to sort these out into three broad, obviously overlapping, categories.

THE BROADWAY THEATRE APPROACH

This type of operation is typified by theatres on Broadway and by shows originating there. It is heavily influenced by the special conditions which have grown up in the Broadway theatre. The practice of treating theatres as real estate ventures to be rented out for a profit, the whole complex situation generated by union labor, and, perhaps most important, the lack of permanent producing companies, have all contributed to a very special way of getting things—including lighting—done on Broadway.

Time and space are hugely expensive. Maximum utilization of theatre time is essential. Equipment rentals and salaries are high. The designer is expected to display maximum efficiency in organizing his lighting, plotting well in advance so that equipment can be rented, and conducting lighting rehearsals with a minimum of lost time. He must work with operators from the union who may or may not remain with the show once it is designed. (Some producers have operators who work with the producer—they do not necessarily stay with a show once it is "up.") Lighting cues are firmly set during rehearsals and given to the stage manager who then feeds them to lighting operators—often not the same operators—who run them night after night. Repetitive precision is essential.

Lighting-control equipment on Broadway is, by and large, primitive. This is the result of the theatre rental situation in which several theatres are still equipped with direct current. Few Broadway theatres are equipped with lighting-control equipment. Touring boards are rented and installed on a show-to-show basis. Because the rental houses want their equipment to be usable in all Broadway theatres to increase its rental potential, the two or three dc equipped theatres have caused almost all rental agencies to stock only resistance-dimmer touring boards, now at least 45 years out of date. A few electronic road boards have been built and are being tried out, but as yet, they have not caught on (see Figures 10-6e and f) on Broadway itself.

Under these conditions, it seems almost irrelevant to talk of designing consoles for "Broadway lighting." The problems arise when the "Broadway system" is applied to other theatre situations which may or may not require comparable operator functions. The Broadway practice often is held up as the ideal on the assumption that what comes from Broadway must be best. Whether or not this is now or was ever true is irrelevant; what is important is to examine the Broadway situation to find what the relationship is between operator and lighting, and discover what this implies for console design. Then, if it can be shown that another theatre situation demands the same kind of relationship, it follows that a similar console might be needed.

Two things are paramount in the organization of Broadway lighting (assuming a high level of artistic accomplishment by the lighting designer): Set-up and rehearsal time must be saved wherever possible; and, once the show is running, accurate repetition of lighting is essential. Furthermore, these things must be accomplished by operators who are not necessarily familiar with the show. Operators have relatively little initiative under Broadway conditions; their job is to repeat cues exactly as given. During rehearsals they are expected to show great ingenuity in getting complex lighting out of primitive road boards, and they usually do. During the run they make few changes of consequence.

A console designed for this situation must focus on efficient use of rehearsal time and ease of repetition of cues, once established. A memory system that "writes" cues instantly when they have been set and will play them back in sequence with great precision answers this need. Since cues in such a situation will be almost all discrete cues, the addition of a simple pile-on control for those situations where more than incoming and outgoing lighting are in operation at the same time, will provide excellent flexibility.

THE AMERICAN PROFESSIONAL THEATRE APPROACH

American theatre "grew up" on Broadway. Only recently has professional theatre attained a status of its own in major centers throughout the nation. Terminology has not yet caught up with fact. Thus we still find such terms as "regional theatre" or "off-Broadway theatre" in use. At best they tell us little about the theatres involved; at worst, they are condescending. Thus this writer has chosen to distinguish between Broadway and the rest of American professional theatre by setting Broadway off by itself instead of the rest of the country.

There are now many theatre centers in the nation as fully professional and capable of achieving a high level of artistry as Broadway. Examples are Las Vegas, Los Angeles, San Francisco, Minneapolis, and Washington, D.C., to name but a few. In terms of technical development, these areas are far ahead of Broadway because they are not hampered by the rental/touring situation or the labor practices which have grown up with that area. The result is that most of the developments in stage lighting technology have happened in these theatres and in the educational theatre.

The situation faced by the lighting operator in these theatres is typified by a greater responsibility for artistic elements, more continuity in employment with the theatre, a greater need to be able to ad lib shows of shorter duration, and the development of theatre architecture which enables him to see what he is doing.

The situation found in Las Vegas is a good example of this: Las Vegas theatre is as oriented to profit and as unionized as that in New York, but with some important differences. Operators tend to be long-time employees of the theatre. Thus their tenure includes the design stages of a production (a more leisurely process in Las Vegas although still pressured), work with the designers and talent, and finally, close contact with the running of the show, making changes as needed from night to night. Their artistic contributions are considerable, particularly during the run of a show when acts may change in order and content within the general framework of the production as it was originally set up. Operators also are often challenged with the task of creating ingenious production devices, for example complicated projector controls, which form an essential part of the production.

The implications of this situation are reflected in the location and nature of the control consoles needed. These consoles are inevitably placed in the back of the house so that the operators can see clearly exactly what is happening on the stage. Although main cues still come from the stage manager, much initiative is taken by the operator who is watching the acts progress and who is expected to make changes as needed.

Another example of a situation in which the Broadway approach is impossible is the "one-night stand." Admittedly not the artistic triumph represented by a carefully designed and rehearsed show, the one-night stand is essential to the economic health of many theatres. This situation is common to all municipal theatres, educational theatres, and any other theatres which are contracted out on short-run basis. It is not unusual in such a situation for the show to arrive at the theatre at four o'clock in the afternoon, install whatever setting it carries, and go on at eight o'clock that night with no rehearsal whatever. There is neither time nor information to set up a series of presets for the show and to arrange cues of more than the most rudimentary sort with the stage manager. This situation calls for a control console which allows the operator to rapidly set up a series of potentially useful lighting patterns and to run them off ad lib as the show progresses, preferably with some cues from someone connected with the traveling group. It is obvious that simple presets arranged to run in serial order will not suffice.

Thus the American professional theatre requires a console designed for great flexibility located to provide the operator with good visibility. The flexible console must be arranged giving first priority to accessibility of control channels for quick change. The operator should be able to arrange lighting in terms of design concepts so that he may ad lib intelligently. Memorizing cues and replaying them or being able to organize a number of presets in advance are desirable adjuncts to the operator, but these functions cannot be allowed to interfere with the operator's essential moment-to-moment artistic control of the lighting. Since timing of cues will need to be under the constant control of the operator who will accelerate or decelerate as art and necessity demand, fade controls and master controls should be carefully arranged with these functions in mind.

THE EDUCATIONAL THEATRE APPROACH

Lighting in the educational theatre is posited on a quite different set of assumptions than that in either type theatre discussed above. First of all it is important to note that the principal activity is *not* merely the training of operators. Obviously this skill must be learned, but the purposes are oriented toward creativity, not mere skill. To the extent that students in the educational theatre become artists in the professional theatre, and this is but a small percentage of the total number of students, the educational theatre is engaged in producing designer-technicians, not operators. (Union operators in the Broadway tradition come into their positions mainly through apprenticeship in the unions.) The remainder of those many students in educational theatre programs ultimately go into other professions enriched by the acculturalizing experience of creative work in the theatre arts. Thus they too, for the time they are in the educational theatre, should experience creative, not repetitive experiences. Since such students may become the most informed members of theatrical audiences of the future, this educational function should not be taken lightly. Furthermore, educational theatre productions seldom run long enough to settle into the highly predictable routine that typifies a good Broadway production.

Therefore a console for the educational theatre should be designed to enable the operator to concentrate as completely as possible on the design concepts with which he is experimenting. He should have at his disposal a variety of methods of patterning the console to facilitate the lighting patterns with which he is working. Since educational theatre is highly experimental as well as creative, consoles for its purposes should, wherever possible, leave the way open for experimentation with new control concepts and control configurations.

The Ideal Console — The Operator as Interpretive Artist

Theatrical attitudes and artistic goals are changing. Designers, particularly those at the top of the profession, are coming more and more to think of lighting in the manner in which Adolphe Appia described it in about 1897. He saw lighting as an infinitely flexible sculpture in time and space in which elements of light are "played in counterpoint" much in the manner of musical melodies. Stop-action designing, in which the designer "sets" a cue and then moves to another which he fixes in time much in the manner of stills clipped from a motion-picture film, is being replaced by patterns of lighting designed to be subtly played against other patterns in constantly changing "light-music." In such lighting, the operator becomes an interpretive artist of the stature of a fine musician. No one would deny the artistry of a Rubenstein, even though he only "plays" the music, and does not compose it. Lighting has far to go before it reaches this happy realm, but the beginnings are apparent. One of the beginnings is the creation of an instrument capable of being played with subtlety. Thus we come to the ideal console: It should be capable of almost infinite artistic manipulation with a minimum of mechanical interference between the interpretive skill and artistry of the operator and the lighting itself. It should be as unobtrusive in the artistry as a Stradivarius is in the hands of a great violinist. And to the operator it should be a hugely flexible instrument upon which he can play with few handicaps and limitations. Such a control console does not exist and probably will not for some time. Nevertheless, it is the measure against which all others should be compared except in those situations where repetition is of the utmost importance and operator artistic contributions are thereby limited. Fortunately, modern technology is capable of meeting both of these requirements reasonably well with the same equipment, although the ideal is still in the future.

Factors Governing Design of Remote-Control Consoles

The basic tenet has already been established: The console should "get out of the way." It should put as little interference as possible between design and execution. To accomplish this end, design of a control console, like the design of a musical instrument, should emanate from an understanding of what it is to produce. Thus we must analyze the kinds of lighting cues which will be operated on our machine.

BASIC TYPES OF LIGHTING CUES

There are three types of lighting cues, each one more complicated than its predecessor.

SNAP CUES

The simplest of all lighting cues are snap cues. They consist of simply turning something on or off. A switch or a series of switches arranged to operate one or more at a time will suffice. Timing is important of course, but it is rudimentary. Although such cues can be easily operated from switches, they are often taken on dimmer circuits because the same lights need to be controlled in more complex ways at other times. This may pose problems, especially with old dimmers which lag, but operators soon learn to anticipate this. The sheer simplicity of snap cues merits them little further discussion.

DISCRETE CUES[3]

Discrete cues are those in which a change in the lighting is performed over a preestablished period of time with clearly established start and finish, and with the rate of change substantially constant throughout this period of time. The change may be simple or complex as to the number of instruments involved, and it may be simple and almost unnoticed or drastic as far as the audience is concerned, but it represents a discrete unit of lighting, separated in time from other changes and homogeneous in tempo.

Such cues are also sometimes known as "stop action" or "set" cues because they are somewhat analogous to a frame clipped from a motion picture; they represent a stable condition which will eventually be replaced by another stable condition. A great percentage of the lighting done today consists of this type of cue. The results of this type of cuing can be exceedingly complex; a high level of lighting artistry can result.

COUNTERPOINT CUES[4]

Counterpoint cues probably have their origin in the works of Adolphe Appia, particularly in his description of the lighting for the second act of *Tristan und Isolde*.[5] Although now over 75 years old, this description still challenges the artistry and technology of modern lighting. Appia was concerned with the production of Wagnerian opera and related his analysis to music. However the concepts prove equally valid for spoken drama although the analysis of the rhythmical structure of spoken drama is somewhat more difficult. Describing this type of lighting is best done in musical terms since it is in many ways analogous to music. Hence we use the term, "counterpoint," to describe it. Counterpoint is a musical technique, exemplified by Bach, in which melodies are played against each other during the same time period. In counterpoint lighting, various elements of lighting (patterns) are "played"

[3] Discrete cues were called "type one" cues in the first edition of this book.
[4] These were called "type two" cues in the first edition of this book.
[5] See Adolphe Appia, *Music and the Art of the Theatre*, transl. Robert W. Corrigan and Mary Douglas Dirks. Coral Gables, Fla.: University of Miami Press, 1962, appendix.

against each other in time and space to form a complex rhythmical structure in harmony with and inseparable from the movements of the actors. "Patterns" of lighting may be such things as arrangements of warm or cool sidelights, keys, fills, special high keys, and the like. Such patterns played in counterpoint in conjunction with the carefully patterned movements of the actors may create a tremendously flexible sculpture in time and space analogous to a musical fugue.

It is obvious that such lighting can be broken down into minute "stills" each of which can be set on the control board as a preset. If these presets are then run off at the proper speed, the results will be a reproduction of the original complex lighting. Similarly, musical counterpoint can be broken down by means of a transcription device into a series of squiggly grooves on a piece of plastic and the music can be reconstructed from these grooves. However, neither the myriad of presets nor the grooves in the record represent a humanly discernible image of the rhythmic structure of the art work. This is the fundamental difference between discrete and counterpoint cues: Breaking discrete cues into presets leaves the rhythmic structure visible; doing the same to counterpoint cues dissolves the rhythm into invisibility. In addition, breaking counterpoint lighting into presets is a prodigious task. It may take as long as several hours to break a few minutes of counterpoint lighting into enough presets to enable an operator to reproduce it satisfactorily. In far less time a sensitive operator-interpreter can learn to "play" the elements of the counterpoint against each other with great effectiveness and the advantage of being able to make moment-to-moment changes to follow the minor variations in actor movement. To achieve this, the operator must know precisely what the lighting design is intended to do and he must have a clear view of the stage. He also needs a console which will facilitate his interpretive efforts.

CONSOLE SIZE

One-man operation of consoles is coming to be the accepted mode, even in Broadway-type setups. As interpretive responsibility on the part of the operator grows, this is more and more inevitable. This tendency is already evident in the reluctance of preset console manufacturers, particularly in England, to make monster consoles containing hundreds of preset controllers. Many of these have been made in the United States (see Figure 10-4). They often exceed the capability of one man to operate them. Such consoles do, when well planned, concentrate the responsibility for major cue operation in one person. Assistants are required to arrange presets and perform other mechanical operations. This should not be necessary in a memory system.

When a console is thought of as an instrument upon which a single operator "plays" the lighting in the manner of an organist at an organ console, the human engineering problems of console design come into focus. It is not enough that the operator have everything within reach; the console must be organized in a manner that graphically relates to what he is going to play on it. Perhaps most important of all, it should take into account the close relationship which exists between the movements of the player-operator and the manner in which he handles the timing of counterpoint cues. An examination of the similar relationship which exists between a musician, the movements he makes at his keyboard, and the way in which he handles tempo in music can be instructive. A lighting operator should be as deeply involved in his interpretation as is a musician and this involvement should result in kinesthetic relationships between his interpretive intentions, his movements at the console, and the lighting. More crudely stated, he should be able to "feel" his way through the console to the proper rhythm in the lighting.

Examination of modern memory consoles reveals only a modicum of this sort of human engineering. Perhaps this is the result of the fact that most console designers are many years removed from active operation of lighting cues and in some cases have never operated any counterpoint lighting at all. Thus it is up to the potential buyer of the console to make his own evaluation of console human engineering. The best way to do this is to run a series of counterpoint cues of the type favored by the producing group on the console experimenting with the various optional methods which the device offers. A demonstration of its flexibility by the manufacturer's agent, while instructive and worth seeing, is not enough. A memory console is no small investment of a theatre's money; it is worth several days of a potential operator's time to sit at the console and run off cues much as a musician might test a new instrument before purchase. If the console is really as flexible as the manufacturer claims, it should be worth his while to make such test sessions available to potential buyers.

COST OF CONSOLE PRODUCTION

It would be nice to be able to say that cost is a nonartistic matter beyond the scope of the lighting artist. Hard reality counsels otherwise. It does help to know that the general cost of the sophisticated electronic devices discussed later in this chapter is being lowered rapidly. Buyers of lighting consoles can help control costs by understanding some of the problems of the manufacturer. The most expensive console is the custom-made variety. It benefits least from the advantages of mass production, even though many of its components are mass produced. Thus manufacturers are taking a modular approach to console design. This means that they try to lump together in one assembly a group of parts which are electrically and operationally related. These assemblies are then manufactured in quantity and stocked. Individual consoles are made up to order by combining the appropriate modules arranged according to the wishes of the buyer. Such a procedure when based on a good analysis of the operational needs of a console and on intelligent engineering, can do much to satisfy the needs of individual lighting artists and still hold costs down. Designers in search of new consoles will do well to study modular systems available before requesting a totally custom-built console. Savings gained by the use of modules may pay for features that would be beyond the budget in a custom console.

PROBLEMS FACING THE PURCHASER OF A CONSOLE

The modular approach promises to offer some relief from the high cost of consoles. However this concept is quite new. Many of the modules advertised are untested and in some cases exist only on paper or as a single prototype. The buyer, with money in hand, faces many hazards before he can smugly sit down to his new console and begin to create masterpieces.

OVERLAPPING TERMS

Reading the glossaries which follow will convince the reader that there is little consistency in the names given to the various parts of consoles. This problem does not merely grow out of the understandable urge on the part of manufacturers to create a proprietary name for their products. Behind this urge are real semantic difficulties: The flexibility of modern electronics exceeds that of language to describe the results. What, for example, do you term a handle that at one moment serves a fader function, at another is a master handle, and still later sets the timing of a lighting change? Such multiple and changing functions are common on modern consoles. In fact, two or more functions may be operating through the same handle at the same time and this arrangement too may be subject to change.

The overlapping of names and multiple combinations of functions tend to lead to a situation where the potential purchaser has no reasonable means of making comparisons between systems, short of time-consuming testing sessions which he may not be ready to undertake with every system on the market. A listing of the functions available in a system, even assuming that terms are defined clearly, is not very much help. Functions which are present but not easily accessible or which cannot be used together, may be nearly useless. On the other hand, two relatively simple functions properly paired with well-arranged controls, may combine into a convenience far beyond the value of either component. Prominently advertised unique gadgets may turn out to be far from the most valuable thing the system has to offer.

Detailed testing is the only solution to this problem. Another advantage can be gained by talks with other theatre lighting artists who have used the same system. Unfortunately any adequate evaluation of the systems available and in price range is a time-consuming task which no amount of study of advertising brochures and data sheets will shorten.

RELIABILITY

Modern consoles are sophisticated electronic devices with hundreds of thousands of parts. One glance at a magnified photo of a memory chip will convince anyone of this. One must approach such a device with the clear understanding that breakdowns are inevitable. Both preventive maintenance and repairs are absolutely essential, and must be performed by highly trained personnel. Fortunately for the operation of a show, these devices are exceedingly flexible. They usually leave the operator with an alternative way of running the cues while the faulty part is being fixed. Indeed, this feature should be carefully checked out before a system is purchased.

Another item to check before buying a console is the guarantee offered by its manufacturer and his facilities for honoring it. Past history is important in this case and should be checked out personally, not via promises by sales representatives. One should also check the probability that trained personnel and repair parts will be available beyond the guarantee period.

A problem associated with the rapid growth and change in the lighting-control industry is that it has been the practice of some companies to make a device for a short time then discontinue it and also discontinue manufacture of parts for it. In other cases companies have gone out of business creating the same situation as far as their products are concerned. These situations throw the purchaser to the tender mercies of the custom parts maker—an expensive, time-consuming way to effect repairs. Careful investigation of past practices of manufacturers and their sales representatives is advised.

DELIVERY

It is not reasonable to expect that a manufacturer will have in stock every variation of console that a purchaser might want. Modular systems often seem to make that promise, but they seldom manage to fulfill it. Thus it is reasonable to expect a manufacturing delay. Nevertheless, a firm date (reasonable in the first place) should be set and the equipment should be expected on that date unless circumstances have changed. Past delivery practices on the part of manufacturers are worth investigating before contracts are written or bids let. Note that it is usually quite legal to write a bid on the basis of a firm delivery date. However, the other side of this problem is that no customer can expect prompt delivery if specifications are constantly subject to change or are not clear in the first place.

PROMISES, PROMISES

Unfortunately, these paragraphs must be written. The lighting equipment and control industry is not totally free of those who will "Promise them anything" to make a sale. Promises or what seem to be promises, are sometimes easy to make. The semantic confusion that surrounds console terminology leaves a wide area open to intentionally fostered misunderstanding. Recourse in law may be difficult. If, for example, the specifications are vague as to what, exactly, is meant by "fader," the seller may be able to show that he has delivered a device which meets the specification, although it may perform few, if any, of the functions the buyer had in mind when he ordered it. Let the buyer beware!

The market is also occasionally plagued by salesmen who are far more eager to condemn their competitor's product than to point out the virtues of their own equipment. There is no justification for buying a piece of equipment simply because it is asserted that everything else is worse.

Glossary of Remote-Control Apparatus — Preset Consoles

The various types of control apparatus which may be combined to make up a console meeting the needs of the cue types lack specific names. Manufacturers in different regions have attached convenient labels to these devices, often overlapping each other's application and creating semantic chaos. The following glossary is an attempt to bring some order out of this chaos, at least for the purposes of this text.

This glossary begins with the most general subdivisions of remote-control equipment and moves toward the smaller units. The three general subdivisions of any remote-control system are the console, the patch bay or interconnecting panel, and the dimmer rack.

Console: the desklike or organlike assembly of control equipment that is used remotely to cause the dimmers and relays in the dimmer rack to operate. A console may have some or all of the following major divisions: manual-control bank, preset banks, card readers, nondim circuit controls, reload controls, houselighting controls, "panic" switch, system locking, and transferring switches, all defined below. Notice that the term "console" is reserved for remote-control apparatus; "switchboard" is applied to direct-control equipment; "control board" is a generic term covering all types of lighting-control apparatus.

Patch bay or interconnecting panel: a device making it possible to operate any load circuit in the lighting system from any dimmer way in the system. It is defined in detail in the text.

Dimmer rack or dimmer room: the rather large and sometimes noisy mass of equipment at the power-controlling end of the lighting-control assembly, usually consisting of heavy steel racks of dimming apparatus, relays, breakers, terminal blocks, and ventilating equipment. In small installations the dimmer rack is often housed in a remote corner of the basement and protected from tampering by a heavy wire mesh cage. In large plants a separate room, often specially ventilated, usually is provided. Acoustic insulation from stage and audience may be necessary.

Package board: the portable unit of lighting control which serves in a small way the functions of the equipment listed above. It usually consists of a "power pack" which contains the dimmers, circuit breakers, patching facilities for loads, and other power-handling parts. Connected to this package by a low-voltage, multiconductor cable is the "console unit." This contains the controllers and master shutoff facilities and may contain presets. In some types of preset package boards, the mastering and fader functions are removed to a third package so that they may more easily serve many console units. In any case it is usually possible to interconnect a number of console units, each feeding its own dimmer pack, to make up large control assemblies.

The following are major parts of consoles.

Manual bank: a set of controllers, one for each dimmer way, that can be used to control the various dimmers of the control system. The manual bank is analogous to the control offered by the rows of dimmer handles on a manually controlled switchboard. Manual banks often are equipped with a master controller that regulates the control voltage to the entire manual bank. Each manual controller usually has associated with it a multiposition switch enabling the operator to place the dimmer way in control of the manual bank, the preset bank or any other control arrangement that may be present.

Preset bank(s): banks of controllers arranged in groups called "presets." Each preset contains one controller per dimmer way. Preset banks may be simply rows of controllers or they may be elaborate complexes of controllers, master selector switches, pilot lights, and other associated paraphernalia. The function of a preset bank is to "remember" a major setup of dimmer readings which may be established on the dimmers by activating the appropriate preset bank.

Card reader: the heart of the infinite preset system. Two card readers are usually required if they are used at all. Each reader is capable of receiving a single preset card (or a similar programming device containing dimmer-reading information) at a time. The information may be in the form of a configuration of holes in an IBM card or the like. In operation, cue cards are fed alternately into one card reader and then the other, with control being transferred from reader to reader by a fader. Card-reader systems are now being supplanted by memory systems, although one card system is still being manufactured in England.

Another variety of "card" consists of a removable assembly of 30 or more miniaturized controllers. Each "card" controls 30 or more dimmers.

Reload controls: small switches that activate the relays controlling the multiple outputs of the dimmers that appear on the interconnecting panel. Activation of these switches in effect "repatches" the loads of the various dimmers. Reload controls often are fitted with master switches making it possible to rearrange the loads of a number of dimmers with the flick of a switch.

Matrix reloading: the system in which complicated patterns of reloading are worked out in advance by arranging pins in a miniature patch panel or operating slider switches in a similar device. When the entire matrix is activated, it signals reloading relays to make all the reloading changes at once. Several matrixes may be available, to be used one after the other to accomplish complicated reloads.

"Panic" system: usually a relay-controlling switch that turns on the house lights by overriding the houselight dimmer. Its purpose is to illuminate the house no matter what catastrophe befalls the dimmer bank. Ideally the panic system should draw its power from a source completely separate from the stage lighting.

System lock and control transfer: usually combined in a key-operated switch that locks off the control voltage to all of the dimmer controls in its off position, turns it on when moved in one direction, and trips a relay when moved the other way. The relay operates a multicontact switch that transfers control from the console to a second control point, often backstage at the stage manager's position. Here the stage manager may operate the lighting within the limits of the particular system.

The following devices usually are found on the manual portion of the console but function electrically as links between the manual and the preset bank.

Fader: an electrical device that makes it possible to activate a preset by gradually feeding control current to it. It also serves to transfer control from one preset to another by gradually turning off control current to one preset bank while turning it on to a second. When the fader is designed properly, this operation can be performed without any perceptible "dip" in the stage lights as the control is transferred. While fader handles resemble dimmer controllers, their operation differs in that a movement of the handle in either up or downward direction can result in the bringing on of lights depending on the position of the preset-control selector switches. A double-handle fader is a desirable refinement which makes it possible to separate the timing of the "off" and "on" portions of the cue. In most situations a double-handle fader is far more useful than a single handle type.

Autofader: the totally electronic device which automatically times and operates long fades. In some memory systems it is the principal fading device for cue operation. Time intervals may be set in advance usually in periods from 1–60 seconds or 1–60 minutes. When the fade is initiated by the operator, it proceeds without further attention unless the operator overrides it and takes manual control. It is an excellent addition to consoles.

Preset-control selector switches: a set of switches for each preset bank.

Usually the set consists of a series of switches operated by push buttons with a mechanical arrangement that prevents the operation of more than one button at a time. They often resemble the station-selector buttons on an automobile radio. The usual arrangement will provide for a button to put the preset bank on "fader up," "fader down," "on," and "off" or "blackout." In some instances the off position may be eliminated by arranging the mechanical interlock between the switches in such a way that depressing two or three switch buttons at the same time disconnects all contacts. Pilot lights or illuminated buttons are often provided to enable the operator to determine at a glance what the condition of a given preset may be.

Electrically the preset-control selector switches determine where the preset bank will draw its control current. If for instance, the "fader-up" button is depressed, the preset bank will draw power whenever the fader handle is moved to the up position. If the "on" button is depressed, the preset will get power no matter what the position of the fader because it is electrically bypassed.

The following parts usually are found on the preset console or are at least directly associated with preset operation of the control board as opposed to its manual operation.

Selective submaster switches: a series of switches arranged in groups, one group for each dimmer way per preset. Each group of switches will usually consist of two or more canceling push buttons similar to those used for preset-control selectors. Depressing a push button will allow the individual dimmer controller for a given preset to draw its control current from one of the submasters provided for that preset. Note that only one submaster may be called upon for current at a time. Thus the controllers of any preset bank may be subdivided into as many groups as there are submasters. These groups are mutually exclusive within the preset in most cases. In a control system involving 30 or more dimmers, four or more submasters per preset are desirable. This arrangement will add up to a sizable number of push buttons to be checked out before the operation of the control board. (For example, 144 buttons are needed for a 36-dimmer board with four submasters per preset.) The control flexibility produced is worth the complication.

Electrically, the preset submaster selectors are simply canceling switches designed to handle the relatively low power of the control system. The selectors are usually mechanically arranged in banks analogous to the preset circuit controllers for purposes of clarity. Placing the selectors next to the individual controllers is probably inviting needless confusion since they are seldom operated during the running of a show.

Preset submasters: found either on the manual portion of the console or associated with the individual preset banks. Either location is satisfactory. Preset submasters consist of controllerlike handles, usually larger in size than the individual controllers, which operate like a normal dimmer. When the handles are up they are on, and when down they are off. They usually are calibrated in the standard 10-point manner. Turning on a submaster will activate whatever preset controllers are switched to it provided the preset itself is getting control current. Thus a single submaster can serve as a master dimmer for the entire preset or for any portion of it depending on the arrangement of the submaster selector switches.

Electrically the submasters usually consist of small autotransformer dimmers arranged to handle the control current. They require the same sort of maintenance as any other autotransformer with the advantage that they usually are asked to carry only a light electrical load. The brushes should be inspected occasionally.

Controller: a device associated with an individual dimmer. On the manual bank it is analogous to the dimmer handle of a manually operated switchboard. On the preset banks there will be one controller per dimmer per preset. Each controller will be calibrated in the standard 1-to-10 manner, often backlighted and provided with a pilot light to tell the operator when it is active.

Electrically, most controllers consist of a resistance device connected in such a way that it represents a constant or nearly constant electrical load no matter what the setting. These devices are known as "potentiometers." Since most control circuitry for remotely controlled dimmers require direct current, each controller usually is equipped with a diode, a tiny device that allows the current to flow in one direction only.

The mechanical arrangement of the moving parts of a controller is of considerable consequence to the operator since it is the "feel" of the device that will determine how smoothly he can fade a single light in or out. Ideally each controller should feel exactly like all of the others in the entire system. At the very least all of the controllers should be mechanically identical and adjusted to similar tensions. A common and undesirable practice on early remote-control systems was to make the controllers on the preset bank simple radially operated potentiometers or simple thumb wheels. Those on the manual bank were much more elaborate linear-movement devices. The rationale for this system was that cues would be taken only at the faders, the submasters, or on the manual. In modern overlapping cue situations this rationale simply does not prove valid. All controllers should be alike.

Control interpatch: a system which allows the various elements of the console to be interconnected as needed. It makes it possible to electrically reconfigure the console to fit the needs of each show. In dimmer-per-load-circuit systems it may also serve to group several dimmers under the same controller in much the same manner that load circuits are grouped on individual dimmers in older systems.

Interpatching may be accomplished in a number of ways. A bay with patchcords may be used, a matrix system can be installed, or the entire interpatch function can be given to logic circuitry in a memory system.

Preset Control: Concept and Elaborations

Early control consoles derived their basic concepts from two sources:

1. The variety or vaudeville show which was divided into neat, separate units capable of being preset and finally activated in one fade up. The control console was the natural sequel to color master and submaster switching which was designed for the same purpose.
2. The engineering staff of the manufacturers assigned to design remote consoles for the simple reason that these people always designed switchboards. Since they were engineers, not lighting artists, their analysis of the needs of stage lighting followed the common scientific practice of reducing the operations to a series of increments. Each increment could be treated as a simple "on-off" or "up-down" operation, separate and distinct from those before and following it. The result of the combination of these two concepts was the *preset-control concept.*

In its purest form the preset console consists of ranks of controllers—one per dimmer per rank. Control of all or any part of the board may be established in any one of these ranks, which are known as "presets." Transfer of control is accomplished by a fader which is attached to the appropriate presets by means of preset-control selectors. The first setup of lighting control for a show may be established on Preset 1 and brought in as the curtain rises by moving the fader from a position without any preset currently attached (say, "fader down") to "up," thus activating Preset 1. During the time this cue is active, or before the show, if necessary, the next cue is arranged by adjusting the controllers on Preset 2. Since this preset is not active, adjustments may be done speedily, and any mistakes corrected without the audience seeing any changes. Previous to the cue to shift to the second lighting setup, Preset 2 is attached to the inactive position of the fader (in this instance, "fader down") by closing its fader-down switch. On cue, the fader is moved to the down position, and control is thereby transferred to the second preset. This operation frees Preset 1 for preparation of a new cue, or it may be held as it is for later return to the lighting condition it already represents.

The simplest workable preset system must have two presets, one of which may be active while the other is being prepared. Such systems, and also the most elaborate systems, will have a manual-control console through which lighting elements that remain constant throughout several presets may be operated. The manual-control console is the usual control position for such items of lighting as "sky backing" instruments behind windows, property lamps which are controlled by actors, and the like. However, any good preset console should also allow continuous lighting to be carried from preset to preset at the same reading with no noticeable change in intensity because of variations in control voltage.

More elaborate preset systems are constructed by increasing the number of presets. Often as many as 10 presets are available to the operator. Under such conditions the console becomes a sort of "memory device" on which the lighting cues are stored and brought into service as needed. Of course, increasing the number of presets also increases the amount of time available to the operator or his assistant to rearrange any given preset before it must be activated. This time increase makes the operation by revolving presets less frantic.

Infinite Preset

The number of presets which may be represented by ranks of controllers is limited. Boards soon become huge and unwieldy, see Figure 10-4. Therefore devices have been sought out which will increase the number of presets without increasing the console size. One of the earliest of these was the punch card. The data is retained on cards, often the standard IBM variety, in patterns of holes punched into the card. The number of presets is limited only by the stock of cards. After being punched to represent cues, the cards are sorted alternately into at least two packs. These packs then are fed into card readers. Cross-fades are accomplished by fading from reader to reader, hence the alternate packs of cards. If pile-on is desired beyond the possibilities of the two readers, another reader may be added.

Although the card system does provide infinite presetting, it offers some undesirable complications. Card decks are susceptible to scrambling. Moving back to an earlier point in a show during rehearsal is bothersome, and revising cues offers some complications because the card must be in the reader in order to view the cue. For these reasons and others, card systems have gone out of favor in the United States. One system is still being manufactured in England.

Another variation on the card system consists of "cards" containing a number of miniaturized controllers, usually 30. This assembly of controllers is plugged into an elaborate socket which connects the controllers into the circuitry. When the card is activated, whatever preset is set on the controllers controls the dimmers. One may have as many presets as one has cards per set of 30 dimmers.

This system is hardly an answer to the needs for infinite preset. The cards are bulky and handling them in quantity presents problems. Chain-driven card-handling systems have been devised to feed the cards into their sockets in sequence, but these have not worked very well. Moreover it is nearly impossible to make a smooth change in setting on one of the controllers in a card—one of the features which originally seemed an advantage for this system. It seems probable that memory systems will supplant these card devices.

Variations and Refinements within Preset Banks

It is seldom that a simple, undivided preset bank will be installed these days, except in the case of infinite presetting which absorbs the functions of the following refinements. Probably the first addition to any preset will be a switch to enable the operator to activate the preset without using the fader. This addition does not necessarily mean that two controllers on two separate presets may be feeding information to a single dimmer at the same time, if this is undesirable, or if it could be injurious to the system. However, it does mean that a given preset can operate a portion of the lighting while other circuits are being controlled by fader action on other presets.

It is but a step from the preset-on switch to a preset master controller. This controller allows the activation of the preset by a fade-in motion instead of switching. From here it is but another simple step to add submasters and submaster selectors (see glossary). At this point a better choice becomes available: The preset master can be eliminated and a series of submasters provided, any one of which can become a preset master simply by placing it in control of all controllers in that preset. The rest of the submasters are inactivated for that preset, but this loss of control refinement is usually minor for the period of time that a preset master is needed. Physically grouping these preset submasters closely, and fitting them with handles easily grasped by one hand, offers the mechanical equivalent of a preset master at no additional cost. The operator is given his choice of two methods of mastering the preset without using the fader.

FUNCTIONS OF PRESET SUBMASTERS

Preset submastering, to a limited extent, serves the same function as increasing the number of presets, because the majority of lighting cues involves only a limited number of dimmer circuits. If, for instance, four preset submasters are available per preset and four sequential cues appear in the lighting plot, each involving different dimmers (not an unlikely possibility), all of this can be done on *one* preset. The operator arranges the four cues on the submasters and activates them in the proper order. Since no fader is available for this operation, extra care must be exercised to avoid "dips" in lighting if cross-fades must be executed between cues. A competent operator can easily learn to avoid dips. If the cues are to be built, one upon the other, the operation is still simpler.

MECHANICAL ARRANGEMENT OF PRESET CONTROLLERS

In the past, preset controllers tended to fall into two categories: (1) those which were intended only as devices for presetting readings to be activated later, and (2) those which were to be used for direct operation of the cues. Obviously the demands for ease of operation were less in the first instance, and costs could be reduced. It was not uncommon to use radially operated potentiometers for this application. In modern lighting practice cues are occasionally taken on a preset bank. All controllers should provide linear motion in a smooth, stepless operation. Preferably, this operation should match in feel the operation of other controllers on which cues may be taken so that the operator will not have any extra adjustments to make. Probably the ideal is to make all controllers identical as far as the operator is concerned. The controllers should all be fingertip operated, allowing the operator to run several with each hand if necessary. They should be instantly readable as to both setting and condition (that is, active or inactive).

Pile-On

So far our discussion has considered only those situations where one controller at a time is feeding control current to a dimmer. This kind of circuitry can be designed by incorporating canceling switches into the console so that only one controller can *ever* be connected and actively in charge of a dimmer at a time, except during the movement of the fader from one position to the other. Incidentally, the wise operator will not hold the fader in its intermediate positions any longer than necessary, because this ties up two presets at the same time and makes dimmer readings exceedingly hard to determine.

There are distinct advantages in making it possible for two or more controllers to be feeding voltage to the same dimmer simultaneously. This situation is called *pile-on* because the electrical effect is to feed the dimmer from two related sources, but not to add up the voltages. The highest controller reading prevails. Any lower voltages feeding to the same dimmer will have no effect on its output. As higher voltages are removed from the dimmer, it responds to the next lower voltage until all are gone.

Electrically, pile-on is accomplished by referring all control voltages to the same neutral point (often ground potential), and arranging all control-voltage feeders in such a way that they vary from the neutral in the same direction.

The following example will further clarify the operation of pile-on control (refer to Figure 10-3). The three ranks of controllers, I, II and III, are each provided with four selective submasters which are chosen by pressing the buttons above the individual controllers. These buttons are represented on this schematic by the circles above each controller.

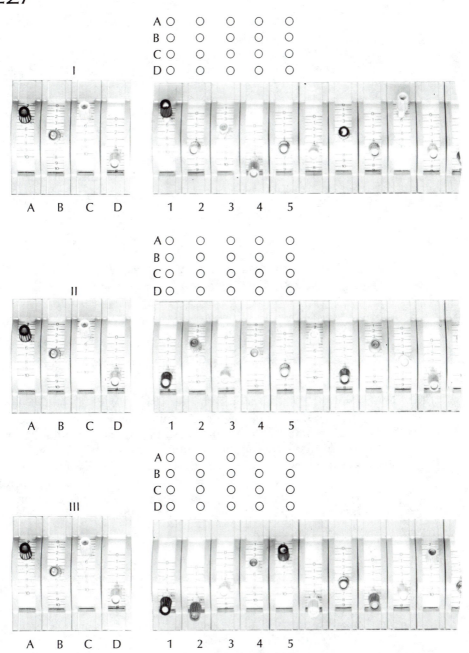

FIGURE 10-3
Control Board Set Up Mainly To Exploit the Possibilities of Pile-On Control. Courtesy of The Superior Electric Company.

The switches are so arranged that any controller of a given rank can be on any one of the four submasters of that rank, but not on more than one at a time.

Assume that the dimmers are circuited to lamps as follows:

Dimmer	Area
1	I left (warm key)
2	II left (warm key)
3	I right (cool key)
4	II right (cool key)
5	Side light left (additional warm key for dramatic emphasis)

These controllers are submastered and labeled as follows:

Submaster I-A: "Warm keys"
Controllers, 1, 2 . . .
Submaster I-B: "Cool keys"
Controllers 3, 4 . . .
Submaster II-A: "Area I"
Controllers 1, 3
Submaster II-B: "Area II"
Controllers 2, 4
Submaster III-C: "All stage left warm keys"
Controllers 1, 2, 5 . . .

(Note that this example has been simplified; the submasters controlling keys, for example, would control many more controllers.)

Given the above arrangement, the operator would set up his cues according to the various functions of the lighting. For instance, the cue "bring all warm keys to 8" would be taken on Submaster III-C. If the controllers circuited to this submaster were at full up (actually they would have been preset to provide proper balance of warm keys at the highest reading to be used), bringing the submaster to 8 would override any other controller-feeding dimmers controlling warm keys if that controller were set at less than 8. Any such controller set at more than 8 would not be affected. Thus the cue regarding warm keys would be superimposed on previous cues making increases only where it overrides.

This will have the effect of retaining the previous cues intact awaiting the removal of the warm key setting or the increase of another function to the point of override.

Submasters shown in Figure 10-3 and not mentioned in this simplified example would be in control of other functions — for instance, stage right sidelights, special 60° key lighting, and so on.

The usual means of setting up pile-on control is to activate two or more presets via the preset on-switch, or one or more of them via simultaneous operation of two or more fader-up or fader-down switches. A combination of these two procedures is also possible. Canceling devices are omitted from pile-on consoles making it possible for every controller on the board to carry current at the same time. Power-supply equipment for the console must be designed with this possibility in mind, although it would be a rarity in practice. Pilot lights indicating which controller or controllers are operative for each dimmer are essential in this system if operators are to avoid making preset movements with active controllers.

The additional complications of this system may seem more likely to produce chaos than artistry. Chaos does not materialize in practice because this system seldom is used in the pile-on mode for revolving preset cues. If revolving preset procedure is being followed because the show falls into discrete cues, pile-on should usually be avoided. The fader can take care of whatever lapping is needed.

The great advantage of pile-on is in the operation of counterpoint cues—those with complicated time factors involving staggered starts and stops and fades at differing paces in counterpoint to each other.

USING PILE-ON

A pile-on console with four submasters per preset is a reasonably flexible control instrument for counterpoint cues. Assuming such a console, the procedure is as follows.

Dimmer ways are divided into groups according to lighting function and organized on the board via the selective submasters, using as many dimmer ways per preset as needed. Occasionally the need will arise for controlling a lamp as a part of more than one function (for example, a blue sidelight that serves as part of a night scene at one point, but as modeling light when mixed with other side lighting during other scenes). This need will necessitate moving to another preset to avoid the problem of nonoverlapping control at the selective submasters. An entire preset will occasionally become a single category of lighting, or it may represent a discrete cue that appears at points in the show where counterpoint lighting is not prevalent. There is nothing mutually exclusive about the two categories of lighting. Operation of cues is performed largely at the submaster controllers, blending the effect of the various functions as the timing and artistic demands of the show dictate. This operation can ordinarily be done by one operator with the occasional aid of an assistant. A distinct asset to this system would be the autofader system.

Analysis of counterpoint lighting for cuing is a highly individualized affair. The categories shown in Table 10-2 will serve as a starting point.

There is nothing extremely new about thinking about lighting in this manner, but the flexibility of modern boards makes it possible for this reasonable way of analyzing lighting to be carried through to its logical conclusion in setting up and running cues. See Figure 10-4 for samples of variously arranged preset consoles.

a

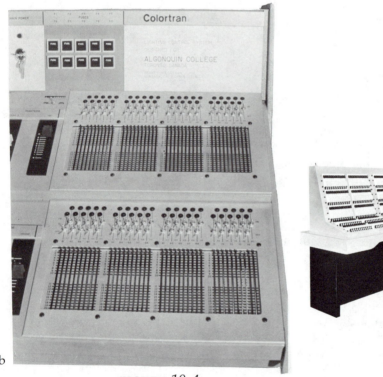

b

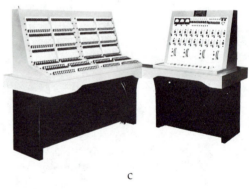

c

FIGURE *10-4*

Preset Consoles. These pictures illustrate some of the many possibilities of preset console arrangement. a, Shows a three-part console. The center section is the main console, the two wings contain the ten rows of controllers, each representing a preset. b, Slider Interconnection of Control Circuitry. This rather simple slider-switch arrangement allows any or all of 40 dimmers to be placed under the control of any 18 controllers. (The last two slider positions are unconnected.) Thus patterns of control can be built up on the controllers. Since these patterns may not overlap within a preset, some limitations are imposed. Nevertheless, each of the two presets may be divided into patterns independently of the other. This board provides a modicum of pattern control. c, A large two-part console

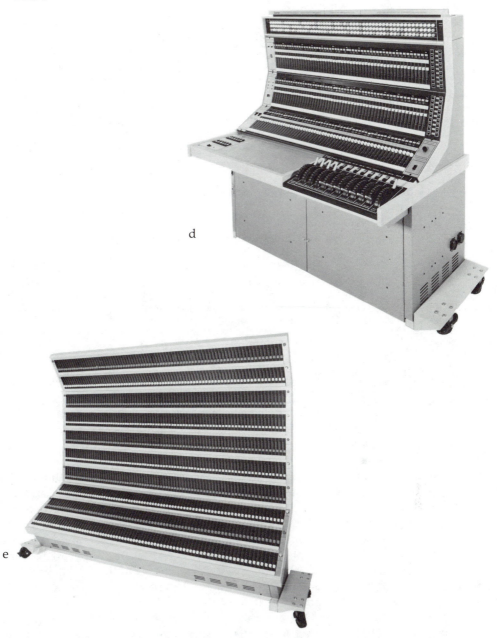

with mastering and submastering controls on the right-hand portion and presets at the left. *d, e,* Show the main console and the preset console of a large preset board designed for use in a television studio. The large field of preset controllers illustrates the difficulties encountered when trying to increase the preset console beyond moderate size. Near-instant location of an individual controller for purposes of emergency change becomes increasingly difficult as size grows. Figures 10-4*a, b, d,* and *e* courtesy of Berkey Colortran; Figure 10-4*c* courtesy of Kliegl Bros.

TABLE *10-2*
Lighting Categories

ACTING-AREA LIGHTING*	CYCLORAMA LIGHTING
Normal (45°) key, left and right	Top and bottom
High (60°) key, left and right	Left and right
Fill, left and right	Color groups—red, green, blue
Side lighting, left and right	Cloud and projected effects
Warm side	
Cool side	
Top or rim lights	
Area groups by left and right sides or together	
Special combinations of areas and their fills which may be arranged without end	

* In many cases the same instruments may serve several functions. For example, the key lights also represent color variations, and when not serving as keys, may be fill. However, it would be a complicated cue indeed in which all of these variations would be in the process of change at the same time.

Pattern Control for Counterpoint Lighting

We have already noted that counterpoint lighting consists of playing a number of lighting configurations "against each other" to produce a design in which change is one of the most important elements. "Pattern control" is the name given to the console arrangement which makes this type of lighting easy to operate. Incidentally, it should be clear that most productions will contain a combination of discrete and counterpoint lighting; therefore a console should be capable of providing both pattern and preset control as needed. Pattern control differs from presetting in the following ways: (1) Several configurations will be active on stage at the same time, each with its own complicated "time line" consisting of accelerations, decelerations and linear changes. (2) These configurations may have many of the same control channels in common, producing what is called a "pile-on" situation. This demands that the highest controller setting take precedence in most instances. (3) Since change is an artistic essential in counterpoint, all or most of the available patterns can be expected to be in the process of change, at varying tempi, at all times. This is completely unlike the preset situation where the normal condition is static, changes being made only at fades from preset to preset.

It is quite possible to devise a console especially adapted to pattern control while maintaining the possibility of handling preset cues, or even returning completely to preset mode if this is wished. In general, standard preset console parts can be used. The first step is the provision of an interpatch system which enables the operator to operate any configuration of controllers from any master. A low voltage patch bay will do this, although there are also several other options. Preset masters, selective submasters, and the like, become "pattern masters" under this system. Each may control any arrangement of controllers attached to it. See Figure 10-5 for such a console. It is also sometimes convenient to make it possible for one master to control several others. This makes color control over cyclorama lighting, for example, much easier. Convenient arrangement of the pattern masters for multiple operation by the hands of the operator is the last main console requirement. Electrically, one thing is essential: Circuitry must be so arranged that current may not flow from one pattern master to another. This can be done by the insertion of diodes (one-way conducting devices) into the circuits leading from the pattern masters to the individual controllers. When this has been done, the same controller may be attached to several pattern masters if necessary.

A system arranged in this manner can be easily converted into a

FIGURE *10-5a*
Control Board for Pattern Control Arranged for Counterpoint Lighting. This system provides 36 channels of control. These are represented by the five rows of 36 controllers shown at the left. These controllers feed from the receptacles shown below in 10-5b. At the operator's right is a portion of the main console showing several of the pattern controllers (large black handles). Any combination of circuit controllers may be placed on any pattern controller by means of the patch system. Channels may be common to as many patterns as is necessary.

FIGURE *10-5b*
Control interconnect board for pattern control board shown in 10-5a. The top vertical rows of receptacles connect to the sixteen pattern controllers shown below in 10-5c. The five closely spaced rows of receptacles near the center feed the channel controllers shown at the left of 10-5a. The lower portion of the board is devoted to multiplier facilities which allow re-patching of the board to a five scene pre-set configuration when this is needed. The patch cords are color coded and provide facilities for multiple patching to a single receptacle when needed.

FIGURE *10-5c*
Main Console of Counter-point Control Board. The operator is shown using 2 of the 16 pattern con-trollers. The buttons below these controllers determine whether the controller will be fed from the line, from the split fader (lower left) or from another patching arrangement which enables any one of the pattern controllers to serve as a master over several others.

regular preset console, if this is needed, by simply connecting each rank of controllers to a single pattern master. The pattern master then becomes a preset master. A more versatile combination is to arrange a number of patterns and perhaps two presets on the same console. This makes both types of control possible.

FIGURE *10-5d*
Typical Multiple Operation of Several Patterns at Once. Operators soon learn to use their hands skillfully to effect complicated changes at varying tempos and in both up and down directions. All photos in this series by the author. Control board designed and built by author and staff at California State University, Northridge.

Packaged Preset Control

Although preset control was originally developed to be permanently installed in theatres, it was not long before manufacturers were making portable packages of this type of control for small theatres. These packages are modular units which can be fitted together to comprise an elaborate, but totally portable system. Generally there are two parts to each package: (1) a power pack containing the dimmers, breakers, load-patching facility and related equipment and (2) a console which con-

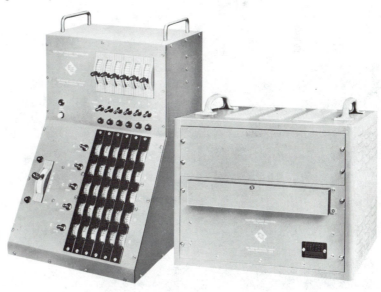

FIGURE *10-6a*
A Five-Scene Preset Six-Dimmer Board (1800 watts per dimmer). The fader is arranged so that several consoles may be plugged together allowing operation from one fader. Courtesy of The Superior Electric Company.

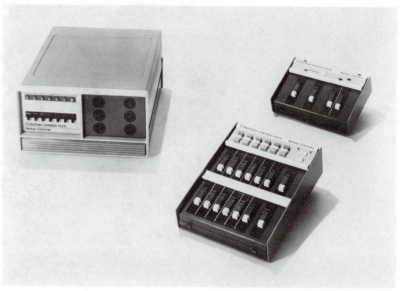

FIGURE *10-6b*
Another Variation Consisting of Three Units. The lower right-hand module is a two-scene preset console with individual preset masters. The upper right-hand unit is a fader module capable of controlling a number of the two-scene preset consoles. At the upper left is one of several dimmer packs available with this system. They range from 1.8 kW per dimmer to 3.6 kW. Each pack contains six dimmers and the power handling equipment necessary for their operation. Courtesy of Berkey Colortran.

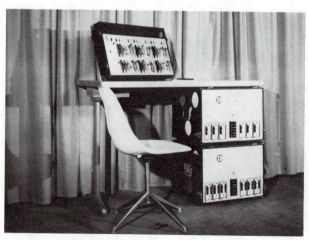

FIGURE *10-6c*
This set of components provides eighteen dimmers and two-scene preset control. Twelve of the dimmers are rated at 2.6 kW each, the remainder at 6 kW. The control console forms the cover of one of the dimmer packs for shipping. Note that each dimmer pack is built in the form of a trunk. Courtesy Electronics Diversified.

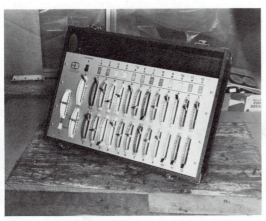

FIGURE *10-6d*
A Portable Scrimmer Console. This console provides two-scene preset control for twelve dimmers with crossfader and scene masters. Courtesy Electronics Diversified.

FIGURE *10-6e*
Modern Road Board. This touring board is designed to meet the special needs of a particular show. It contains five 6-kW dimmers and one 12 kW-dimmer plus three nondim circuits. Only the power pack is shown. The console is similar to those shown in Figure 10-6b. Courtesy of Berkey Colortran.

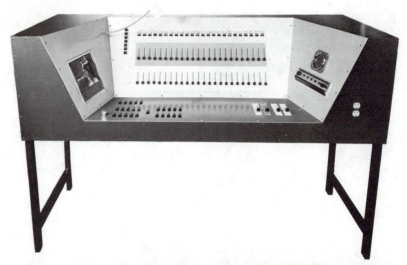

FIGURE *10-6f*
Large-Capacity
Road Board. This
board was specially
built for the Ice
Capades. It contains
three six-dimmer
power packs (1.8
kW per dimmer) and
four 6-kW dimmers.
The console contains
a built-in talk-back
system for communi-
cations. Courtesy
Berkey Colortran.

tains controllers, sometimes masters and/or faders, shutoff facilities, and the like. The two units are connected by a multiconductor low-voltage control cable which may be long enough to reach from the back of the house to backstage in a medium-size theatre. Some systems include a third unit containing faders. This unit is designed to provide fader control over a number of individual console units, making it a master fader unit. See Figure 10-6 for examples of these package control systems, including road boards.

BUYING PACKAGE UNITS

The principal considerations in buying solid-state dimmers have already been discussed. However there are some special considerations that apply when buying portable units. The first is noise from the dimmer packs themselves. Dimmer noise is not a major problem when the dimmer rack is hidden away in the basement. It is a major problem when the dimmers are backstage, in the house, or in a small control booth where operators must work. A well-designed portable dimmer pack should produce a very low hum with no annoying buzz. An actual test in the control location is the best evaluation.

Package dimmers and consoles must be planned for rough handling. They must be expected to suffer all of the rigors of touring and still operate. Not all have come up to this standard in the past. Buyers will be well advised to investigate the experiences of other owners of package systems before buying one. Checking with a reputable theatre consultant will also help.

Package systems represent one of the best buys on the market if they are well made and suited to the needs of the producing organization. The cost per watt of dimmer control will be lower when using packages than with any other system that offers comparable control. Moreover, quite elaborate control configurations can be worked out using these systems.

Summary on Preset Systems

Until very recently the preset console has been the main system of lighting control in large theatres. In the form of package control, and in simplified consoles, it has served small theatres as well. Equipped with selective submastering, it has made a reasonable amount of pattern control possible. However the situation is now changing. Memory systems are pushing preset systems off the market; they already dominate the luxury theatre market and price drops suggest they will move into other markets soon.

Interest in the artistic possibilities of counterpoint lighting is increasing rapidly, especially among top-rank designers. Such men as Josef Svoboda, Richard Pilbrow, and many European scenographers design mainly in this mode and demand that control make possible the high level of operator-interpreter performance necessary to the completion of their designs. Thus as memory devices take over lighting control, it seems probable that pure revolving preset operation will become less and less common.

Memory Systems

As the cost of dimmers lowers, the tendency to install as many dimmers as there are load circuits increases. Moreover lighting systems are growing more complicated in answer to the demand for larger numbers of load channels, and in some cases also from the demands of repertory. A repertory house may need to have instruments for three or more shows up and ready to use at one time. All of these factors point toward more elaborate control at the same time that the art of lighting is moving toward treating a single operator as an interpretive artist instead of a *répétiteur*.

The vast flexibility of computer technology, its huge capacity for handling repetitive data accurately and almost instantly, and the capacity of logic circuitry to organize and, if necessary, repeatedly reorganize complex functions into simple controls, all suggest that memory systems offer an ideal solution to the artistic needs of modern lighting-console design. The final consideration is also becoming more and more favorable; costs are coming down rapidly. Industrial use of computer technology is forcing it into incredible levels of mass production. Firms are carrying as "on the shelf stock" items necessary to the assembly of logic circuitry, memories, and the like. Trained service personnel are available. All of this is part of a major change in industrial technology upon which the theatre can "ride," taking advantage of the technology without having to bear the high cost of either developing or maintaining an industry for a small market.

Thus the computer has entered the theatre, now through lighting, but probably in the future to take control of many facets of production. It is neither a terrifying monster that can take over in the manner of the robots in *RUR*, nor an abject slave willing to do the bidding of any master. Since computers must be "taught" their programs by human beings, they tend to ape the thought patterns of those running them. Ultimately working with a computer becomes something of a test in clear, completely worked out, thinking. If any step is assumed by the human, it will be forgotten by the computer with disastrous results. In lighting terms it comes to something like this: The computer is a creative tool in the hands of the artist but it is one he must learn to use. It makes no assumptions on its own, forgets nothing, and has no initiative. The artistic responsibillity is squarely where it should be—in the hands of the artist.

Glossary of Terms Related to Memory Consoles

This glossary is organized, as nearly as possible according to the procedure which is followed in operating a memory board. General terms come first; then come terms associated with setting up cues and recording them; next are terms referring to the alteration and correction of recorded cues; then follow terms used in operating the show; finally there are terms related to the long-term storage of memory data. Many terms actually refer to several parts of the process and could reappear several times. These are discussed the first time they appear in the normal processes as listed above.

TERMS REFERRING TO THE ENTIRE SYSTEM

Memory: the electronic device which stores the cue information. It may be permanent or temporary.

Main memory: that set of memory apparatus which holds cue information (and program information in some systems) over a long period of time. It is the only place (except for tape or printout) where all of the cue information is in storage all the time. Technically it may consist of ferrite-core devices or semiconductor devices. (There are other possibilities but these are not presently used in theatre systems.)

Buffer; register: either refers to a smaller memory device whose function usually is related to a single cue, preset, or other function which is actively in use. Information is placed in a buffer from main memory or from manual input so it will be available for immediate use without tying up the main memory. The number of buffers determines, among other things, the number of cues that can be active at one time.

Ferrite core: a basic type of memory device. It stores information as "bits." A bit consists of a unit of data in the form of a yes-no, on-off, or +/− piece of information. This is held in the ferrite core as one of two possible magnetic states which the ferrite (an iron compound) can take. Since magnetism is permanent until changed, a ferrite-core memory is called a "permanent" memory; it needs no constant electrical supply to retain its information.

Semiconductor memory: another basic memory device. In this one the data is stored in terms of the electrical state of transistors. They may be in either conductive or nonconductive states, thus handling a bit of yes-no or similar information. Semiconductor memories have the disadvantage of requiring constant voltage if they are to retain their information. However they also have the advantage of producing a constant signal representing the information they contain. They are considered temporary memories and are provided with a battery voltage source if they are utilized as main memories. Semiconductors are more commonly found as buffer memories.

MOS memory: stands for "metal oxide semiconductor." This is a modern semiconductor memory device known for its capacity to pack a very high density of information into a very small chip of silicon. It is also well suited to mass production, forcing the cost of memories lower and lower. These memories are made up on tiny chips of silicon on which thousands of semiconductors and their circuitry are produced by highly refined etching and plating processes. For example, one typical MOS chip is 0.146×0.164 inch in size and contains 256 bits of information.

Cue capacity: refers to the total number of cues (presets) which can be stored in a system. This depends mainly on the size of the main memory and the number of channels of control to be remembered.

Program: the organized body of information and instructions built into a memory system that determines how it will work. Programs determine how information will flow through the system, what alternatives will be open to the operator, what displays will appear when, and the like. Programs are usually expressed as "logic."

Logic: a graphic description of the exact steps which the information in the computer follows as it is processed. Every operation is separated into steps which pose only two alternatives, "yes" or "no." These alternatives can then be represented as electrical circuitry (usually transistors) which conducts or does not conduct. For example at some point in the process of preparing lighting on a memory board, one must decide whether or not to record the data as a cue. This will appear on the logic sheet as:

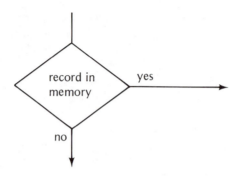

The arrows represent the alternatives. At the point of each would be entered the next step in the process depending on the decision just made. A "program" is a complete arrangement of such logic devised to perform a particular task on a computer.

Hard wired: refers to a computer in which the logic is represented in the system by parts wired together electrically. It cannot be changed without taking the system apart.

Soft ware: roughly the opposite of "hard wired." It refers to information placed in the computer electrically and therefore changeable without taking the machine apart. It may refer to data in a bank or to program material stored in a memory and used to control the flow of information through the computer. A theatre computer system which is so equipped can be changed to fit the needs of an individual performing group by altering the program.

A/D converter or D/A converter: means "analog to digital converter" and "Digital to analog converter," two absolutely essential devices for theatre computers. Lighting information is an electrical analog of the lighting settings. The computer can store only digital information. Thus all lighting data must be converted to digital language before it can be stored and conversely, must be reconverted into analog form for sending to the dimmers. Fortunately these converters are a stock item in computer manufacture.

TERMS RELATED TO THE SETTING UP AND RECORDING OF CUES

Channel: a dimmer, or a series of dimmers operating as one.

Steps per channel: refers to the number of increments into which a conventional dimmer setting (0–10) is broken for purposes of A/D conversion and storage. Within limits, the number of steps determines the accuracy with which the memory records the dimmer readings. For example, one system breaks the 0–10 scale into 64 steps.

Manual: exactly analogous to the manual bank in a preset board. It is a bank of controllers each of which controls a channel directly when it is connected. The manual is one of the common ways of setting up cue information for recording into memory.

Manual-record: a button which, when pushed, almost instantly sends the cue information represented by the settings in the manual bank into memory.

Video display: a main part of one type of memory system. Functions are displayed on the face of a cathode-ray tube (essentially a television tube) and are manipulated by operating a "light pen" on the surface of the tube. When activated by pushing slightly in on its tip, the pen sends a signal into the system which causes it to activate whatever portion of the display is shown under the point where the pen touches the screen. Thus lighting operations, particularly cue setup and channel retrieval, are taken on the face of the tube. Faders are provided for their usual purposes. The advantage of this system is that the video display is part of a soft-ware concept; the program can be altered to meet the needs of the occasion. This simply changes the display on the tube. The tube also displays information on all channels in use; thus it also serves a "mimic" function.

Record lockout: an arrangement designed to prevent unintended recording of information into a system already set up. Such recording could destroy information already stored or could confuse the operator with data he did not know existed in the system. It usually consists of a series of steps which must be executed sequentially. These generally include the insertion and turning of at least one key.

Preset; cue: commonly used to refer to a unit of material stored in memory under a single address number. If the lighting is in the form of discrete cues, these units correspond exactly with the definition of "cue" or "preset" in a preset system. If counterpoint lighting is being used, each "cue" may represent a pattern.

Preset select; cue select: terms applied to the device used to assign address numbers (to allow the computer to identify the cue) to cues. The same names may also be applied to another set of buttons used to call up the cues from memory. The button keyboards usually take the form of the standard 0–9 adding machine keyboard, although some small systems use one button per cue.

Full; overlimit: indicators that the memory is full to capacity. No more information may be recorded until something has been removed or some cues combined. The indicator is usually in the form of a light or lighted sign.

Flag: a signal similar to that above, which can be operated by recording a signal into memory. Thus any cue may be "flagged" to remind the operator that some special action must be taken.

Cue renumbering; cue combining: two functions sometimes supplied with memory systems. Renumbering allows the operator to rearrange cue sequence. Combination allows him to fuse two or more cues into one. These associated functions enable the operator of revolving preset cues to reorganize and save memory space.

Memorized fade time: most systems record settings, leaving fade time to the operator. However it is possible to record the simple duration of fades in memory and feed that information directly to autofaders. The operator then merely initiates the cue. Fades can, of course, be manually overridden.

Mimic; tally; display: terms referring to a set of illuminated numbers or similar arrangement, which light up to indicate some or all of the following:

1. All channels in operation
2. All channels operating in a given cue
3. Channels as called up on manual

The purpose is to allow the operator to know what channels he is dealing with at the moment. Some mimic systems are arranged to have the brightness of the mimic light follow the brightness of the channel it represents. Others depend on a setting meter for this function. Mimic can also be in the form of a display on a video tube.

Setting meter: a voltmeter calibrated in dimmer settings. It can be attached to any channel-control circuit to determine the setting of that channel.

Flasher; blinker: a circuit that can be inserted into any channel control which causes the channel to jump to "full" or, if at "full" to go to "out." In some systems the blinker continues to flash the channel on and off until shut off. It serves to aid in locating a single instrument or instruments attached to a channel.

TERMS REFERRING TO THE PROCESS
OF ALTERING AND CORRECTING CUES

Individual select/record; manual takeover; solo: the process by which a channel is removed from control of memory and adjusted manually. This may involve a matching operation to assure that the setting of the manual controller matches that of the channel in memory. This avoids any sudden change in light intensity as the channel is shifted from memory to manual. The reverse of this process may also be necessary unless the altered reading is recorded as a changed cue.

Cue insertion: a process by which cues are inserted, in proper order, in an already established numerical sequence. For example, it makes it possible to insert cue 24a between cues 24 and 25. Later sequence playback will then play the cues in order.

Rocker switch: one of several systems devised to avoid the matching problem involved in manual takeover. It consists of a three-position switch; center position attaches circuit to memory. Rocking the switch to either "up" or "down" position removes channel from memory and adjusts it in the direction chosen. No matching is necessary.

Fader wheel: another device for manual takeover. It consists of a wheel, designed for hand operation, which rotates continuously in either direction. Automatically picks up (at proper reading) any circuit assigned to it from memory. Movement of the wheel in either direction adjusts the circuit manually. New setting, as in case of rocker switch, must be recorded into memory, if it is to be a permanent part of the cue.

Joy stick: a third device which can be used for manual takeover although it may also be used for fader control. This consists of a vertical handle movable either left or right. It functions much like the rocker switch.

Auto-mod; record in 99; block: terms referring to a process by which a part of the memory can be temporarily used to cause one or more channels to be stricken from every cue in which they appear. This enables an operator to cancel a light or lights from all cues when it is discovered, for example, that the instruments have been knocked out of line. It can be canceled at any time restoring channel to its originally recorded readings.

Blind recording: a process by which cues can be set up and recorded into memory without actually being displayed on stage. It comes in handy in situations where lighting rehearsals are interrupted by long sessions of acting rehearsal, provided the operator and designer know what they want without seeing it on stage. It can also aid in altering cues to avoid using misaligned lamps such as above.

TERMS RELATED TO THE OPERATION OF THE SHOW

Playback; select; call-up; assignment: terms referring to the process by which cues are retrieved from memory, assigned to a fader or master and eventually fed to the stage. These terms may also refer to the entire section of the console where these operations take place.

Preview; next cue: names given to the button and its associated display which call up by number the next cue to be placed on stage. Some of these systems provide a complete display of dimmer readings for each cue, others provide for one-by-one reading of channel intensities, if needed.

Stage; present cue: refers to the cue or cues actually controlling the lighting at the time.

Sequence play: a system for running revolving presets. It automatically calls up the next cue in numerical sequence as the outgoing cue is ended on the fader.

Pile-on: same as in operation of preset boards. More than one preset may be feeding information to a channel at the same time, although no fader is in operation. This is the standard situation when running counterpoint cues.

"+" and "–" buttons: are associated with the use of pile-on through faders. The "+" button causes the fader to add the incoming cue to what is already on stage; the "–" button reverses this process.

Fader: a handle which normally brings in one cue as it removes another. Faders usually are designed to be "dipless"; i.e., they will transfer a channel from one cue to another at the same setting with no visible change in the lighting.

Split fader: a two-handle device which performs exactly as above if the two handles are moved as one. However, if the handles are moved separately, the timing of the incoming and outgoing parts of the change may be separately controlled. Much more desirable than a single-handle fader.

Autofader: an electronic device which will automatically time and oper-ate a fade. Timing may set into fader manually or, in some cases, from memory. The operator initiates the fade and it proceeds auto-matically unless overridden. Usual time settings provide a choice of 0–60 seconds or 0–60 minutes.

Fade meter: a device associated with an autofader which displays the progress of the fade.

Split-handle autofader: a device which combines the functions of the split-handle fader with those of the autofader. Separate incoming and outgoing times may be established for each change and handled automatically.

Cut: has two meanings. (1) It refers to an instantaneous change in light-ing brought about by switching a cue into control instead of operat-ing it through a fader. (2) It refers to a button on one system which assigns ("cuts") a previously called up preset to a fader.

FOH inhibitor; FOH control: a device for overriding memory control of those lights operating in the front of the house. It allows the operator to bring up a cue on stage with the curtain closed and make no changes visible to the audience. The FOH controller then is used to add FOH lights with the operation of the curtain.

TERMS RELATED TO "PERMANENT" STORAGE OF CUES

Long-term storage: although a ferrite core will continue to hold informa-tion almost indefinitely, it is much more economical to remove information which must be kept, but inactive, for months or years to some cheaper means of storage. This cheaper means is usually in the form of a magnetic tape or a punched paper tape, either of which are low in cost and take little shelf space. A teletype printout is also pos-sible. Taped information may be fed back into the system when-ever it is needed. A tape can also be used as a security measure against tampering with the cue data in the memory.

Printout: console may be attached to a special teletypewriter which will type out the cues in written form. The format may be a continu-ous flow of material or it may be arranged according to the lighting setup of the theatre. Such printouts are useful for noting changes in cues which will later be fed into memory by an operator, or for study of cues. It is not very practical to feed cue information back into a memory from a printout because each cue must be laboriously typed back into the teletypewriter.

Memory-to-tape; read memory; dump store: buttons used to activate recording of cue data into a tape device.

Tape-to-memory: reverse of the above. This places information back in the memory usually erasing what was previously there. In some systems this process is fast enough to allow the reloading of the memory between acts. This increases the usefulness of a small memory.

Erase; clear memory; erase all cues: button which clears the memory of all data. It usually is provided with locking device.

The Simplest Memory Systems

Although most memory systems are quite complex, the easiest way to understand the operation of a memory system is to study it in its simplest form. Thus we will first look at a memory which is little more than an infinite preset system in which the cards have been replaced with a memory device. In such a system, cues are originated just as they would be on a preset system — they are built up on the manual bank. When the designer is satisfied with the cue, instead of ordering, "Write it!" and waiting while the preset readings are laboriously written down, he orders, "Record it!" The operator touches the "preset record" button and the cue is almost instantly transferred to the main memory — the operator having given it an address number before pushing the button. All cues are set up in the same manner. During the process, the operator may recall any cue already set up to compare it with the lighting being set at the moment. He may also alter the previously recorded cue, if necessary.

When all of the cues have been set up, or at any point when the designer or operator wishes to see the cues already finished, they can be played back. Let us assume that the operator wishes to play them back in sequence, beginning with cue 1, and wishes to fade from cue to cue. He calls up cue 1 by punching the digit "1" on the cue address keyboard, an arrangement of buttons identical to that on an adding machine. Cue 1 is immediately addressed in the memory and "1" appears in a display above the cue address buttons telling him that cue 1 is ready for assignment to a fader. Assuming that he wishes to start with a dark stage and fade in cue 1 on cue, he will assign cue 1 to the inoperative side of a fader, say fader A-up. He must have fader A in the down position when he does this or cue 1 will flash up on stage. At the proper moment he moves fader A to the up position and cue 1 appears on stage. Displays accompanying these operations will vary depending on the system used. Usually there will be a display which will tell the operator that he has assigned cue 1 to fader A-up and another that informs him that cue 1 is operative on stage. He calls up cue 2 in the same manner as cue 1 and assigns it to the now inoperative down position of the fader. Again on cue, he moves the fader to the down position to activate cue 2. He proceeds through the show in this manner calling up cues and assigning them as he needs them. If he has a second fader, "B," he can assign a cue to it which may then be piled onto the cue active on fader A.

So far the process seems identical to that followed on a preset system with the exception that all cues are instantly available and in random order. However a close look at the process of calling up a cue and altering it will point up one of the major differences between a memory system and a preset system. It will also illustrate the absolute step-by-step nature of computer logic.

The electrical process of storing and calling up information from a memory bank is not as simple as that used to call up the same information from a row of preset controllers. First of all, all modern memory banks are digital devices. This means that the information is stored as digital "bits." The digital system is a system of counting in which there are only two numerals, 0 and 1. All larger numbers are made up of combinations of these. A "bit" consists of a representation of either of the two basic numerals, 0 or 1. The advantage of this counting system is that electrical circuitry can easily be made to represent these two numerals as absolute conditions, off or on. Similarly the same information may be recorded in the form of something that is magnetized or not magnetized, a hole that is punched or not punched, and the like. Such "either-or" conditions have the great advantage of being quite immune to almost all types of interference ("noise" to the communications specialist). But the electrical representation of dimmer settings in a manual bank is not digital information; it is an analog of the light output of the lamp attached to the dimmer, the voltage being proportional to the light output. Therefore, in order to use a memory system to handle lighting cues, it is necessary that the cue information be converted into digital information. The device which does this is the analog-to-digital converter. Fortunately for the lighting industry, these devices are relatively cheap "off the shelf" items in the computer industry.

After the cue information has been converted to digital form, it may be recorded in a variety of memory devices. In order that the information may be retrieved when needed, it must be assigned an "address," a number which will enable the computer to locate it. Since cues are commonly numbered anyway, this presents no great problem.

Playback is somewhat more complicated. This is because it is not typically the instantaneous operation that recording can be. Dimmers require a constantly applied control voltage if they are to hold the setting that they have been given, something we seldom think about when using a preset system. In playback it is also common that the information in a cue will be gradually applied to the dimmers through a fader or master and that it may be combined with information already being given to the dimmers as a "pile-on" operation. Finally, during playback we may wish to make changes in the reading of one or more channels, and will sometimes want to make these changes permanent by changing what is in memory. When a cue is addressed it takes but milliseconds for the computer to scan the main memory and present the information in the form of an electrical replica of the digital information in the memory. This scanning process could be kept going, the information passed through a digital-to-analog converter, and fed via a fader to the dimmers. However this would tie up the main memory making it impossible to tell it to seek out another cue, in addition to creating many other difficulties. Thus an operation is introduced which results in one of the major differences between running a memory board and a preset board. The cue information, instead of feeding directly to the fader and thence the dimmers, is placed in a "buffer." A buffer, or "register," is a small memory, usually made up of transistors. It handles bits of digital information by means of two-state transistor units which either conduct (1) or do not conduct (0). Of course these states could also be arranged in the opposite order. This type of memory is temporary; it depends on a constant flow of electricity to hold the transistors in the proper condition. It can also be made to produce a constant output of signals, via a digital-to-analog converter, which can be fed to dimmers for as long as necessary. The process of assigning a set of cue information to a buffer is deceptively simple: The operator simply presses a button marked with the name of the fader or master on which he proposes to operate the cue and the job is done. He is told that it has happened by the appearance of the cue number in a display associated with the fader. However what has happened is quite different from the similar act of attaching a rank of presets to a fader on a preset board. The cue information has literally been copied and stored in a new location. The main memory has been detached from the system and is now free to seek out another cue. The operator is now working completely free of the main memory which still contains the original cue information, unaltered by having been scanned.

As far as the straightforward playback of cues is concerned, the above information is of little consequence to the operator. It is at the point that he wishes to alter a cue that it becomes important. Again we find the computer refusing to do anything on its own. Altering a cue in a preset situation is straightforward. One simply changes the setting on the appropriate channel controller of the proper preset rank and the job is done. This is the only place where this information is retained (except perhaps in written form outside the system), and the change will automatically be picked up when the preset is activated. This is not so in a memory system. There is no way to simply reach into the memory bank and make an adjustment. The cue being played on stage is not even connected to the memory bank at the time it is being used and, moreover, alterations made to a channel on a manual will not even alter the buffer unless told to do so. Thus the operator must think for the computer, telling it exactly what to do.

ALTERING A CUE

The process works as follows: The operator must first detach the channel he wishes to change from the control of the buffer and place it under the control of a manually operated controller. In some systems this will be a controller on a manual bank, in others a special channel-setting device that can be switched into any channel as needed. If the show is in progress when the operator wishes to make the change, he must be sure that the setting of the manual controller matches the setting coming from the buffer before he switches over. If it does not, the lights will change abruptly as he switches. Some modern systems take care of this matching problem automatically. Having established manual control, the operator may change the light to whatever reading he wishes. But he must remember (the computer will not do this for him) that he has made no change in the information in either the buffer or the main memory. This fact may be an advantage if the change he has made is temporary, caused only by a blocking error or the like. In this case, he may be spared the embarrassment of forgetting to restore the controller to its original setting for the next use of the preset. However if he wishes the change to be made a part of the cue, he must take special steps to make it so because, up to now, he has changed nothing in memory. He enters the change into memory by pressing a button marked "manual record," or a similar designation and the information is changed in the main memory. In some systems the buffer will automatically be changed; in others he must reassign the cue from main memory to accomplish this.

This much simplified outline of the flow of information through the simplest of memory systems will give the reader a rudimentary idea of the kinds of operations he may expect to encounter in using such a console. Many of the operations he has come to take for granted, such as the effect of resetting a preset controller, become more complicated. On the other hand, the tedious job of writing out cues and resetting presets from these written lists vanishes.

It is evident that the construction of a memory system which merely avoids the limitations of a card reader or a revolving preset board is a poor use of the capabilities of computer technology. Much more is possible both in lighting and in other theatre areas. For example, it is clear that computer techniques can aid the operation of counterpoint lighting as effectively as they can handle discrete cues. Given a sufficient number of buffers and a proper arrangement of faders, autofaders, and masters to operate from them, the way is open for the interpreter-operator to manipulate patterns with freedom heretofor uncontemplated. Memory can provide an almost inexhaustible supply of subtle patterns to be called up and worked in counterpoint as needed. Timing of counterpoint can be aided by the use of autofaders and memorized fade time.

In other theatrical areas there is now serious talk of using memory to handle cues in sound, rigging operation, special effects such as projections, and in any other area where the storage of cue data and its instant retrieval can be helpful. Those who are skeptical of the reliability of computer devices, which *do* fail and *do* make mistakes, look upon these possibilities with something approaching terror. Those who are optimistic about improving the reliability of these electrical gadgets see them as a tremendous "assist" for the theatrical artist of the future.

Parts of Memory Systems

Reviewing the material above will reveal that the following are basic to all memory systems:

1. A means of setting the lighting before the information is recorded in memory. There are two systems: (a) The channels may be adjusted on a regular manual bank and (b) channels may be called up, one at a time and assigned to a special intensity controller where they are set. As each channel is adjusted, its setting is temporarily recorded in a buffer. When the cue is complete, the information in the buffer is recorded in the main memory. Both systems have their advantages and disadvantages. The manual-bank system has the advantages of being a familiar way of operating, of providing good back-up for control of all channels in case of memory failure, and of making later retrieval and manual operation of a number of channels at the same time simple. Its disadvantages are that it increases console size inordinantly in large systems, placing parts out of reach of a single operator and that it may prove more costly than the buffer system.

    Advantages of the buffer system are its small size and lower cost compared with a large number of manual controllers. The main disadvantage is that only one channel can be under intensity control at a time. While this need not be a major handicap in setting cues, it is a problem if the channel call-up system is to serve as the only means of operating channels on manual during the run of a show. A possible alternative is to provide a number of manual controllers or "masters" to which channels may be assigned for manual control as needed.

    When the buffer system is being used to set up lighting, it is difficult to ascertain just what circuits are in use or have been set in a given cue. To clarify this, a "mimic" system often is installed. This consists of a field of small lights, one for each channel. These light up as the circuit is placed in use. See the "Glossary of Terms Related to Memory Consoles."

2. The memory bank. This is not evident to the operator except as it does its work. However there are two main types with important advantages and disadvantages. The most commonly used type of memory is the ferrite core. It has the advantage of being a "perma-

nent" memory. This means that it will retain its information indefinitely, whether or not current is supplied to it. However it is costly and bulky as modern memories go. A second type is the semiconductor memory. Most of these at the present time are being made using MOS chips (see glossary). These have the advantage of being very small in size, low in heat output and current drain, simple to install in the circuitry, and low in cost. Their one disadvantage is that they are "temporary" memories. This means that they retain the information only so long as current is supplied. This makes them more adaptable to buffer memories than to main memories. Nevertheless, their other advantages are so great that some manufacturers are using them as main memories and installing battery systems which automatically cut in when the power is turned off or when it fails. In one system, these batteries are designed to sustain the memory for a week. Further back-up is provided by facilities for making a tape recording of the contents of the memory which may be played back into the system whenever it is needed.

3. The playback system. This is the operational heart of the console. It is here that the operator must perform his interpretive function. There are several parts. First, there must be a means of addressing cues. This is usually a numeric keyboard similar to that found on a modern adding machine. It is equipped with a display that tells the operator what cue he has called up. Next, there are a variety of cue-assignment buttons that determine what buffer will receive the cue and thus how it will be introduced onto the stage. Next come the actual operative devices. These may be faders, time controllers, masters, joy sticks, or any combination of these functions. It is here that the human engineering, or the lack of it, on the part of the manufacturer is most evident. See the glossary and the captions of the illustrations of systems in Figure 10-7 for details of the present possibilities. New ideas are appearing regularly.

4. Facilities for altering cues. These are usually comprised of parts from the cue setup system and the playback system; however two additional items are needed. There must be some means of releasing a channel from memory and regaining control over it manually, and there must be a way of recording the altered setting into an existing preset. A variety of buttons and switches are provided for these purposes.

5. Emergency access to channels for manual operation. This may be related to the cue-altering system above, but should include means of controlling a number of channels at the same time and at different readings and timings. A single call-up is not sufficient.

OPTIONAL CONSOLE PARTS

The following devices are optional only in the sense that a primitive memory system could operate without them. In most cases they offer conveniences and flexibility of operation without which the computer system would hardly be worthwhile. (See the glossary for definitions of the terms.)

The sequence player is practically essential for revolving presets if cues come fast on top of each other. When combined with cue insertion to perfect the sequence of cues, it makes Broadway professional lighting as automatic as possible.

The split autofader makes possible the automatic timing of cross-fades with separate intervals for oncoming and outgoing lighting. Both up and down changes start together unless special manual override is used, but they finish separately. This device is as necessary as the sequence player to accurate revolving presets.

FACILITIES SPECIALLY SUITED TO COUNTERPOINT

While the devices mentioned above will solve many of the problems of the operator of discrete cues, they leave the operator of counterpoint lighting with some unsolved problems. (Remember that it is possible to operate counterpoint lighting as revolving presets, but only at the expense of detailed and time-consuming analysis to break it down into a large number of cues.) The most essential aid to operating counterpoint cues is multiple time lines. There must be a number of buffers feeding faders (or other devices) each capable of its own time line. Autofaders are helpful although few counterpoint cues are without accelerations or decelerations. Subtle override must be possible. If it becomes economically possible to memorize accelerating and decelerating fades, these, too would be helpful.

The number of buffers, each capable of a separate time line, is subject to controversy. Obviously, the number of time lines controllable at one time by an operator is the absolute minimum. This is probably at least four to six, if the operator has the help of autofaders. A system equipped with two split-handle autofaders of the time-setting variety and arranged for easy override, is probably the barest minimum for any console considered capable of handling counterpoint. The installation of masters instead of faders may add more time lines at less cost and any two masters provide the same facility as a split-handle fader.

A more reasonable number of time lines for counterpoint control is probably eight to ten. While it is unlikely that the design will call for simultaneous operation of this many time lines at once, it is likely that their operation will be so closely interwoven in complex cues that they should be available to the operator with no intervening "call up and assign" operation.

Identification of Patterns

One of the difficulties with the entire memory concept, particularly where the operator is required to perform considerable ad lib lighting, or in educational theatre where the purpose is the development of designer-technicians, is that the memory system tends to force all reference to the lighting into the form of abstract address numbers. In this instance, the needs of the computer, probably because they coincide with the older practice of numbering rotating presets, have been allowed to dominate the needs of the human operator. The problem is neither apparent nor serious in the case of a *répétiteur* situation although it increases the possibility of undetected errors. It can be acute in the educational theatre where the instructor is trying to get the student operator-designer to focus his attention on the lighting, not the mechanics. It is quite possible for a memory system to memorize and display a more functional identification of patterns than their address numbers. This is consistently done in the case of computer programs which contain written-out notes that aid the programmer in remembering operations. Such a system of cue identification is being contemplated in the control board for the new British National Theatre in London. It deserves much more general consideration.

Portable Packaged Memory Systems

The fantastic reduction in the size of memory devices and their associated circuitry and the concurrent decrease in the cost of these units has brought about the development of the portable memory control console. These units are analogous to the portable preset consoles; in fact they may use the same dimmer packs. However the consoles contain small memories instead of preset ranks. Simplified recording and playback facilities are provided.

At this stage in their development, the number of cues which can be handled by packaged memory boards is rather low and facilities for entering additional cues while in operation tend to be restrictive. For example, one system provides the opportunity for entering new cues while operating on memory. It also provides for the possibility of operating one or more channels manually. However these two functions cannot be performed at the same time. While the need for both operations at the same time might not arise on a large system — many of them have the same limitation — the limited number of cues in the portable memory (18) makes it much more likely that the operator would be caught in this trap.

In spite of their present primitive beginning, the future of portable memory consoles is bright indeed.

Some Modern Memory Systems

The illustrations in Figure 10-7 are examples of the memory systems available late in 1973. No attempt has been made to cover all of the systems available nor even all of the many permutations of the systems illustrated. The purpose of this section is merely to provide an overview of two categories of memory devices: (1) those representing the "state of the art" and (2) some samples of systems designed for theatres with more modest budgets. The entire field of lighting control by means of memory devices is progressing in quantum leaps. New devices are constantly appearing and the basic price of memory storage is dropping rapidly. Information concerning systems currently available and the cost of such systems should be sought from the various manufacturers.

EVALUATING THE MEMORY SYSTEMS

In addition to a brief explanation of the workings of each of the systems portrayed, some attempt has been made to estimate how effectively it might work under the pressures of production. Since all of the systems have been designed around the revolving preset concept, there seems no doubt that they will all handle discrete lighting efficiently. Differences begin to appear when the systems are tested against the needs of counterpoint lighting. One of the most basic elements of counterpoint lighting is the operation of a number of "time lines" simultaneously. A "time line" is an element of counterpoint lighting—basically a design element—which must be operated at its own tempo. It must be capable of accelerations or decelerations independent of other time lines. Thus the number of time lines available to the operator of a memory system is one indication of the ability of that system to operate in the counterpoint mode. Obviously this is a crude measure because many other factors, most importantly human engineering, enter into a complete evaluation of a system for counterpoint.

HOW MANY MEMORIES ARE ENOUGH?

Unfortunately there is no simple answer to this question because of the many variables involved. Moreover, most of the systems discussed below offer a variety of basic memory packages plus the option of additional memories via a tape-recording device. In evaluating a system for adequate memory, at least two general categories of information must be assessed: (1) How rapidly will the style of lighting used by the producing group use up memories? Will the system have at least enough memories to take the production to a point convenient for using the tape storage to refill the memory bank? (2) How fast and convenient is the tape storage unit? Will it be feasible to refill the memory during act breaks? The above is all predicated on a reliable memory and tape system. Such reliability can best be tested by talking to those already using the system. Tape systems, magnetic or punched paper, are subject to failures and must be carefully tested, particularly if their use is to be a regular part of the production process instead of a back-up procedure in case of accidental destruction of information in memory.

THE MEMO-Q SYSTEM

This system is manufactured by Rank Strand Electric of England and sold in the United States by Strand Century, Incorporated. It bears the closest resemblance to a preset system of any of the systems here discussed. A controller is provided for each channel, similar to the manual bank of a preset board. The end of such a row of controllers is seen at the upper left of Figure 10-7a. Cues are built up on these controllers just as they would be on a rank of controllers on a preset board. They may be observed on stage as they are being assembled or "blind recorded" while the stage is under the control of an already prepared memory. Once a cue is ready, it is assigned a number by means of the numerical keyboard labeled "preset select" in Figure 10-7a and recorded in main memory by pushing "manual record." This process can be continued for whatever the memory capacity of the particular system is. For 100 channels this may range from 160 to 640 presets.

Cues are called up by use of the preset-select keyboard. They may be taken manually on the C-D controller by assigning them to the proper

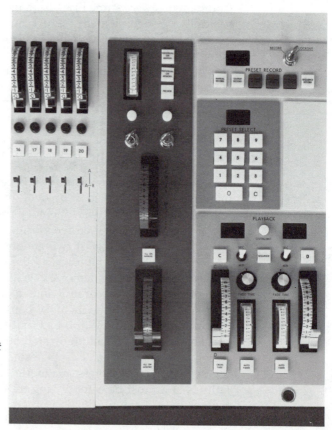

FIGURE *10-7a*
Basic Parts of a Memo-Q System. Close-up shows the end of a row of circuit controllers (left), and the basic record and playback devices which form the main part of the console.
Strand Century.

fader via the C or D select buttons shown on the playback panel of Figure 10-7a. Once assigned, they may be piled on, cross-faded, or faded by means of the autofader at the discretion of the operator. Auto-fader times are set by the dials and activated by moving the appropriate fader to its extreme position. The fade will begin at once and proceed at the preset time. Manual takeover of the fade can be accomplished by moving the manual fader (C or D) to equal the setting of the autofader-indicating meter. This automatically halts the autofade and returns control to the manual fader.

A second set of fader and autofader controls are available as optional equipment. This makes the system capable of four time lines. Cues may be recorded and played either sequentially or at random. In the pile-on mode the highest dimmer reading prevails.

Circuits may be retrieved from manual control at any time by pressing the "individual on manual" button (top center, Figure 10-7a) and at the same time pressing on the channel controller desired. This activates a system which will effect the transfer to manual control when the individual channel controller is moved to match the reading of the circuit in memory. The circuit may be reset and the new reading recorded into the existing memory by pressing "individual record" (top center, Figure 10-7a). This records the change and returns the circuit to memory control. If the change is temporary, the circuit may be returned to memory control at any time by a second operation of the same buttons used to select the channel. Several circuits may be retrieved and changed at the same time, if desired.

Optional features include manual submasters (top right, Figure 10-7b) which have the effect of increasing the number of time lines

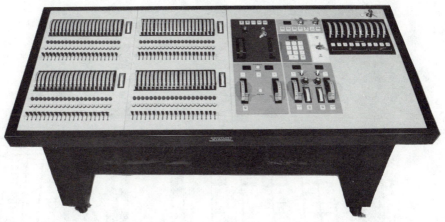

FIGURE 10-7b
A Large Memo-Q System. This system features a double set of faders allowing four time lines, a total of 80 control channels, and an assortment of auxiliary control devices. Strand Century.

available, although not via memory. A tape system is also optionally provided for recording cues for long-term storage.

THE Q-FILE SYSTEM

This system is made by Thorn Lighting of England. It is sold in the United States by Kliegl Brothers. The Q-File system differs markedly from the Memo-Q system, particularly in these ways: (1) There is no manual bank; channels are called up with a numeric keyboard as needed. (2) When cues are piled on, the last cue prevails no matter what the reading of the same channel in the previous cue. (3) Normal operation of cues is by way of autofade devices.

The process of building up cues begins with the circuit controller (Figure 10-7c, right). Circuits are called up, displayed on stage by pressing "select stage" and "set" in a buffer by moving the circuit fader to the required setting. One or several circuits may be set at the same time to the same reading. Calling up a new batch of circuits removes the previously set circuits from the circuit fader's control but leaves the reading established in the buffer. To check the setting of any circuit in the buffer, simply select its number. The circuit fader automatically moves to the reading. A proximity switch in the circuit-fader handle makes it possible to alter the circuit's reading by grasping the handle and moving it in the desired direction. Mimic facilities and a flashing arrangement are available to facilitate circuit setting (Figure 10-7d). The same process may be used for blind recording by using "select preset" instead of "select stage." When the cue is finished, it is recorded in the main memory by means of the "memory controller" (Figure 10-7c, left). The cue is assigned a number at the numerical keyboard and recorded by depressing "record" under either "stage" or "preset," as needed.

Recall and playback of memories is accomplished by the combined

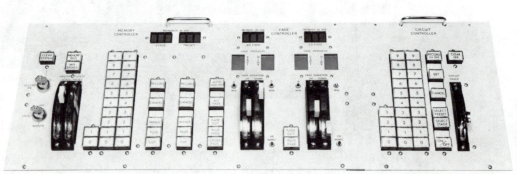

FIGURE 10-7c
Main Operating Parts of a Q-File System. Thorn Lighting, London.

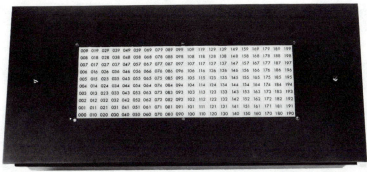

FIGURE *10-7d*
Mimic Panel for Q-File.
This optional device indi-
cates which channels are
active. Thorn Lighting,
London.

operation of the "memory controller" and the "fade controller" sections (Figure 10-7c, center). Memories are called up and assigned to either "AB fade" or "CD fade." Here they are brought into action by setting the fade time and initiating the fade. At any time, fade time may be changed, additional memories may be added, and the fades stopped, if necessary.

Special features are "plus fade" and "minus fade." "Plus fade" piles one cue upon another but with an important difference. The oncoming reading prevails no matter what the previous reading might have been in the case of channels common to two memories. Thus an oncoming cue may have the effect of reducing already established readings as well as increasing them.

"Minus fade" is not the reciprocal of "plus fade." A "minus fade" has the effect of setting all channels active in the cue called for "minus fade" to *zero,* although they may have had higher readings in previously called cues which are still active in the pile-on situation. In effect the last assigned cue has thus captured complete control of all circuits which appear in it and when it is removed as a "minus," these circuits go to zero. This feature may also be used to capture and remove circuits not visibly on in the last assigned cue by setting such circuits to "on at zero" in the cue. This is done by calling the circuit when establishing the cue and giving it a circuit-controller setting of zero.

The "C-D fade" offers much the same control over another set on oncoming and off-going circuits. The "A-B fade" also is provided with a single-handle cross-fade function, if this is needed. Since the faders are really time-setting devices, actual fade progress is indicated in percentages by the large numbers above the "A-B fade" and "C-D fade" controls.

Individual circuit retrieval and alteration is effected by means of the circuit controller. The circuit is selected by punching its number into the keyboard. The circuit fader automatically moves to the setting of the selected circuit and control may be taken merely by touching the circuit fader handle. Changes may then be made as needed.

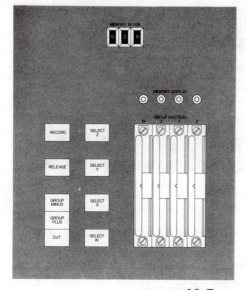
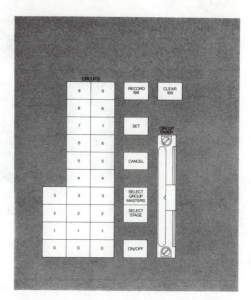

FIGURE *10-7e*

Group Master Facility for Q-File. This optional device allows the operation of four memories at the same time. Thorn Lighting, London.

The basic system of Q-File offers four time lines via memory plus a possible fifth via the circuit controller. Two of these lines will be oncoming and two outgoing at any given moment. There is the possibility of acquiring additional time lines via the add-on feature of the faders which makes it possible to add another memory to an existing fade at any time. Timing for the added memory begins with its addition and continues for the set duration independent of the already started cue. Since fade time can be altered at any time or halted, restarted, or even reversed, considerable flexibility exists at this point.

An auxiliary feature of considerable importance to the operation of counterpoint lighting is the "group master facility." This consists of a second circuit controller for purposes of calling up channels onto the four group masters (Figure 10-7e) in order to balance groups of lighting during set up. During playback, a memory may be assigned to each group master and played back as a single time line. Unfortunately the group masters operate from the same buffers as the regular "A-B" and "C-D" faders making it impossible to operate the faders and the group masters as simultaneous time lines.

Another optional facility is the submaster selection matrix and manual submasters. These provide the possibility of a number of time lines independent of memory. The number of time lines depends on the number of submasters optioned (see Figure 10-7f, upper right). The matrix is operated by inserting the pins which make contact between the individual circuit connections and the submaster outputs.

Q-File offers as an additional option a remote unit (see Figure 10-7g) that allows the setting up of cues from another location—say the middle of the house—by means of a unit resembling the circuit controller. A

FIGURE *10-7f*
Submaster Selector Matrix for Q-File.
Thorn Lighting, London.

FIGURE *10-7g*
Q-File Remote Unit. Portable unit that enables an operator to set cues from a variety of locations. Playback facilities from this unit are limited. Thorn Lighting, London.

FIGURE *10-7h*
*Q-File Tape Unit. This is
typical of magnetic-tape
recording devices for
memory systems. A car-
tridge-tape unit is used to
record cues.* Thorn Lighting, London.

tape-recording unit (see Figure 10-7*h*) also is offered to extend the capacity of the system beyond the basic 100 or 200 cues.

Both of the above systems come with a variety of other functions that
facilitate operation. These include such things as a device that will
enable the operator to inhibit the operation of a channel in all cues in
case of misaligned instruments, for instance, "solo" devices which cut
off all channels but one or flashers which flash a channel to enable the
operator to check its instrumentation, a special flasher circuit for
effects, and a wide variety of indicator devices to inform the operator
of the state of the various functions available to him.

The Memory Center
Lighting Control System

This system is produced by Berkey Colortran of Burbank, California.
It is a very recently developed system, being in the final stages of refinement as these pages go to press. Therefore the following discussion
is subject to change even before the first prototype of the system becomes available for testing. The MC system is basically a modular system, although it offers a great degree of flexibility within the modular
approach. The buyer has the choice of main memory devices. He may
choose ferrite core for maximum security against information loss or
M.O.S. memory (see glossary of terms related to memory consoles) with
a self-charging battery system for sustaining memory. The latter offers
more memory for a lower cost. The total number of memories available

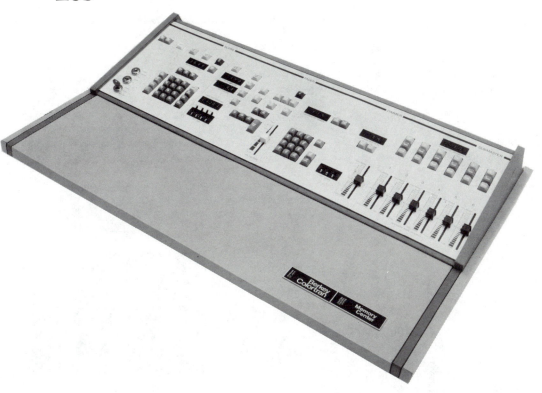

FIGURE *10-7i*
The Memory Center Lighting Control System. This system by Berkey Colortran features memorized fade times in addition to the memorization of dimmer readings. See Figures 10-7j-m for detailed views of parts of the console. Photo: Berkey Colortran.

in a system varies widely depending on the number of channels and the memories desired. The basic module of memory is a unit of scenes and dimmers whose multiple equals 4000. For example, 100 memories times 40 dimmers would be one module. The next increment of increase would be 100 memories times 80 dimmers, or 40 dimmers times 200 memories. Other parts of the console also come in modules; for instance, there may be from one to eight fader modules.

Recording of cues is done on this system much in the same way it is done in the Q-File system described above. Circuits are called up one after the other on a numeric keyboard (see Figures 10-7i, l), adjusted as to level and recorded in a buffer. The entire cue is thus built up, with as many readjustments as needed and, when ready, assigned a cue number and recorded in main memory. A special feature of this system is the ease with which cues may be inserted into an already prepared

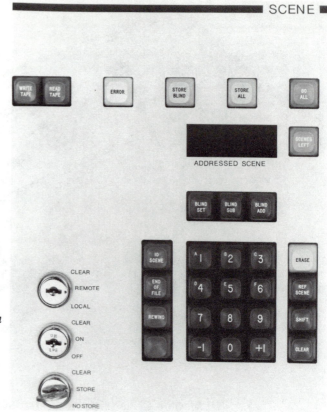

FIGURE *10-7j*
Scene Module of Memory Center System. This section contains the system lock controls, the tape controls and the alphanumeric keyboard for calling up memories. Photo: Berkey Colortran.

sequence. The memory address keyboard which assigns cue numbers is provided with a key labeled "shift" (see Figures 10-7*i, j,* left). Depressing this key after addressing a cue number makes possible the creation of a new cue with a letter designation which will be inserted between the previously addressed cue and the one following it. For example one might address cue 34, then press "shift." At this point cues 34A through 34F may be inserted by addressing them and recording information in the memory under these numbers. The same degree of expansion is possible for each cue number up to the total capacity of the memory. Such a system is particularly important in the MC system because it is capable of recording not only cue information but linear fade times. The latter must, of course, be associated with the cues in sequence.

The basic time or intensity setting device of the MC system is a "joy stick" control whose normal position is at the center of its scale (see Figure 10-7*l* for examples). In center position it exerts no influence over whatever variable may be assigned to it. Moving downward from center causes a decrease. The farther it is moved off center, the more pronounced the change. The upper extreme makes the change instantaneous, the lower extreme stops it entirely. Releasing the handle allows it to return to the center position, removing its further influence from the variable and, if the change has not been completed, control returns to the memory. These devices appear wherever on the console manual control over a variable may be needed.

Once a series of cues has been recorded, the operator may go through them establishing fade times between each pair of cues, or he may choose to call them up, assign them to fader modules, and establish fade times manually as in the systems described above. If fade times are to be recorded, the "load fade" button is pushed (see Figure 10-7k) and an approximate fade time dialed into the "set time" dials. This fade may then be viewed, changed as needed by the "fade override" and, when correct, recorded by pressing the "store fade" button. Recording the fade also establishes a linkage between the present cue and the next cue encompassing the fade and relates the entire operation to the particular fader module on which it was set up so that it will be recalled in proper sequence on that fader for playback.

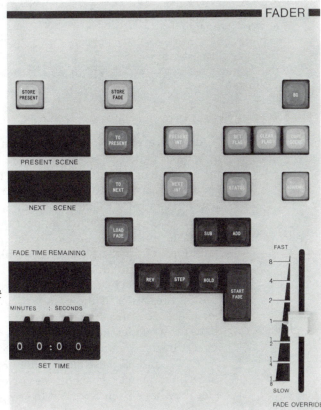

FIGURE 10-7k
Fader Module of Memory Center System. Up to eight of these modules may be included in a system. The module contains fade time setting facilities, various controls for operating cues and the fade time override joy stick. Photo: Berkey Colortran.

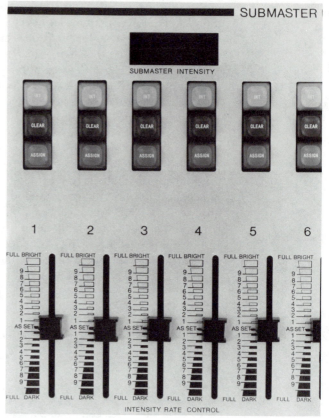

FIGURE *10-7l*
Submaster Module of Memory Center System. Three such modules may be made part of a console. Dimmers may be assigned to a submaster at any time, as need but no dimmer may be assigned to more than one submaster at a time. Photo: Berkey Colortran.

Also, as a part of the cue recording process or afterward, dimmers may be assigned to submasters (see Figure 10-7l). These are available in this system in modules of six up to a total of 18. An assignment to submaster carries through the entire run of cues, no matter what memory is in control. Any number of dimmers may be assigned to any submaster but no dimmer may appear on more than one submaster. Each submaster provides an intensity rate controller (joy stick) which allows variations of intensity setting within the limits established by the memory in control during each cue.

Playback starts by calling up the first needed cue on the scene module (see Figure 10-7j). If the system is in sequence mode and fades have been recorded, this cue and all others in the sequence will be assigned to the proper fader module (see Figure 10-7k) in the sequence previously set up. If, for example, fader module three has been assigned cues 3, 11, 19, 27, and 35 these cues will automatically be called up on module three in sequence. If such a set of cues must be called up randomly after they have been recorded in sequence, the assigned fade times will follow the "present" cue to which they were originally assigned. In random call-up any cue may be assigned to any fader module. The "fade time remaining" indicator will always inform the operator of the fade time available whether in sequence or not.

The fader module contains displays revealing the "present cue," the "next cue," and "fade time remaining." There is a fade time override joy stick for time alterations and "start," "step," "hold," and "reverse" buttons. Each of these actions is reversible as needed. Each module also provides an "add" and "subtract" feature which works like the "plus" and "minus" fade system in Q-file. Thus an "add" cue may cause a channel to change upward or downward in intensity, depending on the setting in the last cue added. A "subtract" cue causes all channels live in the subtracted cue to go to zero regardless of their setting in other memories active in the fader module at the time. It is important, however, to note that this effect prevails only within the individual fader module. If a channel happens to be under the control of two or more fader modules at the same time, the highest reading among the active modules prevails.

The above playback operations are subject to further alteration by

FIGURE 10-7m
Dimmer Module of Memory Center System. The keyboard calls up dimmer channels one after the other for adjustment in setting cues. Adjustment is made by the joy stick control, lower left. The same system may be used to call up and correct a channel during the production. Photo: Berkey Color-tran.

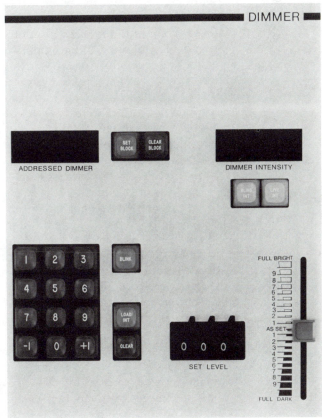

operation of the submasters controlling the dimmers as they have been assigned. This makes it possible, for example, to bring in a cue with part of its channels held to a low reading or zero pending a piece of action on stage, at which point the channels may be brought in manually at a rate following the action. However, it is not possible for the submasters to alter the readings above the limits set by the memory in control at the time.

Retrieval and manual adjustment of circuits may be done in several ways depending on the number of circuits involved and the needs of the situation. A single channel may be retrieved by addressing the channel by number at the dimmer module (see Figure 10-7m) and pressing the "present intensity" button on the fader module. This will cause the system to search the fader modules and set the highest intensity reading of that channel in the intensity display. The same action enables the operator then to use the intensity rate control to alter the channel as needed. Multiple channels may be adjusted sequentially in this manner. If a number of channels must be set into a new pattern of intensities and the change entered into action as a unit, and if time permits, a blind cue may be prepared in buffer and assigned to a fader module for action. This same process may also be used to prepare a set of cues by blind recording while the lighting is in active control of another memory. A third method of retrieval can be made available to those who opt to purchase a set of manual masters and a matrix selection device for assigning dimmers to them as needed. This system operates independently of the entire memory system and can therefore take over control at any time. Any pattern of control may thus be built up within the limits of the masters available.

If one or more channels are discovered to be out of adjustment, misaligned for example, a "block" button (see Figure 10-7m) is available which will set these errant channels to zero in all memory controls until they may be repaired. When the "clear block" button is depressed, the control returns to originally set cues.

The Memory Center Lighting Control System offers up to eight completely discrete time lines of control for counterpoint lighting. Further partial controls are available through the submasters. The unique combination of "add" and "subtract" functions within each fader module and the pile-on "highest reading prevails" relationship that exists between fader modules offers an extremely flexible means of interrelating fades. The recorded fades are linear in nature; no accelerations or decelerations are recorded. However, accelerations and decelerations are available to the operator at each fader module via the fade override joy stick, and some fades may be allowed to proceed at linear rates while others are accelerated or decelerated manually.

The Berkey Colortran system offers a number of additional options, including a tape recording device which will provide long-term and back-up storage for the data in memory. This system is capable of loading into or out of memory in less than two minutes.

Modestly Priced Memory Systems

The systems discussed below represent attempts by manufacturers to provide reasonably flexible systems at prices well under the over-$100,000 class of the large systems above. In both cases the manufacturer has taken a modular approach, manufacturing and stocking console units which can be fitted together to meet the individual needs of customers. This presents some limitations but results in much lower prices. Additionally, manufacturers have tried to utilize more economical circuitry and, in some cases, to eliminate expensive but convenient "extras."

Since the development of modular systems is still quite new — one manufacturer has only a prototype as this goes to press — buyers should investigate systems carefully before making decisions. The information given here can serve only to introduce the general concept of medium-priced modular-control boards; specifics must come from the manufacturers themselves.

THE MMS

MMS is the Rank Strand trademark for their "Modular Memory System." It is sold in the United States by Strand Century. Two versions

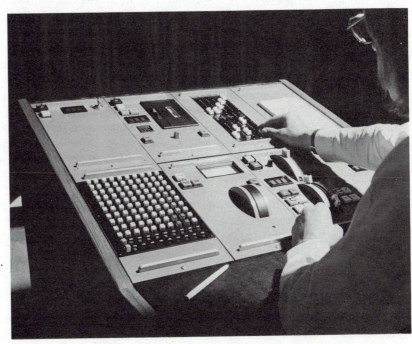

FIGURE *10-7n*
The MMS System. This shows one of the many possible combinations of MMS modules. Rank Strand.

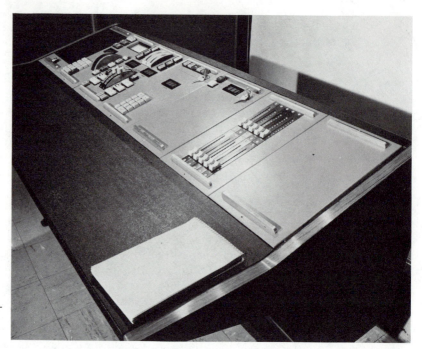

FIGURE *10-7o*
Another MMS Con-
sole Possibility.
Rank Strand.

are shown in Figures 10-7*n* and 10-7*o*. These demonstrate the way in which the pre-manufactured modules can be fitted together to make up consoles. In Figure 10-7*n* the field of push buttons is used to call up channels as needed and serves also as a mimic panel to indicate what circuits are active at any given moment. A numeric keyboard serves the call-up function on the console in Figure 10-7*o;* no mimic system is provided. Both consoles illustrated have split faders, an autofade device, and a special fader wheel (center, Figure 10-7*n*). This device serves as a continuous movement fader which can control any circuit that is assigned to it. The channel is automatically picked up at its present reading when assigned to the wheel, eliminating matching problems. Movement upward alters the reading upward and movement downward does the opposite. The wheel turns continuously in either direction, providing a very flexible way of controlling lighting. Also shown on both consoles are a group of submasters which offer additional time lines. The system shown in Figure 10-7*n* features a tape-recording unit that extends the memory capacity beyond that built into the console.

Q-LEVEL

"Q-Level" is the name applied to the Thorn modular system as it is sold in the United States by Kliegl Brothers. It is known as "Q-Master" in England where it is manufactured. This system (see Figure 10-7p) consists of a set of manual controllers for setting cues and for circuit retrieval. The latter function is performed by moving the manual controller until a pair of indicator lights extinguish. At that point the controller matches the reading in memory and transfer can be effected with no jump in intensity. Circuits may also be permanently held in manual control by means of individual playback/memory switches associated with each controller. A manual master is provided that enables the entire manual package to be treated as a time line for counterpoint purposes. Memories (99 in number) are called up by keyboard and assigned to either of two manually operated playback masters or to an autofader. Pile on is possible. An optional mimic system will indicate what circuits are active and roughly at what intensity. Memories may be piled on by adding a memory on, say fader A, to one on fader B. Three-time-line operation is possible by means of the two manual faders and the autofader. The autofader is equipped with the same plus and minus fade operation explained above under "Q-File" and it operates in the same way: The last assigned cue takes control making it possible to add downward intensity changes as well as upward ones. A minus-fade removes all channels active in the minus-faded cue. However circuits under the control of the manual masters, A and B, will be piled on with the highest reading prevailing. These two functions are not interlocked; if a channel is under control of both fader B and the autofader and the cue on the autofader is minus faded to zero, the common circuit will

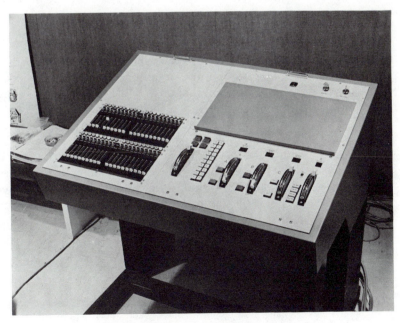

FIGURE *10-7p*
Q-Level System.
This system is known as "Q-Master" in England, hence the label on this particular console. Although not as obviously modular in appearance, this system is also based on a modular concept. Thorn Lighting, London.

remain at its fader. B setting. If, however the circuit is common only to two successive cues on the autofader, it will go to zero.

The above combination of controls offers three time lines in memory with the possibility of additional memories being piled on the autofader. The manual offers another time line.

Summary

It appears that future theatre historians may look upon the introduction of the computer into theatre as an event rivaling the importance of the introduction of electricity. In its recent history, the theatre has often yearned after the artistic superman—the artist who has the vision and skill to exert interpretive control over the entire production. Efforts to do this have been many, and in a few cases the results have been spectacular. Max Reinhardt is an example. But would-be theatre supermen have tended to fail because of their inability to handle all of the many details of theatre art at once. The past solution to this problem, when it has been solved, has been through the selfless dedication of assistants to the "master." Thus the few successful supermen have moved to fame and artistic success over the artistically frustrated bodies of their assistants. The cost to the art of the theatre has often been far more than the gain.

Perhaps the computer offers a solution to this problem. It can be made to handle humanly impossible amounts of data with ease. Once programmed, it can sort, arrange, and retrieve data at incredible rates. Perhaps it is the help needed by that theatre worker who in the old saw, "has 100 things to do, but time for only 10 of them." Perhaps it will allow many more to try their artistic talents as Max Reinhardts.

There has already been serious speculation that the computer can be assigned the task of simulating an entire theatrical production; that setting, lighting, costuming, and even blocking, can be fed into a vastly complex computer-simulator where the theatrical artist can try thousands of combinations, if necessary, before deciding on the one he wants. Note that it is the artist, not the machine, that decides. After the choice has been made, the machine can be instructed to prepare working drawings, specifications sheets, plots, and the like, and eventually to provide a set of memorized cues for running the show.[6]

Much of this is currently possible at the present state of computer development; the rest is certainly possible in the future. Such a device could free the mind of an artist who might then reach new heights of artistic expression.

---

[6] "Synthesized Systems for the Performing Arts." Paper delivered at the 1973 National Convention of the United States Institute for Theatre Technology, St. Louis, Missouri, March 1973 by Jonell Polansky and Robert Slutske.

DISTRIBUTION OF THE CURRENT FROM THE DIMMERS TO THE LAMPS

11

The path of electrical current from the dimmer to the lamp, whether the dimmer is remotely or directly controlled, is usually complex. The path normally begins with output wiring of the dimmer, passes through some type of interconnecting device, travels through permanently installed wiring within the structure of the building, terminating in some type of plug-in device. From this point, the current travels through portable wiring to the heat resistant pigtail of the instrument. Return circuitry follows the same path, eventually returning to the ground bus in the dimmer rack or at the patch bay. Modern innovations have altered this scheme of things somewhat, but our discussion will first follow the conventional pattern; then new developments will be examined.

The Dimmer Room or Enclosure

Dimmer rooms or enclosures are the beginning of our study. In such enclosures, the dimmers are mounted on heavy metal racks, usually in such a way that an individual dimmer may be removed for servicing without disturbing others. Necessary master circuit breakers and individual breakers to protect the dimmers usually are mounted in the same rack. Often houselighting and nondim control apparatus are mounted here also. Since heat will be generated in this mass of equipment even if transformer or solid-state dimmers are used, ventilation is necessary. The usual ventilation device, wire mesh sides and back on the enclosure, may be augmented by forced ventilation of the entire room.

Since most dimmer racks, even autotransformer boards, are a source of noise, they are usually acoustically insulated from the rest of the structure. The floating slab of concrete is frequently used. It consists of a cement foundation resting on heavy acoustic insulation, which rests on the structural floor of the building.

The interior wiring of dimmer racks must, by law, be heat resistant "switchboard wire." This wire is brought to terminal blocks, heavy fiber or plastic blocks equipped with rows of brass terminals to make connections between the internal wiring of the dimmer rack and the wires leading out of it. At such a terminal board, the output wiring of each dimmer leaves the dimmer rack. Live wires are carried out singly; the neutral may be one large conductor representing all neutral leads for the dimmers and the nondim circuits. These wires, now standard plastic-insulated building wiring, lead to the stage.

At the stage, the wires usually terminate at the *interconnecting panel,* a necessary part of every adequate lighting system. There are several types of interconnecting equipment, but all have the common purpose of making it possible to attach any lamp (load) to any dimmer, regardless of the location of the lamp.

Dimmer Utilization: Flexibility and Control Configuration

Two interlocking problems arise when lighting control designers seek to determine how many dimmers should be installed in a system, and what arrangements should be made to attach instruments to these dimmers.

1. Dimmer utilization. Some dimmers will be used almost constantly in the process of lighting a production; others will be in operation only a few moments. This may be uneconomical particularly when the number of dimmers is severely limited.
2. Rational configuration of control machinery. Operation of control boards will be much simpler if related functions can be placed on adjacent operating levers. This cannot be accomplished if dimmers are permanently attached to outlets, and control devices to dimmers.

Economics places limitations on the available solutions to these problems. The problems are most acute where limited funds cause the designers to install relatively few dimmers, and to provide only the simplest of control devices for them. Ironically, the other end of the economic spectrum almost automatically provides solutions through the very elaborateness of the equipment. The range of solutions is approximately as follows.

1. Extremely economical installations designed for quasi-theatrical use. These are installations found in lecture halls, club rooms, etc., where only a minimum of lighting control is needed. Such installations should never be accepted as satisfying, minimal dramatic lighting needs, although there will be those who will claim that they are sufficient.

Minimal installations will usually consist of a few wall-mounted controls permanently wired to the instruments or outlets they control. The dimming devices will probably be autotransformer units in older installations and triac solid-state dimmers in new installations. A variety of SCR dimmers have also been used for such purposes. No utilization or control configuration problems will occur as long as the equipment is limited to its intended purpose. Troubles begin when such equipment is asked to serve theatrical functions. Attempts are often made to add instruments to the system and/or substitute instruments from moment to moment, increasing dimmer utilization. This also complicates the simple control configuration. Where a controller originally had one unchanging function, it may now have several. Such adaptations are made by inserting some form of interpatch device between the dimmers and their intended load. This converts the system from "inflexible" (solidly wired-in loads) to "flexible" easily changeable loads. Flexibility also generates problems. Overloading becomes possible and hot patching is even easier. Solid-state dimmers, particularly those early units installed in just such installations, do not take kindly to these offenses, and often fail. Autotransformers are more tolerant—they will survive years of this treatment if properly serviced. In any event, this limited system will not serve the needs of dramatic lighting.

2. Combination installations principally for public assembly use but adaptable to simple theatrical use. Public school auditoriums, small municipal auditoriums, etc., fall into this category. Unfortunately many eager and growing theatre groups are forced to produce in such pseudo-theatres, and are often expected to mount rather elaborate productions in them. Lighting equipment tends to be a constant source of frustration. The most frequent problem is that such multipurpose buildings are equipped with control apparatus more extensive than that mentioned above, but designed in exactly the same manner. A rather small number of high-wattage dimmers has been wired permanently to borderlights and footlights plus a couple of floor pockets for portable equipment. If the producing group is "lucky" some farsighted individual will have discovered that front-of-house light is good for concerts and lectures as well as theatricals and some form of antiproscenium lighting will exist. It will often be permanently wired to two or three dimmers. Such poorly arranged equipment makes good dramatic lighting impossible although the potential may exist in the equipment itself.

The solution to the above problem is the insertion of a patching arrangement to make the system flexible. Additional protection may have to be provided for the now-detachable load circuits, and the local code may require bringing the entire system up to current safety standards. This could make the project rather expensive, but the results in terms of utilization of dimming equipment will pay off well. It is poor economy to make new installations of this intermediate scale without carefully designed interpatching equipment. Although cost of dimmers is coming down and there should be an effort to install as many as possible, the limitations imposed on such theatres rarely make it possible to install enough dimmers to eliminate interpatching.

3. Completely equipped theatres. These are theatres built with the intention of facilitating serious dramatic productions. Lighting equipment should be elaborate, and mere "adequacy" should be viewed with suspicion. In such installations as these, two alternatives should be considered: (a) It may be possible at present dimmer costs to install one dimmer per load circuit, eliminating any need for interpatching. In this case, the control-configuration problem will need to be solved by some means of patterning the low-voltage dimmer control circuitry—a much easier and less costly job than interpatching heavy load current from dimmers. (b) If a complete set of dimmers is not feasible, some form of interpatching loads *must* be provided. No theatre should allow itself to be trapped between these two alternatives.

Another possibility which may be considered is the purchase of *portable control packages*. These units all come with the interpatching built into them—their portability demands this. The control-configuration problem will be solved by assigning packages to inter-related functions, a procedure which often produces some very rational control arrangements. If minimal assembly halls can be provided with power outlets for package-control units and with a location for the operator—room for control consoles and a view of the stage—such theatres can often serve rather elaborate theatrical lighting needs.

Because package lighting-control units provide interpatching at the dimmers themselves, the package will be a maze of wire. Since most package dimmer units are now remotely controlled (although many like that in Figure 9-3 are still in use), the wires can be in an out-of-the-way corner. Interpatching during a production should be done with care—the chances for error are good—but it can stretch a few dimmers a very long way.

4. Elaborately equipped theatres. These are theatres designed up to the current state of the art. Lighting control will probably include computerlike devices to store cue data, special automatic fader-timers, and other such apparatus. In the area of interpatching, a device is currently being contemplated which would use computer technology to scan a rack of dimmers constantly. Whenever the operator seizes a controller handle or the memory device calls for a circuit to be altered, the scanner almost instantly finds an unused dimmer(s) and assigns it to the circuit to be controlled. It remains so assigned as long as that circuit is at some intermediate reading between full and out. At either "out" or "full" the dimmer is released to the computer for use on whatever other circuit needs it.

Thus the computer serves as a constant "dimmer-utilization monitor" getting maximum use out of each dimmer. It can also be programmed to detect potential overloads and reject them, protecting the dimmers. Engineers suspect that such a system might be cheaper than the installation of a separate dimmer on each of several thousand load circuits in a very elaborate theatre.

Types of Interconnecting Panels

The following summary of interpatch devices will give the reader an idea of what he may expect to find in locations of varying complexity. All types serve to make a limited number of dimmers more useful, and to make possible the grouping of related functions on adjacent operating handles. The various devises shown in Figure 11-1a–e all serve to make possible the connection of any load circuit to any dimmer.

Dimmer-Rack Interconnectors

Dimmer-rack interconnection systems are found where an old, previously inflexible system has been converted to flexibility. Conversion often is accomplished by cutting the connections between the dimmers and the permanent wiring leading to the borders, foots, and the like. Receptacles are installed at the dimmer outputs. Each circuit of permanent wiring is fitted with a short length of flexible cable and a connector to allow it to be plugged into any dimmer. New load fuses or breakers often are required.

Since dimmer-rack interconnections are relatively small and simple arrangements, it is common practice to interplug both the live wire and the neutral in the manner of an ordinary convenience outlet. Interplugging both connectors enables the builder to use standard receptacles and connectors. However, it wastes precious board space and requires the insertion of two breaks in the wiring where one would do. Most of the elaborate systems described below perform the interconnection on the live wire only. Neutral leads from all outlets are permanently connected to a heavy copper bus known as the "ground" or "neutral" bus. Only one conductor per circuit is left to be interconnected.

Telephone-Board Interconnectors

Telephone-board interconnectors derive their name from the general appearance of the unit, which resembles an old-fashioned operator-manned telephone exchange with the dangling connecting cords. Mechanically, it is really simpler than the telephone equipment, but much heavier. Dimmer circuits terminate in a series of single-pole receptacles, the number depending on the wattage capacity of the dimmer and space available at the interconnect panel. Load circuits terminate in a number of flexible, single-conductor cables equipped with plugs to match the dimmer receptacles. These cables usually hang down from the front of the board until they are put into use, forming a

FIGURE *11-1a*
Telephone-Board Interconnectors. A typical telephone-type interconnection system. The dimmers terminate at the single-pole outlets in the center section. Load circuits end in the flexible cords hanging left and right. The breakers left and right protect the various load circuits. At the lower left is a company switch. Patchboard by Strand Century Lighting Inc. Photograph: Herbst.

FIGURE *11-1b*
A Retractable-Cord Interconnecting System. The load circuits terminate in the plugs hanging on the horizontal surface. Cords are neatly out of sight underneath this surface. Dimmer circuits terminate in outlets above, each of which is equipped with a circuit breaker whose handle is so arranged that the plug cannot be inserted into the outlet unless the breaker is off. This prevents hot patching. Kliegl Bros.

FIGURE *11-1c*
Large Retractable-Cord In-
terconnect System. This
large system was designed
for a television studio. Load
breakers surround the re-
ceptacle panel in the center
of the board. Courtesy of
Berkey Colortran.

spaghettilike tangle of cords in front of the dimmer receptacles. Since interconnections somewhat like these have been called "patch bays" in sound-equipment applications, this term is frequently applied to these units (see Figure 11-1*a*).

An improvement over the exposed and dangling load cables is to adapt the telephone-board system of retractable cables (see Figures 11-1*b* and *c*). Weighted pulleys carry the load cables neatly to storage space below the desklike surface of the device. Then only those cables in use are withdrawn as far as necessary.

All neutral lines are permanently connected to a ground bus in these systems, saving space on the patchboard and assuring good connections.

Switch Interconnections

The systems discussed so far have the potentiality of poor connections at the interconnection bay. A careless operator may not shove a plug home, and soon heat will destroy both plug and receptacle. A rotary-switch mechanism has been developed that assures a solid contact. Such switches are available up to 24 contacts, and it is quite possible to use the last contact to transfer control to yet another switch. One or

FIGURE *11-1d*
A Direct-Control Switchboard Incorpo-
rating the Rotary-Switch Device for In-
terconnecting Dimmers and Load Circuits.
No flexible cords or open connections are
needed. Kliegl Bros.

more switches are used for each load circuit, the position of the switch selecting the dimmer. Such a system is expensive and bulky, but does eliminate the possibility of loose connections. The system also reduces the hazards of "hot patching"—making the connection while the dimmer is on—by snap action of the switch, thus, to a large extent, avoiding arcing (see Figure 11-1*d*).

Crossbar or Slider
Interconnection Panels

Crossbar systems, which went out of favor for a period of time in large installations because they were too space consuming, have now regained popularity for exactly the opposite reason. New materials and new technology now make them space savers. See Figure 11-1*e*. In all of these systems bus bars carrying current from the dimmers run in one direction and smaller bars carrying sliders representing the individual load circuits run at right angles to the dimmer bars. Interconnection between dimmer and load circuit is made by moving the slider along until it is over the proper dimmer bus and releasing or depressing it causing it to contact the dimmer bus. High-conductivity mate-

rials and specially designed holding springs make it possible to interconnect heavy loads with relatively small parts. Hot patching is of
course possible, but should be carefully avoided. Since one can theoretically attach all load sliders to the same dimmer bus, precautions
must also be taken to avoid overloading. In this regard a plugging system has an advantage because of the limited number of receptacles
provided for each dimmer. Crossbar interconnects are neat and orderly
because no loose cords are in sight. This makes it easy to determine
which loads are attached to which dimmers at a glance.

FIGURE 11-1e
*Slider Interconnect System. This system makes it possible to connect any of
over 200 load circuits to any of 64 dimmers. The slider is simply moved to
the proper dimmer bus and depressed, making the connection. Circuit load
breakers are at the top and bottom of the panel.* Courtesy of Strand
Century Lighting, Inc.

Using Interconnecting Equipment

Hot patching is a constant problem in all interconnecting systems, because operators are usually in a hurry. The standard practice of the professional stage electrician at his piano-box control board is handy and widespread. He simply drags the load plug along the connections to find the hot one; the plug sparks, and he jams it into place. Actually, if connectors are heavy enough and the dimmers are not sensitive to surges, not much harm is done by this practice. It will, in time, erode the plugs and the surface of the outlets, necessitating more frequent cleaning and maintenance. The greatest destroyer of patching equipment is the loose connection caused by not inserting the plug all the way. One manufacturer has tried with some success to solve both of these problems by fitting each dimmer outlet with a circuit breaker whose handle cannot be turned on unless the plug is in securely. The plug will not go in at all unless the breaker is in off position. This breaker eliminates the problem, but at the expense of an extra step in each plugging operation (see Figure 11-1b).

Reloading Circuitry

Any of the above interconnecting systems, except the first, may be equipped with reloading devices. These devices are most effective with remote-control equipment, but they can also be useful to the manually operated system. Reloading is accomplished by providing two or more sets of outlets per dimmer. These outlets may be activated singly or in groups by operating control switches. Relays do the actual switching. Master grouping of control switches is simple and well worth the trouble, making possible the replugging of a dozen or so circuits with one flick of a switch.

Advantages are several: Manual replugging amid backstage confusion is a risky business. The wrong plug frequently goes into the dimmer receptacle. It also takes time, often more time than is available during a fast scene change. Hasty plugging may result in loose plugs and burned connections. Reloading can eliminate these problems by allowing the operator to set up his replugs in advance and operate them swiftly and accurately from the control board.

One disadvantage is apparent: Reloading makes it even easier to overload dimmers, particularly if the total load on the several reload positions equals more than the dimmer capacity. Ideally, the combined load should always be kept below this point so no damage can be done. But this lessens the flexibility of the system. Operators need to be cautioned and occasionally switches will have to be taped down to prevent trouble.

These reload systems are not complex and require little maintenance if properly installed. The relays are reliable and the switch mechanisms should be sturdy. Diodes (small solid state rectifiers) frequently are used to isolate individual control switches and simplify wiring. The diodes must be of good quality and should be accessible for replacement in case of difficulty.

PROGRAMMED-PRESET RELOADING

The application of computer technology to reloading has already been mentioned. There have also developed a number of quite elaborate systems which fall short of the complications of the computer device. These are "matrix systems." A reloading pattern for an entire control board or some major part of it is established on a miniature electronic replica of the patch bay which is activated whenever this particular pattern is needed. A number of such patterns can be stored depending on the elaborateness of the system. In some cases the replica is actually a plug-in unit which is inserted into a special receptacle and activated. Such patching systems are especially valuable in television studios where a number of patterns must be repeated at frequent intervals, and the cost of studio time for repatching manually is high.

CAUTIONS TO BE OBSERVED WHEN LOADING DIMMERS

No interconnecting system can prevent a careless or uninformed operator from overloading a dimmer. Loads must be computed and double checked. Dimmer-protecting circuit breakers must be sized to take care of occasional mistakes. For those who feel that this possibility of overload is an argument for avoiding the patch bay and wiring the lamps directly to the dimmers, it is only fair to indicate that far more dimmers have been burned up as the result of gradual increases in lamp wattage made by janitors and uninformed users of such foolproof equipment than have been destroyed by occasional overloads imposed by stage electricians. The latter usually catch their mistakes in time. The janitor frequently lets the breaker cool, trips it to on, and goes his way! Or he may simply increase the fuse size, if fuses are used, arguing that more light is needed and the "lines can take it."

How Many Dimmers Are Enough?

This problem has already been touched upon in the discussion of inter-patch devices. Obviously, the more flexible the patching arrangement, the more service can be gained from a given number of dimmers. But this economy exacts its toll. As the number of dimmer ways is limited, more of the designer's time and energy must go to devising ingenious ways of making each dimmer serve multiple functions, often at the expense of the lighting design. Flexibility may improve a nearly intolerable situation or make a limited one more workable, but it is no substitute for adequate equipment in the first place. Ideally, there should be enough dimmer ways available to enable the operator to work the most elaborate production with no during-the-show patching. Note that the number of *dimmer ways,* i.e., channels of control, is more important than the total dimmer wattage available. Total wattage might represent a few very large dimmers or a number of smaller ones. The difference in control potential between these two extremes is tremendous.

Dimmer economics is changing. There is no longer any direct ratio between the cost of a dimmer and its wattage capacity. Cost increases, but only in small amounts, as wattage increases. Basic cost of control circuitry, protective devices, etc., determine the cost of a dimmer more significantly than the power-handling capacity of the SCRs or triacs themselves. The cost of dimmers is dropping to the point where the dimmers represent a much smaller part of the total cost of control apparatus than they once did. Modern theatre consultants are coming to the conclusion that one dimmer per load circuit can now be a reasonable choice. A smaller number of dimmers with interpatching will often cost nearly as much and provide more problems for the designer.

The problem of an adequate supply of dimmers still remains, however, because not all new theatres or renovations of old ones enjoy the services of a theatre consultant. Architects still frequently refer to outmoded "design standards" and specify installations that are obsolete before they are turned on. Such "standards" usually represent what were once satisfactory solutions to individual architectural problems. Abstracting them into generalized recommendations for other theatres has become more and more hazardous as theatre technology moves rapidly into the solid-state and computerized era. Old design standards no longer can be defended on either economic or state-of-the-art grounds.

The local lighting artist may find that he is an authority without strength in situations where he attempts to counter the specifications of an architect and/or a budget-minded bureaucrat. He will often find that the "higher authority" of an outsider will succeed where he cannot. The United States Institute for Theatre Technology (USITT) is an institution capable of assisting in such situations. Its membership includes authorities often able to lend their weight to arguments for employing a reputable theatre consultant to guide the architect in the complicated task of planning the inner workings of a theatre. Such consultants are becoming more and more a standard part of architectural teams along with structural engineering consultants, acoustical consultants, etc. The USITT also maintains a list of such consultants, as does Sweets File.

Package Control

Packaged lighting controls have already been mentioned. They offer an unusually flexible solution to the problem of adequate dimmer ways. This is especially true in structures containing multiple houses where the demands for dimmers may fluctuate widely during the production season. If stages are provided with sufficient heavy-power outlets to supply the power packs of the portable boards, and control cables are permanently installed to the control booths, packages can be shifted from theatre to theatre as needed. If some permanent control equipment is also installed, it should be made to mate with the portable gear. See Figure 11-2.

FIGURE *11-2*

Three Portable Switchboards Installed Next to a Built-In Panel Providing Both Power Feed and Load Interconnection. Power is provided through the heavy connectors at the bottom left of the built-in panel. These outlets are protected by breakers enclosed behind the locked door at the right of this panel. This prevents tampering with the power on. Load circuits on this stage terminate in the male connectors recessed into the upper left of the panel. Just to the right of these are a series of line connectors fed from the breakers at the far right. Thus load lines may be fed directly from these breakers without a dimmer. To provide dimmer control an output cable from a dimmer is attached to the load circuit as shown in the picture. Since all connectors are standard for all wiring in this theatre building, cables are interchangeable and lamps may be fed directly from the dimmer boards if desired.

Note that the bottom switchboard, which contains six 6000-watt dimmers, is provided with heavy duty outlets for large loads in addition to the standard 20-ampere outlets. Equipment by Strand Century Lighting Inc. Photograph: Herbst.

From the Interconnection
Panel to the Lamp

In permanently wired stages, lines from the interconnection panel will run through conduit to the various points on the stage and in the house where instruments are likely to be hung. Hundreds of such load circuits may be installed in a reasonably well-equipped theatre. Since each of these circuits may be operated from any dimmer, and the dimmers will frequently have a capacity of 6000 watts or more, the load circuits will have their own circuit breakers. These devices will be installed at the interconnection panel, easily accessible to the backstage staff.

Number and Location of
Load Outlets

It is probably impossible for a theatre to have too many load circuits. At least it seems that no matter how generously they are provided and how assiduously they are placed, a demand will develop for still more. Since some practical limit must be set, the following precepts may help:

1. Load circuits should be as numerous as possible in those locations most likely to be in constant use. For example, the lighting beams and first pipe positions are almost always used. For a stage with a 40-foot proscenium, 20 to 30 circuits in each of these positions should be a minimum. The circuits should not be duplicates of those in other positions. Preferably each of these circuits should terminate at two places on the beam or pipe. Each termination should have a double outlet. A system that will eliminate many short extensions and the hazard of faulty connections that they represent, is to provide each load termination with a pigtail of 5 to 7 feet of flexible cable ending in a double connector.
2. The practice of paralleling load circuits stage left and stage right in floor pockets should not be substituted for additional circuits.
3. Every permanently installed borderlight or footlight should be provided with extra load circuits over and above those needed to operate the border or foot unit. It should not be necessary to disconnect permanent equipment to obtain load circuits in these locations.
4. Side-lighting locations on the forestage or in slots in the house walls should be generously provided with circuitry and none of these circuits should be paralleled stage right and left. Loads in these positions will tend to increase above estimates.

The best way to determine the load circuit needs of a theatre is to make a detailed study of the lighting practices of the producing group that is to be the principal user of the facility. All maximum requirements should then be exceeded. If any unusual practices become evident that might tend to reduce circuit demands in usual locations, these should not be allowed to prevail. Load circuitry is relatively cheap to install when construction is under way but often prohibitive in a finished building.

The installation of oversized conduits and empty conduits to possible future load demand areas is an excellent practice. However, careful records should be kept of the location and path of such conduits.

Layouts of load circuits provided by reputable equipment manufacturers will offer the stage-lighting specialist a good point of departure and also lend authority to his demands. These generalized specifications should be treated as minimum requirements to be built upon to meet the individual needs of the theatre being planned.

Connectors for Load Outlets

The requirements that must be met by a connector for use on stage are rigorous: It must be able to withstand hard usage, dropping, pounding, being run over by stage wagons, being dropped from a height of 30 feet or more, and all manner of dragging about. It must make a secure electrical connection incapable of being pulled or kicked apart. This connection should be capable of being "hot plugged" (a practice consistently frowned upon and persistently followed!) with neither danger to the operator nor serious damage to the connector. It must be simple to connect in semidarkness or while dangling from the top of a 40-foot ladder. It must meet all code regulations.

PIN AND TWIST-LOCK CONNECTORS

Only two types of connectors are presently available that meet these requirements reasonably well and are within reach of most theatre budgets. These are the *pin* or *stage connector* and the *Twist-Lock connector*.[1] The first, the pin connector, is an old standby in the theatre. It usually consists of a pair of fiber blocks fitted with brass pins (see Figure 11-3a) and receptacles and so arranged that the cover over the terminals serves as a clamp to prevent strain on the cable from being transmitted to the connections. These connectors are made in a variety of sizes and in both "cable" and "asbestos" types, the latter for instruments which must have short leads of motion-picture wire. Stage connectors are conservatively rated, rugged devices that meet all of the requirements except that they may be pulled apart. Stagehands often solve this problem by tying an overhand knot in the cables before plugging the two parts of the connector together. This knot is secure, but hard on

[1] "Twist-Lock" is the trademark of Harvey Hubbell, Inc., whose connectors have been much copied but not well.

FIGURE *11-3a*

Some Typical Stage Connectors. This photo shows some of the more commonly found stage connectors. Although several of those shown are presently obsolete or will soon be declared obsolete because of more stringent safety codes, all of them are presently in use. They are as follows: Top row, left to right: Three-wire 50-ampere Twist-Lock line connector; three-wire 30-ampere Twist-Lock line connector; two-wire 20-ampere Twist-Lock load connector; two-wire 20-ampere line connector; sister clamp (for making temporary connections to bus bars in portable installations); old-type stage, plug-20-ampere, unfused ("half plug"). Bottom row: Three-wire 60-ampere pin connector; two-wire 60-ampere pin connector; three-wire 20-ampere stage connector; two-wire 20-ampere pin connector; modern stage plug, 20-ampere, fused; modern stage plug, 50-ampere, unfused. All of the two-wire connectors shown are to become obsolete soon. The 30- and 20-ampere Twist-Lock connectors have been superseded by the types shown in Figure 11-3b. Twist-Lock is the trade mark of Harvey Hubbell Incorporated. Photo by author. Connectors Supplied by Background Engineering.

cable. A better method is to tape the connectors together or, still better, to tie a short length of cord to the cable just above each line connector. The cord then is used to tie the parts together.

Most older stages will be equipped at least partially with pin connectors, often in several sizes. It is desirable in such cases to convert all cables, instruments, and load terminals to one size, eliminating stage plugs (see below) and the need for adapters.

The Twist-Lock connector is a relative newcomer to the theatre. It is a patented device that meets all of the requirements including that of defying kicking or pulling. The prongs of the load connector are equipped with hooks that engage the line connector when they are inserted and twisted slightly. The connector must be untwisted to release it. When these connectors have been properly installed they will withstand a pull of several hundred pounds. See Figure 11-3b.

Costs of pin connectors and Twist-Lock connectors are comparable. Both types are available in three-wire form where code requirements call for an equipment ground. The Twist-Lock connector will probably win favor in new installations where it can be made the standard unit.

FIGURE *11-3b*

New Twist-Lock Connectors. The connector illustrated here meets the new Occupational Health and Safety Act (OSHA) requirements. Note that many of the connectors in Figure 11-3a above do not. Connectors have hooked blades which interlock preventing accidental disconnection from pulling. Exterior of connector is completely insulated. Clamping device assures secure internal connection even under pressure. Courtesy of Harvey Hubbell, Incorporated.

Pin connectors will probably remain in use in existing installations because cost of a complete changeover is usually prohibitive.

THE STAGE PLUG

This old and now obsolete connector was once standard in stage lighting. It was designed back in the days of arc and incandescent lighting when heavy arc lights were the only powerful sources available on stage. This plug was originally made only in a 50-ampere size. Plugs and receptacles were equipped with a slot-and-pin arrangement to prevent plugging low-wattage incandescent equipment into heavy-duty arc pockets. Later, a 25-ampere "half plug" was introduced that enabled the operator to parallel two circuits out of one 50-ampere outlet (see Figure 11-3a). Many of these plugs and receptacles are still in use. They are obsolete and also dangerous. The danger lies in the very real chance that an operator may touch live parts as he attempts to insert a stage plug into a live receptacle.

Two alternatives are available to the lighting artist faced with a stage equipped with obsolete and dangerous stage plugs. He can convert all receptacles to either pin connector or Twist-Lock receptacles and install matching load connectors on his equipment, or he can leave the receptacles as they are and install modern safety-type stage plugs in place of the dangerous variety. Either change will be costly, but will improve safety significantly. As Figure 11-3 shows, the modern safety-type plug has been designed so that the copper contacts on the plug cannot engage the live part of the receptacle until the plug has been inserted far enough to prevent the operator's hand from contacting the metal parts.

SIZING CONNECTORS

The less need there is for changing connectors or installing adapters the more time will be saved and the fewer bad connections will plague productions. Therefore it is advisable to settle on a single type and size of connector and make it standard throughout the stage. Code restrictions normally limit the size of cables and connectors to 20 amperes for medium lamp receptables and call for heavy-duty equipment wherever mogul receptacles are paralleled to build up heavy loads. Thus a 20-ampere stage connector or Twist-Lock will often turn out to be the standard unit for all but a few 50-ampere circuits for projection equipment.

The old practice of sizing connectors according to the dimmers that fed them should be abandoned. It no longer has any relevance on a stage with flexible control; any outlet may feed from any dimmer.

Portable Cable

No matter how numerous the load circuits and how well they are distributed, any stage will need a large number of heavy-duty portable cables fitted with standard connectors and clearly marked as to length. If equipment grounding is required, these cables will have to be the three-conductor type. As in the case of connectors, all cables should be capable of handling the load (usually 20 amperes) as standardized. The only exception should be a few very heavy-capacity cables for the heavy-duty connectors. Modern stage cables are insulated with rubber, Neoprene, or plastic material. All are rugged and durable, Neoprene being the best in locations where smog may deteriorate rubber. If cables are to be used to rig temporary lighting pipes, weight will be a significant factor and stage cable should be chosen for its lightness as well as its durability.

The final step in providing current to the lamps is the short "pigtail" of heat resistant wire which leads the current directly to the socket of the instrument. This wire must withstand considerable heat. For years asbestos has been the standard insulating material for this purpose. It wears rapidly and often creates shorts or ground faults at the point where the wire enters the instrument housing or when the wire burns off at the socket connection. Modern practice calls for the installation of silicone rubber and/or fiberglass insulation for this purpose. Silicone rubber looks like ordinary rubber but will withstand up to about 600° F. Fiberglass will resist at least this much heat.

Wire burn-offs at the connection to the socket are still an occasional occurrence. Soldering is of little use here—heat is too great. Pressure-applied lugs at the ends of lead-in wires help. However, it is necessary to check the socket leads before instruments are placed in service to detect nearly burned-off wires.

We have now traced the path of the electricity from the service entrance equipment, through the various protective devices, through the dimmer system to the interconnecting panel, and finally, by way of both permanent and portable wiring, to the lamp itself. The return path retraces this same route with the exception that the neutrals usually are grouped together at the interconnection-panel neutral bar. This neutral return is easy to forget in practice but it is vital to the operation of the circuit.

The lighting artist must remember as he faces the complexity of all of this apparatus that its sole purpose is to deliver the electrical energy to the lamps in a way that will enable him to accomplish his artistic purpose. Few arts, even in modern technologically oriented society, can boast (or deplore) such technological array between the artist and his art.

DESIGNING
THE
11 LIGHTING

12 ÆSTHETIC BACKGROUNDS

History of Modern Design Concepts

As we begin our consideration of lighting design, we must recognize our obligation to those who formulated and gave voice to these important concepts. Their influence pervades every aspect of modern theatre; their visions have by no means been fulfilled, even today.

In most artistic efforts, theory has followed practice, often at a respectful distance. Indeed it has sometimes been said that the development of clear-cut theory marks the end of an artistic era, not the beginning. However much support this statement can find in the general history of art, it will find little in the history of modern stage lighting. The fact is that the main body of theory applying to modern stage-lighting design, even to the whole of modern stage design, *preceded* not only the practice, but also the technology by some 20-odd years.

The history of the modern concepts of lighting begins in earnest with the rebellion against the well-made play and its "genuine cardboard mountains." By the middle of the nineteenth century, Europe was rife with fermenting ideas concerning art. Painting, music, architecture, and theatre were all undergoing revolution. Generally this revolution could be typified as antitraditional, anticonventional, and antiornamental. The world was sated with Victorian gingerbread, neat but empty plots, magnificently balanced but sterile landscapes, and the like. "Schools" of the various arts, each with its own aesthetic of rebellion, flourished.

It is no accident that such artists as the Duke of Saxe Meiningen, Henrik Ibsen, Louis Sullivan, and Adolphe Appia came out of this era. Any attempt to trace the origins of an artistic idea or to establish primacy of responsibility would be hopeless. It is much more important that Appia gave clear and emphatic voice to the ideas of modern theatre design than it is that he might have originated some of these ideas. Appia was born in 1862, and he died in 1928. Thus he bridged the theatre from Victorianism to modern antirealism.

His most important work was written in about 1895; it was published in an inferior German translation in 1898.[1] The contents of this book are remarkable in that they contain most of the details of a modern aesthetic of theatre production, particularly lighting and scene design. This concept is still well in advance of practice today, although the modern theatre seems moving generally in the direction Appia outlined. Moreover, the ideas Appia developed for stage lighting and even the equipment he envisioned were some 20 years in the future when he wrote. His concept of lighting required the concentrated-filament spotlight, a device not invented until about 1920!

Appia is commonly credited with the idea of plasticity in lighting and for inveighing against painted scenery. These ideas are present in his works, but they represent practical application of far deeper, and in the long run, more significant aesthetic contributions. Appia had an unusually clear concept of the interrelationship between the parts of an artistically successful theatrical production. Still deeper, underlying this important idea, was a remarkably perceptive understanding of the creative mind and the relationship between creativity and human progress.

Thus Appia was much more than a remarkable prophet of mechanical devices to come, and far more than a writer on the narrow subject of the production of Wagnerian opera, although he centered his attention on the works of Wagner and on music-drama in general.

From 1898 to the present time, there has been a constant development in the art of stage lighting, which appears to be moving in the direction of the fulfillment of Appia's broad aesthetic dicta. Many artists of the theatre in Europe and in the United States have contributed to this movement. Some of the most important are Edward Gordon Craig, Max Reinhardt, Lee Simonson, Stanley McCandless, and Robert Edmond Jones.

Perhaps the most advanced development of stage lighting along Appian lines has been in the Wagnerian productions at Bayreuth. Lighting there was under the general direction of Richard Wagner's grandson, Wieland, until his death on October 17, 1966, and approached the ideal set forth by Appia in his discussions of the staging of Wagnerian opera.

---

[1] Adolphe Appia, *Die Musik und die Inszenierung*, transl. Princess E. Cantacuzène. Munich: Bruckman, 1898. It is now available in an English translation of the original French manuscript. *Music and the Art of the Theatre*, transl. Robert W. Corrigan and Mary Douglas Dirks. Coral Gables, Fla.: University of Miami Press, 1962.

The General Nature of the Discussion of Design

Lighting design is a creative activity. As such, it is like all other creative activity. It is intensely personal, involved with the emotional sensitivity of the creator, and frequently submerged in the subconscious activity of the mind. It is probably ridiculous to speak of analyzing the content of any artist's work. Even phrasing a question on this subject raises semantic difficulties, such as those which prompt the writer to wrap terms in quotation marks, thus hedging the meaning.

Artists often shy away from discussing their creative efforts, fearing that what insight they have may vanish if investigated. Most artists instinctively recoil at the thought of explaining their works. These positions have enough reasonableness about them to prompt many students of stage lighting to treat the mechanical-electrical-optical aspects of the art exhaustively, and give very short shrift to design on the grounds that nothing worthwhile can be said anyway. This writer believes that such an approach is based on an erroneous interpretation of the task of discussing design. It is not the purpose of a discourse on artistic activity to tell the artist how to create a *specific* art work, nor to tell him what artistic content he should put into *any* art work. These are matters for the artist and his psyche. Only he looks through his eyes, feels with his nervous system, and ponders with his brain. Only an individual can inject that human quality into an art work which makes it live. But the *general* nature of the artist's activity, the mode of artistic communication within which he works, the elements which characterize the symbolic devices of the art, and the general steps which must be followed if any art work is to result — these are the province of investigation and discussion.

Procedure

In this section on design we are going to operate within certain basic assumptions concerning the theatrical art. While the assumptions are basic, they are by no means exhaustive, nor are they the last word on the art of the theatre. Probably the best that can be said for them is that they try to deal effectively with the most basic issues concerning our art. In doing so they solve some problems and raise many questions, most of which are not within the scope of this book. The inquiring student of the art of lighting will find himself driven to penetrating and complicated investigation of the aesthetics of theatrical production (see the Bibliography on theatre aesthetics at the end of this book). The further he goes the more fascinated he will be with the complexity and depth of our art, and the more aware he will be of the limitations of our ability even to ask questions, let alone prepare answers, regarding that most deeply human of all human activities — artistic creation.

The Symbolic Nature of Art

Since the basis of the following discussion of lighting design is to be found in modern aesthetic theory which is centered around the term "symbolic," a definition of that term is vital. *The following definition is implied in all applications of the word "symbol" and its variations throughout the rest of this book unless it is specifically qualified in some other way.* Note that this definition, which incidentally must be sketchy because of its complexity, is both broader and deeper than the conventional usage of the word.

It is thought by some authorities that all mental activity except the most direct stimulus-response action (for example, withdrawing a hand from a hot stove) is symbolic.[2] In this sense the term means that the mind has converted the sensory data into a mental *representation* that enables the mind to "think about" these data. "Thinking about" in this case often includes organizing symbolized data into patterns, finding relationships, achieving understanding. Within this context, symbolic transformation—that is, the conversion of sensory data to symbols—is at the very heart of human thought processes.

But symbols do not simply allow man to think about sensory data: They make it possible for him to recreate the emotional circumstances surrounding those data, to recreate by means of the symbol a gestalt of thought and emotion capable of being related to other such patterns. These symbols often are externalized, frequently as words.

ART WORKS ARE SYMBOLS

Artistic activity can be considered profitably to be an extremely sophisticated development of the symbolic transformation process. The artistic psyche pyramids symbols, interrelating them to make still more complex and inclusive structures. In some cases the result is an art work, a poem, a painting, a playscript. All art works have the nature of an extremely complex symbol. It is vital that we recognize the implications of the singular form, "symbol." No matter how great its complexity, an art work will be considered to be a *single* symbol. Within this singularity lie all of the important concepts of artistic unity and harmony.

Artists often make symbols from still other symbols which came, in

---

[2] Among these authorities is Susanne Langer. Her *Philosophy in a New Key* (Cambridge: Harvard University Press, 1951) and *Feeling and Form* (New York: Charles Scribner's Sons, 1953) deal in detail with the symbolic nature of art, making particular reference to the drama. On p. 40 of *Feeling and Form* she writes, "Art is the creation of forms symbolic of human feeling." This definition is further elaborated on p. 51: "In art forms are abstracted only to be made clearly apparent, and are freed from their common uses only to be put to new uses: *to act as symbols,* to become expressive of human feeling." (Emphasis added by this writer.)

turn, from other symbols. The results of such pyramiding can be extremely complex. But the art work will still be singular, still have unity and harmony. This conversion of many symbols into one symbol is also known as symbolic transformation. It is the essential act, the stroke of genius of creative thought, both artistic and otherwise.

WHAT IS A SYMBOLIC RESPONSE?

We will have frequent occasion to write about evoking a symbolic response by the proper use of lighting design elements. What is this response? What are its characteristics?

Briefly, a symbolic response is the act of "getting" the intent of the symbol. The recipient has managed to relate the response evoked in him to his own experience. To say that he now "understands" what is meant by the symbol is only the beginning, if we are talking about the symbolic response to an art work. It is also inadequate to say that the recipient "feels" or "empathizes" with the symbol, although these ideas are part of the result. A symbolic response to an art work is a nondiscursive communication, that is, artistic "content" is not describable in ordinary language. An essential purpose of art is to communicate that which can be communicated in no other way.

If the result of a symbolic response is nondiscursive, is there anything that can profitably be said about it? Probably not in such statements as "The play means . . ." or "This is the theme (or moral). . . ." However, we may gain some insight into the *general* nature of artistic content by examining the nature of the artistic symbol itself. Since this is a book on stage lighting and such an examination is worthy of a book by itself, we can only offer a couple of hints as to what such an examination might reveal.

For instance, the symbolic mode of expression in art evokes both thought and feeling simultaneously. Moreover, these thoughts and feelings will often be in significant and complicated relationships to each other. It is possible to write about these responses but the writing is but a pale image compared to *experiencing* them.

Another discovery made upon examining the nature of artistic symbols is their ability to convey opposite or contradictory material without "canceling out" as this material does when handled in discourse. For instance, in *Macbeth* we are aware that the protagonist is morally a bad man. This knowledge does not cancel out the sense of nobility that surrounds him as a tragic hero. In fact, the opposite reaction seems to take place and our concept of the nobility of man somehow encompasses the possibility of evil.

Still another quality of the symbol is its freedom from the restrictions of material necessity. In art, "being somewhere" does not preclude being somewhere else. Examine *Peer Gynt* for examples. Many writers, including Adolphe Appia, the founder of modern stage design, have been fascinated with the idea that the "logic" of artistic content may be better compared with that of the dream than with that of reality.

Thus the terms "symbol" and "symbolic" and all their variations are to be read in this wide context.

The Symbolic Nature of the Theatre

The theatrical art, like all arts, is essentially symbolic in its nature; that is, its artistic content proceeds from dramatist to producing artist to audience by means of an ever-widening and deepening symbol—the play itself. The essential import of this assumption for us at this stage in the discussion is that we respond to a symbol as a whole. Our awareness of its import to us refers to the entire play as we have received it, not to segments, fragments, or chains of reasoning. We may dissect after this symbolic response, but we have not engaged in aesthetic (artistic) perception of the play until we have experienced it as a whole. Further reflection or repeat performances may well enrich and enlarge this symbol, increasing the depth and scope of the aesthetic experience.

The Communicative Nature of Art

Another assumption underlies the notion that artistic activity is symbolic. This idea, introduced in Chapter 1, is that the artistic activity is somehow *communicative*. It is unfortunate that we have only one word for all the various kinds of communication. Lacking alternative words, we must label as "communication" any activity which involves the evocation of ideas or emotions or both in one or more individuals as the result of the actions of another. What can we learn about communication by an examination of communicative devices?

It is obvious that the requirements of the communicated material will influence the nature of the communicative device, artistic or otherwise. For example, the telephone is a more complicated electrical device than the telegrapher's key because of the more rigorous requirements of voice transmission. However, most nonartistic communicative devices are capable of handling a wide variety of information up to the limits of their complexity. Thus a telephone could be used to transmit Morse code by tapping on it, although this would be a poor use of its capabilities. A corollary characteristic of nonartistic communicative devices is that there are almost always alternate means of communicating the same material. If the voice radio fails, code can take over. Information in language or in mathematical form can be communicated in a wide variety of ways. Some are almost miraculously efficient, such as the communication between computers; others are much slower, but each represents an alternate path for the same kind of information. As communicative devices get more sophisticated, alternate paths become poorer substitutes. In the arts we find a situation in which *no* alternate paths exist. Each art work may be thought of as a communicative device so sophisticated and so specialized that it and it alone can handle the particular material to be communicated. The nature of the material to be communicated and the device which does the job have become completely intermingled. An alteration in either element will result in a different communication. Any attempt to separate these heretofore separable elements will tend to destroy the entire communicative situation.

For this reason the concept of an art work as a symbolic device is helpful; the peculiar interrelationship between art work and content is recognized, and the oversimplified and semantically impossible discussion of form and content—an activity about as rewarding as pondering the old conundrum about the chicken and the egg—is avoided.

FORM AND CONTENT AS A SYMBOLIC ENTITY

We will still find it convenient to use the terms "form," "art work," and "content," but now with the understanding that they are forever linked into a single symbolic entity. As lighting artists we will alter the art work, the symbol. We must always be aware that we are thereby altering, to some degree at least, the content. But this is our business; we must aid in the creation of that master symbol, the produced play. Alteration of the content is inevitable; what matters is the nature of that alteration. To determine the nature of the art of lighting, and eventually to try to assure ourselves that those contributions we make will be positive, not negative, we must begin with an examination of the symbolic nature of the art of lighting. In other words, we will study the communicative device to learn what we can about dealing with the communication which is so inextricably entangled within it. This study is similar to studying the telephone to learn about the nature of the talk that passes over the wires. But we have no alternative—remember that there are no alternative channels open to us when dealing with an artwork.

LIGHTING AS A PART OF THE THEATRICAL SYMBOL

The analysis of the art of lighting begins with a careful look at some of the symbolic devices inherent in lighting. Naturally, the list of symbolic devices cannot be exhaustive for the simple reason that the ingenuity of the artist will continually find new ones. However, we can look at those categories most likely to be basic to lighting art. Our examination of these will fall roughly into two categories—space and time. Consideration of time will bring us back to the artistic complex, space-time. Having looked into these elements of the symbolic process, we will investigate the unifying, inspiring, and controlling factor, the dramatic script. Our knowledge of the nature of the symbolic processes of lighting may aid in our search for clues as to the kinds of symbolic material most likely to provide the lighting artist with the unifying and inspiring forces he needs. It may also enable us to look a bit further into the nature of the dramatic symbol as a whole, and to fit the art of lighting more closely into that master symbol.

Having looked into the nature of the symbolic form, and into the roots of the symbolic development of that form, we will be more nearly ready to trace the steps generally followed by the lighting artist, and to evaluate the various cues, tools, and tricks of his art. We should also be able to make the transition from what perforce must be sequential discussion of the creation of stage lighting to the more realistic understanding that each act of this creative process represents a development in the scope and depth of the art work being created. It is only on paper that the act of artistic creation and the art work that results from it may be separated.

DESIGNING IN SPACE AND TIME

13

The Designer

The creation of the spatial aspects of the theatrical art involves a number of artists—the director, the actors, and the designer. It has become common practice in the professional theatre to separate the design functions of the setting and lighting. This separation has frequently been carried over into the educational and community theatre. There is little to be said for this separation; at best, it represents a division of tasks along technical lines. More frequently it is only a kind of featherbedding already too common in the professional theatre. Artistically, it is very nearly a contradiction in terms to hire a lighting designer and a scenic designer. One or the other is bound to be redundant. One or the other must abdicate his title as designer, and subordinate his creative activities. It is to be assumed herein that a stage designer is an artist concerned with dramatic expression in space, and that he will use both setting and lighting to effect this end, working toward a single artistic goal. Ideally he should be the scenographer, the artistic controller of setting, lighting, costume, and makeup. If these skills are not all within his reach, he should seek enough familiarity with them to effect artistic control over them. Therefore, the term "designer" will henceforth, in this text, refer to the artist who designs at least the setting and lighting and maintains tight control over other visual areas. The aesthetic grounds for this position will make themselves clear as the artistic elements of the work of this designer are developed in the pages to come.

Since this is a book on lighting, discussion of the artistic concepts will move from the design generalities to specifics in the area of lighting. Relevance to specifics in the area of scenery must be left for another time. A stage designer works in space and time. We will study the

303

spatial aspects first, then the temporal, and finally, the fusion of the two.

Dramatic Space

"Stage space" is an indefinite term which can mean building cubage, acting area, space visible to the audience, or the space conjured by the production in the mind of the audience. Since the following discussion cannot afford this kind of confusion, let us agree on some terms. "Stage space" refers to that cubage visible to the audience during the production of a play. "Acting space" refers to that cubage occupied at one time or another by actors during the production. Note that these two terms often completely overlap when the actors range throughout the entire visible space. "Dramatic space" refers to the main subject of our discussion to come — that fluctuating, ephemeral space evoked in the minds and emotions of the audience as the play is produced. The term "dramatic space" may be considered the equivalent of "virtual space" as applied to the theatre by such aestheticians as Susanne Langer.[1]

The "Reality" of Dramatic Space

Dramatic space is a virtual thing, a figment of the mind and the emotions. It has none of the dimensional reality of physical space, none of its Newtonian principles. Thus the *virtual* nature of dramatic space is its *essential* nature. Saying that it is unreal is not describing it negatively, rather this is an indication of its artistically expressive potentialities. To examine these potentialities further, we must consider the symbolic nature of dramatic space. What sort of a symbolic device is it? How does it seem to work? Eventually, and only by inference, we may be able to suggest some generalities concerning the artistic communication which it can achieve.

The Symbolic Nature of Dramatic Space

A symbolic response in the area of art is an immediate[2] and complex response to the perception of an *entity*. This "wholeness" is essential to the entire response. When dramatic space serves as the symbolic device, what is the special nature of the response? What is its probable motivation?

Most effective artistic symbols have their genesis outside of art.

[1] Susanne K. Langer, *Feeling and Form.* (New York: Charles Scribner's Sons, 1953) Chaps. 5 and 6, pp. 69–104.

[2] In this sense, "immediate" means "whole" or "entire" in addition to its usual temporal meaning.

Somewhere under the heavy coating of artistic development there is a core of analogy or even common experiential data that relates the basic ingredients of the symbol with the symbolic content. The existence of this core is what determines the "rightness" of the device in the first place. Seeking out these symbolic devices is one of the prime activities of all artists. It is not true that anything can symbolize anything. The device must be the right device or the artist rejects it. Thus Van Gogh's "Sunflowers" possesses an analogical rightness to the view of the world he sought to express—a lily would not have done the same job!

When theatrical artists set out to achieve expression through the use of dramatic space, a similar rightness may be presumed to exist, and there may be profit in ferreting it out. The theatre artist using dramatic space may be said to be evoking a common experience of all men—our deep-seated response to our existence in space. Space, orientation in it, and the presumption of its predictability are among the fundamental assumptions of life itself. Indeed, the very notion of *being* involves being *somewhere*, taking up space, and having some secure knowledge of the nature of that space. The obverse of this notion—infinity—is not an easy thought. Pondering upon infinity forces man to some uneasy and emotionally charged moments, moments that are dramatic whether they are in the theatre or not.

Dramatic space apparently finds its powerful symbolic core at the point of common human experience: All men to some degree face the emotional and mental conundrum of space and infinity. But the theatre artist cannot stop with this generalized notion; indeed it is his artistic job to build upon it, to wrap this core with layer upon layer of symbolic expressions of insight and emotion. He does this by carrying his audience through a wide variety of vicarious spatial experiences, by weaving in dramatic space stronger, deeper, and more specific artistic content; in short, by using the basic core of common spatial experience to build a dramatic structure of great intensity and significance.

Whether or not the above thoughts concerning the basic relationship between space and artistic expression are acceptable, a little introspection will reveal that, whatever the reasons, appealing to our awareness of space will provoke some strong reactions, and these reactions are desirable dramatic devices. In order to detail the nature of some of these appeals and to show what part the art of stage lighting has in them, we shall ask a series of questions and attempt to answer them one by one. These questions will overlap one another; they will be oversimplifications; they will be incomplete. Nevertheless they should pique the imagination and set thoughts on their way. If they do, they will have succeeded.

WHERE ARE THE EDGES OF DRAMATIC SPACE? WHAT ARE THEY LIKE?

Dramatic space without boundaries brings us theatrically to infinity. Dramatic space, realistically walled off and clearly equated to its stage space, neatly pins us down to a secure relationship with space. This opens the way for other symbolic elements to play the major role. In the first case, the audience is clearly within the dramatic space; in the second, clearly outside it. Between these two is found a vast area of shading. It is here that the theatrical arts, particularly those of acting and lighting, play their strongest roles regarding space and the audience.

Degree of audience involvement in the dramatic space is somewhat parallel to the common concept of aesthetic distance in that our involvement in the emotional crises of the characters often parallels our involvement in the dramatic space. If we "feel with" the characters, we are inclined to consider ourselves within the dramatic space of the play. But this description of dramatic space, like the concept of aesthetic distance, is deceptively simple. It assumes the existence of but one state of mind, one level of symbolic response at a time. The serious dramatic artist abhors this condition because it is shallow and inexpressive. Such a single-minded response may satisfy the creator of a detective drama or a moralizing propagandist, but the serious dramatist, whether tragic or comic, will abhor it. The reason is obvious and significant to the art of lighting. The symbolic potentialities for deep emotion and idea-packed expression lie in the contrasts that may be aroused by putting the audience in a paradoxical position, and thus making them think and feel their way out through deeper artistic responses. The successful dramatist may contrive to place the audience well outside of the dramatic space, but still infuse them with a strong empathetic response toward certain characters. This double state of being is just what dramatic space is fitted to do: Sensing its paradoxical nature is but the beginning of aesthetic appreciation.

The word "horizon" can be appropriately applied as a metaphor to the boundaries established in dramatic space by the lighting, setting, and actors. There is a twofold implication in the word "horizon." On one hand, we think of a horizon as something beyond which we cannot see, as a definite end to our field of vision. On the other, a horizon is a tempting thing to the imagination. Both physically and psychologically it represents a sort of constantly moving, but never overtaken line. This duality accurately describes the nature of the boundaries of dramatic space. As dramatic space is evoked in the minds of the audience, its boundaries are established. At the discretion of the designer, the emphasis can be placed on the limiting aspect of this "horizon" or upon its imagination-tempting quality. However, no matter what the emphasis is, both aspects continue to function.

Macbeth is an example of this duality. The audience both empathizes with and remains outside the dramatic space as Macbeth ponders:

> *To-morrow, and to-morrow, and to-morrow,*
> *Creeps in this petty pace from day to day*
> *To the last syllable of recorded time.*

And all our yesterdays have lighted fools
The way to dusty death. Out, out, brief candle!
Life's but a walking shadow, a poor player
That struts and frets his hour upon the stage
And then is heard no more: it is a tale
Told by an idiot, full of sound and fury,
Signifying nothing.

Consider for a moment the complexity, the variety of simultaneous thoughts and feelings that surround this passage, even in reading, and you have some idea of the overwhelming complexity of the involvement of the audience with the play, the character, and the space in which it all exists. This complexity of response, this being outside the space and within the character, and most of all, the audience's fluctuations in this state of being are major considerations for the lighting artist. The nature of the lighting of *stage* space is frequently the key to the establishment and variation of *dramatic* space. For example, a soft shading off or a strongly directional light so oriented that it involves the audience is often the symbolic key to placing the audience well within the dramatic space of the play.

Again the reader must be cautioned not to assume that being within the dramatic space of the play is tantamount to reducing aesthetic distance, or that it means a singular, emotional kind of involvement. The drama in production is far more complex and inclined to seek subtlety and depth through paradox. Being within the dramatic space at the end of the first act of *The Skin of Our Teeth*, dramatically involved in the saving of humanity from the oncoming ice, does not prevent the audience from extrapolating on the constant repetition of human crises and narrow escapes from annihilation. Indeed, a well-done production of this scene can point to the intensity of both of these reactions as the hallmark of success.

HOW MUCH DRAMATIC SPACE?

We have already raised this question regarding the audience. However, the apparent size of dramatic space, whether or not the audience resides within it, is a matter for further consideration. On the superficial level, dramatic space is often the logical extension of stage space. For example, cramped quarters of *The Lower Depths* may seem to imply a minute and cramped kind of dramatic space. Yet the moment we ponder the example of *The Lower Depths*, this description does not really fit. The dramatic space of that play seems to reach into every slum and ghetto of the world. It is a vile, miserable space, but unhappily all too large for the comfort of those who are outside but dramatically compelled to peer within.

Some interesting paradoxes appear as we consider the symbolic possibilities of larger and larger portions of dramatic space. Audience involvement and emotional response seem to operate at three separate and apparently contradictory levels: First, tiny amounts of dramatic space and huge amounts seem to have in common the tendency to arouse in the audience the uneasy kind of emotional involvement that comes with trying to cope with infinity. At the same time, a second level of reaction often tends to destroy spatial involvement altogether as dramatic space tends toward the infinitely large or the infinitely small. Time considerations may well become predominant, leaving space out of consideration entirely. Third, sharp demarcations of space, whether large or small, may also tend to neutralize the symbolic effect of space, again leaving the field open to other symbolic devices.

Let us draw some examples from *Hamlet*. The staging of soliloquies such as "To be or not to be" offers a study in the first and second kinds of variation. Either a pin spot against blackness, or a space staging technique with horizonless cyclorama lighting may lead us symbolically in the direction of infinity—not an inappropriate concept for "To be . . ."! But it is only a small dramatic step to the second set of circumstances. Space under these lighting conditions may not be a consideration at all. Time may stand still and space evaporate leaving only the intense dramatic moment—a kind of nonspace symbolic mode.

The third condition, sharply divided space, may tend to entirely erase spatial reactions from the attention of the audience during the dueling scene where the dramatic needs of the scene establish clearly defined spatial relationships—the king and queen, the court, the dueling area, and the like.

Note that the many responses to dramatic space will frequently be in operation simultaneously. The contrasts thus provided the artist offer potentialities for dramatic expression of incredible subtlety and depth.

WHAT IS THE TEXTURE OF THE STAGE SPACE?

Dramatic space is not necessarily homogenous. Particularly if it is large, it may be subdivided into a variety of units each having its own qualities. This, for lack of a better term, we shall call "texture." Spacial texture is a factor of lighting variables which operates generally within the framework established by the architecture of the setting. These variables are color, plasticity (light and shade), and distribution of light.

Color tends to be diffuse in its effect on spatial texture. It is likely to increase the homogeneity of stage space. Of course notable exceptions come to mind when strong color is paired with strong contrast in the form of pools of colored light. However striking these effects may be, they are in the minority compared to the subtle overtones of color used in almost every production. While color shadings have a fugitive quality about them that limits their symbolic impact, they can achieve a degree of subtlety exceeding that of most other ingredients of stage lighting.

The interplay between lighting color and setting is not merely a matter of the designer's knowledge of the physiology of color vision. It is an artistic matter. He must carefully seek a balance between compensating for the loss of the symbolic effectiveness of color and excessive and distracting color change. The result of this artistic balancing act, when it is successful, is subtlety. Thus, the symbolic result of the designer's use of color is generally a pervasive overtone, mainly emotional in effect, whose variations within the dramatic space are calculated to keep it just within the consciousness of the audience.

As contributing factors to the texture of dramatic space, light and shade appear to have a strong effect. Again there appear to be two main types of variables: one, subdivision of the dramatic space into units, and two, the hardness or softness of the plasticity within these units. Motivation for these variations may arise from naturalistic considerations such as the natural alterations in lighting that result from stage sunlight streaming through a window, or from expressionistically derived patterns. Whatever the impetus, the deep artistic question concerning these subdivisions concerns their value as parts of the symbolic expression of the drama. Even in the most naturalistic staging, for example, the harshness or softness of the plasticity generated by lighting a window is ultimately a matter to be determined by the artistic needs for this light on the face and body of the actor playing in that area. Naturalism only supplies the general limits for this lighting; study of symbolic implications as light plays upon the actor, will provide the specifics.

The symbolic implications of variations in texture through light and shade are of such great importance to lighting that many pages to come will be devoted to the details of this subject. The underlying bases are of immediate concern to us here: Variations in the texture of the lighting ranging from a soft glow with few shadows to a razor-sharp plasticity, and from a smoothly lit dramatic space to one broken into isolated pools, all derive their primary impetus from the deep human response to our orientation in space. Sharp directionality established by lighting, diffuse glows, and ominous shadows all tend to place us vicariously in space, and to evoke deep-seated reactions as a result.

HOW DOES THE DRAMATIC SPACE FLUCTUATE?

A constant undercurrent has been apparent throughout the past discussion. It has suggested that dramatic space is seldom static. Indeed, the most important implication of each of the previous questions, *change*, has been purposely left until now. Like music, designing in dramatic space is much more a consideration of the relationship between what *was* and what *will be*, than it is a question of what *is*.

FIGURES *a-f*
A few of the many possibilities which lighting offers as a major element in scenography.

FIGURE *a*

Above. Light as Deus ex machina. *This photo and the two figures which follow show a design by Josef Svoboda for the opera* Tristan und Isolde (Wagner). *The spiral ramp and the string background served the entire opera. The pillar of light shown here appeared in the final scene, the well-known* Liebestod. *In this aria Isolde appeared to dissolve into an intense pillar of light as the aria and the opera ended.*

This effect was accomplished by means of a triple row of parabolic reflectors (see Figure b, top facing page) arranged under the circular portion of the ramp. These were directed straight up into the air which was filled with an aerosol dispersion of oil. The aerosol made the circular beam of light visible. As the reflector lamps dimmed up Isolde's figure vanished in the intense light.

Figures a and b were taken before masking was added to the setting, hence the substructure of the setting shows. This production was staged in Wiesbaden, Germany in the 1967–1968 season under the direction of Clause Helmut Drese. Scenography by Josef Svoboda. Photo courtesy Josef Svoboda.

Without the possibility of change, the spatial qualities of stage light-ing quickly diminish to the level of plasticity possible in good portrait lighting. Symbolic value rapidly declines and the special expressive qualities of the stage soon vanish.

Again and again we have applied the word "variables" to our past discussion. For example, we can give more or less emphasis to color; the color itself can be changed to suit the needs of the artist, plasticity can be changed in quality or in kind, and so on. However, change itself must be examined for its symbolic value. It becomes the most subtle and challenging of all the variables in the design of lighting. Perhaps you were puzzled by the strange application of the word "variable" to the word "change." This usage is neither a redundancy nor a play upon words, but an attempt to remind you that change itself may be altered in many ways. In art, no variable can be left to chance; control is the key to success. Therefore, a mere consideration of the start and end of a change sequence is insufficient. For example, we must know that at the start of a given change, the predominant hue of the dramatic space is cool and blue, and that at the end the hue will be warm and yellowish. But this is only the beginning of our design as far as this change is concerned. In fact, the rate of change and the variations of that rate as the change proceeds will probably influence its symbolic value even more than the color alteration itself.

Change involves time and space. In order to treat adequately the symbolic value of changes in lighting design we must investigate the underlying nature of the symbolic use of time and then investigate the complexities of space/time.

The Symbolic Mode of Time

Man exists in space and time. This commonplace pervades every activ-ity, artistic and nonartistic, but we seldom concern ourselves with its

FIGURE *b*

Top, page 311. Detail of pillar of light. Note the reflectors with concen-trated filament lamps arranged with the filaments at the focal point of the parabolas giving essentially parallel beams. Photo by author.

FIGURE *c*

Bottom, page 311. Detail of string setting in Figure a. This photo shows an unusual solution to the problem of providing a rear projection screen without revealing it as such. Svoboda designed the entire surround of the setting for Tristan und Isolde *out of stretched cotton rope about ⅜ inch in diameter. The ropes were mounted on approximately 1½ inch centers by stretching them between a batten on the stage floor and another well out of sight in the flies. The side panels were arranged to allow entrances. The up-stage portion of this string setting concealed a rear projection sheet on which shadow images such as the one shown here were projected. These were supplemented by front projection on the surface of the string itself. The result was screenless rear projection.* Photo by author.

FIGURE *d*

Using Light To Create Dramatic Space. Note how the layers of lighted atmosphere (see caption of Figure a) create a quality of three dimensionality even in a photograph. This shows a production of Svatopluk, *a drama based on Czechoslovakian folk lore. It was staged at the National Theatre in Prague in 1969. Script by Eugen Suchoň, regie: Hanuš Thein, scenography: Josef Svoboda. Photo: Dr. Jaromir Svoboda.*

implications. In the arts the development of the symbolic value of virtual time is equally as important as that of virtual space. Some arts depend more heavily upon one than the other; the art of the theatre depends upon both about equally. The result is great potential for depth of artistic perception, and its concomitant, great potential for confusion.

At the core of the artist's symbolic use of time, as with his use of space, is common experiential ground. All men must cope with the sense of time, its depth and importance, to some degree. Throughout history philosophers have condemned the tendency on the part of some men to live "for the moment," trying to push out of their lives any other sense of time than "now." Of course this is impossible for the sensitive mind. "Now" cannot even be described without reference to "before" and "after." The fact seems to be that the contemplation of time will force the mind and emotions of a sensitive man to the ultimate questions of reality more relentlessly than almost any other activity. However disturbing the idea of infinite space may be, that of infinite time is still more disturbing. Perhaps this is because man is so soon forced to contrast infinite time with his own all-too-finite span. Perhaps, if man were given infinite time, infinite space might become comprehensible. Since this gift is far from possible, man's life is filled with his attempts to deal with time. Sometimes he seems to reach for infinity with every means within his grasp, finding the arts most effective in this search. Sometimes he seems to hide his concern in a search for the moment, in conscious unconcern with anything beyond "now." However, his only escape from the symbolic impact of time seems to be unconsciousness.

It would be ridiculous to attribute such great philosophical import to every subtlety of lighting. Art is not philosophy, neither is it a mystic groping for the hereafter. But it would be equally ridiculous to ignore the powerful, almost subconscious impact of artistic dealings in time. The ordered and orderly temporal elements so powerful in music are certainly not unrelated to the symbolic core of all time symbolism, man's struggle with infinity. Probably one of the chief attractions of the neat, orderly time divisions of comedy, like that of a jolly tune, is the secure moment provided against the darkness of the infinite.

Like dramatic space, dramatic time is a fundamental element in the symbolic process of theatrical art. However, the relationships between dramatic time and the audience are not as easily discussed because dramatic time inevitably encompasses the audience. This makes an analysis along the lines of our discussion of dramatic space meaningless. The alternative seems to be a discussion of temporal variations leading rapidly to the term "rhythm."

Rhythm

Dramatic time may be subdivided, lengthened, shortened, or even stopped in the interest of dramatic expression. Each of these alterations, or any combination of them, will have important emotional and intellectual implications. Ultimately, the powerful nature of these implications is derived from the importance which time has to all men, although this nature may be completely overlaid with other dramatic intent.

Perhaps the best-known concept of the subdivision of dramatic time is that of rhythm. Rhythm consists of the subdivision of time accomplished by stimuli repeated at regular intervals. Time so divided bears a direct relevance to physical time in that the beginning and end of the subdivisions may be marked by the clock. Nevertheless, the subdivided time takes on the aspect of virtual or dramatic time by acquiring its own feeling of duration which may be longer or shorter than clock time, and whose symbolic importance is almost unrelated to the clock time. Rhythm or beat is a physiological as well as a musical phenomenon. Many authorities find a definite relationship between the constant physiological phenomena of heartbeat, breathing, and the like, and those rhythms most common in music. Whatever the case, it is important to note that the communicative aspects of rhythm, either in or out of the arts, lie in change. Sameness of rhythm tends to reduce its attention value to the vanishing point. Change heightens the attention and can be made to carry meaning, both practical and artistic. It is of the essence of all rhythmical communication that the change is *within* the rhythmical pattern; it exists as a variation on a continuum already established. The first step in the development of a new rhythmical pattern must be the introduction of the basic rhythmic structure upon which changes are to be wrought. This basic tenet carries over into the dramatic aspects of rhythm. Variations will be meaningless until the basic patterns are made clear.

DRAMATIC RHYTHM

Since dramatic rhythms tend to have longer periods (the clock-time length of a single pattern) than musical patterns, they are often less obvious. Also since the drama depends upon words for denotative clarity, and this plot-line skeleton is capable of sustaining a larger load of abstraction than a simple rhythmic structure, the drama, unlike music, need not depend directly upon "beat" for continuing the structure. Its rhythms can afford to be more diffuse and less easily perceptible to the casual listener. However, they are no less important to the structure for being buried deeply within it. In fact, the reverse is more likely to be true. The long, rolling, hidden rhythms of dramatic art are vital to its unity in that they tend to reveal the structure of the piece more completely than the shorter rhythms of a percussionist reveal the structure of a piece of music.

Within the rhythmic structure of dramatic time, but rising out of it into singular prominence, is the matter of extending and foreshortening time for purposes of symbolic effect. The artistic skills of a musical composer can often extend and sustain an emotional moment for almost incredible periods. However, this extension usually appears in the form of almost "pure" emotion. The aria "Vissi d'arte" from *Tosca*, for example, offers a splendid extension of powerful emotions through a suspension of dramatic time, but relatively little insight. In the drama, extension of time usually deepens artistic content. Shakespearean soliloquies, for example, almost completely stop dramatic time. Their symbolic content is usually marked by tremendous depth of artistic import, both emotional and intellectual.

CLIMAX

The alteration of dramatic time is one of the chief ingredients of the dramatic form. One is tempted to base a study of the entire climactic structure of dramatic production upon this theme alone. This would, of course, be an oversimplification, but not an unrewarding one. It seems likely that changes in dramatic time, particularly those changes in which the rate of change is carefully worked out, are a major ingredient in that dramatic essential, *climax*.

As far as the designer is concerned, the development of a dramatic climax is inevitably a carefully planned change in temporal and spatial elements. The designer will be as deeply concerned with the rhythm of the change as with the end product. For example, the tempest scene in *King Lear* is a major climax in that drama. Its literary structure seems to imply almost stopping dramatic time to allow minute artistic examination of the tempest raging within Lear. This examination is brought about mainly by ironic contrast with the tempest in the plot itself. It is no accident, but artistic necessity, that the physical tempest on the stage must exist only to the degree necessary to heighten insight into Lear's inner storm. Lear stops in the dramatic time of his life to rage at the injustice of the world, and to reveal how much of man's injustice lies within himself. A moment stands still in the face of the barrage of fast-moving dramatic time before and after this soliloquy. A vital part of this scene is the sense of urgency created by speeding up dramatic time before and after the soliloquy. This urgency carries through the soliloquy as a paradoxical overtone to the arrested dramatic time of the soliloquy itself. The degree to which this urgency contrasts with the soliloquy is largely a factor of the manner in which the change is made through design and acting into the stopped time. An abrupt break with the past will place the emphasis heavily on the need to "get on with the plot," leaving too much unsaid. A long, drawn-out shift will throw too much emphasis on Lear's speculative, inactive nature, or worse still, upon exploitation of the device itself.

Once the duration of the change in dramatic time has been established, the deeper subtleties of change of rate appear. While the setting will provide the spatial basis for change, the actor and the lighting will determine the temporal details. A change that begins rapidly and ends slowly—creeping to a stop—will have a different effect than an early slowing or an abrupt break. There is no point in attempting to detail the artistic effect of these subtleties without reference to a specific production. However, the lighting designer must develop an acute sensitivity to them.

Time and Dramatic Style

It is too easy to jump to the conclusion that slowing down time provides dramatic emphasis and speeding it up provides comic effects. At one level and in certain plays, this seems to be true. However, great speed in dramatic time need not always arouse laughter nor imply shallowness. In *Macbeth,* for example, the sheer rapidity of both dramatic time and plot movement in the opening

FIGURE *e*

Light and Three-Dimensional Design. This production of Prometheus *by Karl Orff was staged at the Munich Staatsoper in 1968. It is an excellent example of a close combination of highly three-dimensional setting, heavy metallic texturing, and carefully angled lighting and projections. The huge cubelike projection upon which Prometheus is fastened is shown in its extended position. It thrust forward to this position early in the opera. Directional lighting has been used to focus the figures and to bring out the metallic texturing, and carefully angled lighting and projections. The huge television projection was used to place the figure of Prometheus "within his own face." The opera ended in blinding light on the metallic surfaces during which the cube, Prometheus attached, disappeared into the steps. Regie was by August Everding; scenography by Josef Svoboda. Photo courtesy Josef Svoboda.*

scenes create a sense of relentlessness that remains an important element throughout the entire play. In satire, rapid movement of dramatic time often contributes to the development of irony by bringing contrasting elements into closer juxtaposition.

Space-Time

The reader will already have noticed that it is impossible to discuss dramatic time without reference to dramatic space and vice versa. Indeed, it seems nearly impossible for the mind to contemplate infinite time without infinite space. For living man at least, the intersection of time and space is *movement*, an activity which occupies both. The actor and the dancer exist at this intersection, and the art of design in the theatre cannot but extend from it. Physically, movement requires time and space. Psychologically, movement on the part of an actor or dancer implies empathetic and often kinesthetic responses on the part of the audience. These, in turn, bring the symbolic impact of movement to the audience. What sort of symbolic device is movement? What kind of artistic import can it carry? A review of the discussion of the symbolic ingredients of design so far will reveal the complexity of the answers to these questions. Probably few other elements of artistic expression are as far-reaching in their implications and as complex in their potentialities as the symbolic use of space-time.

The reader should bear in mind from the beginning that the space and time under discussion are *virtual*. They are the creation of the artist and bear only analogical relationship to physical space and physical time. Thus their origin is human, and their symbolic import derives from the human condition. The potential number of variables in artistic expression through space-time is huge. Moreover, the complexity of interrelationships is beyond mere description. It would be foolish to attempt to enumerate these variables let alone attempt to suggest how they interrelate. One may be specific only when dealing with an individual art work. With the evocation of space-time symbols, deep and fundamental human perplexities and paradoxes come into play, either subconsciously or consciously. The paradoxical nature of the human condition as man hangs between finite life and infinite longings lurks close at hand. Whenever the artist evokes space-time symbolically, the audience is faced with either ever-deepening questions or with conscious shying away from such questions toward the matter of the moment. We may either seek insight or take refuge from space and time, but we cannot escape.

Paradox: The Prelude to Insight

The artistic combination of these powerful symbolic devices affords the opportunity to develop still more perplexing paradoxes. Perhaps one of the greatest functions of the artistic symbol is that it places its audience in paradox—in that untenable situation where the elements diverge and reconciliation is possible only through insight. Artistic symbols often force the emotions and the mind into sharp conflict. Artistic response seems to consist of the human insight reaching into this conflict and bringing out a new relationship, often at a deeper level of insight. This new insight need not be confused with a solution; it may be but a better formulation of a question.

If paradox is at least one essential way in which artistic expression operates, what are the potentialities for the artistic creation of paradox through space-time? Obviously, they are nearly infinite. The mere beginning might be a consideration of the space-time potentialties of the "To be or not to be . . ." soliloquy. Infinite time and infinitesimal space offer a potential worth pondering. What of the possibilities of an artistic comparison of Hamlet's "mortal coil" and infinite space? Or what of the possibility of a Hamlet who addresses the audience directly, including it in his dramatic space and paradoxically in the infinite time of his thoughts? And on . . . and on . . . and on.

Lighting, like the actor, exists in space and time. It also moves, pulsates, and fluctuates. Given the actor's words for specific denotation, it also occupies that vast realm of paradoxical expression: space-time.

NONSYMBOLIC ASPECTS OF LIGHTING DESIGN

14

So much for the artistic or symbolic ingredients of lighting. There are other matters which must be clarified before we can move ahead into the specifics of lighting design. These are the *conditions* of lighting, those requirements which must be met before art can succeed. While satisfying these conditions will not guarantee artistic success, ignoring them will guarantee artistic failure. These are largely psychological and physiological matters having to do with the perceptive apparatus of the audience—its eyes and its kinesthetic senses.

Attention

Of all the spatial aspects of lighting, the focusing of attention is probably the most elementary (a poor word, considering the practical complexity of controlling attention). It precedes most other artistic considerations. The basis for this function is psychological. The human seeing apparatus is arranged to focus its attention on a definite hierarchy of stimuli in an inevitable and nearly incontrovertible order. The artist must work within this hierarchy if he expects success. There is a strong temptation to attribute the precedence of visual stimuli to the animalistic laws of self-preservation. However, if this was once the case, our world has grown more complex and threats no longer arrange themselves neatly in the order in which the eye is designed to perceive them.

The following hierarchy of stimuli is arranged in order of precedence. The highest stimulus on the list will have a strong tendency to take attention from any and all below it, even though the lesser stimuli are multiple.

FIGURE *f*

Controlling Focus of Attention. This picture, from a production of the opera
Aïda (Verdi) done in Basel, Switzerland, illustrates the subtle control that
may be achieved over focus of attention through lighting. The key and fill
light on the figure in the foreground has been carefully adjusted to place
this figure at the focus of attention but not at the expense of the heavily
symbolic background. Scenography: Analies Corrodi. Photo: Hoffmann.
Courtesy Analies Corrodi.

The Hierarchy of Visible Stimuli[1]

1. Intensely colored and lighted moving object
   Example: flickering flame
2. Clearly visible moving object, brightly colored
   Example: actor in red costume moving
3. Clearly visible moving object with little or no color
   Example: actor in gray costume moving
4. Brightly lighted and intensely colored stationary object
   Example: orange upholstered chair in spotlight
5. Brightly lighted object with little or no color
   Example: gray chair in spotlight

As one moves toward the bottom of the hierarchy, the phrase "other things being equal" takes more and more effect. This phrase begs the question somewhat since it is the business of the artist to see that "other things" are *not* equal unless that is what is intended at the moment.

A practical application of the effects of the hierarchy of attention may be found in the sleepwalking scene from *Macbeth*. If Lady Macbeth carries a candle, lit, and with little or no shield around it, the designer will have great difficulty shifting the focus of attention to the nurse and the doctor for their scene unless Lady Macbeth is blocked so that the candle is upstage of her and out of sight of the audience during these lines. The candle may have still other malicious effects as it may upstage Lady Macbeth herself! A far more flexible (and safer from the fire-code standpoint) course is to provide an electrical "candle" with sufficient shielding from the direct glow of the lamp to enable the designer to control the focus of attention by light-intensity adjustments.

Depth Perception

The minute details of facial expression, the larger effects of upstage-downstage crosses, and the three-dimensional nature of setting and properties all depend on the perception of depth on the part of the audience. Contrary to common belief, depth perception in the human seeing apparatus is a rather complex matter involving many interrelated factors and functions. For instance, the usually cited source of human depth perception, convergence of the eyes as they focus on an object much like the lenses of an optical range finder, is not the major element in depth perception except at quite short range. The reason for this is simply that the angular differences becomes so slight as objects are moved more than a few feet from the eyes, that they are imperceptible. Other stimuli take over. Among these are the muscular

[1] Note: Size of the objects has some effect but not in proportion to size.

FIGURE *g*

Acting Area Lighting for Broad Focus. This photo of a production of Julius
Caesar *as produced at California State University, Long Beach, illustrates
the use of a number of acting areas to blend a scene into one unit. Good
plasticity is provided over the entire acting area and individual focus of
actors within the area is left to directorial devices. A secondary problem in
this scene was keeping stray acting area light off the projection surfaces. The
set design was aided in this by blocking the reflection paths from the floor to
the projection area. Direction: Stan Kahan, set design Ralph Duckwall, costumes William Travis.* Courtesy California State University, Long Beach
Theatre Department.

FIGURE *h*

*Combining Key-Fill Control and Focus of Attention. Note in this photo-
graph how the strong directionality of the lighting has been maintained
while still maintaining control over focus of attention. The two figures
center stage hold the focus. (The black and white reproduction tends to
throw some of the focus to the background up right—something controlled
by color in the original.) The production is* Mother Courage *(Brecht)
done at California State University at Long Beach. Direction: Mat Reitz,
set design: Beala B. Neal, costumes: Warren Travis.* Photo Courtesy
California State University, Long Beach Theatre Arts Department.

sensations accompanying the accommodation of the eyes to different focal lengths needed for exact focus on objects at various distances, the mental processes which detect dissimilarities between the two fields of vision as reported to the visual centers of the brain, the nearly intellectual process of noting which items in the visual field overlap which others, and—perhaps almost more important than most of the others to the designer—the application of the laws of perspective (if you know the approximate size of an object, you can estimate its distance with fair accuracy). Incidentally, the "binocular effect" often described in connection with depth perception apparently derives mainly from the mental comparison of the two image stimuli presented to the brain. It depends only slightly on the detection of minute variations in the convergence of the eyes. Moreover, a person with only one eye is able to perceive depth and differences in distance to a remarkable degree. Perspective, shadow detail, and accommodation are all still available to him. The results are not as accurate, but his sense of depth is by no means eliminated.

Two elements of the above discussion of the optical nature of depth perception are amenable to change by the stage designer—*shadow detail* and *perspective*. Shadows caused by strongly directional light striking an object will be visible to some extent to anyone not looking directly along the path of the beam of light. Given the normal angles of lighting we have become accustomed to in nature, we can do a fairly accurate job of determining the shape of an object by noting the shadow patterns it projects. Moreover, the contrast between shadowed areas and highlighted areas is a major source of attention-focusing material.

Shadow Detail

Under stage conditions, shadows are about the only means available to enable members of the audience to perceive fine details of modeling, such as expressions on actors' faces. These hills and valleys forming smiles or frowns are far too small to be measured at any distance by accommodation or convergence. They will be visible only when they cast shadows, and prominent only to the degree that the shadows are prominent. The nature and contrast of these shadow patterns is under the control of the lighting designer. Except in the most intimate theatres a major share of the audience will have to depend entirely on shadow detail to detect changes in facial expressions.

Perspective

Perspective is the science of line-of-sight vision. It determines the apparent height of objects at a distance from the observer, and the convergence of parallel lines in three-dimensional objects as they are seen by the eye or by a camera lens. Since objects that are farther away seem smaller, and since converging lines suggest distant but parallel lines, the designer can exploit the effects of perspective to increase apparent depth on the stage. He can also increase the perceived depth of stage space by attention to those lines and planes which aid the audience most in determining the depth present. For instance, the stage floor or ramps and levels resting on it will provide easily visible lines leading from near the audience to the background. Objects on the set can easily be located on these lines, giving a much clearer picture of the depth of a scene and the size of objects within it than where neither floor nor downstage-upstage horizontal lines are visible. Upstage-downstage crosses are powerful theatrical devices *if* they are perceived as such. However, such crosses are frequently lost on that share of the audience looking at the stage from a sight line that eliminates most or all of the floor.

Lighting and Perspective

These matters of perspective are primarily setting-design considerations, but the lighting artist can do much to improve things by providing changes in lighting texture between the upstage and downstage areas that tend to further emphasize the effects of perspective as the actor moves forward. For example, softer, lower-contrast shadow detail in the upstage areas as contrasted with harder, more contrasting effects in the downstage areas, will heighten the effects of perspective.

It is clearly the obligation of the lighting to reveal the three-dimensionality of those objects designed to increase the effect of upstage-downstage movement. Ramps, levels, steps, and the like, will lose much of their value if not aided by *clearly defined shadows* that reveal their shape and line to the audience.

Painted shadows have lost much of their popularity in the theatre in the last 60 years since Adolphe Appia inveighed against them so vigorously. Fortunately the eighteenth- and nineteenth-century notion of illusion has about vanished. Modern painted shadows are usually intended to be just that: painted shadows. However, they often are painted on fabric, and fabric seldom lies completely flat. If objects with painted shadows are lighted with directional apparatus that casts light obliquely along the surface of the canvas, the result will be unwanted and confusing shadows from the humps and dents in the fabric. These shadows will "give the lie" to the painted detail in an annoying manner. Thus it is still necessary to light painted drops and similar material with as nearly shadowless light as can be arranged. This light, of course, is not the kind that will serve the purposes of the actors and the three-dimensional portions of the setting. Fortunately, modern nondirectional-lighting apparatus offers a degree of control over the spread of light that makes this sort of division of function reasonably possible.

LIGHT AND THE ACTOR

15

As we begin to develop the details of the interrelationship between lighting and the actor, it is necessary to look once again into the recent history of stage lighting. Modern lighting terminology has grown out of this history and can be best understood by examining its development.

The Development of Directional Light in the Theatre

The first indoor stage lighting was essentially nondirectional, that is, no shadows were produced. Banks of candles or rows of gas flames formed borderlights whose light was nondirectional and essentially shadowless. Whatever shadow was cast by any individual flame was wiped out by the light from others. The advent of electricity in the theatre did little to change this because rows of large-filament incandescent lamps were about as shadowless as rows of gaslights. Only the limelight and the arc light were directional. These cast shadows that were visible, and even produced a beam effect to reinforce their directionality. With the invention of the incandescent spotlight, multiple sources of directional light became possible on the stage. It was at this point that two categories of lighting equipment emerged. *General-illumination equipment* was that equipment designed to flood the stage, or a large share of it, with light. Most of this equipment produced no shadow, at least in the manner in which it was used. However, single-source instruments like the early olivette could be strongly directional; that is, they could produce sharply defined shadows visible to the audience. These floodlights were classified as general-illumination equipment because the wide spread of light they produced could not be precisely focused. Rows of borderlights and footlights were more

326

clearly nondirectional. They cast no visible shadows and lighted most of the stage at once. *Specific-lighting apparatus* was the name given to spotlight apparatus and a bit later to beam projectors. Notice that the terms "general" and "specific" imply more concern for the relative amount of the stage that an instrument could illuminate than for the directional potentials of the instrument. The emphasis seemed to be on the size of the brush used in "painting with light," not on the end product.

As spotlight lamps became more powerful and lenses and reflectors more efficient, the fallacy inherent in this categorizing became more obvious. Specific-lighting instruments were now available that could easily illuminate the whole of most stages if placed in the front of the balcony or near the back of the house. The amount of space potentially lighted was no longer a valid criterion.

At this point the terms "directional" and "nondirectional" came to be applied to lighting. While these terms usually are associated with certain types of equipment, the relationship is not fixed. Instead, the emphasis is placed upon the quality of the light produced.

Directional Light Defined

Directional light is light whose direction is clearly apparent to the audience, usually because the light casts visible shadows that reveal the location, or at least the direction, of the source. Occasionally the direction is further revealed by the beam of a powerful instrument as it passes through dusty or smoky air. This effect is not easy to control, but has produced some powerful lighting.

Nondirectional light is that light which produces no shadows that are visible to the audience, because the source is so large that shadows are canceled at stage distances, or because the direction of the light is such that any shadows formed are invisible to the audience. In the case of cyclorama lighting, the effect is also nondirectional because there is no object in the flood of light that will cast a shadow visible to the audience. If the cyclorama is near perfect, a single floodlight will still produce a nondirectional effect on it as long as nothing interferes with the beam. Note that the same instrument in the same lighting setup may sometimes serve both directional and nondirectional functions.

Key and Fill Light

The most conspicuous directional lighting on stage is that kind frequently called *key lighting*. This term comes from photography, where it means the light that produces the brightest highlight and thus predominates by having the strongest directionality. "Key" means substantially the same thing on stage, but with the added complication that the function of key lighting will frequently shift from instrument to instrument. A key-lighting instrument will often

FIGURE *i*

Lighting for Situation Comedy. This scene illustrates some of the requirements which must be met when lighting a rather broad comedy scene in a moderate-sized theatre. Visibility of facial expressions is the foremost concern. Note how the lighting has been especially angled to focus on the face of Falstaff as he conceals himself in the laundry basket. Lighting on his face must be excellent, even when the basket is almost closed; he peeps out at several key moments during the scene. The production is Verdi's Falstaff *at California State University, Northridge. Direction: David Scott.* Scenography and photo by author.

serve as fill at another time. In an earlier day on stage, and still to a large degree in television lighting, spotlights were used to provide key; general-illumination instruments provided the fill.

Fill light is that light which illuminates or fills in the shadows produced by the key light. In photographic media fill light is vital because the film or the electronic gear cannot cope with the contrast between a bright highlight from a key light and a dense shadow in the areas not lit by the key. Photographers often solve this problem with reflectors which pick up some of the key light spilled past the subject and diffusely bounce it back into the shadows. This bouncing reproduces the effect found in nature where sunlight is reflected from a myriad of objects into those shadows cast by its direct beams. Television production has found that reflection is not powerful enough to serve this purpose. The electronic apparatus in the camera works best with a "base light" of no directionality and fairly high intensity, produced by floodlighting apparatus. It serves to fill shadows and to boost the entire level of illumination into the range which suits the television camera best.

In the theatre, the practice of using general illumination for fill light and spotlighting for key lighting has become somewhat outmoded, except in those theatres so short on equipment that the lighting artist must get the most out of the spotlights available. In an adequately equipped theatre, floodlighting apparatus tends to be too limited in function to justify its use; far more flexibility and artistic potentiality can be gained by using spotlights for fill light. For example, a subtle potentiality derived from the multiple use of spotlights on acting areas is that the fill light can also have a directional quality. While the key light is certainly the chief directional element in a given bit of lighting, there is no reason why there cannot be a secondary set of shadows and a secondary directional element. Since the functions may be reversed by dimmer changes, this secondary effect can have great symbolic value. Finally, the directional quality of the key light augmented by the directional quality of the fill will provide further heightening of the three-dimensional quality of both actors and setting. Secondary shadows cast by the fill light add more detail to the objects seen by the audience. Given adequate equipment and adequate control over that equipment, the variations between key and fill light form one of the

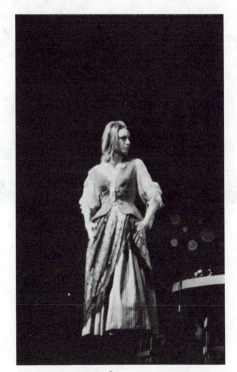

FIGURE *j*
Key and Fill for a Serious Scene. This scene is taken from Bizet's Carmen *as staged at California State University, Northridge. It illustrates good key-fill ratio for a scene of considerable dramatic intensity designed for a proscenium theatre of modest size. The photo was taken about midway in the dramatic build toward the end of the scene.* Scenography and photo by author.

FIGURE *k*
Key Lighting from Below.
This illustrates the some-
what bizarre effect of bring-
ing the key light up from
below and in front of the
actor. Normal shadow pat-
terns are reversed. Produc-
tion: Corruption in the
Palace of Justice *as pro-*
duced at the University of
California at Santa Bar-
bara. Director: Vincent
Landro, lighting: Don
Childs. Photo by Steve
Suess.

most effective artistic tools the lighting artist has at his command. The
following is a discussion of some of the possibilities of this system.

Directional Light and Acting

Unfortunately, many of today's actors, professional and nonprofes-
sional, know little or nothing about the potential contributions of
lighting to their art. To many actors, "being in the light" is the extent
of their awareness of lighting, and seeking the "hottest" spot on stage
constitutes taking the scene. While these are matters of some consequence in the use of lighting by the actor, they reveal only the gross
aspects of the relationship between acting and lighting. Discussion of
the effects of shadow upon the perception of details of facial expression has already indicated that being in the light is but a prerequisite

to the artistic use of the shadows cast by that light. Moreover, directionality, once clearly established for the audience, may have symbolic importance to the scene. Whether or not this potentiality is realized depends upon the actor and his reaction to the light. *In all cases the art of lighting must depend upon the actor for its denotative support.* Given the clarity that the words of the play, uttered by the actor, can provide, the powerful symbolic effect of lighting is available to the actor to heighten and augment his art. *But the actor must be aware of this effect and make the necessary symbolic connection between the general qualities of the lighting and the specific nature of the dramatic material to be communicated.*

While it is not the purpose of a text on lighting to explain how actors should react to light, it may not be amiss to remind the actor that human beings respond consistently and overtly to their lighted environment. Attention is focused almost unconsciously upon areas of bright illumination. Body positions shift to accommodate the eyes to light for reading or to avoid a glare. Darkness produces its effects even with the passing of a cloud over the sun. Light with strong dramatic implications is difficult to ignore. The blazing red of a policeman's light or a flare in the street offer attention-commanding examples. Such stimuli and responses should give the actor the beginnings of his repertoire of responses to light in the theatre. He needs only to add the artistic abstraction and exaggeration that differentiate the art of acting from the nonart of living.

The actor would also do well to spend hours studying the effects of directional light on the face and body. He should develop an acute awareness of the subtle modeling that key and fill light can provide, and a particularly acute sense of the effect of turning into or out of key light as he plays a scene. As he learns of these, he will be more and more aware of the precise control over stage movement that is necessary to the successful execution of subtle lighting while he plays his scene. A turn at the control board can do a great deal to convince the actor that rambling, uncontrolled stage movement will deprive him of an exceedingly effective addition to his expressive repertoire.

The illustrations (Figure 15-1) will reveal a few of the possibilities open to an actor as he uses key and fill to aid in the building of a scene. The notes and dialogue are keyed to the plates to make up for the fact that a series of static pictures cannot express the continuous change typical of such lighting and acting. This series of photographs has been prepared to illustrate the manner in which a shift of direction of a key light can and must be coordinated with the acting. The scene is *Macbeth*, Act IV, Scene 3. The photographs have been focused on Macduff only, since the key-light shift is motivated and utilized by him. Both Ross and Malcolm serve as motivating speakers but visually they remain well in the edges of the visual focus.

The reader must remember that the flow of movement and the changes of lighting from picture to picture are continuous and that the

FIGURE *15-1*

Crossing the Key Light. Pictures a through f (pp. 333–335) illustrate a build in tension produced by reducing the fill light on the actor's left until a strong stage-right key light has been established. Beginning with picture g, a 60° key from stage left is gradually brought in and the erstwhile key from stage right is reduced to a fill light and finally completely extinguished. This key shift is motivated by the actor's turn as he shifts from defeat in grief to anger and seeks revenge. None of these lighting changes can be performed in a linear movement of a single fader because the tempo of each fade or dim-up is independent of the others. Thus the series of lighting changes illustrates a counterpoint cue. Actor: Gilman Rankin. Photographs: Herbst.

---

timing of these changes is found in the characterization provided by the actor. Any attempt to superimpose such a lighting change as this on a scene without the full understanding and cooperation of the actor is doomed to the worst sort of dramatic failure: The lighting will be overobvious. The scene begins in lighting provided by a 45° acting-area pattern with relatively little key-fill contrast.

Light and the Entire Body

Given a costume that reveals the shape and tensions of the human figure, strong key light with little fill can potentially evoke dramatically powerful but abstract material. Unless the audience is very close to the figure, facial expression will not predominate. Reflection of mood and dramatic condition become a function of the whole body, and the response is essentially in the realm of modern dance. Empathy, stirred by kinesthetic responses, is probably at the root of expressions of this sort. Members of the audience will tend to empathize with the figure on stage by establishing muscular tensions that try to parallel those on the stage. Given the denotative power of words, these expressions can be powerful indeed. However, they are not marked by subtlety.

In a more common theatrical situation, using actors and not dancers, there is still the possibility that the expressive potentialities of the whole body of the actor, with no particular predominance of his facial expression, may reach the audience. Again strong key and little fill, plus strong muscular tensions on the part of the actor, comprise the method.

In both instances the direction of the key light is of supreme importance. Key light must strike the figure at nearly right angles to the line of sight of the audience either from the side or from above. Fill, either from reflection or from other sources, must be minimized. The result of this type of lighting is to accent heavily the main lines of the body at the expense of the details. Given these conditions, the rest is up to the actor or dancer.

a

b

ROSS: *Your castle is surprised; your wife and babes*
Savagely slaughter'd: . . .   [a]
MALCOLM: . . . *Merciful heaven!*
What, man! ne'er pull your hat upon your brows;
Give sorrow words: the grief that does not speak
Whispers the o'er-fraught heart and bids it break.   [b]

MACDUFF: *My children too?*   [c]
MACDUFF: . . . *My wife kill'd too?*   [d]

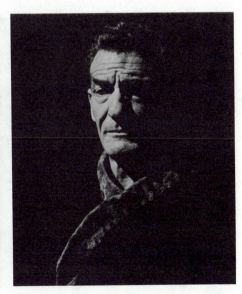

c

d

e   f

MACDUFF: *He has no children. All my pretty ones?*
Did you say all? O hell-kite! All?
What, all my pretty chickens and their dam
At one fell swoop?   [e]
MALCOLM: *Dispute it like a man.*   [f]

MALCOLM: *Be this the whetstone of your sword: let grief*
Convert to anger; blunt not the heart, enrage it.   [g]
MACDUFF: *O, I could play the woman with mine eyes*
And braggart with my tongue!   [h]

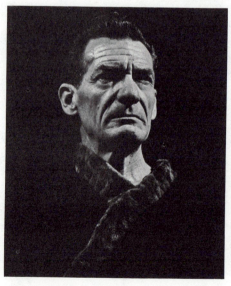

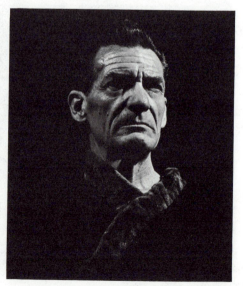

g   h

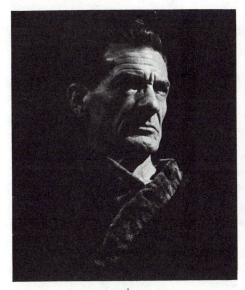

i

j

MACDUFF: . . . *But, gentle heavens,*
Cut short all intermission; . . .   [i]
MACDUFF: . . . *front to front*
Bring thou this fiend of Scotland and myself; . . .   [j]

MACDUFF: *Within my sword's length set him; . . .*   [k]
MACDUFF: . . . *if he 'scape,*
Heaven forgive him too!   [l]

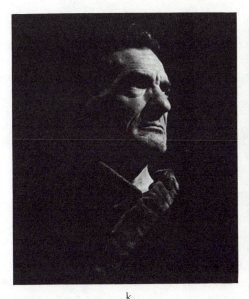

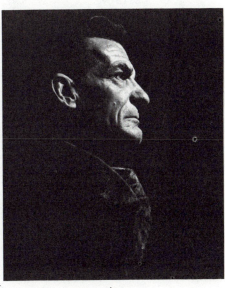

k

l

Obviously such strong and rather abstract effects cannot be of long duration except in the case of dance. Generally the key-fill ratio will soon be reduced and the attention will shift principally to the face and upper body of the actor. Note that this does not mean that "acting from the neck up" is the norm, but that the focus of attention narrows in this direction.

Light and the Actor's Face

As key and fill are gradually reduced in contrast to each other, we arrive at the point where the content of the shadows cast by the key light becomes visible. This point will vary depending on the theatre, the complexion of the actor, the amount of light silhouetting him, and other factors. As shadows are filled, the face comes into prominence. It is only natural that the audience should look into the face of the actor for clues to the emotions of the character he is portraying. The face is where most of our clues of this sort come from every day. The theatre, through the actor, uses these clues for artistic ends. Raw emotion is of no artistic value until it is made a part of the entire symbolic effort of the production. Thus the blends of key and fill which bring the actor's face into prominence serve two functions: (1) They make the expressions of that face visible, and (2) by careful heightening and by the actor's response to the directional quality of the light, they serve to blend the expressions into the entire theatrical expression.

The Designer's Variables

Given the above summary of the various relationships which may be established between light and the actor, it is now appropriate to list the variables which the designer may use to effect these relationships. These will be the practical stock in trade of the designer as he concerns himself with light and actors.

1. Contrast between actor lighting and background
2. Contrast between key and fill
3. Color of key and fill
4. Angle of key and fill
5. Sidelight key
6. Contrast between actors

Perhaps 90 percent of the lighting design done will be in the manipulation of these variables. The bases of these manipulations will be in the aesthetic ingredients of lighting already discussed. In reality these variables represent the extension of the aesthetic matters of space/time symbolism into the practical considerations of lighting design. It is now our purpose to go into detail concerning each of these variables.

Contrast between
Lighting on Actors and
on the Background

Acting space is that space occupied by the actors during the progress of the play. It, plus background and surrounding areas visible to the audience, make up the stage space. In terms of lighting, acting and stage space usually are considered as separate categories. The acting space is subdivided as needed, and the background usually is lighted with general illumination instruments in wide swaths, if not as one unit. Contrast between these two visible elements forms one of the broadest or most all-inclusive considerations in lighting. For the moment we are concerned with the effects which varying this contrast have upon the lighting of the actor.

The two extremes are silhouette, in which no actor light is used, and "pool lighting," where no background light is used. In the case of silhouette, we are back to the situation just discussed in the section "Light and the Actor's Face."

SILHOUETTE: RIM LIGHTING

A special kind of silhouette, "rim lighting," occasionally appears in the theatre and has found a slightly different application in television lighting. The procedure is simple, provided masking space is available. Overhead back lighting is used. Instruments, usually of high intensity, are mounted above and somewhat behind the acting areas. These lights are angled downstage but not enough so that their light passes over the footlight line. The results vary, depending on other lighting conditions and upon the actor's complexion and costume. If the actors are otherwise in silhouette, the rim light produces exactly what its name implies—a rim of light around the upper part of the figure. This rim is most pronounced with light-colored costumes and on blonds. The effect of this rim of light is to emphasize still further the main outlines of the figure at the expense of detail. If actors in rim light are also illuminated from the front, the rim effect is rapidly reduced and, in the theatre, usually loses its value except for special limited area effects. In television, rim lighting serves a different purpose. The electronic necessities of the television camera dictate that the lighting level over the entire set should be quite high. This lighting is accomplished largely by the use of general-lighting apparatus, usually "scoops." Then the actor lighting is superimposed upon this "base light." Since the base light denies the television designer the theatrical expedient of dimming the background to emphasize the actors, rim light, often in huge quantities, is added to get separation between the actors and the rather brightly lit background. Modern improvements in camera pickup tubes and other refinements in television technology are making this technique less restrictive than it once was. In some instances lighting levels have been reduced to about the intensity of stage lighting. However, rim light still finds considerable acceptance because of the contrast-magnifying tendencies of the television camera which increase its effectiveness. The close-up quality of television can bring out those details of rim lighting which would never carry to the audience except in the most intimate of theatres.

FROM SILHOUETTE TO POOL-OF-LIGHT

Ranging from the silhouette toward the isolated pool, there is an ever-increasing emphasis on the actor's face or details of his figure, or both. At the same time there are several kinds of shifts in focus of attention.

Beginning with the silhouette, the attention of the audience can be focused on the actor or upon the background, depending mostly upon whether the actor is moving or stationary. If stationary, he is most

FIGURE *l.*
Side-Back Lighting with No Fill. This photo was taken from the same production as figure k. It shows in close-up the effect of placing the sole light source above and almost behind the actor. Note that facial expression is substantially obliterated and that this would not change if the actor faced the camera. Emphasis is on body tensions and movements; not on the face. Photo by Steve Suess.

likely to fall into place as part of the "picture." As he moves, he normally will hold attention unless the background is "busy," for example, if it is made up of moving or changing projections.

As the foreground is lighted, leaving the background still in light, attention becomes more diversified. Focus will depend upon relative brightness, and movement will predominate over stillness. As more than one acting area is illuminated, shifts of focus will tend to follow the precepts of line, level, position, and the like, commonly detailed in texts on directing. Under these circumstances, lighting becomes only one of a large number of factors influencing the shifting of attention. However, as soon as the background is dimmed down, and one or two acting areas begin to predominate over the others, the powerful effect of lighting again appears. As contrasts increase further between lighting areas, and as the background diminishes in brightness, the effect of line, level, and the like, rapidly wanes. Movement, preferably accompanied by speech, is the only element which can equal light in focusing attention under these circumstances. Thus a moving actor in near shadow can still predominate over a stationary actor in bright light, but only for as long as the shadowed actor moves. All he needs do to give the scene to his competitor is to stop.

As we move still further along the scale of contrasts toward the point where only a pool of light cuts through the darkness, it becomes progressively harder for even the moving, speaking figure to attract attention while in semidarkness. Finally, with a nearly dark background, setting shifts may be made if the tempo and mood are kept within the play's structure. An actor in a bright pool of light can hold attention with only a minimum of awareness being given to the background. Since total blackness broken only by a pool of light is a near impossibility on the stage, the nearly dark background is the limit as far as variations between acting-space lighting and background lighting are concerned.

Contrast between Key and Fill

The following discussion will apply to individual acting areas under all conditions wherein the audience is aware of the actors in lighting other than silhouette. However, the effects of varying the ratio between key light and fill light will be more pronounced whenever the acting area has little competition from other lighted areas on stage. There are two reasons for this: First, outside focuses of attention tend to obliterate details within the acting area in question by cutting down on close study of the area; second, spill light from other sources will dilute the acting-area light, reducing the contrast.

An "acting area" is usually the pool of light formed by focusing two or more spotlights on the same acting space. The result is a head-level pool of useful light roughly in the shape of an ellipse whose longitudinal axis parallels the footlights. This area will usually be about 8 to

10 feet wide, and 6 to 8 feet deep. Somewhat larger or much smaller acting areas are possible.

As far as key-fill ratios[1] are concerned, it will be assumed that both key and fill lights are spotlight sources, and that either may serve as key or fill, depending on dimmer setting. In a simplified form the principles mentioned below may be applied to acting areas wherein the key is a spotlight and the fill is supplied by general illumination. Obviously, reversing the key is an impossibility under these conditions.

THE STANDARD ACTING AREA

For the sake of convenience, let us begin our discussion with a standard lighting area. On a standard lighting area, the actor facing full front will find one spotlight 45° above and 45° to his right, and the other symmetrically placed on his left (see Figure 6-1). Either spotlight may serve as key or fill. The standard acting area produces shadows on the face that most nearly approximate those found in outdoor lighting on a sunny day. If one of the two instruments is equipped with a warm tint, for example, straw, and the other with a cool tint, for example, daylight blue, the effect will be even more realistic. Plasticity will also increase. Moreover, the warm light will automatically become the key and the cool light the fill, simply because of the differences in transmittance of the two color media. Such areas are often run from single dimmers with considerable success. The only difficulty is that the cool fill deteriorates as it is dimmed, destroying both color contrast and the modeling effect of the warm-cool shadows.

KEY-FILL VARIATIONS IN THE STANDARD ACTING AREA

Let us consider a standard area with no color medium and with instruments of equal power: At the full-up position on both dimmers,

[1] Key-fill ratios can be expressed in two ways: (1) light-meter reading (in this case the figures, usually cited in footcandles, express mathematical ratios between intensity readings taken on the key and the fill side of the face); (2) dimmer readings (references to the standard 10-point scale of dimmer calibration). Dimmer readings are quite consistent for linear autotransformer dimmers, but they may vary over a wide range when they refer to the settings of electronic dimmers. Control curves of these dimmers vary widely, depending on the manufacturer and the desires of those buying the equipment. Furthermore, the curves may vary from dimmer to dimmer as the equipment ages.

Actually both systems are subject to many other variables. Color differences, overall lighting intensity which affects the sensitivity of the eye, makeup and skin tone differences, and contrast with costume and background color are the main factors. Since key-fill ratios can only be approximations at best, except in the case of a specific situation, it will be the policy of this text to cite these ratios in terms of settings of a linear-voltage control such as that produced by an autotransformer dimmer or a solid-state device equipped to produce a linear-voltage change. Those experienced with square-law control devices will find it easy to convert this information to square-law terms by mentally increasing the effect of changes at low readings and decreasing that at the 8–10 end.

the area will display nearly flat light with little directionality. However, the moment either instrument is dimmed even as little as one point on a ten-point dimmer scale, a key light appears (the undimmed instrument) and directionality develops. Incidentally, the natural reduction in color temperature as the lamp is dimmed will contribute to a color difference as well as an intensity difference. Stage photographers using black-and-white film will discover that this color difference is often too subtle to photograph under stage conditions; the picture of a subtly keyed scene is left with a flat appearance.[2]

Directionality increases rapidly as one instrument is dimmed, becoming so intense by the time the difference between the two lights is three or four dimmer points (assuming voltage-linear dimmers), that the audience will be disturbed if the actor ignores the directional nature of the light. A turn into the full light becomes symbolic, whether the actor intends it to or not. When there are about two dimmer points difference, the directional nature of the light is available to the actor and can be exploited by him if he is sensitive to it and able to react to it. With differences greater than about five points, the actor *must* use the key light if the lighting is not to call attention to itself.

REVERSING THE KEY

Reversing the key consists of exchanging the functions of key and fill light in an acting area by brightening the erstwhile fill and dimming the previous key light (see Figure 15-1). The tempo or cadence with which the dimming is done will be a matter for careful study each time the operation is designed, but one thing is fairly certain: The situation in which both lights are full up should probably be avoided. This position represents the least expressive use of the area; moreover, at full up for both lights, the overall intensity of the area will probably far exceed that desired in relationship to the rest of the scene. Thus reversing the key will usually consist of a change such as:

Key 8 (as actor turns) to Fill 4 (left spotlight)
Fill 4   Key 9 (right spotlight)

The pacing of the change will be complex. The new key will probably lead off the change, arrive at its new reading at the peak of the actor's turn. Then, starting well after the new key has started, the fill will quite rapidly drop to its fill reading, finishing a second or so after the actor has established his new focus. Obviously this sort of change cannot be made with a single-handle fader. This general pattern will be repeated with variations whether the cue lasts 4 seconds or 4 minutes. The crucial part of the operation is the timing of the oncoming key light, which must be paced with the action and the emotional

[2] Color film will usually exaggerate the warm color, giving a distorted result.

build of the lines. Being either early or late is deadly, particularly if the change is both rapid and extreme. Perhaps the hardest key shift to perform is a complete shift from no fill to full-up key within a time of about 5 seconds. Cooperation between actor and lighting operator will be absolutely essential if this shift is to work.

What is the effect of reversing the key? At its simplest mechanical level, the change provides good facial illumination for an actor who has altered his facing from left to right or vice versa. If this is the only function, the chances are that the design of the lighting has out-stripped the artistic needs of the scene. If directionality has no more significance than the need for adequate light, then complimentary-tint acting-area lighting should almost suffice. In any event, key-fill ratios should be kept near 2:1 or less so that the actors are well lit from either side. However, as the scenes become more dramatic, a polarity usually develops. The characters are drawn toward or forced away from each other. Antagonism to someone or something increases and directional movement becomes significant. Meaningful movement on the part of the actors—a clue for the lighting designer—often calls for meaningful directionality in the lighting. But the beginner is cautioned against leaping rapidly to the conclusion that every slight increase in dramatic tension calls for a dash to the control board. The potential expressive range between 2:1 and 6:1 is tremendous, particularly if the scenes are being played in low background illumination which provides little dilution for the key-fill ratio. The astute lighting artist will begin to build his scene well down the scale with a great deal of background illumination and medium key-fill contrast. His first move in the direc-tion of augmenting dramatic tension will be to increase the focus of attention on the most dramatically significant areas. He does this by subtly taking down background light and light in lesser areas. As the focus narrows, the lighting artist may actually *decrease* the key-fill ratio to compensate for the decrease in spill light which was diluting the key-fill. Compensation for this dilution may have forced the dimmer readings to as much as 10:5, although the appearance to the audience may have been that of 10:9 or even less. As background spill decreases, the lighting artist will find that the dramatic intensity implied by the lighting often far exceeds that required by the play. Thus he increases the fill light to "flatten" the scene. The test of a good lighting artist is, among other things, in his sensitivity to these adjustments.

As dramatic intensity builds, the lighting artist has several courses of action open to him: He can increase key-fill ratios, allowing the actors a strongly directional playing area. This method is powerful *if* the actors can and will use the direction of the light as a significant part of the scene. Such lighting is worse than meaningless if not made a part of the entire play by actor response. Another possibility is to increase or decrease the total brilliance of the area. If other areas are in use, the only choice is to increase intensity, because lowering it would most likely pass the focus of attention to another part of the stage. If the area is the only one in use, a decrease will often work as effectively as an increase. Again, the choice depends upon the scene, the interpretation of the lighting artist and the director, and upon the actor. Increases and decreases are accomplished by raising or lowering the reading of both key and fill dimmers while maintaining the contrast difference between them. The lighting artist will find his eye a surer guide than the numbers on the dimmers because of nonlinearity in controllers, and because at low readings in particular, the eye changes its sensitivity to contrast.

Color of Key and Fill

Of all of the variables usually manipulated by the lighting designer, acting-area color change is probably the subtlest, as a direct result of the subtlety of acting-area colors as they are chosen. However, a difficulty arises because there is such a strong tendency for incandescent lamps to emit only warm light as they are dimmed. The result is that even a minor shift away from a cool acting-area color may result in an entirely warm stage. An attempt to shift the color further in the direction of cool light raises more problems. If the warm side of the area is dimmed enough to make it serve as fill light, the remaining light from that instrument will be very warm and the color medium will transmit it with great efficiency. Thus the fill will end up warmer than it was when serving as key light. The effect may still be warm. About the only sure way to make the scene cool is to bring in to *full* still more cool instruments. Bringing them in part way may only add warm light; the lamps will not produce cool colors until they are most of the way on. Since this method builds up intensity rapidly, lighting artists in need of cool scenes usually accomplish their ends by taking out the warm light and adding cool fill light plus additional cool keys if needed. This procedure is expensive both in equipment and control apparatus. Even well-equipped theatres may be reduced to the use of floodlighting with scoops to build up enough cool light to make mood changes significant. An assist from the setting by way of paint that favors the reflection of cool light will help immensely.

Shifts from cool to warm are much easier to make, but usually suggest a "return to normal" because warmth is the usual condition of stage lighting. Thus they are inclined to be anticlimactic. If a strong effect is needed, something more than acting-area lighting at 45° angles is needed.

As in all cases where color is used in stage lighting in desaturated form, the effects of color changes are fugitive. Five or ten minutes after a quite violent shift to a cool color, for example, the audience will have adapted to this tint so completely that they will think of it as white. Only constant change or stronger color in the background will keep the color "alive," and both of these expedients tend to be distracting about as often as they are useful.

Angle of Key and Fill

Variation in angle of key lighting demands the ultimate in lighting design. In this area, no lighting artist worthy of the name will ever consider the job finished. This is also the area of closest blending of the arts of lighting, directing, and acting.

The first step is the decision that a key light other than a standard 45° unit is needed. This decision is occasionally made simple by the obvious demands of the script, as is the case in *Everyman*. The ascent of Everyman to heaven at the end of the play obviously calls for a special key light of great intensity coming from a high angle. However, such obvious scenes are relatively rare; most Shakespearean soliloquies, for instance, offer no such clear indication to the lighting artist.

The genesis of high-angle key lighting is usually either in design conferences with the director, or during a study of the blocking during early rehearsals. However, the decision that there should be such a light and the act of accurately placing and using it are two vastly different things. Such a light will naturally be an extremely prominent part of a climactic scene. It must be well motivated and blended into the total production if it is not to protrude as an unnecessary element. The actor using the light must be prepared to play it with precision, yet not at the expense of creating a wooden characterization. Such conditions are not easily met, but when they are, the results will be worth the effort.

Location of high-angle key lights calls for special study of the actor to be lighted as he goes through the movements of the scene. Careful attention must be paid to the directional quality which he and the director have already given the scene and also to countermovements opposing that direction. Remember that the high-angle key, if it is also a sidelight, will be reduced to rim lighting as the actor turns away from it. Thus countermovements may require fill light. The scope of movement during the scene to be lit must be studied carefully. A single source is usually desirable from the design standpoint, but it may not cover the area needed. Probably the most important clue to the exact location of the instrument(s) will be found in a study of facial movements and expressions of the actor. Unless the lighting artist has had a great deal of experience with this particular actor, he will be forced to try out lighting angles on him to see how the structure of his face takes the light. For example, deep-set eyes often heighten the tragic quality of an actor's face, but they may become black holes in a high-angle key light if the actor plays with his head down. Obviously a hat that shades the eyes almost precludes high angles unless it can be removed for the scene.

Probably the hardest thing for the lighting artist to evaluate as he thinks through the various possible angles for his key light is the degree to which the actor is going to respond to the light. It will give the actor a powerful directional stimulus to work with or to respond against. Either of these alternatives is desirable; what is completely frustrating is to get no response at all.

Since there are going to be so many unknowns in the arrangement of such specialized lighting, many lighting artists *double hang* an area. This common and very useful practice consists of installing a set of normal 45° instruments for the area and circuiting them separately, giving a complete normal range of control. Then a second set of instruments is hung in a pattern deemed likely to provide the lighting needed for the climax scenes. For example, this may consist of raising the instruments up to the point where their vertical angle approaches 60° and their horizontal angle remains near 45°. The entire scheme may be altered to fit whatever problems the lighting artist anticipates. No matter what their angles, these extra instruments are also circuited separately. With such a combination, the potentialities for variations in modeling light are almost infinite. Any pair of lights can be worked together to produce useful key-fill combinations.

Getting subtly into the single high-angle key-light situation and back out of it are often the most difficult problems the lighting designer faces, once the angle has been determined. The subtlest and by far the most common way to do this is to bring the high-angle key light to a fairly high reading and then slowly, in pace with the action, fade the other lights, leaving only the key and whatever fill is needed. If this fade is to be accomplished without apparent loss of intensity, the key will have to be increased in brilliance as the fade progresses. The total quantity of light will still decrease, but higher contrasts will make up for this as far as the eye is concerned. Getting out of the high-angle lighting can be just the reverse of the above process, although the nature of dramatic climaxes of this intensity is that they usually are followed by a sharp shift of attention to another part of the stage, if not by a break in the play.

A further potentiality of the "double area" lies in the possibility of developing great variety and a gradual increase in dramatic tension over a long speech. The long dramatic speeches in Büchner's *Danton's Death* offer such an example. At the onset of this scene, low-level, high-contrast 45° lighting can be used to set the tragic tone, but leave plenty of potentiality for building later. Gradually, as the speeches progress, and one victim after another is led off to the guillotine, the lighting can gradually shift to the higher-angle key. Finally, as Danton is about to be taken away, only one unit of the high-angle key light can be used, and this at full intensity. The effect is harsh, tragic, and with subtle background lighting, strongly symbolic. Such long sequences point up the necessity for restraint in the use of high-angle key lighting. Its effect is so strongly symbolic that most dramatic climaxes cannot use its power. Overlighting a scene of climax and throwing the focus of attention directly on the lighting is a major artistic sin.

FIGURE 15-2a

Side Lighting Instruments. Three 1000-watt ellipsoidal spotlights mounted to provide a single sweep of sidelights from stage right to stage left. Since this particular set is well off stage, the lower instrument is well above the actors' heads and is angled outward. On a smaller stage with the side lighting closer to the acting areas this instrument would have to be tilted downward. Spotlights by Strand Century Lighting Inc. Photograph: Herbst.

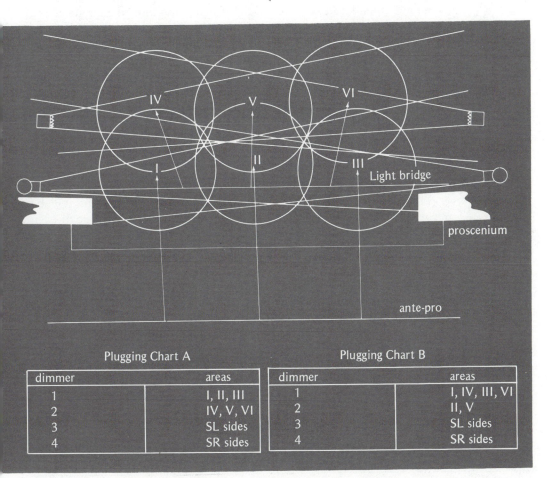

Plugging Chart A	
dimmer	areas
1	I, II, III
2	IV, V, VI
3	SL sides
4	SR sides

Plugging Chart B	
dimmer	areas
1	I, IV, III, VI
2	II, V
3	SL sides
4	SR sides

FIGURE 15-2b

Using Side Lighting to Make an Extremely Limited Situation More Flexible. This simplified lighting plot shows how side lighting can aid in covering the acting space when equipment is severely limited. A total of ten instruments and four dimmers have been arranged to provide coverage of the acting area and some degree of control. Plugging Chart A provides upstage-downstage control over focus while the side lighting offers some degree of contrast control for plasticity. Plugging Chart B offers center side-stage focus control with the side lighting still controlling plasticity. With such limited equipment, the far-right and far-left stage areas are poorly covered by side lighting and the director will have to avoid certain "dead spots." However the center portion of the stage will offer reasonably good coverage and control.

Side Lighting

We have considered key and fill lighting as functions of a single acting area in the McCandless tradition. A similar effect can be created on the actor's face over much larger portions of the acting space by the use of side lighting (see Figure 15-2*a*). For purposes of clarity it will be convenient to treat side lighting as a part of two separate methods of stage lighting: (1) as an adjunct to the McCandless acting area system, and (2) as an essential part of the typical Broadway approach which combines a "wash" of front lighting produced by the use of strong side and front-side lighting. In actual practice there is no need to consider these as mutually exclusive systems.

SIDE LIGHTING AS A PART OF ACTING-AREA LIGHTING

A stage illuminated with a set of well-designed acting areas will be provided with a wide range of key-fill possibilities if each side of each area can be separately controlled. This range will be diminished if control is limited. Faced with an inadequate supply of dimmers, the designer will have to choose from various alternatives:

1. He may "lump" several adjacent areas into large "master areas" and provide key-fill control within these larger units. This sacrifices area control for key-fill control.
2. He can abandon key-fill control in favor of individual area control by circuiting both instruments for each area on the same dimmer. This reduces his key-fill control to choice of color medium, wattage adjustments, and throw-distance changes. These offer only limited control and little opportunity for change, once established.
3. He can arrange full-stage key-fill control at the expense of area control. This leaves him with the possibility for mood changes and general key-fill adjustments but at the expense of losing the attention-focusing value of area control.

FIGURE *15-2c*

Flexible Control Utilizing Side Lighting. This lighting plot has been simplified to show only the skeleton of the area lighting. Over this skeletonized plot, the side lighting has been drawn showing the edges of each beam—something not usually done because of the confusing array of lines generated. It is assumed that all side-lighting instruments are mounted 12– 15 feet from the floor. Careful tracing of the beam lines will show that the main stage area is covered with side lighting offering a wide variety of key-fill effects. Plugging Chart C shows how ten dimmers can be used to provide area control for varying focus of attention and side lighting control for plasticity. Such a system will be sufficient for many productions. Plugging Chart D offers a degree of control that will tax the skill of many student designers. Sixteen dimmers provide separate key-fill control over each area. Side-lighting control then is superimposed over this system to provide a second set of key-fill relationships. If acting-area colors and side-lighting colors are carefully chosen for flexibility in key-fill contrast of actors' faces, a tremendous range of expressive lighting is available to the designer.

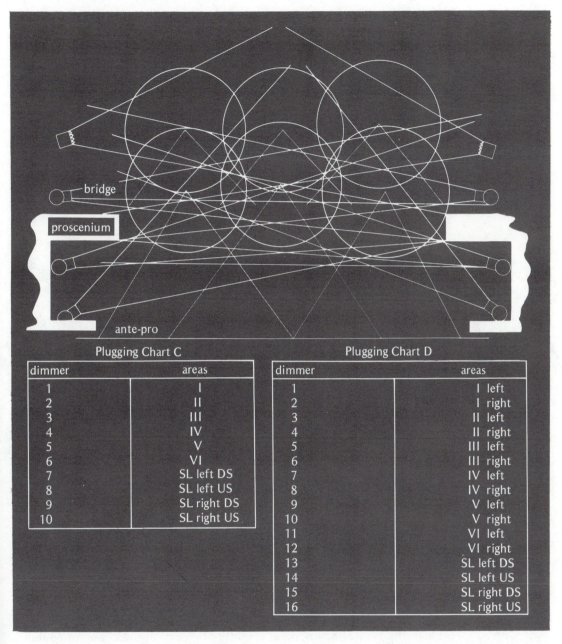

Plugging Chart C	
dimmer	areas
1	I
2	II
3	III
4	IV
5	V
6	VI
7	SL left DS
8	SL left US
9	SL right DS
10	SL right US

Plugging Chart D	
dimmer	areas
1	I left
2	I right
3	II left
4	II right
5	III left
6	III right
7	IV left
8	IV right
9	V left
10	V right
11	VI left
12	VI right
13	SL left DS
14	SL left US
15	SL right DS
16	SL right US

These trade offs can be very restrictive to the designer. The addition of a set of sidelights will often restore flexibility at a reasonable cost (see Figures 15-2b and c and their plugging charts). The designer will also benefit from an additional design element. The side lighting provides more variation in key-lighting angle and color. Such a pattern of area lighting and side lighting is shown in a simplified light plot in Figure 15-2c. This will work best in a setting designed from the beginning with this type of lighting in mind. If this is done, the designer can work out means of controlling the audience view of the large areas illuminated by the side lighting. If, for example, spill on the floor and on vertical portions of the setting can be controlled or concealed, the audience may be led to think that very tight, individual area key-fill control is being used. Remember that side lighting cutting through empty space is visible only where someone intercepts it. As the actor moves through the side lighting at various times in the action, it may appear to the audience that he is being provided with a special key-fill pattern at every location when actually the same instruments are serving all positions.

SIDE LIGHTING AS A PART OF "WASH-AND-KEY" LIGHTING

It is a small step in adjustment of theory from the style of lighting mentioned above to the style used by Broadway professionals in most of their highly effective lighting. However, it is a large step in terms of the number of instruments used and the organization of cues. Professional style has been developed as an adaptation to architecture and union practices of the Broadway theatre, not with any thought about saving equipment. Theatre architecture has largely determined equipment locations. Balcony fronts almost uniformly serve in place of beam or ante-pro positions used by the McCandless system in the educational theatre. This has happened because the balcony-front positions were available and the beam positions were not. Likewise, side-lighting positions have developed from the adaptation of side-stage boxes once used for seating and more recently equipped with "box booms." (These are pipe standards capable of carrying a large number of powerful side-lighting instruments.) Newer professional theatres have tended to perpetuate these practices by providing balconies with built-in mountings for spotlights and the sides of the house with slots for side lighting. In addition to these positions, modern professional theatres are often equipped with ceiling openings for what may be area lighting, specials, or another wash.

Since stages are large and audience-actor distances tend to be large, the tendency of the professional is to work with larger units of space than the typical acting area. (Tightly angled "specials" are, of course, an exception.) These larger areas are washed with color by using several instruments as though they were one, and keyed with still other banks of instruments also angled as one. Often several such combinations will illuminate the same unit of space at different times during the production. Side keys from box boom and tormentor positions are principal sources of key lighting for many of these areas because of the ability of side lighting to operate effectively over a considerable distance, and because such positions are more adaptable to touring or rental-house situations than ante-pro positions which may not be available.

The result of these practices is that the professional designer deals with key-fill relationships on a larger scale than those usually found in the educational theatre. He often tends toward higher light levels, higher contrast ranges, and larger units of stage space. Nevertheless, his concern for the subtleties of the final effect is great, although it has been adjusted to the large, often nearly impossible, playing-area-to-audience distances, and to the vast range of sight lines found in a multibalcony house. He usually must compromise in favor of those audience members on the main floor and perhaps in the first balcony. His concern for their view of the actor is great. The difference between Broadway lighting and that found in a good educational or community theatre should be mostly a matter of scale and terminology, not artistic technique. Scale is important whenever the lighting artist moves from one house to another of different size and different sight lines, whether the house is nominally labeled "professional," "educational," or "community theatre."

SIDE LIGHTING AND LIGHTING THE WHOLE BODY

In spite of the foregoing discussion of light and the actor's face, there are many times when facial lighting is not the primary concern. Such occasions range from fleeting moments when a character's stance is more important or only his presence need be felt, to modern dance where the tensions and shapes taken by the entire body almost always take precedence over the face as the main expressive device. In such situations side lighting may become the main source of actor illumination. Close control over the amount of attention devoted to the face as compared to the body can be had by controlling the degree with which the actor's face receives light visible to the audience. Control is a factor of the location of the side lighting. If it is somewhat downstage of the actor instead of directly to his side, a skilled actor can work with side lighting to shift expression toward or away from his face with great accuracy.

SIDELIGHT AND "DARK" SCENES

A common symptom of the beginning lighting designer whose artistic ideas are still rooted in trying to replicate what he sees in nature, is the design of "night scenes" which results in nearly invisible actors. These are scenes which the dramatist has set in a *virtual* night, a part of the dramatic environment of the play. Only very rarely does the playwright intend that this dramatic night shall reduce his characters to near invisibility. In fact, he often gives them lines which demand

FIGURE m

*Combining Focus on the Face with That on the Whole Body. This lighting
for the dance represents a good balance of focus between the faces of the
dancers and their bodies. This offers a very wide range of expressive potentiality to the dancers. To achieve this effect, light was directed upward from
the platforms and downward from above and somewhat in front of the
dancers. This production was done at the University of California at Santa
Barbara. Choreography: Colleen Franklin, setting and lighting by Don
Childs.* Photo courtesy University of California at Santa Barbara
Theatre Department.

subtle facial expression for their communication. Even when he avoids
this complication, the playwright is concerned with the audience
focusing on the characters' figures as a key point in the dramatic
environment.

The beginner is apt to respond to this dramatic night by reducing
dimmer readings to very low levels, destroying contrast, focus, and
visibility. A more careful analysis of the artistic needs of such scenes
will reveal that what is needed is a *dramatic* darkness—not an absence
of almost all light. The actors may be surrounded by near darkness and
the shadows on their faces may be nearly impenetrable, but actors
should very rarely be almost invisible. The solution to such problems

may be found in the use of side lighting which will highlight the entire figure of the actor and enable him to move his face into darkness although his figure is still revealed and focused. The general levels of such "night" lighting will be low, but the contrast ratio may be very high because of the nearly black background and unfilled shadows. If the scene preceding the night scene is rather bright, the night will seem even darker, although the audience will quickly adapt to the lower light level and be able to focus the night scene.

Side lighting used in night scenes may vary from eye level to a very high sidelight, and from a 90° sidelight to angles well in front of the actors. This wide range of angles offers the designer a great deal of possible shadow-pattern control over the light on the actors, and

FIGURE *n*

Side Lighting to Emphasize Whole-Body Movements. This dance lighting, designed by Don Childs, consists of side lights in alternate lanes. No front fill was used. The result is strong emphasis on bodily tensions and movements and only incidental emphasis on faces. Note how the strong directionality of the light becomes a part of the choreography even in a still photograph. Produced at the University of California at Santa Barbara, choreography: Patricia Sparrow. Photo courtesy University of California at Santa Barbara Theatre Department.

offers the actors a wide but controllable degree of facial emphasis. Interaction between actors and lighting must be carefully worked out with great discipline on the part of actor and lighting-board operator.

Using Lighting To Give
or Take the Scene

Our discussion so far has centered on the problems of the single actor as he moves through the lighted space. However, the actor is seldom alone, although the audience usually is attending to only one actor at a time and he is the one the lighting artist is most concerned about at that particular moment. The shifting of attention from place to place on the stage as the key actor moves or as the attention shifts to another actor is a matter of concern for lighting. There are two general ways in which this shift is accomplished. Either the entire area in which the actor is located is dimmed up or down to accomplish the focus, or the actors move with relationship to the light; the actor "taking the scene" gets the most favored position. At its simplest, this action takes the form of one actor walking out of the brightly lighted space as another walks in. This action is much too mechanical and unmotivated for most scenes and involves too much movement. Given fairly directional lighting, the actors need not walk at all, only shift their positions to give or take. This shift is much like upstaging but often more effective. The principle is that the actor who is more nearly facing into the key light has the scene. Of course, this situation depends upon the key light being angled so that it comes from somewhere near the front of the acting space, but such is usually the case.

Another variation of this giving and taking of the scene consists of the lighting operator making the change by reversing the key. This can be done if the contrast ratio is small and if the actors move slightly to aid the change.

LIGHT AND THE
16 SETTING

No clear-cut distinction is made between lighting for the setting and lighting for the actor for the obvious reason that the actor uses the setting. The more three-dimensional and functional the setting, the more nearly the functions of setting, lighting, and acting blend into one organic whole. Certain aspects of the relationship between lighting and setting can best be clarified by making an arbitrary or artificial distinction as though the setting and lighting could exist without the actor. This distinction is commonly made by the lighting artist as he concentrates on one lighting element or another during rehearsals. Ultimately, all segments must be fitted together, but they are apt to fit better if they have been carefully developed under the concentrated attention of the artist.

To the designer, the first distinction between setting and lighting is largely mechanical: Settings are made of wood, cloth, paint, nails, and the like, and lighting is done with electrical instruments, wire, lamps, dimmers, and so on. The artistic end product is only one thing, the design. Behind this mechanical distinction lie a number of characteristics which the designer must take into account as he fits setting and lights together. The setting is largely a static element. Setting may move or be changed at intervals, but it lacks the continuous mobility of light. The pigments of the setting form a constant colored reflector upon which the changing color of light operates. The shape of the setting is fixed by its structure, to be revealed only by the lighting and the actor.

In some respects the setting is a kind of foundation upon which both lighting and acting are built—literally in the case of three-dimensional level, step, and ramp settings; figuratively, in all other cases.

355

Setting, Lighting, and Dramatic Space

The duality of the horizons of dramatic space has been previously discussed. It is now necessary to discuss the details of the evocation and manipulation of dramatic space. A key point in this complex operation is at the artistic intersection of the expressive aspects of acting, lighting, and setting. For the sake of clarity, we have chosen to enter this three-way interrelationship by examining the interplay of setting and lighting.

The general nature of the horizons of dramatic space must be established early in the design process when the style of the production is decided upon. Actually the horizon is a very significant element in theatrical style when it is considered as a symbolic device. Realism and naturalism, for example, suggest spatial horizons which place emphasis on limiting the dramatic field of vision. The result is usually a rather minute examination of a well-defined segment of space. More nonrealistic styles often have the opposite purpose. But it would be a fatal oversimplification to assume that theatrical styles can be neatly placed on a continuum according to the nature of the spatial horizons they imply. It is much more valid to examine each stylistic decision separately, asking what spatial implications are dictated by the script and whether horizon should be the crucial factor in establishing a style.

In the early formative stages of design, when the designer is thinking in terms of space without distinction as to setting and lighting, he will probably think of the nature of the spatial horizon in terms of the qualities of various theatrical devices. For instance, he may consider the use of a cyclorama whose bottom edge is well concealed behind a three-dimensional setting, and whose top extends well into the flies, obviating the necessity for masking borders. Such "space staging" makes it possible for the actors to suggest a horizon that tempts the mind and emotions in the direction of infinity. The addition of masking borders will reduce this possibility; framing the setting with a false proscenium will usually reduce it still further. The addition of a painted background will emphasize limits instead of infinity.

As lighting is established within the possible variations of space staging, further refinements will appear. For example, soft blending toward darkness at the sides of the cyclorama may cause the feeling of infinity to be still stronger. Strong key lighting on the set and actors, which places the emphasis on strong lines, not on small details, will also cause the horizon to expand. Careful attention to detailed lighting of the actor's face may reduce the infinite quality or may function as a kind of counterpoint to it, depending on the script itself and upon the way the actor handles the words and movement.

All manner of variations on the theme of contrast and counterpoint between the background and the foreground come to mind as one thinks of specific plays. In *The Glass Menagerie,* a kind of "island, within life, within infinity" may be the desired effect. The world of the menagerie, the world outside, and something beyond that are all implied. In *Death of a Salesman,* two concentric kinds of stage space exist, one for the scenes of "reality," another for the dream world of Willy Loman. Outside of these spaces, with nebulous horizons, lies the rest of the world. The ironic interplay between these elements offers opportunity for important dramatic expression.

As the examples above imply, the mechanical technique involved in manipulating spatial horizons involves light blending or separation. Soft, edgeless lighting, accompanied by subtle color change from acting space to the background and a minimum of architectural framing,

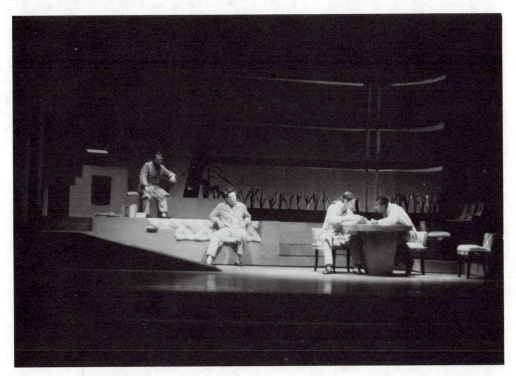

FIGURE *0*
Light and the Setting. Light is as essential to bring out the plasticity of the setting as it is for the actor's face. Note how it has been directed upward from below the up center decorative element to prevent that element from being merely a dim, two-dimensional silhouette. Focus of attention has been carefully controlled to emphasize the actors at stage center but to complete the stage picture with lesser emphasis on the other actors and on the set itself. Production: Don't Go Away Mad *(Saroyan) done at Indiana University. Set: Richard Scammon, lighting: Gary Gaiser. Picture courtesy Gary Gaiser.*

FIGURE p
*Light and the Setting. In this case the light and setting are even more
closely interrelated. Note how the lighted, moving fabric becomes the major
element in this scene relating directly to the actors themselves. Production:*
Celebration *(Jones and Schmidt) done at the University of California at
Los Angeles.* Set, lighting, and photograph by Thomas Hird.

tends to expand horizons. Strongly directional light implies dramatic
space beyond that visible on stage. Sometimes this implied space is
definite, even realistic when sunlight or moonlight is suggested;
sometimes its motivation is purposely vague, throwing the emphasis
on symbolic functions. Since directional light has a specificity about it
that does not exist in diffuse, edgeless light, directional light offers to
the actor, and through him to the dramatist, the potentiality for
expression of considerable depth of dramatic content. A strongly
directional light, playing across a three-dimensional setting and used
as a key light by the actors, comprises a symbolic device worthy of
powerful literary effort. Without the poetic power of good literature,
such lighting and setting will seem pretentious.

Directional lighting interacts with the setting within the acting
space, as well as influencing the horizon. Just as directional light can
chisel the sharp shadows to heighten the features of an actor, it can
also model the setting, if the setting has three-dimensional parts to be

FIGURE 9

Acting Area Lighting for Realism. This photo shows a well-blended set of acting area lights arranged to provide plasticity and a semblance of realism in an outdoor setting. Note that the acting areas have been adjusted to focus the actors with the "sky" discretely in the background although in life the sky would probably predominate. Production: Toys in the Attic (Hellman), director: Richard Scammon, produced at Indiana University. Lighting by Jim Lowry. Courtesy Gary Gaiser.

modeled. Painted "depth" will only be given the lie by directional lighting. However, three-dimensional elements, whether part of a naturalistic setting or an abstract one, will respond to the effects of directional lighting. The result will be an increased sense of depth of the stage space on the part of the audience. This sense of depth, in turn, will add emphasis to upstage-downstage and diagonal crosses of the actors. The result is a heightened symbolic potential for the entire visual production.

Shadow Detail in the Setting

Although the setting lacks the mobility of the actor's face, there is profit in studying the possibilities of controlling shadow detail through careful balance of fill and key lighting. Just as with the face, the outline and principal form of the setting can be emphasized or detail can be brought out. Relatively flat, low-level illumination can be used to neutralize the visual impact of the setting without obliterating it, thus concentrating the focus of attention sharply on the actor. This focus can be achieved provided that the key lighting needed by the actor can be kept off the set. Then separate key lighting can be applied to the setting as needed.

Blending Light

Since every key light in every acting area may produce shadows on the setting and properties, contrast adjustments made to suit the actors may result in a muddle of shadows when this lighting strikes the set. Acting-area lighting can be directed off the set in some instances, but wherever actors must play near setting walls or vertical surfaces, key light will produce shadows whether they are wanted or not. *Blending light* is a partial solution to this problem which also lessens the effect of color change as actors move through complementary-tint acting areas. Blending light is a relatively small quantity of general illumination flooded over the entire acting area and lower part of the setting to reduce shadow contrast. Its color is chosen to match the resultant of the acting-area tints. Blending light will naturally reduce key-fill contrasts, and its effect will be largely nullified by increasing the key to restore the contrast. However, it usually is used in situations where contrasts are to be kept quite low anyway. In a realistic setting, for example, the contrast between key and fill may be entirely the result of complementary tints. If a small quantity of blending light is added, the entire effect can be softened without serious loss of contrast.

Blending light is an element favoring subtlety in lighting, intended to reduce the separation of lighting over the various parts of the setting. Such light affects dramatic space by narrowing or reducing it. Therefore, the designer must eventually base his decision concerning the use of blending light on his estimate of the nature of the dramatic space needed for the play in production.

Colored Light
and the Set

The color of the setting as it appears to the audience is the result of the combined effect of the pigment painted on the set and of the color of the light striking it. Acting-area light will frequently illuminate the walls of the set to above the head level of the tallest actor. The only exception to this occurs when the stage is equipped with a highly reflective floor—something which should never be done except as an intentional stylistic device. Such a floor will bounce acting-area lighting into the setting almost as though the floor were a mirror. Even reversed shadows of the actors may move about on the walls. A temporary solution to this problem is to angle the acting areas from side-light positions sending the bounce light into the wings instead of the back of the set. The only permanent solution is to refinish the floor.

Tonal Light

Whenever acting-area light strikes the setting, its color will alter the color of the setting. Frequently this color alteration is undesirable and uneven. The solution is to add low-level general illumination from a strip of floodlighting instruments which are directed toward the setting. Modern striplights can be used for this purpose with good accuracy because they produce a wedge of light which has fairly sharp edges. The color of this *tonal light* should be selected to bring out whatever color is desirable in the setting. Particularly if the set has been painted with spatter techniques using a variety of colors, the effect will be pronounced. With tonal light the set seems to come alive, almost as though it were moved closer to the audience. Dimming the tonal lighting in or out offers a way of increasing or decreasing the emphasis on the set as the play progresses. Tonal lighting is most effective in those settings with large vertical surfaces that have been spattered in contrasting colors. If the instruments used for tonal lighting are not able to keep this light out of the acting areas, the lighting artist must remember that any props or costumes whose color can be emphasized by the tonal light will attract additional attention. Just how obvious this attraction will be depends on how much other light is striking these objects.

Color Psychology and the Setting

We have already observed that the effect of pale tints of colored light in the acting areas is subtle, but fugitive. Stronger colors are seldom possible in the acting areas because they call attention to themselves instead of the play. However, in those scenes where the impact of the drama is sufficiently strong, strong color in key, fill, or both may be used. This use will almost inevitably result in splashes of color on the setting. Often the designer will find that the splashes of color on the setting will provide almost as many symbolic possibilities as color on the actor without the unpleasant color alterations of his face and costume. The result will be a pool of color designed to strike the set and surround the actor, but supplemented with enough tightly concentrated acting-area color to maintain at least the suggestion of natural skin tones. The variations in this combination and the ironies and contrasts that may be exploited by the actor are many.

The addition of strongly colored key or fill light to either the face of the actor or to a three-dimensional setting will alter the symbolic effect of the three-dimensional characteristics of the lighting. The stronger the color, the more its effect will predominate in the early moments of the scene. As the eye adapts to the color—which it will do to some extent even in the case of saturated color—modeling regains some of its prominence. Shapes again carry a large share of the symbolic import. However, when using nearly pure colors, the symbolic value of the color and that of the three-dimensional elements must be blended together by the words and actions of the actor. Together they form a powerful, but not subtle, symbolic device. Moreover, focus of attention is now a factor of contrast both in intensity and in color. Bright, warm colors will take predominance over bright, cool colors. The most powerful focusing device of all will be a brightly colored moving object of a warm hue whose pigment is supplemented by warm light, but which is contrasted by a complimentary background. A brightly lit red object against a blue-green background meets these requirements, particularly if the red object is reinforced with an additional spot of red light. Subtlety under these conditions is out of the question.

Painting with Light

The use of colored light to "paint" the setting has been a catch phrase since the early days of Edward G. Craig. Color in lighting can, indeed, alter the color of any reflective surface, stage, set, building wall, or the like. The problem on most stages is maintaining the purity of the color while lighting the actors who are playing near the set. Splashes of near-white acting-area color will wash out the deeper color used to "paint" the setting. Cycloramas are regularly colored with light but they enjoy the advantage of being well removed from the acting area.

Language of Color

Strong splashes of colored light on the set inevitably invite symbolic development. In fact, color symbolism in this narrow sense has been a part of theatrical lore for a long time. With the addition of electric light to the theatre it became possible to blend light and to produce colors of a brilliancy previously impossible. This potent attention-getting material led to a good deal of effort to discover or develop a language of color. It seemed unlikely that any stimulus as intense as that produced by brilliant colored light could have only generalized symbolic import. Yet this seems to be the case. Even culturally nurtured color symbolism such as "black means mourning," "white suggests purity," or the like, seems to have little value in the theatre. Black arm bands on costumes will be read as "mourning," but a black costume certainly will not imply anything this specific. Apparently, the most black can do is to appear ominous, and this only if the lines of the costume augment the color. White on stage can suggest almost anything. As to the rest of the spectrum, direct "this-means-this" relationships do not exist beyond the limits of the situation in which they have been set up, that is, within the play itself. Generalizations by the audience from one play to another do not occur.

Warm versus Cool Color

The psychological phenomenon of warm and cool color still remains. This phenomenon is demonstrable and apparently consistent. It can form the foundation for useful symbolic processes but not, apparently, for a generally recognized "language." Thus color symbolism must be a private language that exists for the audience of the individual production, one that is established and used for the sake of its symbolic potentialities within a given production with no intention of generalizing beyond the final curtain.

Such color symbolisms can be established within the audience successfully as long as the basic warm-cool pattern is not broken. For example, it is much easier to make red symbolize war, hellfire, or passion, than it is to make it symbolize peace, heavenly bliss, or repose. The reason for this is in the nature of the color: Its psychological value is warm and any symbolic application must coincide with this. This is but another example of the basic requirement of all symbolic material. There must exist an analogical or experiential validity if symbolic devices are to be "right."

Precautions concerning
Color Symbolism

Color symbolism has a rather blatant simplicity about it that can be deadly. One of the keys to the success of any artistic symbolic device is that with each exposure to the audience, new insight must be added by the symbol. It must grow or die. If we establish red light to mean "war" for the duration of a play and then simply bring in the red on cue every time we wish to tell the audience that war is the subject of the scene, no symbolic development will occur. The symbol becomes obvious, blatant, and ultimately an insult to the intelligence of the audience. At this point the symbol is dead. The nonspecific nature of intensely colored light coupled with the visual impact of its appearance makes it a poor symbolic material. Contrast this use with the literary use of color in such a play as *Macbeth*. Here the symbolic growth can take the form of linguistic development of the concept "red" and the related experiential material "death—bloody death." The variety of word choices, specific images, and potential actor reactions, plus the agility of the audience imagination in expanding the concept of "red" makes this literary symbol far more productive at each return than the physical appearance of a red light. Thus the problem of symbolism and colored light comes to this: The link between color and idea is easily established. The perception is a powerful attention getter, swift in imparting its message. But the effect is of short duration and the simple sensory nature of colored light makes it difficult to build the symbol with each usage. The symbolic use of colored light is more likely to serve as a sort of accent near the climax of a larger and more productive symbolic buildup than it is to serve by itself. Used briefly to cap the climax, its power can be exploited without facing the nearly impossible task of making it grow. For example, a generally ominous, threatening, and disturbing three-dimensional setting design may be revealed as a key visual part of a production of *Macbeth*. These lines and potentialities will be revealed gradually as the play progresses, heightening and gaining symbolic strength from the development of the action. The astute designer would only at the climax be apt to splash red light over his setting.

17 LIGHT AND RHYTHMIC STRUCTURE

We have now studied the functions of lighting as a symbolic device in the master form of theatre production. One subject remains to be developed before we can study the process by which the lighting artist brings about the fulfillment of his design. This subject is *change*. While lighting change can be thought out in general terms early in the design, it can become complete only after the lights have been mounted, angled, and focused. The designer plans for change from the beginning, but he never really finishes designing that change until the last cue is timed. Our procedure will be to study the theory of lighting change first. Then we will take up the apparently more mundane task of deploying the equipment—planning and arranging for the changes to be made later—and finally return to the study of lighting change as we consider the development of lighting cues.

Dramatic Structure and Dramatic Rhythm

Any serious student of dramatic literature is aware that well-written plays, whether in verse or in the most naturalistic prose, have some sort of rhythmic pattern. Reading most play scripts provides only the grossest sort of understanding of the rhythmic patterns, especially if the reader is untrained in the rather complex art of play reading. Even the careful reader, well trained in this task, will find that the aesthetic response gained by reading a script differs in kind and quantity from that gained by witnessing its production. Probably one of the most significant areas of difference between a play read as literature and a play in production is the heightening and sharpening of rhythmic patterns. This rhythm is one of the most important functions of the art of production—and one in which lighting often plays a large part.

365

Concentric Structure

Plays in production tend to have a complex but concentric rhythmic structure. By "concentric" we mean that the rhythmic patterns of a play tend to contain each other, the larger ones encompassing the smaller, and so on until the largest pattern of all includes the others within it. In this manner the rhythm contributes mightily to the artistic unity of the play, giving relationship to a vast and often widely varied assortment of lesser rhythmic patterns. An astute director who has studied his play carefully will give attention first to the smaller rhythmic patterns — building the "French scenes" — then to the larger sections, the scenes within the acts, then to the acts themselves, and finally to the entire play. As his scope widens, he will never completely lose sight of the smallest scene, knowing that it must play its part in the whole.

Climax, Tension, and Conflict

Generally speaking, dramatic rhythms involve a build toward something we rather indiscriminately call "climax." A climax represents some kind of change which involves an increase in concentration of attention on the part of the audience. But there are a number of quite different dramatic techniques for bringing this about. Tension, in the sense of more concentrated audience focus on the play, is a common factor in all of these techniques. Its nature may vary from hilarity in comedy, to stark vicarious terror in a mystery, to a tremendously complex situation of involvement and detachment at the climax of an ironic tragedy. The word "conflict" has been used to describe those situations which bring about this tension or climax. Yet there are scenes in some plays — *The Cherry Orchard*, for example — in which tension is somehow built by something nearly the opposite of conflict.

It seems apparent that any attempt to catalog the dramatic techniques that will produce a climax is likely to be frustrated by any artistic innovator seeking new dramatic material. The lighting artist will be best advised to develop his sensitivity to all available dramatic techniques, anticipating that new ones will come from time to time.

Climax and Anticlimax

Whatever device is used to bring the audience to a state of tension, it is certain that the audience will not be held in that state long without further change. The psychology of attention in audiences seems to be the same the world over. Any stimulus that is sustained without change soon tires the attention and loses its climactic quality. The skillful dramatist knows that even constant change itself will pall, and that only so much tension can be built into any given situation. Thus the dramatist often seeks ways to retreat from the climax before proceeding to another slightly higher than the last. This retreat is the anticlimax, the relief. However, the careful student of the drama will detect something awry here. Anticlimax is not intended to let the audience settle back and ignore the play, or to make it forget the main line of action. Anticlimax is the beginning of the next pattern of climax; the action is anticlimactic only in the sense that the dramatist has shifted his artistic ground a bit and is starting another upward movement toward increased tension. Anticlimax is particularly evident in tragedy where the dramatic movement seems relentless in its progress toward a tension situation of nearly impossible height and complexity. The skilled satirist also weaves his climactic movement in the same manner, but leaves the audience more detached from his characters.

It is possible for us to say that each climax "contains" its predecessors, or at least is built upon them. Earlier climaxes have prepared the audience for the present one, and it, in turn, will aid in preparing them for the next. The effect is cumulative, each development building upon those past. The result, in a good play, is a tightly knit structure whose effect in a successful production is that of a single but complicated symbolic act. The nature of this structure is that of concentricity. The minor "beats" form patterns within the larger groupings, and these in turn fit into the whole. For example, the audience is often aware of only one relentless build from beginning to end of a successfully produced Greek tragedy. Yet the Greek form is almost mathematically divided in its rhythmic structure.

Interaction of Lighting and the Actor in Building Tension

We have already examined some of the techniques involved in contributing to the building of a climax through lighting. We have seen that the key to success in all such efforts is the reaction of the actor to the lighting. Without the denotative power of the actor, the lighting can build only the most generalized and fugitive kind of climax. A subtle kind of interaction takes place between actor and lighting. The lighting artist develops generalized tensions with various techniques of lighting, such as intense focus and dark background, and the actor finds heightened audience response at his disposal. He, in turn, increases his reaction, thereby heightening the effect of the lighting. This interaction can increase the tension until the director feels that the scene is sufficiently climactic, or until the resources of either the actor or the lighting have been exhausted for the particular scene at hand.

As far as the lighting artist is concerned, he needs to develop a very sharp sense of awareness for actor interaction with the lighting, and constantly seek the right balance between the lighting and the acting. For example, in a Shakespearean soliloquy, the actor obviously must hold the attention of the audience with great intensity. Nothing that either the actor or the lighting does must intrude on the intense relationship between character and audience. Anything that will intensify that relationship is artistically desirable. The lighting artist may find himself tempted to increase the contrast between actor and background but the moment he senses that these changes are beginning to move to the center of the audience attention, he knows he has overdone the lighting. On the other hand, leaving the scene in relatively flat lighting, denying the actor the heightening effect of close visual attention on the part of the audience, may depress the dramatic value of the entire scene.

Building a Climax with Lighting

In Chapter 13, we discussed the symbolic mode of building a climax, indicating how space can be varied to increase focus and heighten tension. The symbolic value of these changes will depend on their degree and upon the rhythmic pattern which they follow. In review, the general types of change are those which increase contrast between area and background, increase contrast between key and fill, change to key (and fill) of higher angle, change to sidelight key, alter color of key, fill, or background.

It is now our purpose to study the details of such changes. Change can vary in three main ways: *degree, duration,* and *pace* or *rate.* The effect of these will be interrelated as far as the audience is concerned, but we must discuss each element of change separately.

DEGREE OF CHANGE

Visibility is the most basic limiting factor here. It is seldom if ever justifiable to reduce lighting levels to the point of poor visibility over the entire stage. Some areas may be blacked out as much as possible, but only when others are well illuminated. At the other end of the scale, it is seldom within the limits of artistic expression to create brightness ratios that verge on being painful. Thus intensely lighted white highlights against black velours are usually more of a distraction than an artistic triumph. Similarly, bright lamps on tables or overbright window backings are seldom effective.

Within these extreme limits, the degree of change elected by the lighting designer will depend on a host of interlocked design variables. Some of these are:

1. *Relationship to climaxes to come.* Like the actor, the lighting artist must pace himself, saving something for scenes to come. Thus he will often subdue early changes, holding back the extreme effects

for the more climactic scenes to come later in the play. This technique is particularly useful to the theatre with limited equipment. An extra instrument for a high-angle key light at the final climactic moment may not be available. One side of the regular 45° key area light will have to do. If this is the case, the designer will want to reserve its full effect for the most important moment, even if he feels the need for it earlier.

2. *Number of climaxes.* Some plays seem to move from one tiny climax to another, creating a choppy effect. This choppiness can be diminished by restraining the impulse to light each climax regardless of how small it is. Allow the acting and directing to carry the smaller scenes, saving the lighting changes for the main effort. This method will also have the beneficial effect of reducing the number of cues and making the operation of the show easier.

3. *Emphasis on other theatrical devices for building climax.* Often minor climaxes need only slight heightening from the lighting. Acting and directing techniques can suffice, making large lighting changes superfluous.

4. *Nature of the climax.* Our discussion of the symbolic aspects of light and shade, and the dramatic space they imply, should prepare the designer for making this decision. Tension will be increased more by greater changes than by lesser ones provided that the lighting does not intrude into the attention of the audience in the process.

DURATION OF CHANGE

Duration of change is the total amount of time that the lighting operator takes to complete the change. With the exception of "snap cues" that are motivated by business, such as the operation of an onstage light switch, the dousing of a lantern, or the like, the shortest change period will probably be about 3 to 4 seconds. This speed is about maximum for a cross-fade used to shift attention from one acting area to another, if the lighting is not to become obvious. Even at this speed, the change must carefully pace the movement of the actor who is to be focused. From this minimum of 3 to 4 seconds upward, changes can be extended to the point where their effect is entirely lost upon the audience. Somewhere in the vicinity of 20 to 30 minutes, the effect of the change itself fades out almost completely, and the audience will be aware of the results only coincidentally unless the actors call attention to them. Such slow movements still have profound effect on certain dramatic occasions and should not be overlooked. However, the lighting artist need not worry much about making such long changes continuous. Occasional imperceptible movements of the dimmers interspersed with no movement at all are usually easier to manage and just as effective. Exceedingly long cues are usually timed by the clock[1] for convenience, with adjustments being made periodically to fit the

---

[1] A modern automatic fader is ideal for these cues. In effect, it becomes the "clock."

pace of the scene as it plays for each performance. Shorter changes, on the other hand, are best started and stopped by observation of the business of the actors. Lines will sometimes serve, but since lighting changes usually relate to actor movement, this is the usual source of "start" and "stop" cues.

PACE OF THE CHANGE

Pace is by far the most important and subtle element in making lighting changes. It will determine, more than degree or duration, the artistic effect or nonartistic liability of the change.

In its simplest form pace derives from duration. If, for example, a change is to last 4 seconds, one-fourth of the total change may occur during each second. But things are seldom this simple. Ignoring for the moment the mechanical complications arising from nonlinear dimmer-lamp responses, actor movements and dramatic tensions seldom increase in a linear fashion. They are more likely to start slowly, picking up pace as they proceed, and ending at a rapid clip. The opposite may occur. In the case of shifts of attention from one actor to another (or groups of actors), the pacing may be still more complex as give and take alternate between the groups several times and to varying degrees before the shift is completed.

Such pacing of lighting change derives its pattern from the director through the actor. The director has established these rhythmic movements during the pacing and smoothing rehearsals, planning them to build the climactic structure of the play. The lighting artist can take his cue from these movements or from the director's indication of what he wishes them to be. Ultimately, the pace of lighting is tied to the moving actors, and can be only meaningless and distracting if its changes are not in harmony with actor movement.

Lighting changes often involve far more than one dimmer and one light or area at a time. In the interweaving of changes the rhythmic convolutions of dramatic space evolve. Thus one pace will counterpoint another. Several smaller movements will be encompassed by another longer movement. For example, a number of "follow" changes intended to control focus of attention, may be included in a general dramatic alteration of the key-fill ratio which is intended to build toward a major climax. Superimposed over this may be a still longer change in background lighting whose artistic function is twofold: It is intended to convey the realistic information that the sun is setting and to heighten the climax still more by backing the entire scene with vivid color at the moment of final climax. Such multiple rhythms are common in dramatic lighting usually requiring continuous and precise operation of the control board with a degree of concentration equaling that of the leading actor himself.

18 DESIGN PROCEDURES

We have now discussed all of the elements of lighting design, first in terms of artistic content and then in terms of their general nature. Now we must apply this information to the particular script at hand, evolving an orderly method of arriving at our artistic ends. The lighting designer begins with the script, unifies his concept with that of the director, converts that concept into a visual design, arranges equipment to enable him to execute the concept, and then completes the design by establishing the sequence and nature of changes in the lighting according to the pace of the play.

Developing the Concept of the Play

The first stage in design comes when the designer approaches the script as any other interpretive artist must—alone. He must read and reread the script until he has come to artistic terms with it. In other words, he must respond to it as a symbolic entity whose sole purpose is to evoke aesthetic responses in him (and the other producing artists) in order that he can recreate it in its complete artistic form on stage. As the lighting designer studies the script, he will seek information on two levels. He will need to list all essential mechanical requirements. For instance, if time of day must be established, lighting will often play a part in this. Weather, special effects, and all of the other adjunct elements often used by dramatists will be noted. However, the lighting artist will look sceptically upon this list, making sure that no effect appears only because it seems spectacular. He and the director will ultimately examine every element to evaluate its artistic merits. At the other level of script study, the lighting artist will engage in careful study of rhythmic structure. All of the elements of lighting design will be evoked in his mind at one time or another as he translates the

371

literary structure of the script into the space-time structure of light in dramatic space. Changes in mood as the drama moves toward major climaxes will probably appear first in his mind. Later, detailed study will reveal lesser climaxes and many more details of the interrelationships between scenes. The designer will translate the details into lighted space, changing mood, and emphasis as the play unfolds.

Working with the Director

The second stage in design is the establishment of artistic liaison with the director. Ultimately the director is the artistic leader of the production effort. He must not allow the lighting design or any other element to predominate over the artistic unity of the whole production. Neither must the director allow any element of the production to seek a different artistic goal than the one he is bent on developing. Thus the lighting designer must establish with the director the artistic direction that the lighting design is going to take. He can do this effectively only after he has studied the script himself and developed an aesthetic awareness of its content. The director, of course, must also have established his own artistic liaison with the script. Then director and designer set out to communicate to each other concerning the nature of the art work they are in the process of producing. This discussion is touchy business at best, and both need to be aware of the pitfalls. Glib, easy overstatement can lead to fatal consequences when the lighting is added to the play. Attention to solutions before the problems are agreed upon can create unpleasant surprises later. Allowing personality to dominate over humble awareness of the value of the dramatic script (always assuming that it is a good one) can stifle.

Probably the safest procedure is for both director and designer to spend considerable time making sure that they approach the script in the same way. Each will find that his mode of expression at this point will be that which suits him best—moving, speaking actors for the director, and fluctuating lighted space for the lighting designer—but each should be certain that neither takes the other's attempts at expression for plans or solutions. If both director and designer remember that they are still trying to agree upon the artistic problem to be solved, not trying to solve it, much misery can be avoided.

Ultimately designer and director come to an understanding. First each should feel that he knows how the other looks at the play. Finally they must agree on *one* way of looking at it. Of course, if it comes to a power struggle at this point, the director must win. But this struggle should be avoided if possible; its effect is stultifying. More commonly and more profitably, director and designer can find a view of the play broad enough to satisfy both—one which each will sharpen as the production effort progresses.

Having agreed upon artistic goals, they now proceed to examine the problems which beset them as they strive for these goals. Some problems in the script will affect the director, but not the designer; others, the opposite. Solutions may appear during preliminary conferences. In other cases possible solutions will be agreed upon, their results to be evaluated later. Other problem areas will remain essentially untouched.

As the designer and director move toward attending to the details of the production, they will do well to think first in terms of the moving actor in space. They must agree on the kinds of movement that will typify the play and what the dramatic significance of these movements will be. At this point, they are concerned with generalities. Is the movement the jerky, horizontal movement of farce? Is it the parallel, counterfocus kind of movement often associated with satire? Is it formalized and stylized to create part of a world of fantasy? Is it grand, elegant, royal, simple, dancelike, circular, or angular? What other adjectives describe it? Must the actor move horizontally across the stage? Does he make long upstage-downstage crosses? Must he use elevations? All of these general considerations will help the designer and the director to determine the style of the production and the lighting designer to develop lighting that will augment that style.

Stylistic Considerations

Designer-director discussions about setting and lighting often involve the use of terms that have evolved around the concept of style, a concept that has developed over a great span of time in such areas as literary and dramatic criticism. It has also produced a plethora of categories which often overlap and generate as much confusion as they do insight. For example, where is the boundary between such terms as "domestic tragedy" and "drama"?

In spite of the confusion of terminology, the lighting artist will find that he can gain much information about the proposed production as he discusses its style with the director. Exact definition of stylistic terms is not as important to these discussions as a recognition of the design implications of the terms, whatever their names may be. There are some definite parallelisms between the style of the lighting and the style of the production. Most of these center around the qualities which are given to the highlights and shadows on the actors' faces and to the crispness, or lack of it, in key and fill light as it strikes the setting.

An important implication of dramatic style is the kind of visibility provided for the actors' faces. For instance, the great range and the extremities of emotional expression associated with tragedy will usually call for sharply defined, heavily contrasted facial shadows that tend to reduce the face to rather simple sculptural elements. High comedy, on the other hand, usually calls for visibility of a kind that will reveal the tiniest flicker of subtle emotion on the actor's face. Shadows must be well filled with light but not obliterated, and catchlights—those bright spots of specular reflection from eyeballs, peaks of cheek bones, and the ridge of the nose—should be bright and clear. Every nuance of facial expression should be revealed.

Similarly, set lighting for tragedy and high comedy differ. Tragedy is traditionally dark. However, this seldom means poor visibility. Shadows in the setting may be murky, or even completely blocked in by darkness, but highlights will stand out in high contrast, often in intense color. Key-fill contrast can be very high without large amounts of light when shadows approach total darkness. High comedy will call for more light and seldom require blocked-in shadows. In fact, since characters often "hide" in shadowed areas, only to become the focus of a scene, good visibility in shadow areas is a necessity. Since facial visibility *in detail* is essential, both light/shade and color contrast between setting and actors must be carefully controlled in favor of the actors.

The examples above should reveal the essentials of a discussion of style with the director. Whatever name the director gives to the style, the lighting artist will want to discover the kind of seeing condition this implies. What is to be revealed on the actors' faces? How are we to see their movements? Are masses of figures more important than single faces? Are facial shadows sharply chiseled or revealed in a soft glow?

Acting Space

Just as facial shadows often derive from "style," so may the nature of the acting space. Although this is a complicated subject that involves all of the elements of scene design and lighting, the lighting will be the element that provides the variables within the design and brings unity to the visual production. The potentialities of light for establishing or obliterating them are tremendous. Acting space can "feather out" into infinity, vanish sharply into darkness, be bounded by walls, or be divided into "pools" of light in near darkness, to name but a few possibilities. Moreover these things can change—hard shadows can soften, horizons can close in, and "infinity" can be revealed to be only another wall. Entrances can be a sudden appearance out of darkness or a gradual revelation via softly graduated light. These are matters of prime importance as the director and the designer discuss "style."

Design Considerations within the Framework of Style

Having established the style and clarified its implications, the designer and director can proceed to other details. They can raise questions concerning specific symbolic efforts on the part of the lighting, such as the use of strong color change or key light related to the plot. General limits should be agreed upon as to the share of symbolic content to be handled by the lighting. The lighting designer will do well to avoid accepting too much artistic responsibility here. If his symbolic efforts are to succeed, he will need the support of the actors at all times. On the other hand, a shrewd director can often anticipate limitations in acting talent that need shoring up by carefully controlled lighting operated very close to the line marking intrusion into the audience's attention. Designer and director will have to cooperate closely in the control of such lighting.

Still another area of study is open to the designer and director at the early stages of design—demarcation of the key scenes. Generally there will be agreement at this point, but details of these scenes will be crucial as the development of the lighting progresses. The designer will be on more solid ground if he and the director have studied through these scenes carefully, comparing interpretations and talking over possible ways of handling the scenes. Another reason for studying key scenes is to enable the designer and director to compare their understanding of the rhythmic structure of the play. For example, even minor shifts in aesthetic interpretation of the script may sometimes move the high point of the main climax several lines forward or backward. Checking the location of this point may bring out such differences and lead to closer cooperation.

A good follow-up to the designer-director conferences is for the designer to attend a series of blocking rehearsals. Study of these rehearsals will make concrete many things previously far more abstract than either party thought. Rehearsals will also give the designer what may be his first look at the actors—at their faces, complexions, styles of movement, probable sensitivity to lighting, and other potentialities and difficulties. Frequently the director will be able to make certain concepts clearer as he discusses them with the designer during breaks in the rehearsals and demonstrates as he moves the actors over the rehearsal floor.

Development of the Lighting Plot

As the designer moves from the development of artistic goals to the solution of the problems which those goals present, he will begin to develop a lighting plot. This plan is a drawing intended to indicate where equipment is to be mounted, how it is to be connected, and so forth. In its early form, however, it may reflect more design concept than mechanics of execution. Later, execution becomes paramount and the design concept is often hidden in a myriad of dimensions and electrical data.

The Content of a Finished Lighting Plot

A lighting plot in its final form is a plan of the stage and setting indicating where the various instruments are to be mounted, how they are circuited, what kind they are, what wattage lamps they contain, what color media are used, and where light strikes the stage space. Since over a hundred instruments may be involved on a large stage with a multiset show (see Figure 18-1b), the lighting plot is often subdivided into overlay sheets as a means of reducing confusion. A base plan of the stage with permanently fixed elements of the setting and probably a basic lighting-area plot forms the bottom sheet. Over this, on clear acetate or very thin tracing stock, other details are added. The subdivision may be by acts, by categories of lighting function, or by any means that makes the entire plot more clear.

Early Stages in the Development of the Lighting Plot

The lighting artist will usually develop his lighting plot by working with a roughly scaled floor plan of the acting space and background space. With such a sketch in hand, he may visit the director to determine the general directionality of the acting-area lighting and to reaffirm his understanding of the extent of the acting area. Directors often have a way of eliminating from the stipulated acting-area peripheral zones they later find to be necessary. Such unpleasant surprises can be avoided if the lighting designer queries the director concerning any potential acting areas early in the planning. When in doubt, it is better to agree that such areas *may* be lighted; thus equipment is reserved for them. If the equipment is not needed it will form a reserve against possible last-minute changes or breakdowns. On paper, the result of such a conference with the director will usually be a lighting plot with heavy lines indicating lighting direction and crude ellipses indicating potential lighting areas, especially near the edges of the setting. This plot is little more than a scratch-paper version of the design concepts. The designer then draws upon his technical knowledge of the theatre and its equipment. If he is familiar with the building and its equipment he has a great advantage because he will immediately think in terms of lighting positions and instruments that have served him well in the past. If he is working in a theatre that is new to him or from plans of one he has yet to see, he must rely upon his knowledge of the effect of light on the actor from various angles, trying to reconcile his notion of the ideal lighting angle for each scene with what he infers is possible from his study of the theatre. The blunt truth is that being unfamiliar with the theatre plant is a tremendous disadvantage to the designer. He can anticipate much more trial and error in instrument mounting and circuitry, and much more wasted time.

Planning Acting-Area Lighting

Given adequate knowledge of the theatre plant to be used, how does the designer proceed? The first decision that he must make is the selection of the general pattern of lighting for the show. If he is faced with the situation that confronts many professionals, he will have to plan his lighting around balcony-front and side-lighting positions. However, if his theatre is at all well equipped with lighting-beam positions which enable him to achieve a 38° to 45° lighting angle, he will be able to select the more flexible acting-area plan. In doing this, his first step will be to prepare a scratch copy of the lighting plot on which he will divide the acting space into acting areas. As mentioned in the section "Lighting the Acting Space by Segments: Acting Areas" in Chapter 6, he will subdivide according to the degree of separation he anticipates will be needed. He will take the conservative approach by planning more acting areas than his realistic appraisal of the play tells him will be needed. This will insure him adequate equipment and circuitry for late changes and give some needed flexibility in positioning of instruments for those areas he finally uses.

Lighting plots tend to fall into standard patterns. In general, it is better to use an uneven number of areas since this centers two or more lighting areas on the center line of the setting. Center areas are particularly useful in opera and musical comedy where the down-center playing position often is favored over all others. Lighting areas must usually be plotted in such a manner that they can be made to overlap smoothly on the stage leaving neither dead spots nor hot spots. Actually areas of less than normal light (dead spots) are far from dark in most cases. They often receive light from one of the two instruments assigned to an ordinary acting area, but not from the other. In the case of hot spots, usually three or more instruments illuminate them, raising the intensity beyond the normal level established for the scene and thereby making the rest of the stage seem dead. It is important for the novice in lighting to note that lighting plots do not represent patterns of light on the stage floor; they represent lighted space at head level in the acting area. The experienced lighting technician will walk through the acting area watching the lenses of the instruments to determine which are lighting his face at any moment. A brilliant flare from the filament will be seen when the viewer is in the light. Floor pools are deceptive.

Often the lighting technician who is familiar with a theatre and has operated many shows from its stage will have what amounts to a standard lighting-area plot, which he usually adapts to the needs of the play at hand. He may keep instruments mounted and circuited for such a system, using whatever portion of the whole arrangement he needs for each show as it comes along. This arrangement has much to offer the educational-theatre plant where everyday use of the theatre calls for good general stage lighting. An overall area setup makes it possible to light a piano concert, a speaker, or a musical ensemble at a moment's notice, and frees the staff for more productive activities. Also, since the standard plot will fit into the needs of perhaps 95 percent of the plays to be done, it will save time for each production.

The location of instruments for an acting-area plot is partially a subject for architectural study, as we have already mentioned. The lighting technician normally uses those positions which offer the nearest to 45° lighting for each area. A well-designed and well-equipped house will offer nearly ideal locations for center-stage areas and reasonable compromises for the sides of the stage. In a poorly equipped house, instruments may have to be mounted wherever the structure of the building and the authorities who administer it will permit. Such locations often bear little resemblance to normal acting-area lighting. While this is an annoyance, it need not militate entirely against good acting-area lighting if the designer is willing to experiment with unusual arrangements of key and fill. For example, an acting-area position provided by temporary vertical mounting pipes at the sides of the house near the stage will yield something similar to side lighting. Properly balanced key and fill, using these positions, can produce good modeling on the actors' faces and offers the possibility of strong key lighting at climaxes. Naturalism will have to suffer a bit, but the expressive potentialities are still large.

CHOOSING INSTRUMENTS

Selection of instruments for acting-area lighting will usually be simple. Sharp-edge, low-spill, ellipsoidal spotlights are required for front-of-house positions in beams, light ports, on balcony pipes, and the like. These instruments will put their light output on the stage without spilling into the audience. On stage, Fresnel equipment usually is preferred because of the ease with which areas can be blended and because the shorter throws from lighting pipes require a wider beam spread, a situation which favors the efficiency characteristics of the Fresnel. Many lighting designers have found that wide-beam ellipsoidal spotlights are nearly as efficient backstage and offer greater flexibility when put to other purposes. The final decision will depend on what equipment is available, with the stipulation that wherever spill light would be damaging, the Fresnel spotlight is not indicated. Barn doors and "high hats" or funnels may aid the Fresnel, if it must be pressed into service where its spill is not wanted, but these devices will cut down the efficiency of the instrument.

Wattage will have to be determined by throw, efficiency of instrument, and the amount of light desired on the stage. Often the available dimmer capacity enters this picture whether the designer wishes it to or not. There is no real substitute for experience with the stage and house to be used. Only such experience can tell the designer whether a 1500-watt lamp in an 8-inch ellipsoidal spotlight will have the desired effect or whether he must use 2000 watts. Fortunately wattage adjustments can be made late in the process of lighting a play as long as dimmer capacity is available.

COLOR CHOICE

Selection of color media for acting-area instruments has already been covered in the chapter on color. The designer usually postpones this decision until he can survey the color of the costumes, the proposed makeup, and the paint on the setting. Like the lamp wattage, color media can be changed late in the game.

CIRCUITING AND CONTROL

Circuitry for control of the acting areas is another matter. Particularly if the show is done in a theatre with limited load circuitry, the arrangement must be carefully worked out and may not be subject to much change later. On the other hand, if the designer is blessed with a large number of load circuits terminating handily at acting-area lighting positions and enough dimmers to leave some spares, he can afford to speculate.

Sooner or later, he will usually be faced with the necessity of allocating only one dimmer per acting area. Only rarely will he have enough dimmers to allow him to use one dimmer for each half of every area. Assuming an allocation of one dimmer per area, the designer faces two alternatives. He can circuit the left and right halves of the same area to the same dimmer, giving him overall control of the area but no variable control over key-fill ratio. He can prearrange this ratio by adjusting throw, color medium, wattage, and the like, but once the ratio is set, he must use it as it is. Any key-lighting changes have to come from a third instrument on another dimmer. The other alternative is to circuit by key and fill. The left halves of two or more areas are circuited to one dimmer and the right halves to another. Obviously there is an additional advantage here if only large dimmers are available because several areas can be handled by two dimmers. This combination leaves the designer with a wide range of key-fill control at the expense of separate area control. He can ease the "general illumination" effect of this combination considerably by grouping the areas controlled by a given pair of dimmers according to probable use patterns. For example, he may lump upstage and downstage center areas together, left stage areas together, and right stage areas together. In a play in which emphasis is not going to depend on area-to-area intensity differences, this grouping may provide as much separation as the designer will need. Using warm and cool tints in key and fill makes color variation possible with this system.

Depending on the wiring of the theatre, the designer will indicate the grouping of two or more instruments together at the patch panel or at the circuit termination near the instruments. If he must group two or more instruments on the same load circuit, he must exercise additional care to see that those circuits which are often old and low in capacity are not overloaded. In many theatres such considerations, plus limited dimmer capacity, will reduce the acting-area combination to the one pattern which is safe to operate. This arrangement is usually theatrically poor; its only advantage is electrical safety.

The exact angling of acting-area instruments will have to await the mounting and circuiting of the instruments. However, the designer will indicate the approximate angle and focus of each instrument on the light plot. Angle is indicated by vertical mounting position, including elevation above the stage floor if this is not well known and permanently fixed, and horizontal position on the mounting pipe. Sectional drawings of the stage and house are seldom a part of a lighting plot, although they may be necessary to the designer in the computation of close lighting angles and sight lines.

The lighted area provided by each instrument is indicated on the plot by an elliptical or circular figure. Whatever the shape of this figure, it is only an approximation. Ellipses are somewhat more accurate, but the exact usable shape of the area will vary with angle and spread of the light beams. Usually the designer will draw a line from the center of each instrument location to the center of its lighted area. The practice of drawing lines representing the sides of the beam is less desirable because it doubles the number of direction lines on the plot—a drawing already suffering from overcrowding.

It is common practice among designers to adopt a set of simplified symbols for the various types of equipment found in the theatre,[1] often letting the size of the symbol indicate the design wattage rating of the instrument. Thus a large outline of an ellipsoidal spotlight may represent a 2000-watt design wattage instrument and a small outline a 750-watt design size. Note that the designed wattage of the instrument may not indicate the wattage for the particular use because most instruments will operate well using lamps several sizes smaller than their designed capacity. See Figures 18-1*a* through *d* for a typical lighting plot of acting areas.

Planning Specials and Sidelights

The sequence of events in the development of the lighting plot will vary depending on the needs of the particular show and the whim of

[1] Commercially precut templates are available to ease the work of the lighting designer as he draws up his lighting plot.

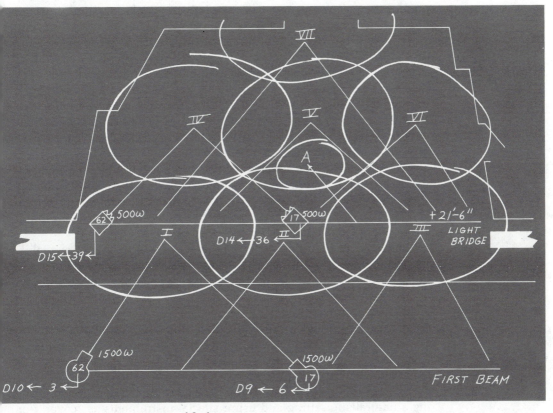

FIGURE *18-1a*

Typical Lighting Plot. This drawing is a simplified version of a typical light-ing plot for an interior setting in a proscenium theatre. Only Areas I and IV have been completed, for the sake of clarity.

Notice that this plot is arranged for the use of a lighting operator at the back of the house. Thus the lighting areas have been numbered from this operator's left to right. If the lighting were to be operated from backstage, it would be more sensible to number from stage left to stage right. The lighting areas themselves have been given Roman numerals to reduce confusion in cues where Arabic numerals must be used to refer to dimmer settings and frequently to time. The special pool, stage center, has been given a letter designation to separate it from the areas patterns. Areas I and IV have complete notation giving instrument type (the outline), wattage (this could be indicated by the outline of the instrument if practice is consistent), the color medium (in this case Brigham gelatine numbers have been used), and the circuitry. This circuitry designation tells the reader the number of the load circuit used to supply the instrument and the dimmer from which this circuit gets its power. The elevation of the light bridge (or light pipe) is given because this is variable. The height of the beam is fixed by the archi-tecture of the building and assumed known.

Only the most skeletal outline of the setting is included and in this case no furniture is shown because the completed lighting plot with all side-lights, specials, and so on, will be confusing in spite of all efforts to simplify it. Furniture must be shown if its location determines lighting areas.

the designer. However, after developing the regular area lighting, the designer will probably want to consider special acting-space lighting, since he will usually think of these instruments in connection with the acting areas. The term "special" refers to any instrument or group of instruments whose function is to augment the acting-area lighting (or in some cases, temporarily supplant it) during particular scenes. Such instruments usually are placed with even more precision than the acting-area lighting and are circuited separately and carefully adjusted during rehearsals to closely fit the action. Specials may be used to provide additional focus of attention within an area, to enable the designer to change the angle and color of the key lighting, particularly when no key-fill control is available in the area lighting, to meet special needs within the plot, to augment realistic motivating sources, and the like. In a complicated production, specials are usually plotted on an overlay of the basic area lighting.

The choice of instruments for special areas will vary with availability and the needs of the actor who is to use the special. Usually sharp definition is needed to heighten the directional effect of the special and to make it stand out from the acting-area lighting more clearly. Its edges may also need to be cut to fit a doorway opening or some other setting feature. For all of these purposes ellipsoidal spotlights offer the best solution. The framing shutters of the ellipsoidal can be adjusted to almost any geometrical shape needed. Focusing or defocusing the lens element with relationship to the aperture will produce either a sharp edge or a soft edge to fit the particular application. When lighting a naturalistic setting and using special instruments as "cover" for motivating sources such as table lamps, a soft edge may be desirable. A Fresnel instrument best serves this purpose.

FIGURE *18-1b*

Professional Lighting Plot for Repertory. This lighting plot contains the information for four operas. Since a repertory situation does not afford the luxury of separately hanging, focusing, and gelling each production, the designer has devised a scheme where each instrument serves several needs. Instruments used as area lighting also serve as a wash and as specials as needed. Color changes are accomplished by adjusting the additive mixture of area and side lighting. Individual areas were lighted or left dark depending on the configuration of the four different settings.

Control under these circumstances had to be very flexible. The designer began with the concept of using one dimmer per instrument. The plot shows that this was partially achieved although "two fer" instructions appear on the plot and ganging instructions on the plugging chart, Figure 18-1d. Although much less than one-dimmer-per-instrument, the control is extremely flexible.

Note particularly the heavy complement of side lighting equipment. There are proscenium booms, tormentors, and a double set of ladders at each side of the stage. In contrast, there are but nine instruments in the ante-pro (ceiling) position. This is a typical professional approach; key lighting is provided by side lighting, heavily instrumented and carefully angled.
Courtesy Jonell Polansky.

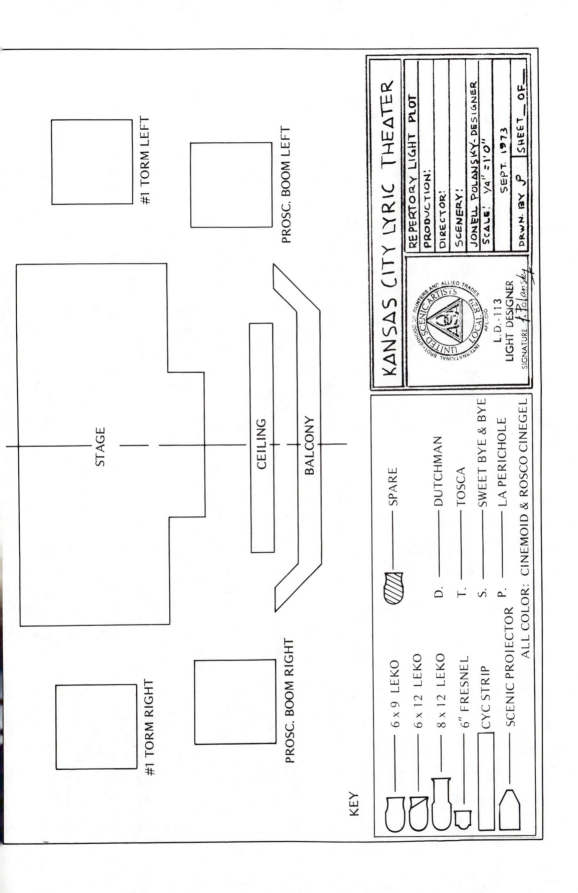

#1 TORM LEFT

PROSC. BOOM LEFT

STAGE

CEILING

BALCONY

#1 TORM RIGHT

PROSC. BOOM RIGHT

KANSAS CITY LYRIC THEATER

REPERTORY LIGHT PLOT

PRODUCTION:

DIRECTOR:

SCENERY:

JONELL POLANSKY-DESIGNER
SCALE: ¼" = 1'0"   SEPT. 1973
DRWN. BY JP   SHEET ___ OF ___

L.D.-113
LIGHT DESIGNER
SIGNATURE J. Polansky

UNITED SCENIC ARTISTS
INTERNATIONAL BROTHERHOOD OF PAINTERS AND ALLIED TRADES
LOCAL 816 AFL-CIO

KEY

— 6 x 9 LEKO

— 6 x 12 LEKO

— 8 x 12 LEKO

— 6" FRESNEL

— CYC STRIP

— SCENIC PROJECTOR

— SPARE

D. — DUTCHMAN

T. — TOSCA

S. — SWEET BYE & BYE

P. — LA PERICHOLE

ALL COLOR: CINEMOID & ROSCO CINEGEL

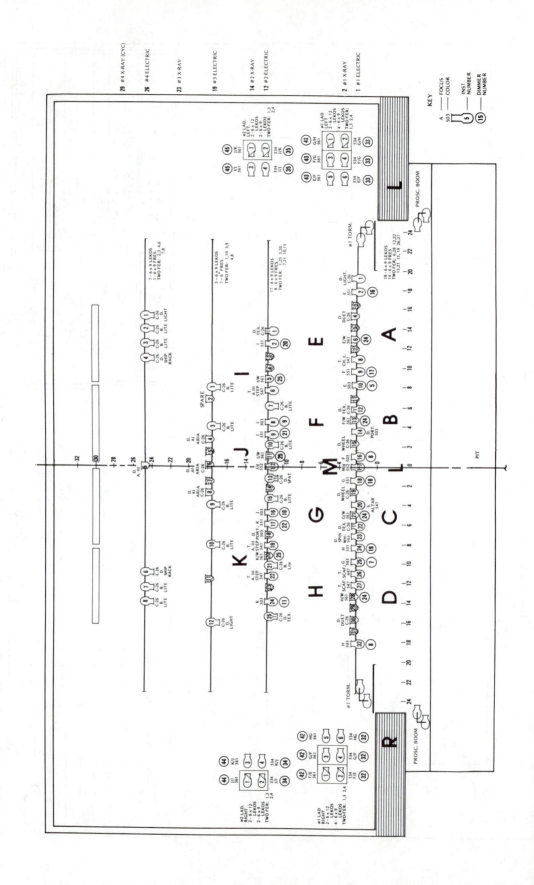

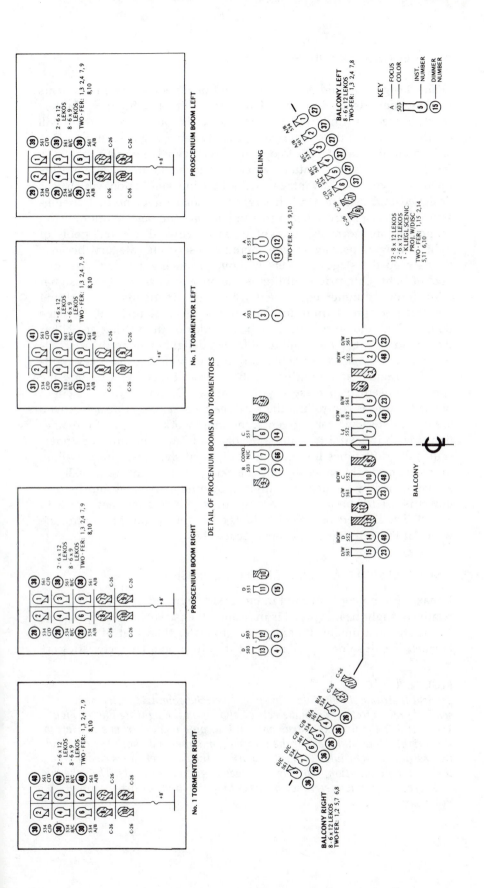

DETAIL OF PROCENIUM BOOMS AND TORMENTORS

The designer should be cautious about using ellipsoidal instruments for long periods of time at full intensity with the framing shutters nearly closed to produce "pin-spot" specials. Such instruments will overheat, warping the shutters and possibly damaging the reflector. One solution to this problem is to operate a relatively large instrument at a fraction of its normal wattage when it is to be shuttered down. This operation will take advantage of the housing ventilation which was designed to dissipate a much larger heat load under normal circumstances. Special narrow-beam instruments are the best solution.

Specials are normally thought of as downward-directed pools of light. Sidelights usually are considered as a separate category, because they sweep the stage in layers without producing a sharply defined pool of light. Often side lighting is the only recourse for the designer with limited dimmer equipment who must circuit his area lighting one area per dimmer in order to control focus of attention. If the stage floor is dark and unreflective, and the sides of the setting are either dark or so arranged that spill light from sidelights will not be distracting, the designer can use side lighting to provide the main key lighting. The regular area lighting can be used to focus attention and the sidelights used to increase key-fill contrast. Of course this system is not as flexible as controlling the key area by area; therefore actors who are to be defocused for a given scene must work upstage of the sidelights. Such inflexibility is not a major handicap if the director understands the difficulties imposed by equipment shortages and is willing to compensate by altering the blocking. Side lighting usually is accomplished by the use of relatively powerful ellipsoidal sources. The power is needed because of the long throws which often measure 40 to 50 feet. The shutters of the ellipsoidals allow the operator to control the width of the side-lighting beams accurately.

THE BEAM PROJECTOR AS SPECIAL OR SIDELIGHT

If maximum power is needed in either side lighting or a special, and a relatively slight beam spread is indicated, the parabolic beam projector is a useful instrument. Its efficiency is greater than that of either the Fresnel or ellipsoidal spotlight, and its directional characteristics are

FIGURE *18-1c*
Typical Instrument Schedule. This page from the complete instrument schedule refers to the "second electric" shown on the lighting plot in Figure 18-1b. It lists the first 20 instruments on that pipe reading from stage left to stage right. Note that most of the information appears on both the plot and the instrument schedule. This extra work by the designer saves costly crew time in the preparation, hanging, and focusing of instruments. The schedule also serves as a quick reference in case of malfunction. Courtesy Jonell Polansky.

INSTRUMENT SCHEDULE

PRODUCTION _____ KANSAS CITY LYRIC _____

PG. __7__ of __10__

DATE __6-73__

REV. _____

LOCATION	UNIT #	TYPE	USE	COLOR	CIRCUIT	DIMMER	NOTES
#2E	1	6"L	D Texture	C-26			Template
#2E	2	6"L	Area I	551		20	
#2E	3	6"F	D. Senta Plat	C-26			Spare
#2E	4	6"F	D. Senta Plat				Spare
#2E	5	6"F	I Wash	561		25	
#2E	6	6"L	T Act III Steps	547			
#2E	7	6"L	B. Lite	C-26		63	
#2E	8	6"L	Area I	503		9	
#2E	9	6"L	Area J	551		21	
#2E	10	6"L	B. Lite	C-26		64	
#2E	11	6"F	J Wash	561		25	
#2E	12	6"L	J ¢	552		65	
#2E	13	6"L	D Spatter	C-26			Template
#2E	14	6"F	P. Act II Stairs	547		65	Spare
#2E	15	6"L	B. Lite	C-26		64	
#2E	16	6"L	Area J	503		10	
#2E	17	6"L	Area K	551		22	
#2E	18	6"F	D. Portrait	503			
#2E	19	6"L	T Act III Steps	547			
#2E	20	6"F	K Wash	561		25	

excellent. It is the best instrument when "beam-of-light" effects are desired. Since its beam is nearly parallel, it cannot cover much area even as a sidelight, but its efficiency often makes up for this.

CIRCUITING SPECIALS AND SIDELIGHTS

Special instruments almost inevitably require independent control at the dimmer board. Since allocating a dimmer to an instrument which will possibly be operated only for a few seconds during the entire show is extremely wasteful of what is usually an insufficient supply of dimmers, replugging of specials is a common practice. Several specials, whose use is well separated in time, are allocated to the same dimmer, fed from the dimmer in sequence as needed, and then removed. The crudest way of replugging is to station an assistant at the patch bay who performs the necessary interplugging as he is cued by the switchboard operator. On a manually operated board, the operator himself may perform this operation if time is available. A refinement of this system on a manual-control board is to provide each dimmer with several outlets at the patch bay, each outlet controlled by a switch. Note that load circuit breakers should *not* be used for this function. Then all specials to be operated from a given dimmer are permanently plugged into the switched outputs and turned on in proper sequence. This method reduces the chances that the harried assistant will pick up the wrong load line, but it makes it easier to overload the dimmer by turning on more load than it can take. Remote-control boards usually are equipped with patch bays backstage. In this case, the replugging operations can be performed by a backstage assistant if necessary. A better but more expensive way is to equip the control board with a system of relays controlling the output receptacles of each dimmer. These relays can be activated singly or in groups as needed. The danger of overloading will still exist.

Since side-lighting loads tend to be large and because sidelights usually find extensive use throughout a production, often far exceeding that originally envisioned by the designer, they are usually circuited into dimmers and left there. Circuiting patterns will vary with needs, but usually the operator will separate the sidelights at least by stage-right and stage-left groups. Further subdivision into upstage

FIGURE *18-1d*

A "Hook-up" Chart. This is another name for a plugging chart, such as those shown in Figures 15-2b and c, although it contains more information. Note that several instruments shown on the second electric in the lighting plot (Figure 18-1b) and the instrument schedule (Figure 18-1c) also appear here. The function of the plugging chart is to enable control board operators to circuit the proper instruments to the proper dimmers and, conversely, to determine what instruments should come on when a dimmer is operated.
Courtesy Jonell Polansky.

DIMMER	CIRCUIT	LOCATION	UNIT #	TYPE	USE	COLOR	NOTES
21		#2E	9	6"L	J	551	
22		#2E	17	6"L	K	551	
23		Bal. Rail	1, 5 11, 15	8"L	A-D Wash	561	
24		#1E	6, 13 21, 28	6"F	E-H Wash	561	
25		#2E	5, 11 20	6"F	I-K Wash	561	
26		R. Bal. Rail	3, 5, 7	6×12L	B/C C/B D/A	534	
27		L. Bal. Rail	1, 3, 5	6×12L	A/B B/C C/D	534	
28		Prosc. Torm R	2, 4 6	6×12L 6×9L	B/A C/B D/C	534	
29		Prosc. Torm L	2, 4 6	6×12L 6×9L	D/C B/C A/B	534	
30		#1 Torm R	2, 4 6	6×12L 6×9L	B/A C/B D/C	534	
31		#1 Torm L	2, 4 6	6×12L 6×9L	C/D B/C A/B	534	
32		#1 Lad. R.	2, 4 6	6×12L 6×9L	F/E G/F H/G	534	
33		#1 Lad. L.	2, 4 6	6×12L 6×9L	G/H F/G E/F	534	
34		#2 Lad. R	2 4	6×12L 6×9L	J/I K/J	534	
35		#2 Lad. L	2 4	6×12L 6×9L	J/K I/J	534	
36		R. Bal. Rail	6, 7, 8	6×12L	B/A C/B D/C	561	
37		L Bal. Rail	2, 4, 6	6×12L	A/B B/C C/D	561	
38		Prosc. Torm R	1, 3 5	6×12L 6×9L	B/D C/B D/C	561	
39		Prosc. Torm L	1, 3 5	6×12L 6×9L	C/D B/C A/B	561	
40		#1 Torm R	1, 3 5	6×12L 6×9L	B/A C/D D/C	561	

and downstage control patterns is helpful. Since it often takes three or more instruments to properly sidelight a portion of the stage, this group of instruments can usually be treated as a unit and operated from one large dimmer.

Planning Background Lighting

The designer often will find it convenient to consider separately the lighting of those areas not occupied by actors, but still visible to the audience. He will continue to think of these as a separate category as he works out cues and may even want to separate them at the control board if this is possible. Background lighting tends to be nondirectional, concerned with constant color mixing, and related to the setting in a different way than the acting-area lighting.

Background lighting can vary in complexity from a fill light in a doorway or an alcove to a complete cyclorama setup with projected scenic effects. Usually it becomes quite simple when an indoor realistic setting is in use. If "sky" is to be seen through windows and open doors, a sky drop of some sort is used and lighted with floodlights in one or two colors depending on the need for day and night effects. Often a "sunlight" or "moonlight" directional instrument is aimed through openings in the set to catch on drapery or produce a realistic splash of light on the wall. If a shadow pattern is wanted from such lighting, an ellipsoidal spotlight or small beam projector must be used. The light source should be placed as far from the window or doorway as possible to make the instrument approximate the parallel beams of sunlight or moonlight. If only a catchlight of color is needed on the drapery, a short-range instrument can do the job. Such window and door combinations often are circuited together on the same dimmer.

Outdoor settings or space-staging techniques offer a greater challenge to the designer. Here a cyclorama or at least a full sky drop is essential. Lighting this may offer a real challenge. High-power equipment with even light distribution is essential. Furthermore, unless the cyclorama is free of imperfections (this usually means a plaster sky dome), there must be enough equipment to allow wide overlapping floods of light to obliterate shadows from wrinkles, bumps, and the like.

CYCLORAMA LIGHTING

Two systems of cyclorama lighting are common: cyclorama borderlights with footlights, and groups of floodlights. Both have their advantages and disadvantages, and both can produce highly satisfactory results if the equipment is adequate and the designer careful.

Cyclorama borderlights and footlights are an expensive and space-consuming but very effective way of producing sky effects. These instruments are relatively high in wattage. Lamp wattages may range up to 500 watts per socket on large stages. Well-designed instruments will produce an even distribution of light over a cyclorama when hanging quite close to the top or when mounted near the bottom. These units are expensive. A price of $40 to $50 a lineal foot is not uncommon. They are heavy and unwieldy; therefore they must be permanently mounted on counterweighted line sets at some optimum position with regard to the cyclorama. Moving them upstage or downstage, like moving the cyclorama itself, is a major project involving several days' work for several men. If the cyclorama lighting is continued around the sides, as it should be to provide proper lighting distribution, special hanging arrangements must be made for the upstage-downstage portions. These units will then occupy space frequently needed for wing arrangements. Cyclorama footlights, which are almost mechanically identical to their borderlight counterparts, are often mounted in troughs in the stage floor. This arrangement is expensive but offers storage for the units as well as an ideal place to operate them. However, the fixed location of the trough limits movement of the cyclorama. An alternative arrangement is to mount the footlight units on casters so that they can be rolled away when not needed. Storage of these bulky units then becomes a problem.

The alternative system is to light the cyclorama with several groups of three or four scoop floodlights arranged in front of the cyclorama in such a way that they cover the surface smoothly. To produce an ideal distribution of light these instruments should be farther from the cyclorama than borderlights. Of course no scenic elements can be mounted in the intervening space. More fly space is used during the actual operation of the cyclorama. The compensating factor is that the floodlight units are much lighter in weight, take up less storage space, and can be used for other applications when not needed as cyclorama units. They can be handled by one person and mounted at the ends of regular pipe battens to light the sides of the cyclorama. If floodlights are to be used from the floor position, they will present more of a problem. Masking and mounting are more difficult. However, the storage problem is much smaller.

Either type of cyclorama lighting will usually use red, green, and blue primary colors plus possibly a second circuit of blue or a near-white circuit. Note that the designer is not faced with much show-to-show choice in the use of cyclorama equipment. The decision is made when the theatre is designed and equipped, and the lighting designer must live with it. In the case of traveling shows he will be faced with the same problems compounded by the shipping difficulties, or else he must make do with the permanently installed equipment in each theatre he uses.

Design of cyclorama lighting consists mostly of choice of color to be applied to the cyclorama with the possibility that the designer may wish to depart from the usual three-color primary arrangement when he does not need its flexibility but does need high efficiency within certain color ranges. If, for example, an abstract space-staged play calls for only yellow and blue background, the designer will probably find it far more efficient to use these color media than to mix his colors from the three-color system. The decision to use bottom lighting on the cyclorama for a particular play is a matter for the designer to ponder. Realism dictates that the horizon portion of the sky should be brightest for sunsets and sunrises. In abstract settings this area of the cyclorama will often need to be brighter to aid in focusing the attention of the audience downward toward the acting space. On the other hand, many settings cover the lower one-third of the cyclorama, making horizon-line lighting unnecessary or perhaps a little ridiculous. Others require that the actors use the floor space quite near the cyclorama, making cyclorama footlighting impossible. In many productions the designer will deem footlighting the cyclorama unnecessary because intensities will not be high enough to make it possible for the cyclorama to control focus of attention. In such instances footlighting the cyclorama will tie up equipment better used elsewhere and clutter the stage as well.

Like area lighting, cyclorama setups are frequently held in readiness from show to show. Particularly if a floodlight arrangement is used to light the cyclorama, a great deal of time will go into blending the fields of the individual instruments to produce smooth color mixing. Once this job is well done there is a strong temptation to keep it. Since the floodlights are light in weight, they may be left on the battens in position, while curtains, drops, and the like, are mounted beneath them. Occasional lamp and color-medium replacement will be all that is necessary in many cases.

The designer may wish to stipulate that the sides of the cyclorama be controlled separately from the upstage portion. Separate control is usually not much of a problem because cyclorama lighting loads are large and must be subdivided anyway. The possibility of separate side-cyclorama control opens new potentialities to the designer. He can focus attention, take light off unwanted side or back areas, and perhaps most important, use the cyclorama lighting to blend projected cloud effects into the stage picture. (See Appendix I on projected scenery.)

BLENDING ACTING-AREA AND BACKGROUND LIGHTING

Probably the greatest challenge to the artistry of the designer as he considers background lighting will be in the provisions made for careful blending of foreground and background. Blending is especially important in amphitheatre arrangements where the audience looks down on the stage floor and is acutely aware of the edges of the acting area. However, some attention must be given to this matter in almost any theatre. The artistic considerations have already been discussed; they develop from the designer's concept of the horizons of dramatic space as related to the show at hand. As he develops the lighting plot, the designer must keep clearly in mind the variations in the horizons of the dramatic space which he wishes to effect. He then chooses equipment designed to produce subtle blending or sharp demarcation, taking into consideration the nature of the setting as it limits the dramatic space. For example, if the play demands sharply defined dramatic space, the setting will probably consist of realistic walls which should be lighted to emphasize their apparent solidarity and the natural boundary which they create. Actors may play directly against a wall and acting-area light will spill onto it above head level. Instruments chosen for these acting areas will usually be Fresnels, whose soft edges erase the upper limit line of the acting-area light.

An example of the opposite extreme in lighting the horizons of dramatic space occurs when the setting has no walls at all, and is placed in front of the cyclorama in such a way as to obliterate the line marking the intersection of the floor and the cyclorama. Under these conditions, acting-area light must be held away from the surface of the cyclorama to avoid diluting its color and destroying its horizonless effect. Often a band of partially lighted space 6 to 12 feet wide will be established between the cyclorama and the limits of useful acting-area lighting. Such a band of lighted space can symbolically become a kind of "limbo" in dramatic space, useful to the drama and susceptible to a considerable variety of lighting. Choice of instruments and colors for such an area may be complex. Sharply focused ellipsoidal spotlights may be used to create special color or key light. These sharp-edge instruments can be precisely angled to just miss the cyclorama. Such effects can create in the audience the appearance of great distance and almost limitless horizons. Ultimately the lighting of the edges of the acting space is a matter that must be coordinated with the setting design; neither design concept can afford to ignore the other.

CIRCUITING BACKGROUND LIGHTING

Background lighting, with the exception of occasional small window and door effects for sunlight and moonlight, tends to add up to very heavy electrical loads. Cyclorama wattages over 100,000 watts are not unusual; 30,000- to 50,000-watt loads are common. Scenic projectors often draw from 2000 to 6000 watts. Thus circuitry will usually be dictated by the availability of large dimmers. Electrical-code requirements will keep most individual load circuits down to 20 amperes, but many of these will operate in tandem to feed one cyclorama color. Usually wattages will vary with color, the blue circuits drawing at least twice the wattage of the red.

If enough heavy dimmers are available, the designer will want to subdivide the cyclorama lighting as suggested in Table 18-1.

TABLE *18-1*
Subdivision of Cyclorama Lighting

LEFT	CENTER	RIGHT
Red	Red	Red
Green	Green	Green
Blue	Blue	Blue
Blue*	Blue*	Blue*

*The extra blue circuit is a great advantage in efficiency because a slight dimming of incandescent lamps cuts off all blue output.

Additional circuits will be needed for projected effects and any special cyclorama lighting such as a flare of red light from below. The minimum number of circuits will be three, one for each primary color.

The Completed Lighting Plot

Figures 18-1*b, c,* and *d* illustrate the degree to which a professional lighting plot may be developed. Such elaboration is necessary in the professional theatre where every effort must be made to save expensive stage time and where most of the equipment must be rented well in advance of the production. The plot and the various schedules are prepared by the designer and the equipment is ordered from this information. This tends to limit the designer to the equipment he has stipulated on his plot. Therefore the canny designer plans a number of "spares" into the plot to enable him to meet late changes. Such a degree of plot elaboration and schedules may not be necessary in educational and community theatre situations. For example, an educational theatre designer may feel it beneficial for the student lighting crew to abstract the information in the instrument schedule from the lighting plot. They may gain a better grasp of the process of reading lighting plots this way. Similarly, a designer working at a community theatre which owns its own equipment need not plan for "spares" to assure the availability of equipment. Finally, many theatres will have permanently located equipment which need not be plotted in detail. In no case should the lighting plot and its associated schedules be more complicated than the situation demands.

Mounting the Lights for the Show

Once the lighting plot is finished, the designer will find that he has accomplished about as much as can be accomplished without moving to the stage. Occasionally a designer who is fortunate enough to be working with a technically well-trained director will talk over the finished lighting plot with the director. To technically knowledgeable people, a lighting plot is a clear indication of design intent. To the uninformed it is only a confusing mass of lines.

If the sequence of theatrical events is such that the designer must wait until late in the production schedule to hang the lighting apparatus, he can put some of the intervening time to good use by touring the production areas, examining costume color, paint details, and other details. From these examinations he will be able to make final decisions concerning acting-area tint combinations, and the necessity for blending and tonal lighting. This information can then be added to the lighting plot. An assistant can tote up the number of color frames of each color and prepare a cutting guide so that color media can be made ready. Instruments can be checked out, repaired if necessary, and the inventory of lighting equipment assembled in readiness for mounting.

Mounting the instruments for a complicated production can take anywhere from a couple of hours to as many days depending on the convenience of the theatre, how much equipment is already in place, and on the skill and efficiency of the workers. A good procedure is for the entire lighting crew to go over the lighting plot, dividing up the work and making sure that everyone understands his job. Then battens are lowered, including the light bridge, if one is available. The designer may mark location of instruments with chalk on the pipes and helpers can assist him in mounting the equipment. Lamp wattages are checked if this is necessary, and all instruments are hung, finger-tight, on the batten before any of them are roughly aimed and clamped. This method makes it easier to move the instruments slightly if the spacing is not quite right. Then the instruments are roughly angled and firmly clamped into place with a wrench. Shutters of all ellipsoidal instruments are opened to make sure that none will be turned on while completely shuttered—an oversight which can cost a lamp and reflector in short order. Equipment then is circuited. If a plugging strip is available, instruments are simply plugged into outlets as already planned, or into the nearest outlet, which is immediately recorded as the load circuit for that particular instrument. As equipment is connected, it is good procedure to connect each instrument in turn to a nondim circuit at the plugging panel to check out the connections. After checking, the load circuit can be inserted into the dimmer way planned for it on the lighting plot, or held for later plugging.

If the equipment is to be mounted on a batten, and stage-cable circuits run from the instruments directly to the control board or to some offstage terminal point, it will be easier to run the longest lines first, tying up the cable as far as the next instrument, then including the second cable, and so on to the end of the batten. When running such cables a foresighted worker will coil up about 4 to 6 feet of cable near the instrument and tie it to the batten before plugging in the instrument lead. Then minor shifts of the instrument's location can be made without the necessity of untying the entire bundle of cable to get some slack. The only precaution is that the coil of cable must not be allowed to touch any hot instrument housings. Extra precautions must be taken to support the end of the bundle of cable where it drops to the floor.

After all hanging instruments have been mounted, the batten is counterweighted and raised to trim position. Angling and focusing then begin. If a light bridge is available or if a rolling ladder can be moved along under the instruments as each is turned on, the processes are easy. If the instruments must be repeatedly raised and lowered to get the proper angle and focus, much time and energy will be wasted.

Before acting areas can be angled from the onstage position, it will be necessary to angle and focus those areas whose instruments are in or over the house. If lighting beam positions are used, the chances are that equipment in these positions will already be mounted, needing only minor adjustment. If balcony pipes are used, they will be prepared and circuited along with the onstage equipment. The general procedure is to work from downstage areas to upstage areas angling each separately, then checking its blending with those around it. A switchboard operator plus a man to position the instruments form a minimum crew. Usually the designer will remain on stage calling out instructions as he checks the lighting by walking through the areas being adjusted.

If a setting is to be erected under the onstage lighting in a way that will prevent the lights from being lowered for later adjustments, pre-liminary arrangements must be exact. In most instances, the designer will want to see a few rehearsals under the acting-area lighting before he will declare it satisfactory. Minor adjustments will often be necessary.

19 CUES

Light cues are necessary if the operator is to perform the various functions of lighting a show in proper sequence. As lighting gets more complicated and the various operations tend to overlap, the basic function of cues may easily get lost in the sheer complexity of trying to find a system of notation equal to the job. Indeed, it is not at all unusual for a beginning light crew to become so engrossed with the cues and the mechanics of the control board that they forget to look at the stage to see what effect their efforts are having.

The theory of cues seems simple: Cues should tell the operator exactly what operations to perform, when to perform them, and at what pace and duration. Furthermore, the cues should do this with the least possible distraction of the operator from his basic task of operating the lights. Finally the lighting cues should reflect the artistic intent of the lighting artist so accurately that the operator will have a clear grasp of the subtleties of the lighting, and will thus be able to make the various minor adjustments in pace and emphasis that performance-to-performance variations in the production require. This theory is a large order, far beyond the capacity of any system of cue notation so far devised.

Music comes to mind as an art form in which a complicated but successful system of notation has made artistic communication relatively simple. Indeed, it is possible to attribute much of the rapid progress of Western music to this factor alone. Talented musicians still chafe under what they consider to be major inadequacies in their system of notation, but these problems are small when compared to the situation in stage lighting. The basic ingredient of successful notation which has benefited music is not presently available to stage lighting. This ingredient is the standard musical scale, applicable to all instruments. This scale is further standardized for each type of instrument by consistent keyboard arrangements, fingering positions, and the like, making

397

it possible for a pianist to perform on any available piano. Minor variations exist for some instruments, but these are well within the grasp of a well-trained performer. The situation is almost exactly the opposite in the case of lighting. No "scale" exists that enables the lighting artist to refer with any degree of accuracy to a lighting condition in space. Such a scale would be analogous to the use of musical notation to refer to a harmonic situation in a chord. Moreover, there is no standardization in lighting-control boards, the "musical instruments" of lighting. The only standardization in lighting is the 10-point dimmer calibration which is susceptible to a wide variety of differences within these 10 points.

The stage-lighting artist might do well to examine the principles of musical notation to see if any of these might be adapted. However, such an examination is doomed to early frustration until a greater degree of standardization can be achieved in control boards, lighting positions, and the like. Without such standardization the situation is analogous to an orchestra in which each instrument is designed with a different musical scale. Incidentally, such standardization need not result in any stultification of artistic efforts. The opposite should be the case. Consider the infinite variety of tonal and harmonic arrangements possible in a modern symphony orchestra. Each instrument has its own voice and range, but all are unified by the musical scale.

What Can Be Expected of a Cue System?

All cue systems are compromises, many of them poor ones. The art is reduced to depending on the facile memory of skilled and sensitive operators who memorize the lighting, using cues only as a memory-jogging device. Any hope of communicating artistic intent through any present system is vain indeed.

What, within the present limits of the art of notation, are the characteristics of any good cue system? The following list includes some of the more important ones:

1. The cue system should offer minimal reading problems for the operator who must concentrate on the control board, not upon reading.
2. It must lead the operator's recall rapidly and directly to the lighting operation which he is to perform—*not* merely to the mechanical operation of the control board.
3. It must reflect the timing of the operation as clearly and in as much detail as will be needed to enable the operator to remember the rhythm of the cue.
4. It must be keyed to the script of the play in such a way that the operator can focus his attention on the play—not the cue sheet—and still get all the necessary information.

5. It must contain a reasonably effective system of warning the operator of impending cues.
6. It must remind him of any operations which must be prepared in advance, giving him the information early enough to make it possible to double check the prearrangements.

As a general rule, the cue system should be no more complicated than the needs of the show require. Simple comedies often are adequately cued by means of a cue card or two telling the operator what he must do when the stage manager starts the play. At the other extreme, a constant flow of cues written in the script and read to the operator by an assistant may barely suffice for a complicated play.

Various Systems
Cue Card

Several systems are commonly in use. Each has its place and its limitations. The simplest system is the cue-card system, little more than the refinement of the old-time professional operator's cue sheet. The cue sheet was often a printed program for the production with a few scrawled notations on it for each scene. The sheet was impaled with the handle of a little-used dimmer and referred to occasionally to check out a cue. Since most of the timing came from the stage manager who held the book and gave adequate warnings, the electrician frequently devoted most of his attention to the potentialities of the backstage poker hand he held. Such a cue-card system is adequate for a play in which the lights are set for each act and no major changes are made during the time the curtain is up, with the possible exception of a time-of-day fade or increase usually suggesting sunset or sunrise. The operator prearranges his lights for the coming scene, with the exception of the antiproscenium lighting, before the curtain goes up. The anteproscenium lighting he brings in on cue as the curtain rises. Then he retires from the scene until the end of the act when he reverses the process and makes whatever changes are required for the act to come. The occasional sky fade or build is timed by the clock after being started by the stage manager.

Cue Sheet

An elaboration of the cue card is the "cue sheet." It includes line or business cues from the script and enables the operator to perform the operations in synchronization with the action of the play. Frequently he is still under the direction of the stage manager for timing and uses the cue lines merely as a double check. Or if timing must be precise, he may get the warning from the stage manager and take the cue directly from the line as he hears it. If he is backstage, business cues are difficult because he can see so little of the action. Usually the stage manager or an assistant will have to peek around the tormentor and relay the information to the board operator. Timing is difficult but not impossible under these conditions.

Script Cues

The next most complex cue is the script cue. In this system the lighting cues are written in the margins of a playbook with the exact "takes" marked in the script. The operator follows the script, making the changes as they appear. This system meets the needs of the fourth item on the list of cue characteristics far better than the more primitive systems above. It can also lead to difficulties when cues come thick and fast. The operator frequently must lay down the script and concentrate on the control board to operate his cues. Before he can get back to the book and find his place, other cues will have been passed up. The cue-book system works best with a play in which there is a steady flow of cues, well spaced but closely tied to the lines. An alert operator with a good memory will follow the book as needed and feel free to abandon it for a page or more, trusting his memory for cues at those points. The degree of concentration required for this feat is much the same as that required of the leading actor.

Card Plus Script Cues

The ultimate degree of complexity consists of a retreat to the cue-card system combined with the use of the script. In reality, two sets of cues exist, a complete set in the script and an abbreviated set on the cards. This arrangement of the cards will depend upon the kind of control equipment being used. Assuming for the moment a manually operated board backstage, the cards will be subdivided according to the number of operators needed to perform the cues. Often several operators are used because of the size of such boards and the weight of the dimmer mechanisms which must be moved. Each operator has cue cards with those cues upon them which have been assigned to him. Cues are numbered and the references are all by cue number. Either the stage manager or a member of the lighting crew follows the book closely, calling out warnings and cue "takes" to the operators. At each warning all operators check their cue cards to see what if any operations they must perform when the take is given. When the take comes each performs the operation according to the timing on his cue sheet.

One of the advantages of this system is that a variety of timings can be worked into a single cue by adjusting the timing of the individual operators. All start at the same time but do not necessarily finish together. The system also provides a means of careful attention to the progress of the play because one person does nothing but keep track of the place and the timing. Finally, it is about the only method of coordinating complicated cues on a large manually operated board. Someone must "call the plays" and keep things moving.

Front-of-House Control as It Affects Cues

A major change takes place in cue systems when the control board is moved from backstage to a position where the operators can see the stage clearly. First of all, the stage manager is removed from the picture. In fact he often knows less accurately what is happening on the stage than the lighting operator. Only an occasional cue which depends on anticipating an entrance started backstage, or an effect which begins behind unopened curtains, will originate with the stage manager. Of course he will start the acts, often with the help of the lighting operator who can see when the last spectator is in his seat.

The majority of lighting cues are taken from business, not lines. The operator in a booth at the back of the house is in excellent position to take such cues directly and in exact rhythm with the movements of the actors. Thus no matter how simple or complex the system, he will probably take most cues directly. However, he may need help to ascertain what operations he should perform and possibly to set up cues on a preset system.

Cues with Preset Consoles

Usually the removal of the control board to the back of the audience also means that remote-control equipment has been installed. However, in intimate theatres this may not always be true. When it is, the nature of the cuing system will have to take into account the requirements of the remote-control system in use.

Almost all remote systems are intended to be operated by one person although that person may need the assistance of one or two others to prepare preset operations and follow cues. Let us consider cuing with a typical preset remote-control board. Even with a two-preset board there is the possibility of rotating from preset to preset. Rotation will be accomplished by operating one or more cues from Preset I (several will often be possible if submastering is provided) while preparing Preset II. Preset II is then placed into operation and one or more cues are operated on it while Preset I is reset for further use. The show proceeds on this rotating basis. Cues will be of two sorts: those which are taken by the operator on the appropriate preset and with the proper submaster if this is available, and preset cues. The first type of cues will be handled like cues for a manual board with the addition of the information as needed to direct the operator to the proper controller for each operation. Cue cards, sheets, a cue book, or a combination of these will do. The second type of cues will tell an assistant or the operator himself, if he has the time, what changes to make in the controllers of the inactive preset in order to ready it for its next operation. These cues must refer the operator who is making the changes to a specific time for starting his work and then tell him exactly what should be done. No timing or reference to the actors is necessary unless it be a warning that the changes must be finished by a certain line.

In the case of complicated shows with a multipreset console, the work will have to be divided. The operator will take cues, receiving the warnings and the takes from a cue reader who follows the text. A third person will arrange the presets in advance, starting when cued by the cue reader. This third person often assists the operator when overlapping cues of differing paces are to be operated.

The addition of infinite-preset card-reading apparatus eliminates the need for the third party since all the necessary information can be sequenced in advance on the card stacks. The problem of overlapping cues with different pace still remains.

The above discussion is most relevant to discrete cues (see Chapter 10). Counterpoint cues can be operated within the pattern of a revolving preset arrangement, particularly on an infinite-preset console, but the amount of analysis necessary to break these complicated cues down into revolving sequences will often frustrate the designer's attempts to concentrate on the artistic elements of the lighting. A better solution is open to those lucky few with consoles generously supplied with submasters in each preset. Four or more submasters per preset are desirable under these conditions. It is also most helpful to have the console arranged to allow pile-on.

Given these refinements, counterpoint cues will best be organized by establishing various functions on the submasters, for example, stage left 45° keys, stage left 60° keys, stage right sidelights, moonlight sidelights, and so on. Cues are then written in terms of functions and timing, the operator blending the various functions as needed while taking his timing from the action. Additional refinements and variations within the various functions are handled by making changes in the various preset controllers. This works best if these controllers are identical in size and feel to those on the manual bank.

Figures 19-1a and 19-1b illustrate one designer's approach to the problem of plotting, and scheduling a major repertory season of opera. Note particularly the detail in the plot and the various schedules (see also Figures 18-1b, c, and d). Such meticulous work saves valuable crew time during lighting setup. This opera company used a variety of lighting control equipment installed backstage. Figure 19-1b shows a cue sheet for one of the operators, while Figure 19-2 shows a preset cue sheet used to prepare the console for coming cues.

KANSAS CITY LYRIC THEATER — 1973 SEASON　　　DESIGNERS'
JONELL POLANSKY — LIGHTING DESIGN　　　　　　CUE SHEET

PRODUCTION_____ TOSCA _____ PG. _5_ OF _60_

CUE _15_　DESCRIPTION — TOSCA'S ENTRANCE

COUNT _20_

1 A 503 ⑥	25 In III 561 Wash	101 #1 503	121
2 B 503	26 R Rail 534 ⑥	102 #2 503	122
3 C 503	27 L Rail 534 ⑥	103 #3 503	123
4 D 503	28 R Pro 534 ⑤	104 CYC 547	124
5 E 503	29 L Pro 534 ⑤	105 #1 547	125
6 F 503	30 R Torm 534	106 #2 547	126
7 G 503	31 L Torm 534	107 #3 547	127
8 H 503	32 #1 Lad R 534	108 Cyc 545	128
9 I 503	33 #1 Lad L 534	109 #1 561	129
10 J 503	34 #2 Lad R 534	110 #2 561	130
11 K 503	35 #2 Lad L 534	111 #3 561	
12 A 551	36 R Rail 561 ⑦	112 CYC 561	
13 B 551	37 L Rail 561	113 #1 519	
14 C 551	38 R Pro 561	114 #2 519	
15 D 551	39 L Pro 561	115 #3 519	
16 E 551	40 R Torm 561	116 CYC 519	
17 F 551 ④	41 L Torm 561		
18 G 551	42 #1 Lad R 561		
19 H 551	43 #1 Lad L 561		
20 I 551 ⑧	44 #2 Lad R 561		
21 J 551	45 #2 Lad L 561		
22 K 551	46 3E Back		
23 In I 561 Wash ⑧	47 4E Back		
24 In II 561 Wash ⑧	48 Bow 552		

Auto Transformer — 6 Packs

51 Act III Steps	61 Bal. R.	71
52 Act III Steps	62 Bal. L.	72
53 Act III Steps	63 Madonna	73
54 Scaffold ⑧	64 Glow	74
55 Couch	65 Scarpia Sp.	75
56 Candelabrum	66	76

FIGURE 19-1a

A Designer's Cue Sheet For Repertory. This cue sheet is related to the lighting plot shown in Figure 18-1b. It reflects a highly organized effort by the designer to expedite lighting in a repertory situation. All instruments in the standardized lighting plot (Figure 18-1b) are preprinted on the cue sheet. Changes representing each cue are then entered as the cues are worked out. One sheet serves for each discrete cue. Courtesy Jonell Polansky.

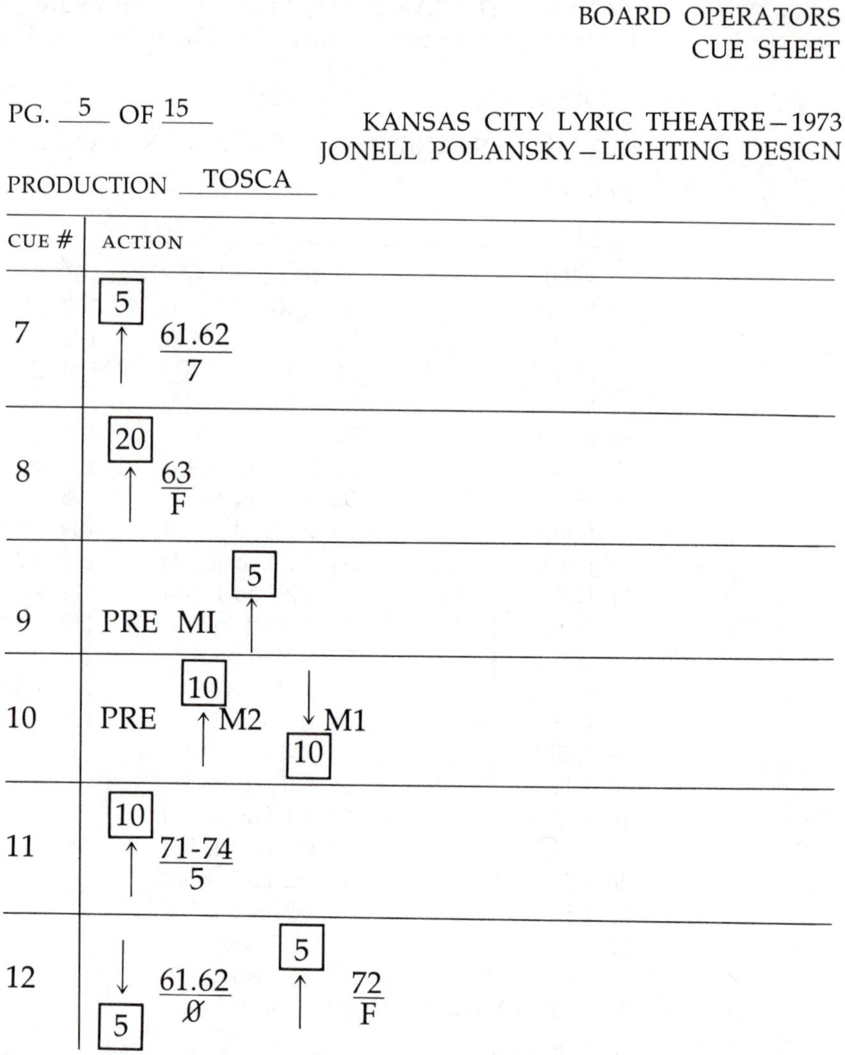

BOARD OPERATORS
CUE SHEET

PG. __5__ OF __15__

KANSAS CITY LYRIC THEATRE – 1973
JONELL POLANSKY – LIGHTING DESIGN

PRODUCTION __TOSCA__

CUE #	ACTION
7	⑤ ↑ 61.62 / 7
8	⑳ ↑ 63 / F
9	PRE MI ⑤ ↑
10	PRE ⑩ ↑M2 ↓M1 ⑩
11	⑩ ↑ 71-74 / 5
12	↓ 61.62 Ø ⑤ ↑ 72 / F ⑤

FIGURE *19-1b* (above)

A Board Operator's Cue Sheet. This cue sheet was devised for the use of a backstage board operator during the repertory season referred to in Figure 18-1b. Only basic information is given in this cue sheet. Note that the designer has followed the typical professional roadshow practice of referring to dimmers instead of lighted areas on stage. Cue seven would translate as follows: "On a count of five raise dimmers 61 and 62 to the reading of seven." Cues nine and ten refer to preset masters instead of individual dimmers. See Figure 19-2 for a preset sheet. Courtesy Jonell Polansky.

FIGURE *19-2* (facing page)

A Presetting Sheet. This sheet contains no regular cue information involving immediate changes in the lighting on stage. Instead it is a set of instructions for rearranging preset controls which will affect lighting when a preset master is operated as in cues nine and ten, Figure 19-1b. Note that the operator must know when to begin to make these changes thereby avoiding accidentally working on an active preset. Controllers without entries are not changed. Courtesy Jonell Polansky.

KANSAS CITY LYRIC THEATRE- 1973
JONELL POLANSKY- LIGHTING DESIGN

PRESET 5 / AFTER CUE 7 / SCENE 1

1	2	3	4	5	6	7	8	9	10	11	12	13	14	15	16	17	18	19	20	21	22	23	24
5		5	5	5			F	F	F				4		8		7	F	F				

25	26	27	28	29	30	31	32	33	34	35	36	37	38	39	40	41	42	43	44	45	46	47	48
6	6	6			6	6	6	6				F	F	F					7		7	7	

PRESET 6 / AFTER CUE 8 / SCENE 2

1	2	3	4	5	6	7	8	9	10	11	12	13	14	15	16	17	18	19	20	21	22	23	24
F		F	F	F			6	6	6			5	F		3		6	8	8				

25	26	27	28	29	30	31	32	33	34	35	36	37	38	39	40	41	42	43	44	45	46	47	48
4	4	4			8	8	8	8												5	5	5	

Cue Sheet for
Series 2000
Q-File

Production:_____   Act_____   Scene_____   Page_____   of_____

CUE NO.	MEMORY	ACTION	FADER & TIME	FINAL MEMORY	NOTES

FIGURE *19-3*

Cue Sheet for a Memory System. This is one type of cue sheet which has been devised for operating a memory console. It is adapted to the operation of discrete cues. Compare it with the manual board operator's cue sheet, Figure 19-1b. No dimmer readings are needed in a memory-system cue sheet. Since this sheet was devised for Q-File, a console which allows the adding of memory after memory via the same autofader action, the entry, "final memory," is especially important. Operation of counterpoint lighting on this console might involve a more elaborate cue sheet. Courtesy Kliegl Brothers and Jonell Polansky.

Cuing with Memory Controls

Memory systems are relatively new in the theatre. They are still changing, taking on many diverse forms. New devices are being added and old ones placed into new relationships with each other. Thus cuing is even less standardized when using memory than when using preset. One thing is certain: There is no need to spend time laboriously writing out dimmer settings for presets. These can be instantly stored in memory. In some systems it is also possible to store additional information, for example, duration of fades and flags for special manual operations.

The least difficulty is encountered in devising a cue system for handling revolving presets (see Figure 19-3). Cue numbers in a script, either in the operator's hands or those of the stage manager, usually serve. They must, of course, be properly anticipated by warnings. Two problems may arise: (1) The normal error-detecting-and-correcting process that takes place when an operator identifies cues as lighting changes on stage, may be further lessened because of the multiplicity of cues and the abstractness of address numbers. In a show with a great many presets it is unreasonable to assume that the operator will memorize the lighting for each preset without some more concrete identification than a number. (2) Whenever it is necessary that the operator of the board operate in an ad lib mode, he will need to prepare some sort of catalog telling him what lighting combinations he has set on which cue number so that he may call these up as he needs them.

Cues for Counterpoint Lighting

The problem of cue identification is further aggravated when counterpoint lighting is in use. Since the very essence of counterpoint is in the subtle blending of lighting elements in a complex time pattern, it is vital that the operator know at every moment with what patterns he is working. Cue numbers alone are an inadequate reference for this purpose.

CUE CATALOGING

The immediate solution to the problem of cue identification, whether operating discrete cues or counterpoint, is to develop a catalog of cues. This should list cues by number, indicating what lighting preset or pattern is represented by the cue. For example, in preset lighting:

Cue 1——afternoon exterior
Cue 2——evening exterior

In counterpoint lighting:

> Cue 1——stage left cool sides
> Cue 2——stage left warm sides
> Cue 3——60° keys—front areas

If the show is quite complicated, the catalog should be further broken down by acts and scenes for easy reference.

The purpose of such cataloging is clear: The operator must know at every change exactly what is being done to the lighting on stage and what the artistic purpose is for doing this. He is then capable of comparing what he sees on stage with what the cues tell him he should see. He can make intelligent adjustments if they are needed in preset lighting. In counterpoint, he then has the information needed to adjust the tempi of the changes.

MEMORIZED CUE INFORMATION

We have already mentioned that it is quite possible for a computer to be programmed to handle the catalog information as part of its memory function. Such a system would present the operator with the cue information he needs as well as the memorized dimmer readings necessary to operate it. This information could be brought up with the "next cue" button and transferred to the "stage" display as the cue moved to the stage. Such a system is being comtemplated for the new British National Theatre in London. It should be seriously considered elsewhere.

How the Designer Prepares for Cuing the Show

Once the equipment is all mounted, focused, and circuited, and color media is installed, the designer is ready to prepare his preliminary cues. Whatever cue system the operators are going to use, it is almost inevitable that the designer will work from the script. The only exception to this will be those very simple productions in which there are but one or two lighting changes. In such cases the cues will usually be set by the designer during rehearsal and written by the operator.

However, in more advanced and more challenging productions, the designer will find that some preliminary cuing will be a great asset. Often an experienced designer can approximate dimmer settings for major scenes by estimating on the basis of past experience. He will simply set down in his copy of the script the readings he feels will do for the job. The beginner will probably do well to run a series of trial settings on the lighting as soon as the set is up and painted, but without the actors. He can take readings from these trial runs that will be approximately right for the lighting rehearsals. Such readings will then be combined with information gathered from the director about cues that are mandatory within the script itself. For instance, the darkening of a room as twilight progresses can be preestablished from the script even to the approximate timing of the cue. Plot-motivated lighting changes will be located in this manner and approximate settings entered in the designer's book. Action lines indicating the start of such cues can be marked by the director. Still other lighting effects that have been agreed upon by the designer and director can often be precued before any lighting rehearsals.

Once the designer has gone as far with precues as the show will allow, he has these preliminary cues transformed to whatever cue system the operators plan to use. All of this work is, of course, tentative and subject to any amount of change.

Training New Lighting Operators

Since this text is intended for the use of educational-theatre personnel, a digression is appropriate at this point concerning operators. The introduction of the back-of-house remote-control console has made great changes in the teaching of lighting (particularly in the training of console operators). Previously, with the board backstage, the operators were frequently little more than robots whose hands were glued to a couple of dimmer handles. They took orders from the cue reader and seldom had the time or the inclination to reason why. Only in those rare moments when they were allowed to see the production from the front while someone else played robot could they understand what it was all about. Things have changed. The addition of a fine view of the stage from the lighting booth offers an excellent chance to bring out the theatrical sense of many a neophyte. He is now a part of the show and can see his contribution—or his mistakes.

Since educational theatre meets its objectives only by training the neophytes, reliance on old hands at the control console is poor pedagogy. It is also risky business because the old hands graduate and are no longer available. How does one train the beginner who knows only that the console is related to the lights by some magical process? Set up the console and let him follow the action! This method sounds like tossing a nonswimmer off the end of a pier for his first swimming lesson, but it is not nearly as dangerous. First of all, the console should be carefully prearranged by an expert. Controllers should be plainly marked according to the *lighting areas* they control. This arrangement may change later when the beginners have learned the console, but for the first lessons let them operate by area notation alone. Explain how the controllers work. Allow them to try them. Caution them about any potentially dangerous operation they might stumble into—although the expert console operator should be able to forestall such exigencies by careful planning. Finally, explain to the director and the actors that the lighting changes they perceive for the next rehearsal or so have little if anything to do with the final lighting except that they will enable the cast to have the advantage of trained operators. Then determine a reasonable amount of emphasis for the area of greatest attention—say three dimmer points—and establish a general background lighting level for all other areas, making it high enough to avoid darkness, and let the new operators take over. If several operators are to be trained, let them take turns so each has complete responsibility for a period of time.

At this point the designer-teacher will do well to leave the control area and go to the house. Telephone communication should be established from there to the control board for purposes of answering questions and offering suggestions. Then the designer should watch carefully. At first the neophytes will be several seconds to a minute behind the action of the play. Although they should be instructed to study the script and to attend a rehearsal in advance of their first work on the console, it will often develop that they have not done so. Thus they will be learning both the play and the console. However, watching the results of their efforts will motivate some fast learning. It is an unusually dense operator who will not be following most of the action by the third session. Actors will trip him up by false starts and he will occasionally get the wrong controller, but a sense of the rhythm of the play's movement will begin to appear. If the designer is going to choose the regular operator for the show from one of the candidates learning the board he will look for the person who senses the rhythm of movement and begins and ends his changes with the movement of the actor. He will watch for the operator who keeps his eye on the stage as much as possible, only referring to the console when necessary. Another likely prospect is the fellow who sees possibilities for performing these operations more effectively by using the various submasters and preset arrangements that he is now beginning to understand.

Frequently such teaching sessions will produce some lighting arrangements worth incorporating into the lighting of the show. However, whether this happens or not, the designer will provide the crew with detailed cues after they are reasonably familiar with the console and ask that they try to run these.

"Technical Rehearsals"

The experienced theatre-lighting designer will have noted that there has been no indication so far of a "technical rehearsal." This device is a convention of the professional theatre where union restrictions and high costs, plus the elimination of the necessity for training personnel, make the longer, more relaxed, more rewarding system of lighting a show impossible. In a technical rehearsal, lighting, sound, setting changes, special effects, and all other mechanically complicated elements are added to the production in one huge effort, often lasting until dawn. Actors run through lines stopping for each technical change and repeating until it is set. Then they move to the next. These rehearsals are tiring, nerve-wracking sessions, but with a team of experts they get the job done. Educational theatre can often avoid this situation by adding lighting and sound well ahead of technical rehearsal time, thus converting the technical rehearsal into a rather intensive blending and smoothing rehearsal which will also serve to check all cues. The presence of soundproof lighting-control booths and good telephone communications from the director and designer to these booths will aid greatly. With the telephones, instructions can be quietly relayed to the operators without disrupting the play, and further rehearsal time is still available for making corrections.

Setting the Lighting Cues

Whatever the procedure for training the crew, the time comes for completing the design job. Completion involves setting all cues as to readings, timing, pace, and sequence, and requires lighting rehearsals, whether they are part of a technical rehearsal or come earlier in the production process. However, the more subtle and complicated the lighting, the earlier it should be blended into the action of the play.

The location of the designer during lighting rehearsals will depend upon the architecture of the theatre. He must place himself approximately in the center of the audience. Preferably he should be able to move from this position, taking his communication gear with him. At his "base position" he will need a work light, dim, yet bright enough to read and write by; a telephone with connections to the lighting booth, backstage, and to the director, if the latter is not close by; a copy of the script with preliminary cues in pencil; a copy of the lighting plot with all circuitry up to date; and an inexhaustible supply of pencils and black coffee!

The designer bases his decisions, as he moves through the lighting rehearsals adjusting and readjusting the lighting cues, on his study of the script and his understanding of the aesthetic content of that script as he and the director have discussed it. All of his major decisions at the time will be aesthetic in nature, although he may coincidentally solve technical problems.

Setting Static Scenes

During early lighting rehearsals the designer will seek to establish "pictures" in the lighting. That is, he will concern himself with setting contrasts to focus attention, adjusting overall color for mood, and establishing dimmer readings that will hold through static scenes. He will not try to develop and refine sequences until he has the static scenes worked out. It is impossible to work out a change until you have fixed the point from which the change must move. There may be long, overlapping changes in the show, but at this point the designer will simply set up the various segments of these long sequences as static lighting. Later he can arrange the rhythm of the changes to come. For example, a simple sunset fade which carries through a dozen other cues will merely be established at the beginning and changed to the "finish" reading at the end of the lines involving the sequence. Overlapping cross-fades may be treated as "snap cues" at this point so that the designer can study the facial contrasts and focus of attention. Such preliminary designing of cues can take place without stopping a smoothing rehearsal if the director will permit and the lighting-control booth is soundproof.

As contrasts are set and approved, a member of the lighting crew writes them down. The contrasts are subject to change, of course, but must be reproduced at each rehearsal to enable the designer to refine them. Since the designer will have the light operators make many trial changes that he will promptly reject, it is common practice to instruct the cue recorder to write nothing until the command "Write it!" has been given. This practice will avoid confusion the next time the cues are operated.

If the theatre is equipped with memory control, the cue writing is reduced to the act of noting the cue number and its intention in terms of lighting, setting the number on the cue assignment keyboard and pressing the "cue record" button. Nevertheless, nothing should be recorded until the designer gives the word.

It would be more efficient for the designer of the lighting if all costumes and makeup could be used for each lighting rehearsal. This is seldom possible, particularly if the lighting is to be inserted into the production well ahead of the traditional technical rehearsal. Often the best the designer can do is to request the cast to avoid wearing white or brightly colored rehearsal clothes unless these are the colors they will wear during the production. Makeup will have to come later and adjustments will have to be made for it.

Sequencing the Cues

After contrast ratios, focuses, and mood lighting have been set up in a preliminary way, the designer is ready to sequence them. To sequence he needs rehearsals in which the action will play continuously for considerable periods, preferably without cutbacks. A "cut" from the director right in the middle of a long, involved, lighting sequence will try the designer sorely. His concern at this point is rhythm. He is adjusting the pace of cues to the dramatic structure of the play as this particular cast is playing it. He will instruct the operators to keep the cues in pace with the play even if this means jumping the lighting occasionally. Such jumps will have to be adjusted later.

Communication with the operators is critical. At this point in the lighting design the operator must be apprised of the artistic concept of the lighting if it is to be successful. Frequently the designer will want to have the operator merely watch a scene while the designer explains what is to happen. Student operators in particular should be allowed to view the play from the designer's seat and have changes explained to them in detail as frequently as possible. This practice is not only good pedagogy; it produces more sensitive operation of the cues.

Sequencing lighting cues is to the lighting as polishing the blocking is to directing. Moreover, the two are inextricably interlocked. Each pattern of lighting worked out by the designer at these rehearsals will be built upon the foundation of the blocking already set by the director. Any deviation from that blocking will tend to destroy the effectiveness of the whole. The amount of ad lib movement that can be tolerated will depend on the lighting contrasts which are being used and the size of the lighting areas used for focusing attention. Brilliant comedy lighting with general key light over wide areas may offer the actors a lot of latitude. Precise "pool lighting" against a near-black background calls for precision. Sometimes a movement of an inch or so is too much.

Not only will the designer build upon the blocking, he will try to pick up and intensify the dramatic mood of the scenes. He may try many of the various devices for building a scene with lighting before he hits upon one or a combination of several that works. He will consult with the director frequently about the degree of emphasis and the amount of build to be given to a scene. Often the designer and director will try to estimate what degree of emphasis an actor can tolerate at a given moment.

Another aspect of lighting and directing that will be completed during sequencing rehearsals is the defocusing of groups of actors as the director wishes to "take them out of the scene." Timing of such dims is crucial if key lines are not to be clipped.

Shifting attention in multiple-focus scenes, such as the agent-object scenes so common in satire, may have to be worked out with split-second precision to carry the audience's attention to the right group at the right moment.

During all of the lighting rehearsals, a constant barrage of technical considerations will harass the designer. Dead spots will appear mysteriously where none existed two hours before, and presetting or mastering operations on a remote-control board or replugging efforts on a manual board will "swamp" the operators, making them incapable of running the cues. Finishing touches will be added to set and costumes, altering well-made plans for lighting angles, and so forth. The designer will take copious notes of these things, fixing only the most vital ones during rehearsal. The rest will be adjusted after rehearsal or before the next lighting session. Frequently reangling and regelling sessions will develop at the last moment if the theatre is new to those working in it.

Final Rehearsals

Final lighting rehearsals, like final dress rehearsals, should be a time for firming up cues already well established. Last-minute changes should be minor and few. Directors must understand that lighting-board operators are no more able to change their cues at the last rehearsal than actors are to learn a new set of lines. During the last few rehearsals the designer should remain off the telephone leading to the lighting operators or should refrain from giving them instructions from his position behind them. He should take careful notes of sequencing problems, cues missed, and mechanical problems still to be solved. These must be worked out before the next (often the last) rehearsal.

Cue systems—whether card, book, cue reader, or whatever—should be nearly superfluous by the final rehearsal. Operators should be free to watch the results of their work without panic-stricken reference to "the book" for the next cue.

20 EVALUATING A LIGHTING DESIGN

Evaluation of any artistic activity tends to be a shaky business at best. However, critical judgments have to be made, particularly by those who seek to improve their art. Sometimes evaluations have to be tentative, even hedged, and almost completely counterbalanced between praise and condemnation. Other times they can be direct, specific, and can suggest specific alternatives whose probability for success is much higher. The nature of the script itself will often determine more than any other factor whether critical judgment can be tellingly made. A script that is artistically unclear or one whose artistic merit comes from nontheatrical elements will leave the critic, like the interpretive artists before him, with little upon which to build. On the other hand, a script that is manifestly clear, has great artistic depth, and falls squarely in the realm of theatrical art, provides a point of departure for artist and critic alike.

Categories of Criticism

Generally speaking, critical evaluations of lighting will fall into two categories: that performed by the artist and the rest of the production staff for purposes of improving their arts, and "outside" critical opinions rendered up by those not part of the production effort itself. Both have their place, although the present discussion will be centered mostly on those judgments made by producing artists themselves. As a critic, the producing artist has both advantages and disadvantages over the "outsider." To his credit he can claim a degree of familiarity with the script that is seldom the property of the playgoing critic. He has a clearer picture of the reasonable potentialities of the particular production at hand and is thus less likely to apply standards which are ridiculously out of proportion to the individual case. On the other hand, he certainly cannot claim any degree of objectivity, he is liable

415

to see unsuccessful efforts only in terms of the difficulties which impeded his progress toward a solution, and his view of the play may be tinged with nonartistic considerations.

Recognizing these advantages and disadvantages, how can the producing artist go about a reasonably rewarding job of evaluating his own work? Can he exploit some of the advantages of his position and "neutralize" some of its disadvantages in such a way that he can at least make judgments that will help him to do a better job next time?

Within the limits of the number of times the production is performed there is a reasonable chance that such worthwhile judgments can be made. That is, if the artist has a chance to develop even a little objectivity to his work by observing it as a finished production for some period of time after his efforts have ceased, he can make useful judgments. However, if he is limited to "opening-night critiques," the chances are slim.

Return to the Script

Probably the most helpful thing that the lighting artist can do to prepare himself for an evaluation job is to return to the script for a fresh look at its artistic content. If he can revive some of the aesthetic response that originally guided him in his design conferences with the director, he will have something to go by. Of course, this possibility depends on the script, and is worth little effort if the script is inartistic.

Having done his work with the script, the artist may wish to apply some or all of the questions below. These questions are not intended to outline an aesthetic for criticizing lighting, but to raise issues which will tend to make the artist measure his lighting against the artistic goal of the lighting design with which he started. The more basic question of an evaluation of the original goal will often grow out of these.

1. How did lighting, acting, and directing blend together? Was it ever possible during the performance for the audience to separate these items? (Of course, this question refers mainly to acting-area lighting, but even background lighting should usually be seen by the audience as an extension of the action instead of an end in itself.)
2. Given a reasonably good blend of lighting, acting, and directing, were the results of that blend better for the part the lighting played than they would have been had the play been performed under good work lights? (This question is aimed at the "do nothing" kind of lighting design whose virtue is innocuousness and whose artistic contribution is simply getting out of the way.)
3. Was the lighting technically smooth? Did the production manifest technical facility that cleared the way for artistry? (Good artistic intentions, like other good intentions, merit little reward unless they are carried through to successful completion.)

4. Did the lighting follow convention meticulously and effectively? Was there a clear indication that the lighting artist made his artistic decisions out of conformity? (These are basically negative questions if the purpose of criticism is to advance the art of lighting. On the other hand, a meticulously handled but completely conventional lighting job often has artistic merit.)
5. Finally, the ultimate question: Did the lighting make a positive contribution to the symbolic transformation that must occur in the audience in every successful production? In different words: If the audience responded to the production as it should to a work of art, did the lighting share in motivating that response?

In one sense the last question is related to the problem of conventionality. Any artistic experience is new and unique; it represents something new and important in the life experience of all who share it. Thus it cannot be conventional. Art, in this sense, grows by rebellion against the established order, against the already known, against the sated palate, the jaded sense of taste, and most of all against the nonventuresome soul who fears the possibility of a new insight, perhaps because that new insight will destroy an old prejudice.

In an art that is technically as new and undeveloped as lighting, there is plenty of room for the rebel and the experimenter. Dogma is difficult to support in the area of lighting—and it should be! However, the critic should deplore and the artist beware of mere novelty or mere rebellion and should encourage artistic experimentation in the only honest way one can—by judging the results stringently but encouraging the experimenter to rise to better things the next time.

APPENDIX
I

PROJECTED SCENERY

Projected scenery provides one more reason for combining the tasks of the scenic designer and the lighting designer. It falls squarely between these two areas depending on the technology and the aesthetics of both for its success.

Aesthetically, scenic projection is another vastly flexible addition to the artistic tools of the designer. It offers him a range of brilliance of hue that paint cannot achieve (only translucencies can match it); an entirely new element, variability; images which can change at will; and the possibility of developing images in space in a manner that cannot be approached by conventional techniques. In spite of the fact that scenic projection has been in use in the theatre (particularly in Europe) for a long time, it is safe to say that its potentialities have only been touched upon. Its aesthetic is therefore incomplete.

Technically, scenic projection makes large demands on stage lighting. Projectors represent large loads, often special loads not amenable to regular dimmers. The problems of controlling ambient light on projection surfaces require special adjustment of the lighting design. Projector locations and the necessity for maintaining a clear space between the projector and the surfaces upon which the image appears make special demands on the arrangement of scenery.

The ideal is that the same artist design the scenery, the lighting, and the projections. Only then will a totally unified artistic result follow.

Scenic Projection Defined

The methods of projection are so varied and the new developments so frequent that only the broadest possible definition will remain operative. Thus we define as scenic projection any process which results in an image that is perceptible *as an image* to the eyes of the audience. This includes "images" formed by arranging spotlights in a manner that builds up a pattern of light on a surface visible to the audience, and images built up by insertion of "gobos" (simple slides) into ellipsoidal-reflector spotlights. It also includes images developed by such exotic devices as lasers and computers. The key thing is that there be an image and that it be visible *as such* to the audience. The existence or absence of a slide is not critical to our definition.

Aesthetics of Projected Scenery

At its present stage of development, both in the United States and in Europe, scenic projection seems to be following two somewhat divergent aesthetic paths. While these are not mutually exclusive, they do represent quite different approaches to the use of projection in production and can best be dealt with separately.

The Didactic Approach

The didactic style of production generally accompanies the use of theatre as a device for political statement. Plays of Brecht and Weiss are typical. The audience witnessing such plays is asked to make intellectual connections between events portrayed by actors on the stage and those represented on the projection screens. The material on the screen may be taken directly from life, as opposed to having been created for the theatre, although the skills of the film editor blur this distinction considerably. In any case the projection screen serves the play much in the same way that a projector and screen serve a teacher in a classroom. Hence the term "didactic" is used. Instead of making any attempt to blend the screen into the setting or to utilize projection in a manner that will blend visually into the rest of the visual production, the screen is simply treated for what it is—a device for the presentation of visual material for the intellectual consumption of the audience. Such material may at times be accompanied by a sound track as in the showing of clips from news films in the production of Weiss' *Vietnam Discourse*.

Multiple screens, variable picture sizes and shapes, montage techniques, and other film techniques often are used to increase interest and to bring various pieces of visual matter into ironic juxtaposition. Relationships between actors and the projections are direct and intellectual. Actors refer to materials on the screen or enact scenes idealogically parallel to or contrasted with the pictures. In this manner the carefully chosen "facts" of real life are brought to the stage and commented upon in the theatrical mode.

FIGURE ſ

*Projection in the Didactic Style. The setting for this production consists of
48 cubes, each capable of handling a separate image from a rear screen
projector installed in the cube. Eighty slides were provided each projector.
The entire assemble was controlled by means of a keyboard and scored as
music. The design concept was to use the repetition of images to produce a
grotesque effect highlighting the absurdity of "civilization." Production:
The Susanna Play produced in Frankfurt, Germany. Regie: Jaromír
Pheskot, scenography: Josef Svoboda.* Photo courtesy Josef Svoboda.

The essential elements of this aesthetic approach center around the
didactic and/or ironic purpose of the entire production. Any device
which furthers this purpose is desirable. Often the recognizable reality
of the pictures is their most desirable feature. Film clips of politically
famous people making political statements are a good example. The
projection techniques are selected to heighten the realization in the
audience that they are seeing actual film clips, not staged pictures.
Presentation in television or newsreel format is a common device.

It is interesting to note that the same technique can be used in productions which ape the didactic style of the political theatre without its
strong political slant. In such cases the projected material is prepared
in the manner of didacticism for the sake of style.

FIGURE *s and t*

Die Soldaten (*The soldiers*) *These two pictures show two of the many patterns of images used in this production to present a vision of the effects of war. Repetition was used to increase impact. At the end of the play the screens moved away in every direction to reveal a futuristic war machine in blinding light and with ear-shattering music. Note that the productions illustrated in this section of pictures are sound and projection presentations with living actors, although they are not shown in these detail photos. Regie for* Die Soldaten: *Václav Kašlík, scenography: Josef Svoboda. Pictures courtesy Josef Svoboda.*

FIGURE *u*
Projection on Three-Dimensional Objects. This example of didactic use of projection illustrates the distortion effects which may be gained by using three-dimensional objects as a projection surface. This technique offers an extremely wide variety of artistic possibilities to the designer willing to experiment. The production is Atomtod *(Atomic Death) by G. Manzoni as staged at Piccolo Scala. Regie: Virginio Puecher, scenography: Josef Svoboda.* Photo courtesy Josef Svoboda.

Projection as an Integrated Scenic Element

The second approach treats scenic projection as another element to be blended into a highly integrated artistic whole. It achieves its ends most fully when there is no awareness on the part of the audience that projection is being used as a separate element.

The visual potentialities of projection, its fluidity, its wide range of brightness values, its ability to exist as three-dimensional space, and its variability in time are utilized by the designer to extend the overall design possibilities open to him. Perhaps the most famous exponent of this style of production is the Czechoslovakian scenographer, Josef

Svoboda. See the production pictures in this Appendix. Projection is an important element in his vast array of devices for making the staging into a flexible, three-dimensional expression of the dramatic script. Professor Svoboda uses projection as a part of the total scenic environment, sometimes carefully blended with the rest of the scenic elements, sometimes as an accent clearly identifiable as projection.

An interesting application of projection is its use as a device for changing the shape and texture of entire settings, even actors. It can be made to flow over three-dimensional objects, through layers of gauze, or across the stage floor, giving variable dimension and texture to everything it touches. As a space-changing device it can define, divide, integrate, texture, and even expand or contract the virtual space of the production.

Another application of scenic projection also falls into this category of integrated images: the use of projections as a part of spectacle. Musical and extravaganza productions, such as those found in Las Vegas theatres, use projections because of their brilliance and rapid changeability. A stunning variety of projected backdrops, some of them with moving parts (e.g., a showboat with rotating paddle wheel!) can be produced to follow the rapid pace of such shows. These images are integrated into the production by their brightness, the style of the art work from which they originate, and the pacing of the show. No attempt is made to blend them invisibly into the remainder of the elaborate scenery of an extravaganza.

Economics of Scenic Projection

One of the most disabling illusions about scenic projection is that it offers the theatre a method of saving time and money because it will avoid much of the cost of painting drops. Particularly at the outset of work with projection, nothing could be further from the truth. Equipment will prove to be expensive, either in money or in time to build it. Preparation of image material will consume great quantities of time, or cost a lot in professional fees. Designers will find that, until they have become thoroughly accustomed to utilizing the special aesthetic possibilities of projection, it takes longer and may produce poorer results than conventional techniques.

The worst thing a producing group can do when first utilizing projection is to plan to work it into the production during the normal technical rehearsal period. Both in terms of design and as a technical element, projection must come first, not last. Extra time and extra financing must be made available early in the production calendar. The ultimate results after several productions by the same team can be both aesthetically and economically satisfying. Experienced production groups do, indeed, save time and money with projection, but only after a considerable period of heavy investment of both.

FIGURE *v*

Projection as a Part of Decor. This photo illustrates the use of projections of conventional scenes and decorative elements to create some semblance of realism. Panels form the stage space providing entrances and variety in the space itself. Production: Eugen Onegin (Tschaikovsky), *regie:* Vačlav Kašlík, *scenography Josef Svoboda.* Photo: Dr. Jaromír Svoboda.

FIGURE *w*

Opposite. Projection as Acting Area Lighting. This production of On A Sunday in August (František Hrubín) *was done at the Tyl Theatre in Prague. Note how the projections on the stage floor serve the function of acting area lighting. This calls for careful arrangement of the image material to make the light serve both purposes. Regi: Otomar Kresče, Scenography: Josef Svoboda.* Photo: Dr. Jaromír Svoboda.

FIGURE *x*

Projection Through Open Mesh Materials. This picture should be compared with Plate X in the color section. The images are projected on strips of wire screening, twisted to take shapes which need no framing. Opaque and mirrored surfaces were added to complete the design. Production: Pelleas and Mellisande *(Debussy), Royal Opera House, London. Regie: Vačlav Kašlík, scenography: Josef Svoboda.* Photo courtesy Josef Svoboda.

FIGURE *y*

Opposite. Projection on Reflective Surfaces. This is a detail photograph from a production of Tannhauser *(Wagner) produced in London at Covent Garden. It illustrates a highly sophisticated treatment of dramatic space through the use of irregular shaped reflective surfaces capable of carrying projections and also of reflecting the images of actors stationed below them in "pockets" formed by the setting pieces. The scene shown is part of the Venusberg sequence in the opera.* Scenography and photo by Josef Svoboda.

FIGURE *aa*

Projection by Linnebach Projector. This photo shows a scene from Waiting
for Godot *(Becket) as staged at Indiana University. The projection was
used only for a short period during Lucky's long speech and during his attempted suicide. It was achieved by means of a Linnebach projector hidden
behind the elevation up stage. Set design: Max Beatty and Tim Weinfeld,
Lighting: Gary Gaiser. Photo courtesy Gary Gaiser.*

FIGURE Z

Opposite. Scenography for a Production of Macbeth *(Opera by Verdi). The
scene shown is the "show of kings." Note how the setting has been arranged to provide physical separation between the setting where acting
area light must prevail and the cyclorama where the projections must be
protected from ambient light. Scenography: Analies Corrodi, Basel, Switzerland. Photo: Hoffmann.*

Earlier and Simpler Applications of Projection

Early application of scenic projection was in the area of realistic skies. Clouds, sunset, lightning flashes through storm clouds, fires in the distance—all were possible with the early scioptican, or "effects projector." This instrument was an auxiliary fitting for a plano-convex-lens spotlight, consisting of extra condenser lens to narrow the beam from the spotlight to near-parallel rays, a slide carrier for relatively large slides, and an objective lens. The whole unit attached to the front of a standard spotlight, the latter becoming the light source for the projector. Revolving disk mechanisms driven by clockwork or electrical motors offered the possibility of movement opening the way for "rain," "fire," "rippling water," and a dozen other stylized and often wooden effects—many still available today.

Modern adaptations of this system are still available and in use today, particularly in Germany. The firm Reiche and Vogel, makes a complete line of adapters which make it possible to convert their basic spotlights into projectors.

Movement of such images is almost always fatal to the focus of attention on the actors. However, slowly creeping clouds or a slowly changing sunset could be very effective. Such effects usually are projected onto whatever serves as a cyclorama. If this cyclorama is a plaster dome or a wrinkleless cloth, the results may be good. If the surface is poor and low in reflection, poor results may follow.

Recent developments in scenic projectors represent a huge amount of progress over the scioptican. Modern units are efficient, powerful, and often include elaborate devices for moving the effects or changing the slides. Since background projection has become a standard and effective device in motion-picture work (and also to some extent in television), most of the technical progress in the United States on projectors has been motivated by these industries, the theatre reaping the profits of success along with the photographic arts.

The Linnebach Projector

Another early development in the art of projected scenery was the Linnebach projector which was an adaptation of the Japanese shadow box. The device has no lenses and works on the basic laws of light emanation (see Figure I-1). It takes advantage of the fact that light travels in straight lines from its source and that it emanates from a point source according to the law of squares. Any opaque object placed between the point source and the projection surface will produce a shadow image magnified according to the law of squares. This projector has been developed into relatively sophisticated versions which will be discussed below.

The Pattern-Projecting
Ellipsoidal Spotlight

The pattern-projecting ellipsoidal spotlight is basically a lighting instrument modified to take advantage of the simple objective lens system of the ellipsoidal spotlight. The modification consists of adding a rugged slide carrier at the aperture of the spotlight. This carrier generally is provided in addition to the usual framing shutters. Any projection material able to survive the heat at the aperture may be projected with the limitation that the lens system is extremely crude. The resulting image will often be fringed with chromatic aberration and appear fuzzy.

Coverage from ellipsoidal-reflector spotlights being used as projectors will vary with the beam spread of the spotlight. Even wide-beam ellipsoidals will produce only limited coverage since they are intended for acting-area lighting. Optical efficiency will be high. The simple lens system has been designed to gather a lot of light and put it on the stage.

Technical Problems of
Theatrical Scenic
Projection

Background projection in the legitimate theatre probably offers the most nearly insurmountable optical obstacles of all projection situations. In contrast to this, motion-picture studios have been especially designed for the "process shot." The camera "looks" at the projection from only one angle at a time, and this angle can be mathematically computed to eliminate perspective errors, lens flare, ambient light problems, and a dozen other things which plague the theatre. Thus, the adaptation of background-projection apparatus from motion-picture work to the theatre must be done with a clear understanding of the special difficulties encountered in the theatre. As we examine these difficulties, we will let the word "screen" stand for whatever surface or surfaces are intended to be covered by the projected image. Projection distances are given as measurements from projector to screen. There is considerable "give" in these figures because the lens will produce an acceptably sharp picture over several feet on either side of the plane of sharpest focus. The depth of this area of acceptable focus is known as the "depth of focus" of the lens.

1. *Projection distance.* Optical laws require that the distance from the projector to the screen bear a definite relationship to the focal length of the lens. The larger the image must be, the farther away the projector must be placed, or the shorter the focal length of the projection lens must be. Theatres seldom afford even minimum projection distance, let alone that which optical experts would con-

sider "optimum." In fact, few theatres offer more than a few feet behind the cyclorama. This space limitation completely eliminates the rear-projection techniques usually used in movie studios. Even in those rare theatres where rear-projection space is available, it is seldom deep enough to allow the use of "normal" focal-length lenses.

2. *Ambient light and image brightness.* Motion-picture theatres operate the projector in a nearly dark room. Home movies are shown in darkened rooms. Slide projectors require relative darkness even when the slides are shown by machine in repeated sequence on a ground-glass screen. But theatre background projectors must work against acting-area lighting, whose intensity is often ten or more times that of a well-lighted office. Moreover, the light on the stage is directional and much of it is directed toward the projection surface. The technical term for this situation is "high ambient-light levels," which simply means that there is a lot of light which tends to wash out the picture on the "screen."

3. *Poor projection surface.* Motion pictures are usually shown on a screen whose surface is especially treated to improve its reflectance. On the other hand, theatre projectors usually must throw their image on the dull surface of a cloth cyclorama. Much of the light is absorbed, still more passes through the cyclorama; some, but not much, is reflected toward the audience.

Types of Scenic Projectors

Any discussion of scenic projectors must be based on the use of these devices. In general, two categories of usage are found:

1. Single-projector applications where one very wide-angle projector is used to produce the entire effect seen by the audience at any one time. Changes are made by fading from projector to projector in alternation. This is typically an American theatre technique. It is probably an outgrowth of the technique of the motion-picture process shot. Here the use of a single projector simplifies perspective problems and eliminates any problems of matching separate portions of an image. The single, powerful projector working on a rear screen works well for process photography; there is adquate projection distance behind the screen in a large picture studio and plenty of space in front of the screen to solve ambient light problems. When the same technique is transferred to the legitimate theatre this space is no longer available. The results are often poor.

2. Multiple-projector techniques. This method consists of building up the image to its desired size from smaller images produced by a number of projectors. It accepts the vignetting problem, often converting it into an advantage by treating the breaks between images

as design elements. Since each projector need only cover a limited area, the optical difficulties that arise from seeking extra-wide coverage are alleviated. Similarly, the power of the individual projectors need not be very high to build up a bright image.

Except for some projections on a complete cyclorama or a large rear projection screen which contain a great deal of line detail, the single-projector approach seems to have little justification. Even on a full cyclorama, soft images such as clouds are easily blended allowing the use of multiple projectors.

Adopting the multiple-projector approach still does not solve problems of wide spread in little throw distance. Most theatres are so short of space that the problem remains acute. Thus the following description of the ideal projector remains relevant.

The optical prescription for a projector to be used in the theatre is nearly impossible. The projector should have extremely high power, high efficiency, very short throw, and high resolving power to make a sharp image. Moreover, it should operate noiselessly, change slides remotely, be able to "crawl" images at exceedingly slow speeds, be able to operate on the same slide for hours without heating it to dangerous temperatures, and it should not cost too much!

Recognizing that the above projector exists only in some distant Utopia, let us examine some of the optical problems involved and see what solutions can be wrought.

Efficiency in a projector is analogous to efficiency in a spotlight. If high power is desired, lots of light must be produced, gathered up, and passed to the slide, and then the bright image must be sent to the screen with little loss. Light sources should be as powerful and efficient as possible to get as much light and as little heat as possible. Slides should be large—the larger the better—to pass large quantities of light without concentrating too much heat in too small a slide area. Objective lenses should be "fast." Their f number should be $f/3.0$ or smaller. They must have very short focal length to spread the image rapidly and smoothly over a huge cyclorama or projection sheet and they should be able to withstand high temperatures.

The following discussion is not intended to suggest that the technical problems regarding scenic projection have been completely solved. The basic problem of reconciling high ambient-light levels with short throws and poor projection surfaces remains even with the best available equipment. However, a number of workable compromises exist, which are discussed below.

Lensless Systems:
Square-Law Projectors

One simple solution to the wide beam spread problem in scenic projection is to resort to the law of squares. Extreme magnification can be had in short projection distances by this technique. Moreover, possible distortion problems arising from improper alignment of the projector with the projection surface can be overcome.

THE MODERN LINNEBACH PROJECTOR

The shadow-box projector in the theatre was invented early in the development of electrical lighting on the stage. It is simply a light-tight metal box, painted dead black on the inside to remove spurious reflections and equipped with a concentrated-filament lamp. Light from the lamp passes out through the front of the box through a glass slide on which images may be painted (see Figure I-1). Light emanates by law of squares until it strikes the projection surface. This projector is the simplest of all. Its great virtue is this simplicity, since anyone can make one and almost anyone can make slides for them.

Images from Linnebach projectors are usually rather crude. The detail that can be projected depends on the size of the filament of the lamp and the distance between the slide and the lamp. The smaller the filament and the farther away the slide, the sharper the picture. There is a limit, however, to the reduction in size of filament that can be achieved without reducing the power of the instrument below a usable level. Likewise, moving the slide farther from the filament

FIGURE *I-1*
Modern Linnebach Projector. This simple sheet metal device is a modern adaptation of Linnebach's earlier design. The lamp must be a concentrated filament lamp of the greatest power and smallest filament dimensions possible. Glass slides about 18 inches square are inserted into the slots at the front. Courtesy of Kliegl Brothers.

increases its size according to the square law and soon makes the slide too large for convenience.

Since Linnebach projectors usually are operated at either the floor level or hung well above the center of the projection surface, light distribution and distortion can be a problem. The distance from the bottom of the screen to the projector as compared with the distance to the top may result in a much dimmer picture at the top (assuming the projector is on the floor). If the slide and the projection surface are not parallel to each other, distortions will occur. If they are parallel, filament to slide distance may vary unreasonably. Thus, the Linnebach projector pays for its simplicity and wide beam with other defects that may mitigate against its use.

DIRECT-BEAM PROJECTORS

A more modern adaptation of the Linnebach principle is the direct-beam projector. This instrument also works on the basic principle of the square law, using the spherical emanation from a concentrated filament as its source. However, at least part of the time it converts the sharpness versus slide-distance problem into an asset from the liability it is with the Linnebach. The direct-beam projector consists of a well-ventilated lamp house, painted black on the inside and usually equipped with a 2800-watt, 60-volt lamp. This lamp is used because it has the smallest filament dimensions for reasonably high light output. The front of the lamp house is open. Light emanates from this front and is passed through a series of large slides mounted at varying distances from the lamp. Those slides nearest the filament are smaller and contain image material planned to have a very soft focus. Those slides farther from the lamp house carry images larger in size and intended to be progressively sharper as their distance from the lamp increases. The result is that a picture may be projected with multiple "layers" of sharpness, similar to the multiplane techniques used in an animation stand for making animated cartoons. Slides usually are painted on clear acetate instead of glass and are merely hung on a frame in front of the lamp house.

This direct-beam or filament projector is obviously a very flexible instrument. It is also quite efficient because the lamp is powerful and because the large slide size transmits lots of light. The biggest problem is bulk. Most stages simply do not have room for such a device. Some community theatres have been built with special balconylike structures for these projectors. Slide detail can also get to be a problem in that the multiple layers and large size make photographic reproduction techniques difficult.

The xenon lamp (see Chapter 2) offers the possibility of making a nearly ideal square-law projector. Before the hazards of xenon lamps were so well known, the Festspielhaus at Bayreuth devised projectors around them which were incredibly effective. A xenon lamp was sur-rounded by a half-cylinder of clear plastic upon which designs were painted. Using only a 2800-watt xenon lamp it was possible to cover the entire cyclorama with an image bright enough to resist the ambient light from bright stage lights. The small source size produced an image of great sharpness and the curved slide solved many of the distortion problems normally encountered in projecting on a cyclorama. Such a projector would be illegal in the United States today. The hazards of working with an essentially unenclosed xenon lamp are too great. However there is the possibility that safer lamps will become available or that methods of enclosing xenon lamps in transparent material that is safe will be worked out. Results of such developments could be spectacular. The xenon lamp and its recent descendants are also used as sources for lens projectors. This is dis-cussed later in this Appendix.

POOR MAN'S LINNEBACH

A miniaturized version of the Linnebach projector is worth mention-ing here because of its sharp image and adaptability to small stages. This projector uses high-intensity lamps. These are commonly used in desk lamps and similar applications where a small, highly efficient source is needed. They come in a wide variety of light output and life ratings. For projection purposes, it is possible to operate them through a transformer at approximately 20 percent over voltage. The result is a high-intensity concentrated light source which will cast a brilliant image. Since its sharpness exceeds that of any other lensless projector except xenon, the illusion of even greater intensity is achieved.

The housing can be an adaptation of the Linnebach unit with the slide mounted in slots in the front, or the direct-beam principle can be applied by mounting the slide separately. As usual, the inside of the housing must be dead black.

Since the lamps are operated over their normal voltage, they will draw more than the rated current and have short lives. Wiring must be heavy enough to carry the extra current and runs should be kept short by placing the step down transformer at the projector. The lamp life problem is not acute. Lamps are cheap. Any lamp that is badly darkened should be immediately replaced.

Those who work with these transformer-operated projectors must remember that electronic dimmers cannot normally be used to dim them. The distorted wave form produced by the dimmer will prevent the transformer from working properly unless it is a special trans-former made for just this purpose. Dimming with an autotransformer dimmer is a more practical solution if these dimmers are available.

This instrument is not intended to replace more powerful instru-ments on large stages. It is, instead, fitted to small theatres where a small, efficient lensless projector can be used for experimental staging with little expense.

Lens Projectors

Modern lens projection in the theatre is a costly and somewhat ponderous affair. The optical and physical demands of theatrical projection are stringent and no standard equipment has been developed. Much of the equipment used is hand built, custom designed, and highly expensive. The decision to use scenic projection by means of lens projectors is thus an expensive matter. Rental of such equipment is possible, but unless the designer is familiar with the equipment and the relatively obscure arts of slide preparation, short-term rental is unlikely to produce artistic results commensurate with the cost. In fact the opposite may be the case: The production may get bogged down in the details of developing the projected effects and turn out to be worse than it might have been without it. However if funds are available or can be carefully hoarded over several productions until a number of projectors can be obtained, much more is possible. Given a basic set of equipment in the hands of a designer over a considerable period of time, the artistic potentialities and the economics of scenic projection both become more favorable.

THE IDEAL LENS-PROJECTOR SYSTEM

Present projection systems are far from this ideal, but a statement of an ideal will provide some basis by which to judge what is available. The ideal lens projector should produce a bright, evenly illuminated and sharply focused image over a wide surface at a short throw. An increase of 1 foot of picture width for every foot of throw is not an unreasonable demand. The projector should be capable of being dimmed with regular theatre dimmers, should operate noiselessly, and should offer no unusual hazards. It should be widely adaptable as to slide material, variety of movement of images, sharpness of focus, correction of optical distortion, and color change of image. It should be relatively compact, easily mounted and handled, and rugged enough to withstand backstage usage. Preferably it should be economical to operate, using lamps common to stage equipment and requiring no more electrical know-how than any spotlight requires.

AVAILABLE SYSTEMS

A number of projectors are available commercially, some of which are illustrated in Figures I-2a–m. They vary considerably in the degree to which they approach the ideal. Generally, the more rugged the optical

FIGURE *I-2*
Modern Scenic Projectors. These pictures illustrate some of the types of lens projectors available today. (a) 10,000-Watt Incandescent Projector. Note the grid in the slide carrier. This is used to prepare slides by indicating distortion. Courtesy of Pani of Austria.

FIGURE *I-2b*
Stage Projector Equipped with a 5000-Watt T-H Lamp. Slide carrier takes a 17-cm square slide. Courtesy of Pani of Austria.

chain and the more versatile the aperture space, the better the unit. Efficient optics will vary with the lenses used from job to job. Some of the more critical elements in lens projectors are discussed below.

THE OBJECTIVE LENS FOR SCENIC PROJECTION

The optical demands placed on lenses for scenic projection are almost diametrically opposed to the optical laws governing the design of any lens system. Solutions to the resulting optical dilemmas are relatively

FIGURE *I-2c*
Stage Projector with Special 4000-Watt Metal-Vapor Lamp. This projector and those shown in I-2a and I-2b are sufficiently large and heavy to necessitate the attached castered base and tilt mechanism. Courtesy of Pani of Austria.

FIGURE *I-2d*
2000-Watt Projector with T-H Lamp. Note the accurate tilt adjustment and the detachable lens assembly. Courtesy of Pani of Austria.

FIGURE *I-2e*
5000-Watt Projector Equipped with Zoom Lens. This lens can produce gradually increasing or decreasing images by operation of its electric drive. Courtesy of Pani of Austria.

FIGURE *I-2f*
10,000-Watt Projector Fitted with Special Double Disk-Drive Mechanism. This will produce fire, rain, fog, snow, cloud, and water effects. Courtesy of Pani of Austria.

FIGURE *I-2g*
4000-Watt Scenic Projector with Two-Slide Changer. Courtesy of Strand Century Inc.

few and exceedingly costly. Since the demand for lenses of this complexity has been small, little research has been done and the theatre has had to make do with those lenses developed for other purposes which happen to partially fit its needs.

The basic optical problem of scenic projection is related to that discussed under the optics of the ellipsoidal spotlight. Since a bright image is needed to offset the effects of high ambient-light levels and a poor projection surface, the lens must gather up as much of the light coming from the slide as possible and efficiently focus it on the "screen." This projection calls for a "fast" lens, that is, one capable of transmitting a large amount of light. At the same time the image must be greatly magnified, preferably from as large a slide size as possible. Again, the purpose is to handle as much light as possible and to get a large image at short throws. These last two requirements are optically incompatible with the first requirement. "Fast" lenses, although they tend to have short focal lengths, by their nature usually cover only small slide areas. Thus, an *f*/1.2 lens is common for 8-mm photography but nearly unheard of for larger sizes. Likewise 35-mm cameras often are equipped (at considerable cost) with *f*/1.9 or *f*/2 lenses. However, an attempt to use such lenses on a press camera taking a 4 × 5 inch picture would result in blurred corners of the picture. The general rule is that fast, short-focal-length lenses have limited covering power; slow,

FIGURE *I-2h*
Same Projector Equipped with Multiple Remotely Controlled Automatic Slide Changer. Note the flare shield around the objective lens. Courtesy of Strand Century Inc.

FIGURE *I-2i*
High-Power Lens Projector.
Lenses are interchangeable.
See Figure I-2k. Note dou-
ble fans for lamp and slide
ventilation and separate
circuitry for lamp and fans.
Courtesy of Kliegl
Brothers.

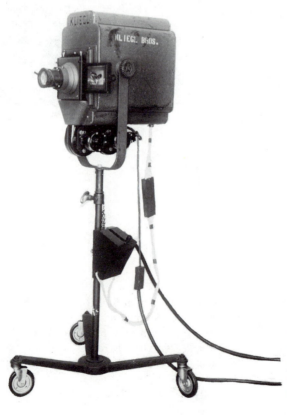

FIGURE *I-2j*
5000-Watt Scenic Projector
for Medium-Sized Slides.
Courtesy of Kliegl
Brothers.

FIGURE *I-2k*
Set of Interchangeable Lenses for Projectors Shown in I-2i and I-2j.
Courtesy of Kliegl Brothers.

long-focal-length lenses cover more slide or picture area but do not provide either the required picture size or the brilliance of image.

Two partial solutions to this lens problem have been devised. One is the use of an auxiliary or "collector" lens; the other is the development of high-powered, special lenses. As these two are discussed, the reader must consider one more special demand of projection service: The lenses must handle large quantities of heat as well as light. Many photographic lenses that have the speed and some degree of the slide coverage will be destroyed by the heat load which a projector imposes upon them.

The collector lens is a relatively simple lens, often a plano-convex unit, which is placed between the slide and the objective lens. The result is a reduced focal length for the entire lens system that varies with the distance between the objective lens and the collector. The focal length is always shorter than that of the objective alone. Moreover, the variable focal length feature is an advantage to the theatrical projector where various image sizes may be needed in different settings. Still greater variety of magnification can be obtained at reasonable cost by changing the focal length of the relatively inexpensive collector while keeping the same objective.

The drawbacks to this system are also numerous. First, the quality of the image tends to deteriorate because of the optical crudity of the collector. The collector also wastes light—at least 10 percent—and often it is difficult to get a collector-slide-objective combination that does not result in part of the light from the collector striking the barrel of the objective and spilling around it.

Although there are many manufacturers of lenses for general projection service, there are few makers of specialized lenses for very-short-throw, large-slide-coverage applications. These are the lenses commonly sought for scenic projection. In the United States, the principal supplier of new lenses of this type is the Buhl Optical Company. This firm makes several lenses that are adaptable to theatre work. One of the most useful is a 4½-inch retrofocus lens. This is basically a 9-inch lens of high quality fitted with an auxiliary lens system which halves the focal length without changing the lens-to-slide distance. The additional parts slow the lens considerably, but the result is a lens capable of covering a large slide and producing image spread of about 1 foot for every foot of throw distance. The retrofocus feature is also an advantage when a multiple-slide changer of the flopover variety is to be used. Such a changer has almost unlimited slide-carrying capacity because additional slides can be accommodated by simply increasing the number of links in the slide-carrying chain. Although dramatic productions will seldom have need of the large number of slides which such a system can accommodate, the space behind the retro-focus lens offers the ingenious designer the opportunity to install a wide assortment of special-effects machines such as lightning devices, kaleidoscopes, double-plane fire effects, and the like. This Buhl lens is not expensive as special-purpose lenses go, but many theatres will still find its $400 price almost prohibitive. Moreover, it is a bulky lens weighing about 10 pounds that is likely to unbalance some projectors.

Another useful lens, still available but neither as economical or as simple to get as it once was, is the 4½-inch Aereo Ektar. This lens was common on surplus markets after World War II. Many thousands of them were sold for as little as $25 each although they had cost the government much more when they were part of an aerial camera. Such lenses are still occasionally available on the second-hand market. If they are in good condition they make fine projection lenses. There are also a number of second-hand barrel lenses, often unmarked as to manufacture, available. Some of these may have a focal length in the vicinity of 4 inches and sufficient speed for good projection. The user will have to take his chances on their ability to handle the heat load which a 2- or 5-kilowatt lamp can produce.

One of the critical factors in the choice of any lens to be adapted to projection service is that the rear element be large enough to make it possible to collect into it the light from a large slide. If necessary a supplementary lens may be added to improve collection. It will usually be about 8 × 15 inches and will be placed as close to the slide as possible.

In general, if one must have about a foot of image width for each foot of throw distance, one must start with an objective of about 4-inch focal length and insert another lens between the slide and the objective (in addition to the one near the slide). It should be about 5 × 9 inches and must be moved toward or away from the objective to get the focal length needed. Each movement will also require that the entire lens package be moved to get the image back into focus. If not as much picture width is needed, a longer focal-length objective may be used with or without the extra lens as necessary.

Sometimes satisfactory results may be achieved with no special

FIGURE *I-2l*
Modern Xenon-Source Scenic Projector. This 4200-watt unit uses a xenon lamp like that shown in Figure 2-6. Since the basic lamp house is designed for use as a source for 35 mm movie projection (requiring a small pool of light at the aperture), the first lens to the left of the lamp house is a spread (negative) lens which widens the beam. Other lenses bring the light into convergence on the slide and eventually into the back element of the objective lens.

FIGURE *I-2m*
Closeup of Projector in Figure I-2l. This shows the converging lenses, the slide and slide changer, the slide cooling blower, and the retrofocus objective lens. This Buhl lens has a focal length of only 4½ inches, but operates at a distance of eight inches from the slide, thus providing room for the flop-over slide changing mechanism. A large number of 4" × 5" slides may be handled in the chainlike changer. Projector, Background Engineering.
Photo by Author.

objective lens at all. Several plano-convex spotlight lenses can be arranged to form a lens of sufficiently short focal length and coverage to produce the desired image. Distortion will be rampant in such a lens but it may be turned into an advantage by utilizing it to soften and change the image. For example, crude daubs of translucent paint on a slide can be transposed into a wide variety of cloudlike patterns by adjustment of such a simple lens. The range of variation is so great that the same slide may serve several purposes if overall color is changed by adding gels.

The ingenious designer will want to experiment with such things as pieces of embossed clear plastic, pressed glass, punched metal, and the like. Focusing and defocusing such items with a regular lens and also with a simple distorting lens made from spotlight lenses produces almost endless possibilities.

MULTIPLE-PROJECTOR TECHNIQUES

The use of multiple projectors to cover large-screen areas reduces the demands on lens projectors. Heat loads on slides are lessened and lenses are not asked to perform near-miracles. Preparation of slide material is easier because distortion can be dealt with piecemeal by making each slide parallel to the surface that it covers. Focus can also be individually adjusted projector by projector, providing additional artistic control. Likewise, portions of the image can be changed without disturbing the remainder.

Unfortunately even the installation of multiple projectors does not usually completely solve the short-throw problem. Space for even partial coverage is limited. Short-focal-length lenses are still likely to be needed.

Obviously a multiple-projector system will be at its worst when it is necessary to produce a linear image over a large surface, all parts closely matched. If it is necessary to change such an image in unison the situation is nearly impossible. Motion-picture techniques are available that will do this job, but at very high cost.

LIGHT SOURCES AND LIGHT-GATHERING EQUIPMENT

Light sources for lens projectors have become more varied than in the past. Originally only two were available, the incandescent lamp and the carbon arc. The carbon arc has largely disappeared from usage. The incandescent lamp is still by far the most common source. It has the great advantage of being standard in the theatre and can be controlled with standard lighting-control apparatus. The only exception to this rule is that incandescent lamps operating at over normal voltages can be dimmed by solid-state dimmers only if provided with specially designed transformers. Relatively new light sources include the xenon lamp which has now been in use for a number of years and the very recent "dirty-arc" lamps (called "HMI" lamps by one manufacturer) which offer at least partial solutions to some of the problems encountered in the use of xenon. Both the xenon and the new arcs offer levels of efficiency unapproached by the incandescent lamp. Increased efficiency means that more light can be produced with less heat. The tiny source size available with xenon lamps and their descendants also increases the optical efficiency of the projectors, making it possible to achieve high-screen brightness at remarkably low input wattages. For example, an 1800-watt xenon unit can often be equated with a 5000- or even a 10,000-watt incandescent unit, depending on operating conditions. The HMI lamp is even more efficient.

In spite of these spectacular improvements in exotic sources, the incandescent lamp will still be the most common projection light source for some time to come. Conventional stage lighting or projection-service lamps usually are used, often with stepup transformers and forced ventilation. Lamp life is thereby shortened, but light output and color temperature are improved enough to make up for this loss. However, operators should note that there is relatively little advantage in stepping up the voltage to the lamp if the slide is mostly warm colors. The lamp is already highly efficient at this end of the spectrum and little will be gained for the lamp life lost. Tungsten-halogen lamps offer a distinct advantage to scenic projection service. Their higher efficiency and color temperature make it unnecessary to overvoltage them. In fact, increasing the voltage above normal increases the somewhat remote risk that the lamp may explode. All T-H lamps operate above atmospheric pressure even at normal voltage.

THE LAMP HOUSING

Housings for projection service tend to be bulky. They must contain the lamp, the reflector and condenser system, often a heat filter, and inevitably a blower or perhaps two. Additional electrical equipment usually is added in the form of speed controls for the fans, the voltage-boosting transformer for the lamp, and possibly an interlocking relay to prevent the operation of the lamp without the fans. The latter is a good addition to any projector because one mistake can break enough lenses to exceed the cost of installing this relay.

Since the housing is the only defense against fan noise, it should be acoustically insulated to reduce reverberation as much as possible. This insulation will also tend to keep the outside of the instrument relatively cool—something that will be appreciated by those who have to work near a hot projection machine in cramped quarters. Mounting provisions should allow for the tilting of the machine up and down. More elaborate supports are usually best left to the needs and ingenuity of the using theatre.

Light-gathering and focusing equipment in the lamp house should be as flexible as possible. Slide size and distance inevitably vary. Also the possibility of controlling the distribution of light over the projection field is desirable. Sometimes a hot spot can be converted into an asset if it is movable. The installation of a piece of heat-filtering glass between the condensers and the slide or between the condensers themselves is often desirable. Such a filter should be removable because it will waste some light that may be critically needed at times. It will also tend to raise the color temperature of the light striking the slide. The heat filter should be removed when the projector is to be operated at reduced voltages with warm-colored slide material.

CONDENSING LENSES

Condensing lenses are usually simple plano-convex lenses of a quality somewhat better than those used in ellipsoidal spotlights. The latter lenses are a reasonable substitute if better lenses are not available, but they will have a higher breakage rate and not be quite as effective as light gatherers. Probably two or three condensers will be needed to focus the light on the slide properly. Of course, each air-to-glass surface wastes light, so the condensers should be as few as possible. The problem is that condensers of short focal length are usually too susceptible to heat breakage because of their thickness. Often two lenses of long focal length will stand up where one lens of short focal length would fail. See Figure I-3 for a typical arrangement.

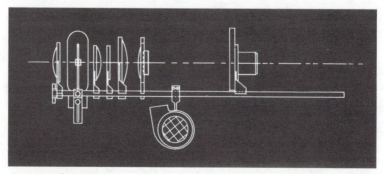

FIGURE *I-3*

Working Parts of a Typical Scenic Projector. This outline drawing shows a typical arrangement of the main optical parts of a scenic projector. From left to right they are: spherical reflector, lamp, collector condenser, heat filter, second condenser, front condenser, slide (directly in front of front condenser), and the prime objective lens. A blower is shown in position to cool the slide. Supplementary lenses often are added to the prime objective lens. The distance between the slide and the front condenser frequently varies greatly from this illustration. The mounting of all optical parts on heavy rods, approximating an optical bench, is a good practice. Courtesy of Universal Screen Company.

The condensers are properly adjusted when the pool of light they produce just covers the diagonal of the slide and then narrows to fall within the confines of the rear element of the objective system.

APERTURE EQUIPMENT

The devices for holding and changing the slide material will vary with the needs of each production and with the nature of the material itself. Thus flexibility is the rule. It should be possible to accurately align glass slides with the aperture, to change them rapidly, or to abandon them entirely in favor of moving systems that enable the image to be "crawled" either horizontally or vertically, as needed, at any speed. Furthermore, the entire carriage mechanism should be demountable to allow the installation of various Polaroid-effect machines and devices of the designer's invention.

Crawl devices are designed to move an endless belt of projection material through the aperture at varying speeds. For theatrical use, extremely slow speeds are likely to be most useful. For instance, *Amahl and the Night Visitors* requires the Star of the East to move across the stage during a period of some 60 to 80 minutes. This movement represents a travel at the aperture of from 5 to 7 inches, depending on slide size. Slow but variable speed-gear motors operating on direct current are commercially available which will produce excellent results with either rotary or crawl devices. Their speed controls include a dc supply and the circuitry to effect speed control. It is possible for an experienced electronics expert to construct such controls at considerable saving. Ideally, the motors should vary over a wide speed range in either direction and be capable of starting or stopping with no jerking. Obviously the remainder of the mechanism must be made with considerable precision if wobbles or vibrations are to be avoided. Any vibration will be multiplied by the throw distance. A tiny movement at the projector may appear as a highly visible jerk on the projection surface.

A possibility little explored at this stage in the art of scenic projection is the use of multiple planes of projection material in the aperture. Moving and stationary material can thus be accommodated and the sharpness of focus can be varied from plane to plane. Potentialities here are little more than speculation at this time.

Operating Lens Projectors

A standard procedure for placing lens projectors into operation should be followed to avoid damaging equipment. The greatest hazard is that the lamps may be turned on without the blowers. This will usually destroy the entire condenser system in perhaps 10 seconds—sometimes even faster. Standard procedure should require that fans be turned on and checked individually to see if they are in operation before any lamps are turned on. It is not enough to listen for the sound of fans unless only one is in use.

Since fan noise may be a significant part of the noise environment of the production, it may be advantageous to turn on all fans before the audience enters the theatre and leave them on for the entire production. Thus the audience will become accustomed to the fan noise as it does to air-conditioning noise. Sometimes an autotransformer dimmer can be inserted into the fan circuit as a speed control and the entire array of fans slowed slightly. This will reduce the noise a great deal because air noise tends to vary with the third power of the velocity. Fans should be carefully checked for overheating if this is done, and the projectors themselves should be checked for adequate ventilation.

Before each performance each projector should be checked to determine the state of the slide. Most slide materials tend to fade and must be replaced periodically. The fade rate will vary with the intensity of the lamp, the time on, and with the nature of the source. High ultraviolet sources such as xenon have a greater tendency to fade slides than incandescent lamps.

If crawl or rotating devices are involved, these should also receive nightly checkouts before the house opens. Finally, the lamp should be checked nightly or, if it is a T-H lamp, a rough log should be kept of time on at "full up" and replacements should be scheduled at intervals short enough to avoid any failures. Projectors are usually key devices in a production and should not be operated with anything but the most reliable of lamps. If xenon lamps are in use, they will have to be replaced on a regular schedule. If xenon lamps are operated past their rated life, they become highly dangerous because they are increasingly apt to explode. Many xenon-lamp power supplies are provided with operating time meters to assist the operator in keeping track of lamp life. *Xenon lamps should be handled or replaced only by authorized, trained personnel using approved safety gear.* It is dangerous merely to open the lamp house without proper equipment.

The Projection Surface

When a screen is used as a projection surface it will have to meet the requirements listed below. Frequently there will be no "screen" as such; the images will be reflected from scenery, the stage floor, actors and costumes, or special materials designed into the setting as a foil for projection. For example, the designer may include varied layers of gauze or scrim in the setting specifically for the purpose of projecting images onto and through this material. The results will be strikingly three dimensional if the projectors are properly angled. Still another example is the use of closely spaced cotton cord, a device often used by Josef Svoboda. This may be placed in front of a projection sheet to allow the use of rear projection without any visible screen, or it may serve as a low-efficiency projection surface itself, or both.

If projections are being used as didactic devices, a screen or screens will be much in evidence. No attempt will be made to blend such didactic screens imperceptibly into the setting. However if there is a visible screen other than a cyclorama, which by its encompassing nature blends itself into the setting, and this screen is not treated as a didactic device, the designer will encounter a problem. A screen generally refuses to look like anything except what it is; a large blank space occasionally filled with images. The best solution is to avoid getting into the problem in the first place. Svoboda's rear projection screen concealed behind a string curtain is a good example of a way to avoid the problem. An ingenious designer will arrive at other equally good solutions if he begins with the premise that a screen, unhidden, will not do.

The following discussion of projection surfaces describes the technical requirements they must meet if they are to work well. Designers will have to work within these conditions or adjust for their absence.

EFFICIENCY OF PROJECTION SURFACES

Front projection screens are related in terms of "gain." For this purpose a standard reference material is used. This is a block of pure magnesium carbonate, a very white substance with nearly perfect diffuse reflection. A material that equals the surface of this block in reflection is said to have a gain of "1." Many screen materials have a gain number greater than 1. This means that they selectively reflect a greater portion of the light back toward the source than does the standard reflector. Thus viewers at the axis receive a brighter picture at the expense of those far on the periphery. Since it is not practical to view a screen at angles near 90° to the axis of projection anyway, such gain is a distinct advantage. A beaded motion-picture screen, for example, will increase the brightness of the projected image greatly over a reasonable viewing angle and drop off rapidly beyond that angle. However, viewing angles for scenic projection cannot always be so carefully controlled as those in a motion-picture theatre. It usually becomes necessary to sacrifice high gain for wider dispersion if those on the sides of the house are not to view a very dim picture. From this point of view, the matte surface of a muslin cyclorama is a relatively good projection surface. It will provide wide dispersion although its reflectance may be rather low.

SPECIAL SURFACES FOR FRONT PROJECTION

Ideally a front projection surface should have wide dispersion over the entire angle of view of the audience. It should also have high reflectance. White matte surfaces meet these requirements. However another problem may enter the picture; the reflective surface may also be highly susceptible to ambient light making it difficult to light the actors properly.

Cycloramas usually meet the specifications for front projection rather well, if they are clean. They are also generally far enough removed from the acting area to reduce ambient-light problems to a tolerable level. When the designer seeks to use other scenic elements for front projection surfaces the problem gets more difficult. He must choose surfaces which serve the needs of the stage design and only occasionally can these surfaces have the reflectance he needs (assuming he can solve the ambient-light problem). More often the designer will have to use low-reflectance materials and brighten the image by the use of higher-powered projectors. Fortunately modern equipment can offer him this option, if he has the equipment. If not, he will have to avoid the use of low-reflectance surfaces.

SURFACES FOR REAR PROJECTION

Rear projection surfaces face the same problems with an additional complication. If the light passing through the screen is not sufficiently diffused, a hot spot or flare will be visible to those in the audience who are on a sight line that includes the projection lens. In extreme cases the lens itself will be visible as a bright spot of light. One solution to the problem is to place the lens where no one can see it, but this usually results in a dim picture for everyone. A better solution is to use a screen with a high dispersion rating. Unfortunately such screens tend to have low transmission factors. Preferably the rear projection screen should also transmit light from the front, enabling it to absorb ambient light from the stage lighting. This principle is similar to that used in the construction of "black-front" television tubes. It is one of the great advantages of rear projection over front projection.

FRONT OR REAR PROJECTION

It is unfortunate that this alternative will not be available to most existing theatres. Obviously, if there is no space for rear projection, the question is academic. However, new theatres are being built, especially in the educational theatre. It is often possible to design such theatres with storage or construction space directly upstage of the acting area sufficient to allow rear projection. Such a theatre offers the designer the option of either system.

Given his option, there are no set rules that will apply to all cases. One can only cite the advantages and disadvantages of each system, leaving the relative weighing of these items to the designer as he approaches each production.

The three advantages of rear projection are its efficiency, its economy of acting space, and the ease with which distortion of the image can be controlled. The rear screen is highly efficient when properly designed because it can absorb and eliminate ambient light that would destroy an image of the same intensity on a front screen. It is theoretically possible to make front screens more efficient, but they may become too susceptible to ambient light.

The rear screen saves acting space by eliminating the shadow zone which must be kept clear in front of a front projection surface if actor shadows are to be avoided. Such a shadow zone is often 15 feet in depth. In the case of the rear screen, the actor can approach to within a foot or so of the screen if he may be lighted by side lighting only.

It is almost inevitable that the projector for front screen use will be placed far off the optical axis of the system. It is usually above or to one side of the projection surface, thus producing great distortion and light distribution troubles. A properly designed rear-projection system will allow the projector to be placed on or very near to the optical axis, eliminating most of these difficulties. Often the projector is "aimed" at a point in the center of the audience to produce the greatest image brilliance over the greatest audience area. This aim usually produces little distortion.

The two disadvantages of rear projection are the need for a considerable space behind the projection surface and the necessity that the surface itself be especially designed to transmit light instead of reflecting it.

Front projection obviously eliminates the disadvantages cited above. Its greatest value is that it can operate where rear projection cannot even be considered. An efficient cyclorama surface is all that is needed.

The disadvantages of front projection are mostly centered around the problems in handling ambient light on the projection surface and in locating the projector.

Given a good translucent projection surface and sufficient space for rear projection, there is no reason that front and rear effects cannot be combined. Such a good surface will still reflect enough light from its front to allow remarkably effective blending of images and lighting. There is also the possibility that such usual handicaps as actor shadows may not always be a negative feature—experimentation offers many possibilities.

One thing seems certain: An attempt to force an image through a muslin cyclorama from the rear is doomed to failure. Any muslin good enough to make a good cyclorama is too opaque.

The designer working with rear projection should experiment extensively with the blending effects that can be achieved by projecting images from the rear of the sheet and softening these with cyclorama lighting from the front. Indeed, this seems to be one way to control the attention value of the projected image. Dimming the image alone is seldom satisfactory since it leaves the projection surface dark and susceptible to every stray beam of light that comes its way. Moreover a dark background is not always artistically desirable.

Location of the Projectors

Scenic projectors can be made to operate remotely. During the actual run of a production remote operation is highly desirable because the presence of an operator will introduce vibrations that will jiggle the image. However, these machines require almost constant adjustment during the preparation of a production and frequently need servicing even between acts. Thus an inaccessible projector is usually an impossibility. Since any sway or vibration will be magnified in the image from the projector, these machines are seldom hung from above except from the heaviest and steadiest of light bridges. The best mountings are those planned as an architectural part of the building to be as free from vibration as the structure itself. Some modern thrust-stage theatres have had such positions designed into the building as walk-in locations for both projection and lighting equipment. These locations are mainly designed for use in front projection. Rear-screen projectors are usually mounted on a scaffoldlike structure that raises them to a position near or on the optical axis. Lens flare must be carefully masked from such locations by means of baffles cut to fit tightly around the lens barrel.

Operating noise will sometimes govern location of a projector. In this case, rear-screen mounting retains the advantage by being farther from the audience. Usually a better solution to the noise problem than letting it govern projector location is to reduce the speed of the fans slightly and to provide more acoustic treatment of the lamp housing.

In no case should a projector be mounted in an enclosure without adequate ventilation. Large amounts of heat are generated by the lamps in these units and this heat must be rapidly moved away from the instrument.

Lighting While Using
Scenic Projection

Arrangements of stage lighting for use with projectors will depart from normal because of two necessities: (1) the lighting artist must bend every effort to reduce ambient light on the projection surface. He may still provide cyclorama lighting on the sheet itself as a blending agent or to produce sky effects in those scenes not requiring projections, but he must angle every acting-area instrument so as to avoid bouncing light into the sheet inadvertently. (2) The aesthetics of a luminous projected image will require a different degree of balance in the acting-area lighting. Higher contrast ratios will often be needed and in all cases the lighting artist will want to have enough acting-area light at his disposal to make sure than he can control the focus of attention, directing it away from the projections and toward the actors.

Generally these two requirements are not incompatible. Acting areas will often need to be angled at more than the normal 90° horizontal separation to throw the spill light into the side stage areas where it is more easily controlled. Likewise, the vertical angles will tend to be steeper. Both of these changes will have the effect of increasing shadow contrast on the actor's face. Key light should not need to be substantially reduced provided the projector and surface are of good quality. However, blending light from general illumination instruments will often have to go. Overall intensities may be trimmed slightly by using less fill lighting and fewer area lights at any given moment. In no case, however, should projection dictate an overall effect of near darkness backed up by a bright image unless the artistic demands of the production call for sharp focus of attention on the image material instead of the action. The greatest improvement in stage lighting for use with projection will come with careful elimination of those rays of light that are doing little or no good anyway. Generous use of barn doors, hoods, and flare-cutting shields of special design will often do as much as relocating instruments at no loss of light that is really needed.

Lighting areas close to the projection sheet can be done with ellipsoidal spotlights adjusted for sharp cutoff. Top- or side-lighting positions can be used effectively, provided floor and setting do not bounce too much light.

Just as effective as changing the angles and quantity of lighting and often less limiting to the production, is the treatment of reflective surfaces on the stage. All floor surfaces not visible to the audience should be painted flat black. Those surfaces visible to the audience should be as dark and diffuse in reflective characteristic as the design of the setting will allow. The stage floor itself is usually the worst offender and often the most difficult to treat. Light wood finishes, particularly glossy varnishes, are taboo. Dull, dark wood filler is the best finish. A near-black canvas ground cloth would be the ideal floor covering as far as projection is concerned.

In extreme cases special floor-surface treatments may be used to prevent reflection of light into the projected image. Josef Svoboda cites a case in which portions of the stage floor were covered with a rubber material which consisted of closely spaced short tabs of black rubber standing vertically from the surface. These served as light traps cutting reflectance nearly to zero. When walked on, the tabs flattened out, springing back when the foot was removed. The material made it possible for an actor to work directly in front of a rear screen and be lighted. Black carpeting with thick nap would serve almost the same purpose.

FIGURE *bb*

Lighting and Scenic Projection. This photo of a production of Das Elfte Gebot (Samberk) *at the Theater des Staatlichen Films, Prague shows a typical arrangement of lighting to avoid ambient light on the projection surface. Note that the acting areas have been located well down stage and that angles of key and fill have been so arranged that little light is reflected from the floor or props in the direction of the screen. In severe cases, when actors must play very close to the projection surface, special non-reflective floor covering may be used. Direction: Alfréd Radok, scenography: Josef Svoboda.* Courtesy Josef Svoboda.

Vertical surfaces occasionally turn out to be giant reflectors sending ambient light into the projection sheet. Usually a minor change in angle will solve the greatest part of this problem. Costumes will not offer any difficulties unless the actor must play very near to the sheet while wearing highly reflective clothing. In this case he may be surrounded with an unwanted "halo" of spill light. A dark costume or reblocking is the only solution.

Since at least some of the stage lighting must bounce somewhere, the designer will be well advised to provide "light traps" in the setting. These will be areas of rough, dark texture whose low reflectance and dispersive effect will dispose of bounce from side lighting and area lighting.

Blending of the Projection and the Setting

Blending of projections into the *mise-en-scène* is a difficult matter far beyond the scope of this discussion even if it were a fully developed art, which it is not. Only a few hints can be offered. First, color har-

FIGURE *CC*

Interaction between Live Actors and Projected Images. Several levels of dramatic symbolism may be developed by this technique. A montage may be created in which the same actor who is seen "live" on stage is also seen in the projected image(s). Dramatic interaction may then provide the director a vast range of possibilities. As many as three or four levels of visualization may develop. Production: The Last Ones (Gorki), *Scenography: Josef Svoboda. Photo: Dr. Jaromír Svoboda.*

FIGURE *dd*

Controlling focus of attention and spill light. This picture illustrates a happy solution to what might have been a difficult problem. The actress on the rope bridge must be well lit while playing in front of the projection surfaces. This must be done without spilling light into the projection screens and must provide a good key-fill ratio for the scene. The high-angle side lighting shown here solves the problem nicely. Note that similar high angle lighting has been used to light the two figures on the floor stage left. The production is the Caucasian Chalk Circle (Brecht) *as done by the University of California at Santa Barbara. Direction: Ted Hatlen, scenery and lighting: Don Childs.* Photo courtesy University of California at Santa Barbara Theatre Department.

mony between the overall tone of the projection and the tone of the setting and lighting is necessary. In this regard, projections of vivid multicolor photographs are usually undesirable unless these are to be seen as a realistic panorama through a window. Often single-color or two-color images are far easier to handle. Second, the border between the projection surface and the rest of the visible stage space should be emphasized as little as possible. Of course, the obvious exception to this rule is the "through-the-window" scene. Generally, any setting device that tends to blur or diminish the line of demarcation is desirable. Third, and by far the most important, the projected material should be a vital part of the entire scenic environment. It should elicit a response from the actors as a part of their essential dramatic environment and become almost an indistinguishable part of the total *mise-en-scène* for the audience. It is fatal to add projections as a sort of "added attraction."

Preparing Image Material for Scenic Projection

Hand-Painted Slides

There are still available in Europe several specialists who have the skill and patience to hand paint projection slides. This is an art which closely resembles that of the miniaturist. Such slides, when properly done, become masterpieces in their own right. Since the originals are used in the projectors, they must be carefully handled and stored. Replacement is often difficult, if not impossible. (Many European theatres have files of slides dating back many years which are still used in their repertory. In some cases the original artists have long since died.) One or two slide painters can also be found in the United States.

Most designers have neither the skill nor the time to hand paint slides. Fortunately it is no longer necessary. The photographic methods described below can produce the same degree of precision and artistry and with the great advantage that the original need never be placed in the production.

Photographic Techniques

The conventional way of preparing slide material for use in background work in motion pictures and television is photographic. Original material is selected or drawn, depending on the nature of the subject, and this material is copied photographically, Eventually, after several photographic steps, this material is made into a slide. For instance, a motion-picture process-shot background is often a photograph taken on location, made into a slide, and projected by rear projection on a screen which forms the background for the process shot. Perspective is maintained by meticulous care in the placement of the taking camera with relationship to the camera in the original photo. The results sometimes defy detection.

Art work (as opposed to photographs) prepared for professional use is usually made up to a standard size determined by the aspect of the finished image and the technical demands of the photographer. Flat-but smooth-finish paper stock is used to avoid paper textures and reflections. Colors are carefully adjusted to compensate for distortions that will occur later in the process. When the art work is finished, it is photographed, usually in color, and the film is specially processed to produce slide-contrast ranges. The photographer seeks a very thin, clear image, allowing some color distortion to occur. Hopefully, this distortion has already been compensated for in the original art work. During the photographing of the material, distortion can be intro-duced to compensate for the position of the projector in relation to the screen, if this is known. Finally, the developed image is stripped from its backing and adhered to a piece of glass, making a slide. Cost of such a process for photographic work alone often runs to $25 per slide and duplicates cost about as much as originals. Several days to a week must be allowed for photography and processing, plus whatever inter-val is required for shipping.

The results of this professional process will be precise, properly scaled as to density, and as scientifically accurate with regard to the original art work as it is possible for a fine photographic craftsman to make them. But the artistic worth of these slides will all derive from the original art work. The designer will have no control over any of the intermediate processing steps during which he might make adjust-ments to augment his art work.

Preparation of full-color slides by the designer himself is usually impossible unless he is a specialist in the field of color development. Usually far too much room and equipment will be needed and the process will take up too much of the designer's time when he can ill afford it. However, the preparation of black-and-white material is not nearly so difficult and time consuming. Neither is it so costly. More-over, the black-and-white image need not be projected in black and white unless that is what is needed. The transparent portions of the image can be colored simply by placing a piece of color medium over the projector lens. The image itself can be toned to produce several colors by photographic means. There are also available a number of nonphotographic processes by which copies of the image material can be developed in color on a transparent base. These copies can then be superimposed to produce a multicolored image. Such nonphoto-graphic processes are discussed below.

All of these processes, photographic and others, are contrast-increas-ing procedures. An increase in contrast makes it possible for the designer to make desirable alterations in the image during intermedi-ate steps which have the effect of reducing contrast. The contrast then is regained later in the processing. For example, an image can be pho-tographed in long-scale black-and-white film and developed for low contrast. This process will often catch detail that might otherwise be missed. After various photographic steps in which the desired parts of the image are brought out, the final image is prepared on high-contrast material that produces a slide of the proper density but with the image material as needed.

If the designer is doing his own photographic work, or is in the darkroom as it is being done, he can control every step of the process and extend his influence over the finished material. He can perform such photographic manipulations as dodging while enlarging, localizing development, selecting various papers and films whose characteristics match his needs, and adjusting time and temperature during development processes. He can superimpose images from more than one source in various sizes on the same film if this is necessary. He can determine whether to project a positive or a negative image of the material as the final product. Images of clouds, for instance, are often best worked up in negative form and then reversed during processing.

Final preparation of the slide material from the processed negative should be reduced to a repeatable mechanical process so that as many duplicates as are needed can be produced. A reliable supply of duplicates to replace those lost to heat damage or accidents will be assured.

It is obvious that the designer wishing to work in the area of scenic projection should familiarize himself with photography, particularly the many techniques commonly used in the darkroom to alter the original image.

Other Materials and Techniques

There are a number of rewarding ways of preparing slide material that do not involve the use of an ordinary camera or the photographic darkroom. Some of these appear to be flexible and useful techniques often useful by themselves or in combination with the photographic work. There are two general categories: Xerox processes and ammonia processes.

XEROX

Xerography depends on the transfer of images by means of electrically charged plates of special materials whose charge distribution is altered by exposure to light. The image thus formed is then transformed to whatever base is needed. While the common Xerox machine is usually a 1:1 copier, a camera unit is available that will increase or reduce image size by 50 percent per operation. Further size adjustments are made by rephotographing. Xerography is basically a high-contrast, line-development process, but some gray-scale work can be accomplished. The degree of flexibility will depend on the skill of the operator. Costs are relatively high if this machine is to be used only for producing theatrical images. However, if this use can be combined with other functions—for instance, the preparation of duplicate library cards from filmed originals—the cost can be shared and thus reduced.

Although Xerox offers a fine means of making copies on transparent stock from a wide variety of image sources, tests indicate that the Xerox image itself does not survive well in the intense heat of a scenic projector. The image material, carbon black, absorbs heat rapidly and destroys the base material ruining the slide. (Dense black-and-white photographic images suffer from a similar fault.) Therefore Xerox serves best as an intermediate step leading to an image finally reproduced on a more durable material.

AMMONIA PROCESSES

Many designers will already be familiar with the basic ammonia processes; they are those used to reproduce working drawings usually known as "blue-line" or "black-line" prints. However, manufacturers of these materials make transparent stock that can be developed by the same ammonia processes. When developed, this material produces positive images in a wide variety of colors. The background is clear and quite heat resistant, making it possible to use these materials either as intermediate image material or to produce the final slide. The technique is simple: A "master" made up of either lines or simple gray scales is placed over a piece of the sensitized material and the whole exposed to light, preferably light rich in near-ultraviolet radiation. After sufficient exposure to destroy the sensitive materials in the lighted areas, the latent image is developed by placing it in a chamber containing ammonia gas. No liquid developer touches the material and the finished image is dry and immediately usable with no further treatment.

The trade name of one of these materials is Chromtex. It offers the designer many opportunities for experimentation. Certain limitations must be noted. First, the process is a direct positive process. Either a negative must be made on special diazo material supplied for this purpose or a photographic negative must be made. Second, enlargement or reduction of the image is difficult. A photographic enlarger will not produce enough near-ultraviolet light to allow reasonable exposures. Again, the solution is to return to photography. Finally, these materials are best suited to the reproduction of line drawings. They handle gray-scale materials only moderately well. Considerable increase in contrast is inevitable when using these materials. This contrast is not always a disadvantage because it allows the designer to "develop away" many minor blemishes and erasures in his art work.

There are several advantages obvious at once to the experimenter in scenic projection. The cost is low, in fact almost insignificant, once the experimental stage is over. The equipment needed is simple. A blue-print printer is desirable but not vital. Any source of ultraviolet light will make an exposure, including a fluorescent desk lamp at close range. Any simple enclosure such as a large jar will serve as the developing chamber. A large, clear plastic tube with a bottle of ammonia at the bottom is ideal. The final results can be as effective as the patience and ingenuity of the designer will allow.

The amount of color developed up in these materials by the ammonia depends on the exposure. The more light that strikes the stock, the less image will be developed at that point. Thus the shadow of a dark line on the master produces a dark line on the copy—no negative is involved. The designer is left with two variables to control as he determines the contrast and detail he wants in his slide: He can control the contrast in the original art work and he can adjust the exposure of the slide. Generally, the third variable usually available to the photographer, time and temperature of development, is not available in this process. The materials are designed to be developed to completion and no "stop bath" is available to remove whatever undeveloped materials remain. The only way to produce clear highlights with ammonia materials is to develop them up completely.

A process developed by this writer may be worthy of further experimentation by readers: The original art work is done on frosted-plastic color medium. Either soft frost or heavy frost can be used depending on the amount of texture desired in the final product. Soft frost produces no visible texture; heavy frost can be made to produce some texture if properly handled. The images are worked up on the frosted surface using a soft lead pencil or a red crayon pencil. The latter produces subtler effects but will not block the printing light completely. The graphite from the pencil can be blended with the fingertip or with the corner of an eraser. It can be erased completely if desired. After the image is built up to the desired contrast and detail, it is copied on Chromtex. The copy can be made in either primary or secondary colors or in several other tints. If the slide has been worked up in the same size as the finished material, all that remains to do is to mount the image. The Chromtex image, if it is in black or yellow, can be placed in a photographic enlarger and enlarged or reduced as needed on photographic stock. It will be reversed in this process and can be then printed reversed, if desired, or reversed again photographically before returning to Chromtex.

These Chromtex images withstand the heat of scenic projectors to a remarkable degree. A single deep-blue image will often last through an entire performance and still be usable for at least part of another. Other colors are usually even more durable. The base material is flame resistant.

Mounting of these images will depend on their proposed use. If stationary images are desired, the Chromtex can be bound to glass backings with cellophane tape leaving two sides free to expand or shrink with the heat.

Probably the greatest hazard in the entire process is the use of the 28° Baumé ammonia, a powerful, corrosive liquid whose fumes can paralyze the breathing apparatus. If the liquid is spattered on the skin, it burns like any other strong alkali. It can be exceedingly dangerous to the eyes. However, this ammonia rapidly loses its strength when left exposed to the air and is easily washed away with water. In normal use as developer for Chromtex, it soon loses its strength and must be replaced. Replacement is not expensive and the nearly exhausted ammonia makes fine cleaner for spotlight lenses. Use in a well-ventilated room.

Any translucent or transparent material can be transferred to Chromtex as long as it will pass near-ultraviolet light. Drawings done on tracing paper with a soft lead pencil or painted with India ink work well. Photographic negatives or positives work well. If the photograph is on glass, such as a professionally prepared projection slide, it can be duplicated by simply placing the glass slide over a piece of the Chromtex and exposing the "sandwich" to sunlight or light from a fluorescent lamp at close range.

Chromtex images can be superimposed when bound to the glass backing to make a multiple-color image. Graduated fields of color such as those intended to suggest the shading of the sky near the horizon can be developed up on a separate piece of Chromtex and superimposed over other material as needed. However, all-over color is best produced at the projector by placing pieces of gelatine or plastic color medium in front of the lens. This method is more efficient because the heat absorbed by these gels is dissipated outside of the aperture and does not damage the slide. Moreover, it now becomes possible to change the color of a slide from scene to scene without preparing a new slide.

These processes are offered in the hope that they will inspire the reader to pursue them further and to develop his own techniques in the still infant art of scenic projection.

APPENDIX
II

ORDERING LAMPS FOR STAGE USE

Economics

Purchase of incandescent lamps for use in stage-lighting instruments will represent a sizable portion of the total operating budget of many theatres. Since the economics of lamp purchasing favor the large institutional order, careful planning ahead as much as a year in advance of need will often result in large savings. Schools, colleges, and municipalities will often make their lamp purchases for general service use on the basis of a lamp contract made annually or biennially as the result of competitive bidding. If stage lamps can be included in this contract, savings of approximately one-half of the usual retail lamp cost can often be effected. However, such savings can usually be accomplished only by the purchase of case lots of lamps.

The above discount conditions, plus the necessity for special ordering of some types of stage lamps no matter what the price, make it necessary that the stage-lighting artist plan his lamp inventory carefully to avoid emergency buying. Such emergency purchases will always be made at the highest price and often result in the use of the wrong lamp because the proper one is not available immediately.

The first step in organizing lamp purchases is standardization. As few different lamps as possible should be stocked. Base types should be as consistent as possible throughout the stage. Other lamp configurations should be held to as few as possible. This will facilitate case-lot ordering and make it more feasible to keep an adequate supply of lamps on hand.

Current Lamp-Ordering Data

465 The only practical way to keep abreast of new developments in the manufacture and distribution of lamps is to keep on hand a copy of

the latest lamp-ordering bulletin of at least one of the major lamp-manufacturing companies. Such bulletins are published frequently, twice annually in the case of the General Electric Company. They may be received by having a salesman from the company place your name on the mailing list or by writing directly to the manufacturer in the name of the organization purchasing the lamps. Since such bulletins are expensive to publish, they are not usually sent to anyone who inquires; instead they are reserved for potential customers. Consistent buying from one company will guarantee continuous receipt of up-to-date bulletins.

When ordering lamps from a manufacturer's bulletin, it is necessary to use the code designation for the lamps needed and to indicate the date and/or number of the bulletin from which you took the information.

Data Needed for Purchase of Lamps

Stage lamps are precision instruments; they cannot be ordered by wattage alone as are household lamps. A somewhat standard method of coding the information about lamps is known as the ANSI code. It consists of a series of three letters which apparently bear no analogical relationship to the data they represent. Thus a common 500-watt T-H lamp for ellipsoidal-reflector spotlights is known as EGD. Not all manufacturers use this code, however.

Since lamp manufacture is in a state of rapid flux many new lamps, including retrofit types with overlapping applications, are coming on the market. The only solution is an up-to-date lamp substitution manual such as the GE *Stage/Studio Lamps*. A list even a few months old may already be out of date.

The following list of data is provided as a sample of that which is needed when ordering a lamp without the use of a special code number or catalog number. However the best way of being assured of getting the proper lamps is to establish contact with a reputable supplier who keeps up with the almost daily changes and will take the time to pursue the exact details of your requirements.

Filament type: monoplane or biplane or several others (for example, C 13 or C 13-D)

Distance from filament center to tip of base (known as "Light Center Length"; abbreviated LCL)

Wattage at rated voltage (specify both)

Base size and type (for example, medium bipost)

Envelope size and type

Optimum operating position

Color temperature at rated voltage

Average life at rated voltage, often expressed as "spotlight service" or "floodlight service"

APPENDIX
III

ALLOWABLE AMPERAGE IN COMMON STAGE-LIGHTING CONDUCTORS

This table reflects the usual allowable amperages for stage-lighting service for portable cables, asbestos "motion-picture" wire, and the like. The lighting expert should consult local codes before computing the allowable load for permanently installed wiring, or for special applications involving motors, unusual power-factor conditions, and the like.

CURRENT (AMPS) FOR WIRE SIZE (AWG)	CURRENT (AMPS) FOR INSULATION (TYPES R, R-W, RU, RUH, T, TW)	CURRENT (AMPS) FOR INSULATION (TYPES A, A1, A1A)
18	6*	—
14	15	30
12	20	40
10	30	50
8	40	65
6	55	85

467 *Property lamps only.

APPENDIX IV

LIGHTING THE ARENA AND THRUST-APRON STAGE

Recent developments in theatre architecture offer new challenges to the theatre-lighting artist. These developments reflect a tendency on the part of theatre architects to eliminate the aesthetic separation implied by the proscenium wall. The new design is more than a simple move away from the "peep hole" theatre of the past century. It represents a complete revamping of the concepts of audience-play relationships. Instead of a theatre being a place in which one *witnesses* a performance, it is considered a place in which one *participates in* a dramatic experience. Drama and audience are no longer separate; they are combined into a single organic totality.

In general, the theatres designed around these concepts fall into two broad categories: (1) The arena theatre or theatre-in-the-round and (2) the thrust-apron stage. The arena theatre has been characterized as small, intimate, and highly theatrical because of the fact that the play is completely surrounded by the audience. Arena theatres have tended to carry the idea of play-in-the-audience to its logical extreme by placing action in the aisles, in the circular space outside the audience area, and even within the seating itself.

A number of large arena theatres seating 2000 to 3000 people have been developed for the use of professional groups doing musical comedy. Even opera has been attempted in these edifices. They offer the producer a large seating capacity in a relatively economical house with a minimum of staging costs because scenery is kept to a minimum. These theatres suffer from the same sight-line problems as their smaller counterparts, but usually not from the cramping proximity of the first rows of the audience. Acoustics and visibility from the more distant seats are problems.

The thrust-apron stage is characterized by seating on three sides of the acting area, or at least the front portion of it. It is difficult to establish any clear line between the thrust-apron stage and the pros-

cenium stage because all degrees of apron staging exist, from a proscenium with large forestage area and conventional space behind the
proscenium to theatres with a thrust platform and no proscenium at
all. The situation is further complicated by the addition of elevators,
removable seating, and even movable partitions that make it possible
to change the configuration of the theatre from play to play.

As far as lighting is concerned, any stage which juts out into the
audience to a sufficient extent to make it necessary to light the front
acting areas from three sides can be considered a thrust-apron stage.

In terms of aesthetics, the arena and thrust-apron theatres and the
concepts that motivate them can mean nothing but more artistic
freedom for the designer. The possibility of increasing the flexibility
available to the artist in his manipulation of dramatic space and his
control over audience involvement in the play can only be regarded as
beneficial. For instance, the lighting artist will find a challenge in the
potentiality of directly involving the audience by means of the powerful mood effect of color and pattern in and surrounding them. The
possibility of getting the actors close enough to the entire audience to
make the most subtle key-fill changes effective without resorting to
the magnification of the photographic arts can be equally rewarding.
However, the architectural results of these aesthetic concepts concerning audience and play have not always produced theatres in which the
lighting artist can pursue these ideals. Innovation, as is too often the
case, has brought as many limitations as freedoms.

The most limiting factor imposed upon the designer in the arena or
thrust-apron stage is that he is forced to cater to a wide divergence of
sight lines. Once the sight lines of the audience have exceeded the 90°
separation of the acting-area lighting, which they do in both the arena
and the thrust-apron stage, the lighting artist finds that the directionality of his lighting is reduced to whatever effect the vertical
angles may have. Those in the audience "looking down the beam"
from seats directly under the instruments will see only those shadows
representing the vertical angles of the beams. There will be many more
of these viewers in an arena or thrust-apron stage than in a theatre
with conventional sight lines.

As the audience moves still further around the playing area, even
the directionality of side lighting is reduced. Part of the audience will
be looking down the beam of the sidelights and another part will be
looking almost directly into the beam. For both of these groups, the
designer's intentions will be badly distorted. Moreover, there is a real
danger of blinding parts of the audience with flare from instruments
aimed very nearly in their faces.

With the effectiveness of horizontal angles reduced, the designer
will find that there will be a tendency to increase the vertical angles.
The result is often too many heavy shadows in scenes that do not call
for them.

The degree of artistic limitation imposed by staging scenes in the aisles will depend upon how the designer and the director approach these scenes. If they seek the traditional separation between actor and audience, they will encounter insurmountable problems. If they choose to light the audience itself as an integral part of the theatrical effect of such staging, new possibilities will open. Ultimately their success will depend to a large measure on the work of the playwright who must produce a script that can function and thrive under these circumstances. In fact, the playwright is at the heart of the entire aesthetic of these "new" theatres. Transplanting traditional dramatic concepts based on separation of play and audience into these environments is risky; the separation may be impossible both aesthetically and mechanically. The concept of unifying audience and drama into an integrated experience begins in the script itself and then must extend throughout all aspects of production.

Still, the possibility of combining some of the elements of theatrical separation of audience and play with the intimacy of "total theatre" is intriguing. Moreover, there seems to be no reason why intimate theatre need always produce sight-line problems that defeat the designer. Another configuration, the wrap-around stage, offers interesting potentialities that have yet to be extensively explored. In this theatre the play is "wrapped around" the audience by placing it on playing space surrounding a large share of the seating. The audience is just as thoroughly included in the dramatic space and sight lines are much more favorable. Multiple stages, pivoted seating, and even reversible seating have been tried. More experimentation may offer new possibilities to the designer.

Practical Considerations

The wrap-around theatre will offer no additional practical difficulties that cannot be solved by adding more equipment to light the additional acting space. The arena and the apron theatre are a different matter. Sight lines hamper key-fill control. Close relationship between audience and play make flare and spill-light problems. Action in the aisles cannot be well lighted for visibility. Equipment is inaccessible during performances.

Key-Fill Problems

These have already been introduced above since they mar the aesthetic of these theatres. Practical solutions are partial at best. Arena staging acting areas are usually four-sided, that is, the standard acting area pattern is repeated completely around each area by mounting instruments at 90° intervals. Attempts to conserve equipment by using a 120° separation usually fail because three segments of the audience

FIGURE *ee*

Key and Fill on the Thrust Stage. This photograph, taken from a production of The Lion in Winter *at California State University, Northridge, illustrates the kind of problem encountered while designing acting area lighting for a theatre with a thrust stage. The necessity of lighting the actor's face for a viewing angle over 180 degrees tends to cause the designer to separate his acting area instruments by a horizontal angle of more than 100 degrees. The shadow area on the near side of the actress' face is a typical result. In this particular instance the resulting shadow pattern is appropriate to the seriousness of the scene and works as an advantage. However the same arrangement would not serve well for a less dramatic scene. Reducing the key-fill ratio at the dimmer setting will not solve the problem; the lighting must be reangled and another instrument will probably be needed. The production was directed by Gilman Rankin.* Lighting and photo by the author.

are subjected to lighting which leaves a shadow area down the middle of the actor's face as he faces them. Occasionally these areas can be located in the aisles, but this usually hampers flexibility of seating and lighting-instrument placement.

Control and dramatic development of the directional quality of light in the arena theatre will be mainly limited to what can be done with vertical angles. Both the wide sight lines and the proximity of the audience to the playing space will force this upon the designer. Often there will be only a foot or so of space between the playing space and the nearest rows of seats. Lighting instruments must be so placed that they will not blind those occupying the front seats and usually so that little light will strike the audience at all. This demands steep lighting angles with instruments that can be precisely controlled. Fresnel spotlights equipped with oval beam lenses, flatted risers, and often with hoods, will be the most useful. Wide-beam, short-throw ellipsoidal spotlights will also prove very effective. Since throws are short, wattage will be low. A normal load is 500 watts. The instruments usually are mounted over both the audience and the playing area as needed. Little or no attempt is made to conceal them. Wiring is usually brought in from above the ceiling or plugging strips are hung just under it. Circuits are often duplicated 90° around the playing space to facilitate the four instruments per area. All of this equipment and wiring will be inaccessible during the performance. Safety standards must be high and lamps should be changed often.

Thrust-apron stages will tend to offer less difficulty in the mechanical arrangement of equipment; lighting beams often are provided. Throws will be longer and wattages higher. The areas will frequently be three-sided, still at 90° intervals. Side lighting may occasionally be possible, depending on the architecture.

Lighting the Aisles

Arena theatres often have no entrances to the playing area except through the aisles. Since these entrances must be long, especially in large theatres, the tendency is to begin and end scenes in the aisles. Bits are often played entirely in the aisles while the main playing area is being prepared for another scene. This staging calls for illuminating a narrow aisle, usually without blinding any of the audience. The usual solution is only partial. Ellipsoidal spotlights are angled up and down each aisle and shuttered off the audience. This arrangement produces a certain amount of illumination but still leaves those looking in at 90° to the aisle with poor lighting. Top lighting will only occasionally be possible for the aisles.

If the aisle scenes can be treated in a manner sufficiently theatrical to allow a blending of lighting off into part of the audience, better solutions are available.

Design Procedures

Illumination will be paramount in the early consideration of lighting design for the arena theatre. Until the designer has provided a smooth pattern of areas with reasonable plasticity for all of the audience and no flare in anyone's face, there can be little concern for directionality, color, or special pools. Given this base, the designer can then proceed much as he would in a conventional theatre. Key-fill considerations will be limited to high-angle key lighting. Color choice for acting-area lighting will be much the same as in proscenium staging with the exception that paler tints will often be more effective at close audience range. Related-tint schemes are often most effective.

Given a script that will not only survive but grow under the aesthetic conditions of the arena or thrust-stage theatre and the proper equipment and mounting positions, the lighting designer will find that his knowledge of the design of lighting will not only serve him well, but will expand with the added flexibility and intimacy these theatres provide. Further experimentation with theatrical forms may well offer as many new ventures for the designer as for the playwright.

BIBLIOGRAPHY

General Stage Lighting

Bentham, Frederick. *Stage Lighting*. London: Sir Isaac Pitman & Sons, 1950. Useful text on British practices. Second edition, 1968; much recent information updating first edition. Considerable treatment of scenic projection.

Fuchs, Theodore. *Stage Lighting*. Boston: Little, Brown, 1929. Basic text. Now far out of date.

Heffner, Hubert C., Samuel Selden, and Hunton D. Sellman. *Modern Theatre Practice*, 3rd ed. New York: Crofts, 1946.

McCandless, Stanley. *A Method of Lighting the Stage*, 3rd rev. ed. New York: Theatre Arts Books, 1947.

McCandless, Stanley. *A Syllabus of Stage Lighting*. New Haven: published by the author, 1949. Advanced lighting information in syllabus format.

Parker, W. Oren, and Harvey K. Smith. *Scene Design and Stage Lighting*. New York: Holt, Rinehart and Winston, Inc., 1963. Detailed treatment of stage scenery.

Pilbrow, Richard. *Stage Lighting*. New York, Van Nostrand Reinhold, 1971. An excellent treatment of lighting from the standpoint of the British theatre.

Rosenthal, Jean and Lael Wertenbacker. *The Magic of Light*. Boston: Little, Brown and Company, 1972. More of a personal statement than a text, but an important addition to the works on professional lighting in the United States. Good presentation of professional practices of the Broadway Stage and the atmosphere of theatre in that area.

Ruben, Joel, and Lee Watson. *Theatrical Lighting Practice*. New York: Theatre Arts Books, 1954. Valuable information on the professional aspects of lighting.

Selden, Samuel, and Hunton D. Sellman. *Stage Scenery and Lighting*, rev. New York: Appleton-Century-Crofts, Inc., 1959.

The Aesthetics of Stage Lighting

Appia, Adolphe. *La Musique et la Mise en Scène*. This work is available in the original French manuscript in microfilm from the New York City Public Library. Available in an English translation by Robert W. Corrigan and Mary Douglas Dirks which includes all of the material in the French microfilm version plus a section heretofore available only in the German translation (long out of print). The translation is titled *Adolphe Appia's "Music and the Art of the Theatre."* Coral Gables, Florida: University of Miami Press, 1962.

Craig, Edward Gordon. *On the Art of the Theatre*. Boston: Small Maynard, 1925. (Now out of print.)

Craig, Edward Gordon. *Scene*. London: Humphry Milford, 1923. (Out of print.)

Craig, Edward Gordon. *The Theatre Advancing*. Boston: Little Brown, Inc., 1919. (Out of print.)

Craig, Edward Gordon. *On the Art of the Theatre*. Boston: Small Maynard, 1925. (Now out of print.)

Hospers, John. *Meaning and Truth in the Arts*. Hamden, Conn.: Archon Books, 1964.

Langer, Susanne. *Feeling and Form*. New York: Charles Scribner's Sons, 1953.

Langer, Susanne. *Philosophy in a New Key*. Cambridge: Harvard University Press, 1951; New York: New American Library, 1948.

Light, Color, and Human Vision

Adler, Francis H. *Physiology of the Eye,* 3rd ed. St. Louis: The C. V. Mosby Co., 1959. L. C. No. 59-13528.

Evans, Ralph M. *An Introduction to Color*. New York: John Wiley & Sons, 1948. Best general introduction to color theory.

General Electric Company, Cleveland. *Fundamentals of Light and Lighting*. Excellent discussion of light and color.

I.E.S. *Lighting Handbook*. New York: Illuminating Engineering Society, 1952.

Jacobson, Egbert. *Basic Color*. Chicago: Paul Theobald, 1948. The Ostwald color theory.

Luckiesh, Matthew. *Color and Its Applications*, 2nd enlarged ed. New York: D. Van Nostrand Co., 1921. (Out of print.)

Luckiesh, Matthew. *Light and Shade and Their Application*. New York: D. Van Nostrand, 1916. (Out of print.)

Munsell, A. H. *A Color Notation,* 10th ed. Baltimore: Munsell Color Co., Inc., 1946. Munsell color theory.

Scenography

Burian, Jarka. *The Scenography of Josef Svoboda.* Middletown, Connecticut: Wesleyan University Press, 1971. Important treatment of a major figure of the theatre world. Profuse illustrations clarify the Svoboda concept of the scenographer as a total artist of the visual production. Lighting, setting and projections blend into an expressive unity.

Projected Scenery

Kingslake, Rudolf. *Lenses in Photography: The Practical Guide to Optics for Photographers.* New York: A. S. Barnes and Co., Inc.; London: Thomas Yoseloff, Ltd., c. 1963. Kingslake is director of optical design, Eastman Kodak Company. L. C. No. 63-9367.

Kook, Edward. *Images in Light for the Living Theatre.* New York: 1963. Privately mimeographed report of a project sponsored by the Ford Foundation. Contains valuable summary of present attitudes toward scenic projection. Data on projection equipment out of date.

Manufacturers of Equipment related to Stage Lighting

Since this field is rapidly changing and any list of manufacturers published herein would rapidly become uselessly out of date, the reader should consult the current American Theatre Association Directory for up-to-date information.

INDEX

Numbers in italics indicate illustration page numbers.

A Acting area defined, 113, *114*
Acting area lighting, 377
Acting space, 110, 374
Additive system, 100
Aesthetics of lighting, 295
Alignment of spherical reflector, 59
Alternating current (ac), 131
   vibration of, 164
"Alzac" process, 51, 53
Ambient light, 432
American professional theatre lighting, 209
Ampere, definition of, 128
Angle of incidence, *50*
Angle of key and fill, 344
Aperture
   of projector, 449
   of ellipsoidal reflector spotlight, 85
Appia, Adolphe, 295
Arc light
   carbon, 15, 111
   xenon, *39*, 447
Arena lighting, 468
Attention, control of, 320
Autotransformer dimmer, 177

B Back EMF, 134
Back lighting, 337
Background lighting, 390
Base, lamp, *24*, 25
Beam projector, *65*, 386
Bipost base, *24*, 25
Blacklight (ultraviolet), 44
Blending light, 360
Border light, 53
Brightness, 92
Broadway theatre lighting, 208
Brush (slider), 182, 184

C Cable, 290
Carbon arc follow spotlight, 111
Carbon monoxide hazard, 15
Card reader, 219, 224

Cartridge fuse, 152
Cellulose acetate color medium, 94
Change (in lighting), 368
Chroma, 92
Chromatic aberration, 72
Circuit, series and parallel, *127*, 129
Circuit breaker, 149, *151*, 153
Circuiting, 388
Circuiting background lighting, 393
Circuiting and control, 379
Climax, building with lighting, 315, 366
Coleman lantern, 14
Collector lens, 443
Color
   contrast, 104
   filters, 93–95
   identification, 91
   of key and fill, 116, 343
   map, 98, *Plate III*
   mixing, 96
   names, 103
   psychology, 361
   symbolism, 363
   temperature, 16, 105, *Plate VIII*
   triangle, 99
   wheel, 91, *Plate VII*
Colored light, 89, 93, 96
Colored light on colored objects, 102, *103*
Complementary color, 100
Complementary tint system, 116
Concentrated filament lamp, 19
Condensing lens, 76, 448
Conductor, 124
Connectors
   pin, 287
   Stage plug, 289
   "Twist-Lock," 287
Console, *207*
Contrast
   between actor and background, 337
   key-fill, 339
Converging lens, 76, 448

Cool color, *Plate VII*
Core losses, 135
Cost of electrical power, 129
Counterpoint cues, 213, 253
Craig, Edward Gordon, 362
Criticism of lighting, 415
Cues, 397
Cue card, 399
Cue sheet
    memory, *404*, 406
    operators, *404*
    preset, *403*, 405
Cuing counterpoint lighting, 407
Current, electrical, 123, 125
Cycle (Hertz), 133
Cyclorama lighting, 391, 394

D "Dark" scenes, 351
Depth perception, 322
Design procedures, 371
Designer, 303
Designer's variables, 336
Diazo (ammonia) process, 462
Dimmer
    loading, 283
    master, 175
    multislider, 185
    number of, 283
    remote control of, 185
    room, 273
    utilization, 274
Dimmer, types of
    autotransformer, 177
    resistance, 174
    SCR, 196
    triac, 197
Direct beam projector, 435
Direct current (dc), 132
Directional light, 326, 330, 336
Director, the, 372
"Dirty arc" lamp, 447
Discrete cues, 213
Double-flatted reflector, 62
Dramatic rhythm, 315
Dramatic space, 304, 356
Dramatic style, 316

E Educational theatre lighting, 211
Efficiency of spotlights, 57, *58*, 61
Electric arc light, 15, 39, 111, 447
Electric current, 123
Electrical heat formula, 131, 160
Electrical safety, 160
Electrical shock, 165
Electricity, nature of, 123
Electron flow, 125
Ellipsoid, 60
Ellipsoidal reflector, 60, *61*
    maintenance of, 62
Ellipsoidal reflector spotlight, 43, *85*
Emergency lighting, 144, 159, 168
Equipment ground, 167
Establishment of mood, 5
Evaluation of lighting design, 415
Eye sensitivity to color, 105

F *f* number system, 72
Filament, 18, 22, *26*
Fill light, 108, 327
Flatted ellipsoidal reflector, 62
Flexible and nonflexible switchboard, 172

Floodlight, 52
Fluorescence, 43
Fluorescent lamps, 43
Fluorescent ultraviolet sources, 45
Focal length, *71*
Focus of attention, 5
Follow spotlight, carbon arc, 111
Follow spotting technique, European, 111
Foot-candle, 12
Footlights, 54
Four-wire system, 141
Fresnel, Augustin, 79
Fresnel lens, 79, *80*, 84
Fresnel spotlight, 81
Front projection, 451
Functions of lighting, 4
Fuses, 149, *151*
    cartridge, 152
    Fusestat, 152
    plug, 152

G "G" lamps, 20
Gaseous discharge lamps, 37
Gating, 193, *195*
Gelatine color medium, 94
Generator, ac, 126, 131, 132
Glass color medium, 93
Glossary
    memory devices, 240
    preset devices, 218
Ground fault detector, 161, 205
Grounded common neutral, 139, 144, 167
Grounding, 139

H HMI lamp, 447
Halogen cycle, 29
Heat formula, 131
Hook-up chart, 389
Hot busbar, 144
House lighting supply, 144
Hue, 92

I Ideal console, 212
Incandescence, 13
Incandescent lamp, 18, 22
Incidence, angle of, 50
Index of refraction, 66
Infinite preset, 224
Instrument schedule, 387
Insulators, 124
Interconnecting panels, 277
Interconnectors
    crossbar (slider), 280
    dimmer rack, 277
    switch type, 279
    telephone board, 277

J Jones, Robert E., 296

K Kelvin scale, 16, *Plate VIII*
Key and fill, 108, 115, 327, 340, 470
    color of, 116
Kilowatt hour, 130

L Lamp bases, *24*, 25
Lamp efficiency, 26
Lamp life, 26
Lamp ordering, 465
Lamps
    blacklight, 44

Lamps (continued)
fluorescent, 43
incandescent, 18
mercury vapor, 44
tungsten-halogen (T-H), 25, 31, *35, 36*
xenon, 38, *39,* 447
Langer, Susanne, 298
Language of color, 362
Lens projector, 437
Lenses
collector, 443
condensing, 76, 448
converging, 76
Fresnel, 79, *80*
objective, 438, *443*
plano-convex, 69, 74, *75*
projection, 437, *443*
retrofocus, 444
Light
and the entire body, 332
giving and taking scene, 355
measuring, 11
nature of, 9
as physical phenomenon, 89
and the setting, 355
visible, 11
Light plot, 375, *381, 383*
Lighting, building tension with, 367
Lighting cues, types of, 213
Linnebach projector, 430, *434,* 436
Load outlets, 286
Load sensitivity, 171, 174, 204
Lumen, 12
Lumen maintenance, 27

M McCandles, Stanley, 113
Magazine (fuse or breaker), 154
Magnetic amplifier, 194
Main switch, 142
Manual control of lighting, 170
Master dimming, 175, 183
Master switching, 189
Mastering as a remote control concept, 189
Matrix reloading, 283
Memo-Cue system, 256, *258*
Memory Center System, 262, *263*
Memory cue sheet, *406*
Memory systems, 239, 247
package type, 254
parts of, 251
Mercury vapor lamp, 45
Mixed reflection, 51
MMS, 269
Motor driven dimmers, 190
Mounting instruments, 394
Multiple projectors, 446
Multislider dimmer, 185
Munsel system, 92
Mylar color medium, 95

N National Electrical Code, 157
Neutral, 139
Neutral bus, 144
New operators, training of, 409
Nondim circuits, 189
Nonspectral hue, 90
Normal, defined, 50

O Objective lens, 438, *443*
Ohm, 128
Ohm's law, 128
Operating position

Operating position (continued)
of Conventional lamps, 28
of T-H lamps, 34
Optical center, 71
Optical density, 66
Ostwald system, 92
Output curve (dimmer), *206*
Oval beam fresnel spotlight, 83
Overcurrent protection, 149
Overload, 161

P Package control, 235, *236,* 284
Package memory control, 254
Package preset control, 235, *236*
Painting with light, 362
Panic lighting, 168
PAR lamps, 55
Parabolic reflector, *63*
Paraboloid, 64
Paradox, 319
Parallel circuit, 127, 129
Patch board (bay), 279
Pattern control, 232, *233,* 253
Pattern projecting ellipsoidal spotlight, 85, 431
Perspective, 324
Phosphors, 43
Photographic projection slides, 459
Physiological bases of lighting, 6
Pigtail tester, *146*
Pile-on, 226, 227
Pin connector, 287, *288*
Plano-convex lens, 69, 74, *75, 80,* 443
Plastic color medium, 94
Plasticity, 107, 108
Plug fuses, 152
Plugging chart, *389*
Point source, 20
Portable control boards, 235, *236,* 254, 284
Portable wiring, 290
Power formula, 129
Power transformer, 137
Prefocus base, 22, *24*
Preset control (glossary), 218
Preset cue sheet, *405*
Preset submasters, 225
Primary color, 97, 100
Projected scenery, 418, 423
Projection distance, 431
Projection surface, 450
Proportional dimming, 176
Psychological bases of lighting, 6

Q Q-Level, 270
Quartz-halogen (iodine) lamp, 29

R "R" lamps, 56
Radiant energy spectrum, 9, *Plate I*
Reactance, 134
Realism in lighting, 6
Rear projection, 452
Reflection, 48
diffuse, spread, and mixed, 51
law of, 49
Reflector lamps, 55
Reflectors
efficiency of, 51
ellipsoidal, 60, *61*
parabolic, *63*
specular, 57, *58*
spherical, 60, *61*
Refraction, 66, *69*
Regulation, dimmer, 203

Reinhardt, Max, 296
Related tint system, 118
Relay, 188
Reloading, 282
Remote control, 186
Remote dimming, 189
Remote switching, 187
Resistance dimmer, 174
Retrofit lamps, 23, 34
Retrofocus lens, 444
Reversing the key, 333, 341
Rhythm in lighting, 5, 314, 365
Rim lighting, 337
Rise time, 199
Risers, lens, 81, 84
Road boards, 236, 237
Roundel, 93

S Saturable reactor, 191
Saturation, 92
Saxe-Meiningen, Duke of, 295
Scenic projection, lighting for, 454
Scenographer, 303
Scioptican, 430
Scoop, 52
SCR. See Silicon Controlled Rectifier
Script cues, 400
Secondary color, 100
Selective submastering, 221, 225, 230
Sensitivity of eye to color, 91, 97, 105, Plate II
Series circuit, 127, 129
Service entrance equipment, 142
Sequencing cues, 412
Shadow detail, 324, 359
Short-arc lamps, 38, 447
Short circuit, 161
Side lighting, 112, 346–348, 351, 353
Silhouette, 337
Silicon-controlled rectifier (SCR), 196
    dimmer, 196ff
    noise, 199
Simple circuit, 125, 127
Single color system, 120
Slide changer, 445, 449
Slides, scenic projection
    Chromtex, 462
    diazo (ammonia), 462
    hand-painted, 459
    photographic, 459
    Xerox, 461
Snap cues, 213
Solid neutral, 167
Solid state control, 195
Solid state switch (triac), 197
Space/time, 318
Specials, 380, 381
Spectra, 11, 90
    incandescent, 16
Spectral and nonspectral hues, 90
Spectroanalysis, 92
Spectrogram, 92, Plate IV
Specular reflection, 49, 57
Spherical emanation, 48
Spherical reflector, 57, 58
Spotlight
    efficiency of, 78
    ellipsoidal reflector type, 85, 86
    Fresnel type, 81
    plano-convex type, 77

Spread reflection, 51
Square law projector, 433
Stage plug, 288, 289
Standard acting area, 114, 340
Standard candle, 12
Step lens, 84
Step-down and step-up transformer, 136
Striplight, 55
Stroboscopic effect, 38
Style, 316
Stylistic considerations, 373
Sublimation, 27
Submaster, 221, 225
Subtractive system, 100
Surge protection, 202
Svoboda, Josef, 422
Switch
    selective submaster, 221, 225
    solid state (SCR, triac), 196
    "T" rated, 184
Symbol, defined, 298
Symbolic response, 299

T "T" lamp 22, 82
"T" rated switches, 184
Technical rehearsals, 410
Telephone board interconnector, 277
Testing for hot and neutral, 145
Texture of stage space, 308
T-H. See Tungsten-halogen lamps
Theatre as symbol, 300
Theory of color vision, 96
Three-phase four-wire system, 141
Three-wire system, 141
Thrust-stage lighting, 468–473
Thyratron tube dimmers, 193
Thyristor, 196
Tonal light, 361
Training new operators, 409
Transformer, 133, 137
Triac, 197
Tungsten-halogen (T-H) lamps, 21, 25, 35
    dimming, 31
    life of, 31, 36
"Twist-Lock" connector, 287, 288
Two-wire system, 140

U "U" ground outlets, 167
"UL" label, 158
Ultraviolet light, 44

V Visible light, 10
Volt, 128

W Wagner, Richard, 296
Wagner, Wieland, 296
Wall dimmers, 198
Warm and cool color, 363
Wash and key lighting, 350
Watt, 130
Wavelength, 9
White light, 105
Wire size, 164, 467

X Xenon lamps, 39, 447
Xerox process, 461

Y Young-Helmholz theory, 96